MW00461275

ARNSPARGER'S

COACHING
DEFENSIVE FOOTBALL

ARNSPARGER'S

COACHING DEFENSIVE FOOTBALL

BILL ARNSPARGER

FOREWORD BY DON SHULA

S^t_L

St. Lucie Press

Boca Raton Boston London New York Washington, D.C.

Library of Congress Cataloging-in-Publication Data

Catalog information may be obtained from the Library of Congress

International Standard Book Number 1-57444-162-0
Printed in the United States of America   2 3 4 5 6 7 8 9 0
Printed on acid-free paper

CONTENTS

FOREWORD

I've known Bill Arnsparger for many years. We first worked together on Blanton Collier's coaching staff at the University of Kentucky in 1959.

A year after being named head coach of the Baltimore Colts, I asked Bill Arnsparger to join my staff in the spring of 1964 to help Charley Winner and later Chuck Noll coach the team's defensive squad. We shared six winning seasons in a row that were filled with a sense of accomplishment as well as some disappointment.

In 1964, prior to league expansion and the introduction of the first Super Bowl, we advanced to what was then the big event, the NFL Championship. Not bad for our first year together as a team. Unfortunately, we lost to Blanton Collier's team. He had become the head coach of the Cleveland Browns. Going up against our former boss and mentor presented an interesting benchmark and a challenge that we would face again and again.

In 1968, following league expansion, we finally won the NFL Championship against Blanton Collier's Cleveland Browns and advanced to Super Bowl III. Unfortunately, we lost to Coach Weeb Ewbank's New York Jets. It was the new American Football League's first Super Bowl win and a game quarterback Joe Namath made even more famous with his bold guaranteed victory statement to the media.

In 1970, following my appointment as head coach of the Miami Dolphins, I asked Bill to become my defensive coordinator. I've known and competed against a lot of great coaches over the course of my career. Yet even today, when I think about defensive coaches, the first name that comes to mind is Bill Arnsparger. He was special. The measure of a great coach is getting the most out of his talent, and he certainly achieved that objective. Bill Arnsparger was the architect of the Miami Dolphins' "No Name Defense" that contributed to the team's first Super Bowl appearance in 1971 and back-to-back Super Bowl victories in 1972 and 1973. The 1972 "No Name Defense" was the #1 defense in the NFL and contributed to the only undefeated 17–0 season in NFL history. In 1973, the "No Name Defense" held our opponents to a record low 15 touchdowns, and they were again the #1 defense in the NFL.

In the early 1980s, Bill Arnsparger developed another great Miami defense, called the "Killer B's," which contributed to the Dolphins' fourth Super Bowl appearance. His defenses ranked first or second in the NFL for fewest points allowed in nine of his eleven seasons with Miami. In 1983, Bill's final year with the Dolphins, the "Killer B's" allowed an NFL low 15.6 points a game. These great defensive squads that I've described weren't blessed with a lot of superior natural talent. Bill Arnsparger helped each player realize his full potential and as a unit helped them to define the word "teamwork." That's what made Bill and the teams that he coached so special.

In the 1990s, Bill developed yet another great defense for the San Diego Chargers, which contributed to their first Super Bowl appearance in 1994.

Nobody can inform at any level of football better than Bill Arnsparger. Whether you are a young aspiring coach, an experienced coach who wants to learn more, or a football fan interested in the "nuts and bolts" of the game, you'll find that Bill makes it both interesting and exciting.

Bill did a great job for me in our Super Bowl years, and now he is going to do a great job for you, the reader. Enjoy!

Don Shula

Former Head Coach of the Miami Dolphins and Baltimore Colts

INTRODUCTION

Not long ago, I sat with my mother on a gorgeous summer day, discussing our lives in general. She looked over at my husband and father, who sat smoking cigars and talking football, and said to me, "I wish you liked football."

I laughed and replied, "I do like football, sort of, but I don't know a tackle from a lineman!"

She laughed and rolled her eyes and cried, "A tackle is a lineman!"

That should tell you how much I have learned through osmosis in a football household. There is a picture of me when I was a baby with a football in my lap—which is as close as I got to a football for the next 16 years. It is a long-standing joke among my family that I am probably the only person to attend six Super Bowls who sat among the roaring crowds and calmly read romantic novels. And, over the years, I have tried to figure out why I never took an interest in this game that so fascinated my family.

During my college years, I came to the conclusion that my disinterest may have been, in part, because I always felt some resentment that my life was so regulated by this game. It so often demanded a schedule that conflicted with my wishes and desires. More importantly, it took up so much of my father's time! I am in all ways "Daddy's little girl," and in my child's brain, football was a competitor for my father's love and attention. So it is not surprising that at a young age I chose to show my displeasure by resisting all attempts to learn even the smallest detail about the game.

In the third grade, I joined the first girls' soccer team in Miami Lakes, Florida, and to my delight I discovered that I loved sports. Because my father is a great dad, he always made time to come see me play in whatever sport I chose to compete. As often as he could, he took off early from work and flew home late on Friday nights so he could be in the stands (or in a lawn chair) on the sidelines. My resentment always was against football and never against my Dad. He had less time on weekends than most of the fathers of my teammates, and yet he made more games in the next ten years than most of them did. If my brother and I had games on the same day, he would go to one, my mother to the other, and they would switch at halftime.

Why tell stories of my childhood? Well, my father asked me to write the introduction for a book I will never read because I cannot understand it. Nor do I have any desire, even now as I approach 30, to understand the game. I learned to enjoy it as a spectator during his years at LSU and lost interest until he went to San Diego. Once again, I picked up a spirit for his team. The only time I watch football now is when my husband has people over to watch a Florida State game. I feel it would be too rude to go into the bedroom and read!

But this book is about my father's expertise in a complicated game that is just as much about mental talent as physical. And, when it comes to a mental talent for football, my father has something that is rare and elusive. He has been called a genius for as long as I have been able to read articles about him. As it pertains to football, I will have to take other people's word for it (and his record). He has always been a genius to me insofar as being a dad is concerned. Although he made me crazy at times and the 40-year generation gap just about drove me to distraction during my teen years, I have never believed he was anything other than brilliant. He is the type of man who comes along only once in a great while. It has been my honor to be his daughter and even when I am most angry, he has always made me proud.

So, if he has given to the game of football even half as much as he has given to me and his whole family...If he has brought not just his talent but a degree of respect and honesty to the field...If he has given young men a sense of purpose and well-being...If he has enlightened anyone's mind and kept even one person on the right path...And, if he has helped in any way to make football a sport that people can not only love but feel proud of, then I suppose any resentment I have carried from my childhood is just that—childish.

I encouraged my father to write a story about his life, the people he has been blessed to work with, and some of the stories he knows. He has done that in the final chapter of this book, and it makes for very interesting reading. Other than that chapter, don't mind me if I sign off now and never read any further. I think I hear a romance novel calling my name!

Mary Susan Arnsparger Klein

PRE-GAME WARM-UP

Why write a book? This is a question I have asked myself and have been asked by others many times. I firmly believe that this one question and the answer to it have forced me to keep my focus on what I hoped to accomplish.

When I explain why and my thoughts to others, the usual reply is, "I thought it would be a book of stories about the individuals, coaches, and players you were involved with during your coaching experience." As my experience covered over 40 years, that could have been a possibility. Such a book would provide interesting reading for the average fan. It would probably also appeal to those with a desire to learn more about the happenings in college and professional athletics, specifically football.

When I explain that what I decided to write is a technical book on football, another question arises: "For whom?" This book is for the college student interested in coaching, the young coach, the experienced coach, and the fan who is interested in the "nuts and bolts" of football.

What I have actually written is a book that I searched for repeatedly as a student–athlete interested in coaching. As a young coach, I would have liked to have had this type of book available to help me expand my knowledge. As an experienced coach, this book would have proved valuable to me to compare my thoughts with those of the respected author. We all learn from others; I most certainly did, and we all do to some degree. We learn through books, lectures, listening, discussion with others, and, of course, through trial and error. All of these forums were valuable to me, and now, in retirement, I have the time to discuss my coaching thoughts, my ideas, and my ideals with others.

I ask no one to accept verbatim what I say or what I believe. My purpose is to create a base for discussion. What I say and what I believe come from my experience, through working with my many mentors, the assistant coaches, and the players with whom it was my pleasure and privilege to associate. Each group played a part in directing and forming my coaching philosophy. This was true in the beginning, as a player in high school and college, and it continued throughout each opportunity as an assistant, a head coach, and a director of athletics. Basically, I have tried to put into words my philosophy, the details of coaching in general, and specifically coaching defense.

I have been involved in athletics for more that 40 years, from 1950 through my retirement in 1995. There were changes during that time span—changes in personnel, terminology, alignment, technique, ownership, and administrators—but the basics of playing winning defense remained the same. Proper alignment, controlling the blocker, finding the ball, pursuit, and tackling, together with the proper mental attitude and physical condition, were the constants in every situation.

My approach in this book is to walk the reader through material that in many ways resembles the notebook a coaching staff would prepare for the players. This is material that I have used and believe is fundamental and necessary for a successful defensive package. From time to time, there will be slight changes based on the personnel available. However, as I explain, the basic thought and objective remain the same.

The following pages contain the basic alignments, keys, and assignments for all positions in each front, coverage, and blitz. The same is true for short yardage and goal line defense. Special defense and special situations are also covered. Special defense includes five, six, and seven defensive backs, and special situations include two-minute offensive group formations and unbalanced line adjustments.

In addition, illustrative stories or events are included to make the material more meaningful. This material may pertain to discipline, motivation, a specific technique, personnel, or other factors that are necessary for success. Throughout the TEAM concept, the proper attitude and work ethic are stressed and emphasized as keys to gain the edge and WIN.

I have thoroughly enjoyed putting this book together. Several people were very helpful to me, and I want to thank them for their time and effort. First, my son, David, was of tremendous help. He not only has a coaching background, but also has an excellent command of proper English. His expertise in both areas was very helpful to me. His coaching background began as a student assistant at Gainesville High School in Gainesville, Florida, then graduate assistant at the University of Florida, followed by a graduate assistantship at Notre Dame University. He was then defensive backfield coach at Alabama A&M and later the receiver coach at Northeast Louisiana University. Presently, he is the defensive backfield coach at Cornell University. Being trained in and thoroughly aware of both offense and defense, he was really a great help in making sure that I properly explained every part of the defensive package. He often called my attention to a technique or an assignment that needed a more detailed explanation. My heartfelt thanks to David. Next, Connie Sullivan, wife of Jerry Sullivan, my receiver coach at Louisiana State University (now with the Detroit Lions), taught me the proper use of a computer. Needless to say, before starting the book I was computer illiterate. Connie spent many hours with me, explaining and working out the problems that I would create. I thank Connie for her patience and for continuing to stress to me the importance of proper self-expression. And last, but by no means least, were my wife, Betty Jane, and our daughter, Mary Susan. My wife allowed me to completely take over the den upstairs. She fully understood my project, and she showed considerable restraint in never moving a single sheet of paper from where I had left it the night before. I am sure she will be happy that I am finished and she can once again use the vacuum cleaner in the den. Both Mary Susan and my wife encouraged me to continue. Mary Susan has written several short stories, and she no doubt felt a sense of urgency in my continuing to tell my story. To all, plus the many coaches with whom I have worked and the players who performed on the field, I say thank you. Believe me, without their support, it would have been impossible to complete this book.

I hope that you, the reader, at whatever level, will benefit from the material in this book. I hope the book will prove valuable in your search for increased knowledge and understanding of defensive football. I believe that if you can pick up a few useful ideas through reading a book, attending a lecture or clinic, or studying a game tape, the time spent is worthwhile. And now, let's share the journey through a defensive football package that was successful and is still used today.

THE KICKOFF

50 YEARS OF THOUGHTS!

The following thoughts and statements have been a part of my coaching career from the beginning. Through the years, I added to the list, and each became more meaningful. I have tried to correctly note the originator in each case. As I read them now, memories return, and the words become more meaningful in my coaching philosophy and life in general. I hope they will prove equally helpful to you.

"You never learn anything, until you accept it to act upon."
    —William H. Kilpatrick, *Theory of Learning*

"You either get better, or worse, you never stay the same."
    —Woody Hayes
        Head Coach, Miami University (1949–1950)
        Head Coach, Ohio State University (1951–1978)

"You can accomplish a lot if you don't care who gets the credit."
    —Blanton Collier
        Head Coach, University of Kentucky (1954–1961)
        Head Coach, Cleveland Browns (1963–1970)

Consistency is the same behavior under similar circumstances.

Each play is the most important play in the game. If the play is a success, that is good; celebrate, and get ready for the next. If the play is not successful, that is bad; put it behind you and get ready for the next. You never know which play will be the play that wins the game.

Like the play, each game, each season is a new experience. Win or lose, put it behind you and get ready for the next.

"**Success** is never final, and **failure** is never fatal."
  —Don Shula, Head Coach, Miami Dolphins (1970–1995)

OPPORTUNITY IS NOWHERE! As written, "nowhere" is one word, but it's your choice how to read it: opportunity is nowhere or **opportunity is now here**. Attitude is what you SEE, THINK, FEEL. You have the ability to control your attitude. It is your choice—POSITIVE or NEGATIVE.

Have a **CONVICTION**, a belief, a vision, of what you want, of what you expect. Establish boundaries, set objectives. Set a standard—**PERFECTION**.

MENTAL error   NOTHING BUT AIR keeps the player from carrying out a MENTAL assignment.

PHYSICAL error   Is caused by the opponent. (Example: the opponent is stronger, faster, quicker.)

We can tolerate the PHYSICAL error; however, we must win our share of the battles. We must ELIMINATE the MENTAL error.

PERFORMANCE dictates response: If it is good, complement and encourage. If it is bad, correct and redirect.

When asked, **don't guess**. If you don't know, say you don't know!

The TEAM concept   Together   Football is a TEAM game. Every
                        Everyone   player depends on the player in
                        Accomplishes   front of him, beside him, and
                        More   behind him to be successful.

Scoreboard for a Winner
(author unknown)

A winner says, "Let's *find out*"; a loser says, "Nobody knows."

When a winner makes a mistake, he says, "*I was wrong*"; when a loser makes a mistake, he says, "It wasn't my fault."

A winner credits his *"good luck"* for winning—even though it isn't good luck; a loser blames his "bad luck" for losing—even though it isn't bad luck.

A winner knows how and when to say *"yes"* and *"no"*; a loser says "yes, but" and "perhaps not" at the wrong times and for the wrong reasons.

A *winner works harder* than a loser, and has more time; a loser is always "too busy" to do what is necessary.

A winner makes *commitments*; a loser makes promises. A winner shows he is sorry by making up for it; a loser says "I'm sorry" but does the same thing next time.

A winner says, *"I'm good, but not as good as I ought to be"*; a loser says, "I'm not as bad as a lot of other people."

A winner *listens*; a loser just waits until it's his turn to talk.

A winner *respects those who are superior to him* and tries to learn something from them; a loser resents those who are superior to him and tries to find chinks in their armor.

A winner says, *"There ought to be a better way to do it"*; a loser says, "That is the way it's always been done here."

It's All in the State of Mind
(author unknown)

If you think you are beaten, you are;
If you think you dare not, you won't;
If you like to win, but don't think you can,
It's almost a cinch you won't.

Life's battles don't always go
To the stronger or faster man,
But sooner or later, *the man who wins*
Is the fellow who thinks he can.

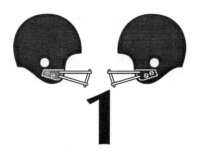

1

BASIC INFORMATION

THE BASICS

As the term implies, *basic information* is important because it is a tool that proves useful to the staff and players in "getting everyone on the same page." This chapter contains information regarding terminology and other items basic to all personnel. Through the years, experience has taught me that it is best for all staff and position players to use the same terminology in referring to offense, defense, and special teams. This allows for better communication between groups and gives each individual a better understanding of the overall system in use. If for no other reason, it eliminates possible error on game day, when vital information is discussed and transmitted between groups. First and foremost, the team needs to be together in all phases of the program.

This section is written as it might appear in the players' notebook. The coach will be talking directly to the player and making him aware of his responsibilities as an individual, a member of a unit, and a team member.

A. Why Do We Have a Playbook?

1. It carries out our theories of learning. We learn by seeing, writing, listening, reviewing, and by practicing on the field. **To be the best**, it is essential that you study this playbook.

2. It puts everything on record. Both the coach and the player have a record of everything that is needed for the individual position, the unit, and the team.
3. It aids with understanding terminology and with indoctrinating new players.
4. It serves as a review for returning players.

B. Mental Attitude

1. To win, you must believe you can win!
2. To become **champions**, you must have the desire. Championships do not just happen; they come from within each and every individual. *Unless you have a specific assignment that takes you elsewhere, do you run to the ball?* That is our test for desire.
3. You must be willing to pay the price to win, both on and off the field. Set high personal goals and take **pride** in achieving them.
4. All improvements will come from you as individuals. Coaches only organize practices to help you improve yourself. Devote most of your time to weaknesses, rather than your strong points.
5. We will not drive you. We will retain only those who do everything possible to win. (The last sentence is more of a pro attitude than would be true in college or high school.)
6. We will not accept anything but your best effort: in the classroom, your notebook, warm-up activities, and in practice. Prepare yourself for the opportunity to **BE THE BEST**.

C. Health

1. Good physical condition and proper mental attitude go hand in hand.
2, Periodic checkups and physical examinations are necessary to protect yourself. Keeping your weight under control means a longer life—and a longer career!
3. We expect you to be in better physical condition than your opponent.
4. You must not permit circumstances that lead to accidents or ill health (e.g., not taping ankles, not getting proper rest, etc.).
5. If injured and working out to get back in shape, do not exercise or stand near groups practicing, where you might become reinjured or cause a player to be injured.
6. As a ball carrier, never relax near the sideline when running. This is where many injuries occur. Keep running away from the sideline.

D. Form in Running

1. Put a lot of power into your first few strides for maximum acceleration. These should be short driving steps. Your back should be parallel to the ground.
2. Lengthen your strides and gradually come up a little higher as you progress.
3. Drive with your arms from the start. Keep the elbows close to your body, and make movements parallel to the leg action. Arms should be bent at the elbow at a 90-degree angle. Hands, arms, and upper torso must be relaxed.
4. Keep your glutes under your body. Arm movement should be a "hammer" action.

E. Tackling (Eyes at the Numbers)

1. In a ball game, tackle the ball carrier any way you can. Nothing sets the tempo like a good sharp hit and gang tackling. First man—eyes up and hit through. Second and third man—strip the ball carrier (under and up) and get the ball. This is another way we can **gain the winning edge**.
2. To achieve this mark, use the following techniques in making an individual tackle:
   a. Take a good **fundamental position**. Be under control and cocked.
   b. **Get close**, and put your eyes at the numbers in front of the man. Never use the helmet to tackle. Specifically, do not use the top of the helmet. By using proper technique and keeping your eyes at the numbers, you will avoid serious neck injuries.
   c. **Explode up** and **through** the ball carrier. Use the weight of your body and the power of your legs
   d. **Grab 'em**—anything you can get hold of. Wrap the opponent up, and continue to drive through.
3. Very few front tackles are made. Therefore, much of our practice will be from the angle. Give the ball carrier only one way to go. In coming from the angle, we will use the same techniques. Emphasis will be on **head in front** and **eyes at the numbers**, using the same driving force up and through the ball carrier.

F. How to Run Stationary Signals

This is the team phase of practice. We want to time-up the offense and have the defense review alignments and assignments. Although the defense goes at two-thirds speed, it is still a valuable period. Both groups must understand the objective and work hard to improve their technique and assignments. Stay off the ground—the key is to keep your feet moving. Proper practice procedure must be explained, and the coach must continually demand that the proper procedure be followed. This period must not be a scrimmage; we do not want to tackle the ball carrier. (This is important for the defense as well as the offense.)

1. Wear and use all protective equipment assigned.
2. The defense must go at two-thirds speed. Take proper alignment, know your assignment, give resistance, and use proper technique as you move with the opponent. Have a controlled charge and flow with the play.
3. **Run to the ball**, be in good position, and strip the ball (under and up). This is good practice.

G. Team Starts: Defense

1. **TEAM STARTS** is a drill used to warm up, but important fundamentals are reviewed at the same time. Different fundamentals will be stressed during this period. As an example, it is a good time to review the huddle, the huddle call, seeing the snap of the ball, not hearing the cadence, and the assignment of a blitz charge.

   To begin, a coach spots the ball on a yard line. The middle linebacker is given the defensive call and repeats the call to the huddle. The team breaks the huddle and aligns by position. The coach calls the cadence and snaps the ball. The team executes the defensive call and sprints ten yards.
2. Objectives of TEAM STARTS:
   a. To form and improve the appearance of the huddle.
   b. To give the middle linebacker an opportunity to make a defensive call and to give the team an opportunity to call the formation and strength.
   c. To give the team an opportunity to see the opponent's formation and break the huddle ("READY").
   d. To review alignment and assignment, usually a blitz call or a regular call, and to practice the "check-it" call.
   e. To improve stance and readiness to move. **Watch the ball**.
   f. To simulate the opponent's cadence and to emphasize movement of the ball, **not the sound of the quarterback's voice**. Deep backs will begin to backpedal (at least four yards), then recover and sprint forward.
   g. On a blitz call, the line and linebackers coordinate the assignment. Deep backs simulate bump and run or regular blitz alignment.
   h. On a regular call, the line reacts to ball movement. Linebackers and defensive backs simulate a pass drop, recover, and sprint forward.

i. To warm up, establish defensive pride, and **set the tempo.**
j. To improve quickness on movement of the ball. **Don't guess!**
k. To simulate the assignment. Everyone sprints ten yards. Jog back outside and regroup. **Be the best**.

H. Pursuit Drill

1. Huddle, alignment, and movement are the same as team starts. In addition, a ball carrier lines up wide to the right or left to simulate a sweep.
2. On the snap, come to your point at the line of scrimmage. Locate the ball and run to it (nose to the ground). Two-hand tap on the ball carrier.

I. Intercept Drill

1. Huddle, alignment, and movement are the same as in team starts. In addition, the coach drops back and throws the ball downfield to a defensive back or linebacker. The coach may at times throw the ball to a lineman.
2. Rush the passer in your lane. When the ball is thrown, turn and locate the interception. Form a return blocking pattern at the numbers. Go to meet the returnee, turn, and locate an opponent (**eyes at the numbers**). We have the ball. SCORE. **No penalties**. Come off the field.

J. The Winning Edge

1. The difference between winning and losing often lies in the failure to do the little things necessary to win. Not everyone can be an all-star, but everyone can **run to the ball** and be a **team player**.
2. We are looking for players who will become **winners**—ones who make the play, do their jobs, and help win the game!
3. Study the following tips and decide if you will do the things necessary to be a **winner**.
   a. Always **play the defense** called. Don't guess. The **alignment/assignment** gives you an opportunity to win the physical battle.
   b. Every lineman, linebacker, and defensive back must run to the football once it is in the air. Your presence could mean an interception, a recovered fumble, or a game-saving tackle.
   c. Linebackers need to play **down and distance** on long yardage plays by increasing their depth.
   d. All positions must know the **defensive progression:**

- Proper alignment
- Control the blocker
- Locate the ball (usually look inside first)
- Run to the ball
- Tackle

e. On long passes, the player nearest the defender must call "BALL! BALL!" at the last moment. This must be practiced.

f. Defensive backs must not allow the receiver to make unnecessary yardage by making a futile attempt to break up a pass that would not give the opponent a first down.

g. Linebackers and defensive backs must **hustle on every batted ball.** You must stretch or dive and intercept.

h. Defensive backs and linebackers must make a determined effort to **intercept low passes.** Too many low passes are incomplete because the defender thinks he cannot reach the ball.

i. **Return** every intercepted pass in **the designated way** we have planned for that opponent. This increases our chances of gaining extra yardage. A sideline return is basic.

TERMINOLOGY

I have tried to keep terminology and definitions to a minimum. However, it seems that the number increases annually. Actually, this is probably good, because no one takes anything for granted or assumes that the information is understood. This truly represents improvement and the changes needed to improve as coaches and as players.

Each off-season, each position coach is asked to review the terms used in his position and to make sure that all necessary terms are included in the update for the coming year. Experience has shown that this section is more clearly defined by dividing it into the basic areas (for example, formation, personnel, backfield action, general, alignment, charges, and an additional catch-all category). Before we proceed, it is important to note that both coaches and players can become overwhelmed by terminology. Therefore, as I learned early in my career, if it's important, it should be written down. Writing it down puts it on record, which means that it can be easily reviewed, updated, or eliminated as necessary.

The following provides an example of terminology that one might expect to see in a playbook. As I mentioned above, terms are added and deleted daily as additional material is added during the year. The terminology in this section is intended as a guide to keep the staff and players "on the same page."

A. Formation Terms

REGULAR (REG): Tight end and "Z" are on the same side of the formation (= strongside)

SLOT (S) or OPPOSITE (OPP): Tight end is away from "Z." "Z" and "X" are on the same side of the formation (= strongside).

STRONGSIDE (SS): The side of a formation where two receivers are aligned. Example: Tight end and "Z" or "X" and "Z."

WEAKSIDE (WS): The side of a formation away from two receivers.

CLOSE (C): "Z" is one to three yards outside the tight end.

FLEX (FX): Tight end is flexed three yards from the offensive tackle.

NEAR (N): A wide receiver aligned away from the tight end aligned one to three yards from the offensive tackle.

FAR BACK: The back aligned on the side away from you.

NEAR BACK: The back aligned on your side.

STRONG BACK: The back on the strongside of a formation.

WEAK BACK: The back on the weakside of a formation.

B. Personnel

MIKE (M): Name used to designate the middle linebacker.

N: Nose tackle aligned on the center.

SAM (S): Name used to designate the outside linebacker to the tight end.

S/C: Corner aligned on the strongside of a formation.

S/E: End on strongside of a formation.

S/S: Safety aligned on the side of the tight end. The letter "S" is used in drawings.

S/T: Tackle on the strongside of a formation.

TED (T): Name used to designate the inside linebacker to the tight end in a three-man alignment.

W/C: Corner aligned on the weakside of a formation.

W/E: End on the weakside of a formation.

WILL (W): Name used to designate the outside linebacker away from the tight end.

W/S: Safety aligned on the side away from the tight end. The letter "F" is used in drawings.

W/T: Tackle on the weakside of a formation.

C. Backfield Action

$\boxed{B}$: Symbol for backfield triangle: quarterback and two remaining backs.

BOOTLEG: An action by the quarterback away from the backs and tight end, to the side of "X."

FLOW: Both backs to the strongside of the formation, regardless of quarterback action.

FRANK: Both backs to the weakside of the formation, regardless of quarterback action.

ROLL: Both backs and ball (quarterback) to the weakside. Action must definitely be outside the offensive tackle area.

WAG: An action by the quarterback away from the backs, to the tight end.

D. General Terms

BUNCH: Term to define a pick relationship by #1, #2, and #3 in a close alignment.

CHECK-IT: Term used to call off a coverage or blitz. The front will stay and use verbal and visual signals to denote a change in coverage.

CP: Coaching point; an additional note pertaining to the alignment, key, or assignment of a player.

I'M GONE: Term used by the linebacker aligned behind the line, to tell linemen that his coverage forces him to leave his normal alignment responsibility.

LOS: Line of scrimmage

OMAHA: Term used to call off a line or linebacker charge or stunt.

RENO: Term used to alert the front to the possibility of a run.

VEGAS: Term used to alert the front to the possibility of a pass.

E. Linebacker Alignment

CRACKBACK: Term used to describe the alignment of an outside linebacker, on the line of scrimmage, facing in toward the ball and the backfield formation. This position will allow the linebacker to beat the crackback block by an offensive player aligned outside the defender.

GIANT: Term used to tell WILL his alignment. Approximately one to two yards off the line of scrimmage and outside the W/END.

I: Term used to tell outside linebacker his alignment. A position half-way between the offensive tackle and the onside receiver and deep enough to SEE both positions.

OUT: Term used to tell outside linebacker his alignment. A position aligned inside and off the outside receiver in a position to delay the receiver.

TIGHT: Term used by a linebacker to tell linemen to return to normal from OVER or UNDER alignment.

BLITZ ENGAGE: Linebackers faking a blitz to keep the running back from releasing. Cover back man to man if he releases.

BRACE: A double technique on the #2 receiver on the strong or weak side. The deep defender will use an inside technique.

CLAMP: A double technique on the #3 receiver strong. The deep defender will use an outside technique.

DESTROY: A coverage technique used by linebackers that is backed up by inside and outside help in zone or man.

HANG: Linebackers covering back from a depth (five yards) on defensive side of ball.

HOLD: A call to SAM linebacker by strong safety to cover "Y" if he blocks.

HUG: Linebackers closing to coverage immediately on the offensive side of the ball when back blocks.

IN/OUT: Linebacker and another defender covering two receivers, using in/out techniques on the release of the receivers.

OMAHA: A call to call off a stunt or blitz to a standard front or coverage.

SMACK: SAM and MIKE blitzing. WILL has coverage.

SWILL: SAM and WILL blitzing. MIKE has coverage.

WHAM: MIKE and WILL blitzing. SAM has coverage.

F. Defensive Line

CAGE: Responsibility to contain the passer.

CHASE: Either by alignment or stunt, you have trail responsibility behind the line of scrimmage.

COLLAPSE: Technique of squeezing offensive blocker down the line of scrimmage on a play away.

CUT-BACK: Responsibility for inside cutback on play away. A two-gap responsibility.

DOWN: Call to the defensive end or defensive tackle by a linebacker to cover the next inside lineman.

HUG: Call by linebackers to the end which tells the end he has coverage on the back to his side or a second back across the formation.

INDIAN: Call in all situations to place the outside linebacker and end or end and tackle in an inside gap charge.

LOOSE: A call directed by the outside linebacker to the end and tackle to take a wide alignment. (Example: End moves to head-on to inside tight end, and tackle moves to outside shoulder of guard.)

MOVE: A call to initiate movement from one front alignment to another.

PROWL: An individual movement of a player from one alignment to another and returning to the alignment called.

SHOW: A call to line up in one front and move to another. Usually used to show a blitz. When to move is made by a "MOVE" call.

SOLID: A call in over/under defenses to cover the offensive tackle by the defensive end and to cover the offensive guard by the defensive tackle.

TIGHT: Call to an end by an outside linebacker to move him from a loose alignment to a head-up-to-outside alignment on the offensive tackle.

TUFF: Call to an end (usually the bubble end) to control the "B" gap.

WIDE: End aligns one yard outside the outside tackle. (Example: Under front alignment.)

G. Line Charge

BAM: Outside linebacker and defensive end in a "C–B" type of charge.

LION: An exchange in responsibility between the defensive end and WILL or SAM. The defensive end will have contain and WILL or SAM will have C-gap responsibility.

OUT: Tackles in an even front in a B-gap charge.

PINCH: Tackles in an even front in an A-gap charge.

RAM: The bubble-side defensive end in OVER/UNDER front in a B-gap charge.

SLICE: A combination call —RAM and SPIKE type of charge in an odd front.

SPIKE: The odd front tackle over the offensive guard in an A-gap charge.

TOM: Even front, split side tackle in an A-gap charge.

TOMY: Even front, tight-end side tackle in an A-gap charge.

H. Defensive Backs

ANCHOR: Corner lines up left or right and stays left or right.

BAIL: Drop to a deep zone from a press technique.

BANJO: Man-to-man coverage, where two defenders are in and out on two receivers, when aligned in a pick relationship.

BUNCH: A pick relationship by #1, #2, and #3.

"C" TECHNIQUE: Man-to-man technique used in playing with a post player.

LOCK: Stay on your man, man to man.

OZ: Term used in man coverage to play zone.

POST: A call in three-deep zone and man to man with a post player to handle deep crossing receivers.

PRESS: Alignment by coverage. Line up as close as possible without being offside.

THE HUDDLE

The huddle is where the play begins. The shape is not important, although I have always felt comfortable with a rounded, closed huddle because it promotes attention to the signal caller as well as a feeling of unity and togetherness. However, many successful teams have used all shapes of closed and open huddles. As is true in many areas that we will discuss, the coach and staff must feel comfortable with the type of huddle chosen and must stress its importance with the players. Whatever the decision, closed or open, rounded or square, it is the beginning of our demand for perfection and attention to detail.

HUDDLE

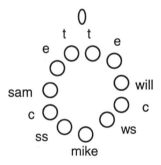

The huddle is pictured above, along with the important points that must be emphasized in the huddle and at the line. The original call for the front, coverage, or blitz is made in the huddle. If a change in the defensive call is necessary, it must be changed at the line of scrimmage. The change must be made quickly and communicated to all defensive players. In some cases, the change or check-off refers only to the front or only to the coverage or blitz. To communicate the check-off, both VERBAL and VISUAL signals are necessary. Each player must continually communicate the new call. To place added emphasis on this phase, the defense from time to time is asked to use only VISUAL signals. We want to be prepared, and we want our players to feel comfortable with both VERBAL and VISUAL signals. To accomplish both, the technique of communication must be practiced.

In order to be successful, what you believe and feel must first be taught and then continually stressed. The attitude and discipline of the team often can quickly be read by watching the huddle. It is the trademark of a team.

A. In Huddle

1. **Form the huddle quickly**. Don't be the last man in the huddle.
2. **Keep a constant huddle**. The two tackles (NOSE and TED—30 defense) form the huddle on the ball. The shape and hands-on-knees appearance are the responsibility of each individual.
3. MIKE does the talking. All others look at him. MIKE talks straight out, not up in the air or down at the ground. SEE the players.
4. **Huddle procedure**: Give **alignment** first, **coverage** second, and any **special alerts** third. (Example: UNDER—cover ONE.)
5. After the call, MIKE will say "READY" and then pause. All clap hands. This is the signal to break the huddle and concentrate on the opponent's huddle. **Watch the opponents break their huddle**. Find the TE, know the STRENGTH (side of two receivers).

B. At the Line

1. **Watch the opponent's huddle**. See the strength of the formation as the opponents break. The side of the two receivers will be the key to strength. (TE and "Z" or "Z" and "X"). If there are four wide receivers, the strength will be designated by the game plan (personnel or wide side of field).
2. **Call the strength** as the opponents break the huddle. (Example: STRONG RIGHT.)
3. **Call the formation** as the opponents set at the line of scrimmage. (Example: "I" RIGHT.)
4. It is important for all to KNOW and CALL the strength and set of the formation. Your alignment and assignment will be determined by these two factors. **This is your first responsibility as a defensive player.** *Nothing but air* keeps you from carrying out this part of your assignment.

C. Defensive Check-offs

1. LINEBACKERS will make the call to change the FRONT. The SAFETY will be responsible for the COVERAGE change. The S/S will usually have this responsibility, because he is in a better position to communicate with the team. When making a change, use both **VERBAL** and **VISUAL** signals.

2. The change must occur quickly, first by the **designated signal caller** and then **repeated by everyone**.
3. LINEBACKERS and SECONDARY must relay the call by both **VERBAL** and **VISUAL** signals. As a TEAM we must make sure that all team members **know the defense** we will play. TALKING and SIGNALING will eliminate the possibility of a mental error.

D. Personnel Changes

1. Substituted personnel take the places of the players they replaced in the huddle.

FORMATIONS

A. Regular Personnel

The terminology used by both the offense and the defense should be the same. The offense is responsible for establishing the terminology that concerns the offense, and the defense has a similar responsibility. Throughout my career, I have heard arguments pro and con regarding this philosophy; however, a true team attitude begins when the staff is together. With this as a starting point, we will go over all formations and the terms used to describe each.

SPLIT R

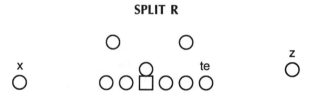

Backs are aligned in **SPLIT** position. "Z" is aligned outside to the strongside, "X" is aligned outside to the weakside. The strength is **RIGHT**.

I R

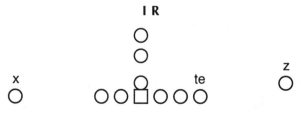

Backs are aligned in **I** position. "Z" is right, "X" is left. Strength is **RIGHT**.

WEAK R

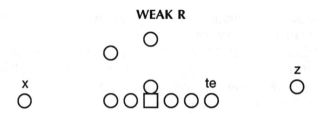

Backs are aligned in **WEAK** position. "Z" is right, "X" is left. Strength is **RIGHT**.

STRONG R

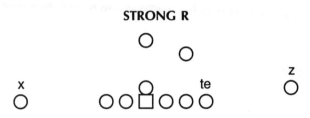

Backs are aligned in **STRONG** position. "Z" is right, "X" is left. Strength is **RIGHT**.

I R SLOT

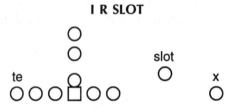

The other backfield alignments as described above may be added to describe the following: **SPLIT R SLOT, WEAK R SLOT, STRONG R SLOT**. In the diagram above, the SLOT is right, and the TE is aligned to the left. Normally the receiver in the SLOT is "Z," with the "X" outside. Strength is **RIGHT**.

DOUBLE R

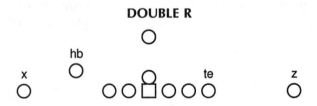

DOUBLE: Back moves up to the wing position weakside, away from the tight end. "Z" is right, "X" is left. Strength is **RIGHT**.

DOC R

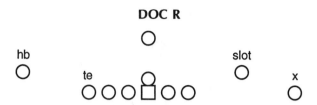

DOC: Back moves outside to the tight end side, SLOT is right. Strength is **RIGHT**.

FLOOD R

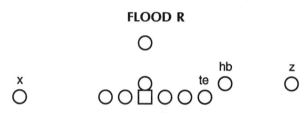

FLOOD: Back moves up to the wing position strongside, to the tight end. "Z" is right, "X" is left. TE may be flexed with back aligned inside. Strength is **RIGHT**.

TIGER R

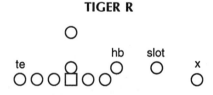

TIGER: Back moves up to the wing position, away from the TE and to the side of the SLOT. The back may be aligned inside or outside the SLOT position. Strength is **RIGHT**.

ACE R

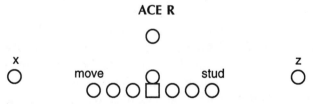

ACE: One BACK and two TIGHT ENDS. One TE, usually the best blocker, is designated the STUD TE and is the TE that normally remains stationary. The other TE, usually the best receiver, is designated the MOVE TE. The defensive front normally aligns on the STUD TE. In the above diagram, the TE aligned to the right is the STUD TE. "Z" is outside right, "X" is outside left. Strength is **RIGHT**.

ACE DOC R

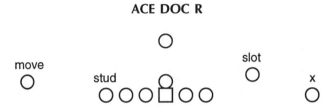

ACE DOC: The SLOT is right. The MOVE TE is aligned to the left, outside the STUD TE. Strength is **RIGHT**.

TEXAS R

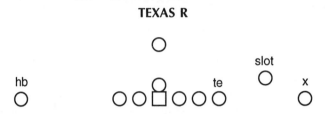

TEXAS is a gimmick formation. The back is aligned as the wide receiver outside to the left. The tight end and the two wide receivers ("Z" and "X") are aligned outside the TE to the right. Strength is **RIGHT**.

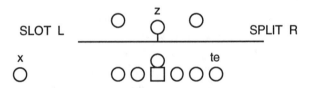

"Z" is aligned in the backfield. As the diagram shows, movement to the side of the TE is SPLIT R. Movement to "X" is SLOT L. If "Z" remains in the backfield, coverage will be called by plan: (1) strength to field, (2) strength to "X," (3) strength to TE, and (4) no strength. In the case of the fourth choice, I have used **cover 2**, which proves useful and also makes for a simple plan. If "Z" moves out of the backfield formation, **cover 2** will stay or the plan may call for a return to the original call.

The same strength calls are good regardless of the personnel, as the third man in the backfield. **CP:** The TE, "X," or a third back could be aligned as the third back. The plan should always say what we will do if presented with this formation. If you are aware in preparation of the regular T formation, more specific plans may be necessary.

B. Substituted Personnel

QUEENS R

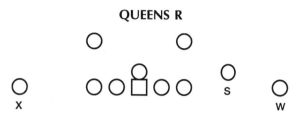

QUEENS: Three wide receivers, two backs. The two backs may be in any alignment: SPLIT, I, WEAK, STRONG, DOUBLE, or FLOOD. The QB may be in regular alignment or in shotgun. Strength is **RIGHT**.

KINGS R

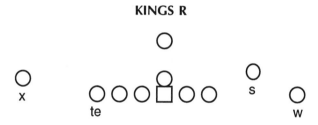

KINGS: Three wide receivers, one tight end, and one back. KINGS personnel, DOC alignment. The remaining back may be aligned on the side of the TE or the side away from TE. The QB may be in regular position or in shotgun. **CP**: The best run threat aligns the back to the side away from the TE. Strength is **RIGHT**.

KINGS TIGER R

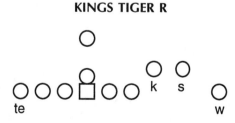

KINGS personnel, **TIGER** alignment. Three wide receivers away from the TE.

JACKS DOUBLE R

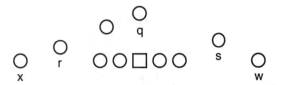

JACKS personnel: Four wide receivers, one back. The QB is shown in shotgun, but may be in regular position. **CP:** Receivers may be aligned in FLOOD (three to onside). Strength is by game plan: (1) the best receivers, (2) wide side of the field, or (3) any other tendency that may be shown in the breakdown.

SPREAD R

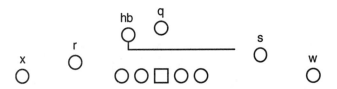

JACKS personnel: Back moves to either side, to **SPREAD**. The same movement by the back may also be used with KINGS personnel. Strength is by game plan, based on the formation before movement to SPREAD.

PAIR weak r

PAIR personnel: **Two tight ends** or **one tight end and "X,"** aligned with "Z." **CP:** One TE will be assigned the STUD term. By plan, the FRONT may or may not be aligned by the STUD definition. The backs may align as previously described: SPLIT, I, WEAK, STRONG, DOUBLE, or FLOOD.

DIAMOND double r

DIAMOND personnel: **Three tight ends**, one wide receiver ("Z" or "X"), and one back. **CP**: It is usually best to align the FRONT where there are two tight ends. DOUBLE is shown above, but FLOOD may also be used. Strength is **RIGHT** for coverage.

CLUBS strong r

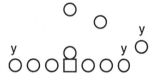

CLUBS personnel: **Three tight ends** and **two backs**. The backs may be aligned in SPLIT, I , WEAK, STRONG, DOUBLE, or FLOOD. Strength is the side of **two TEs**.

C. Movement of Personnel

The following terms are used to describe the movement of personnel.

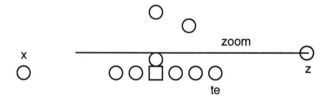

ZOOM is "Z" moving across the formation to create SLOT. Strength changes from strong right to strong **LEFT**.

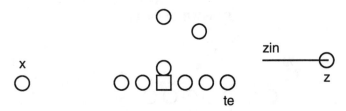

ZIN is "Z" moving toward the formation. Strength does not change, strong **RIGHT**.

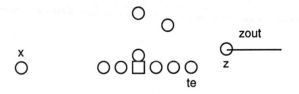

ZOUT is "Z" moving away from the formation. Strength is **RIGHT**.

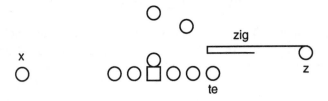

ZIG is "Z" moving to the formation, and then moving away from the formation. Strength is **RIGHT**.

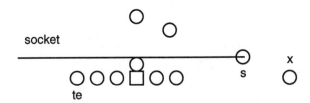

SOCKET is the SLOT moving across the formation to create a regular set. Strength changes from right to **LEFT**.

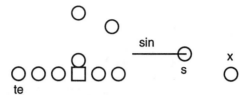

SIN is "S" moving toward the formation. Strength is **RIGHT**.

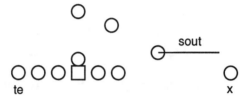

SOUT is "S" moving away from the formation.

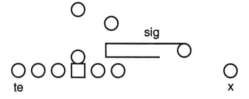

SIG is "S" moving to the formation, and then away from the formation. No change of strength, strength is **RIGHT**.

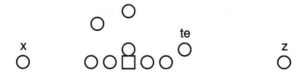

YO is "Y," the TE aligned off the line of scrimmage. Strength is **RIGHT**.

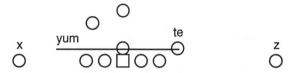

YUM is "Y" moving across the formation. Strength changes from strong right to strong **LEFT**.

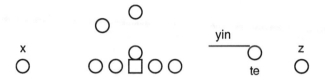

YIN is "Y" moving toward the formation. Strength remains **RIGHT**.

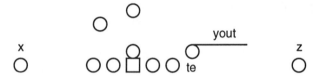

YOUT is "Y" moving away from the formation. Strength remains **RIGHT**.

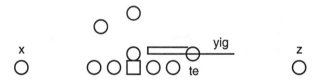

YIG is "Y" moving to the formation, and then away from the formation. Strength is **RIGHT**.

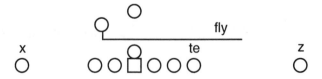

FLY is either back moving to the strongside to create FLOOD formation. Strength is **RIGHT**.

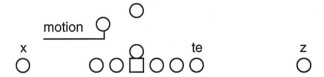

MOTION is either back moving to the weakside to create double formation. Strength is **RIGHT**.

D. Formation Strength

Strength of the formation is very important to establish a strongside and a weakside for coverage definition. The designated strength for regular formations is normally the side of two receivers ("Z" and "X" or "Z" and "Y"). However, if there are several personnel groupings, this rule could result in a problem. To prevent confusion, let's discuss those personnel groupings and a suggested method to establish strength for coverage.

Pair, Pair "Z," and Diamonds

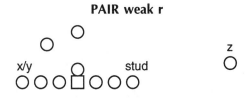

PAIR: FRONT and COVERAGE strength is the side of two receivers. **CP**: If the STUD TE aligns away from the two receivers and a run threat exists, moving the FRONT by the STUD alignment may be considered.

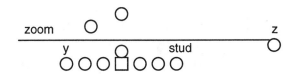

PAIR–ZOOM is a change of strength. Regular to **SLOT**. If using a double-digit call (for example, 36), the coverage would go from the first-digit CALL (3) to the second-digit CALL (6). STRONG CORNER will come across with movement.

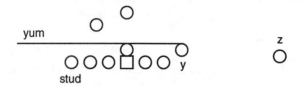

PAIR–YUM is a change of strength. SLOT to regular. If using a double-digit call (for example, 10), the coverage would stay with the second digit. The WEAK SAFETY would stay with the "move TE" and SAM would stay on the stud.

PAIR–the FRONT is aligned on the STUD. **Pass strength** = STUD and "Z," STUD away = SLOT.

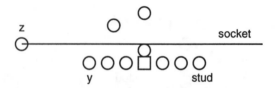

PAIR–SOCKET is a change of strength from **SLOT** to **REGULAR**. If using a double-digit call, the coverage would go from the first digit to the second digit.

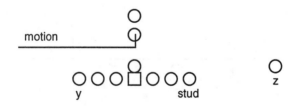

PAIR–motion **to DOUBLE** is either back moving to the weakside to create DOUBLE formation. There is no change of strength.

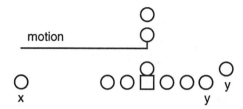

PAIR "Z": **Two TEs** together designate strength **RIGHT**. There is no change of strength on motion to **DOUBLE**.

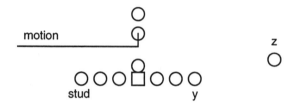

PAIR: Formation is aligned as **SLOT, FRONT** is aligned on **STUD**. Motion is to **DOC** formation. There is no change of strength.

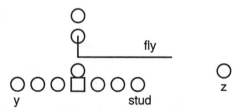

PAIR–fly to FLOOD is either back moving to the strongside to create FLOOD formation. No strength of change.

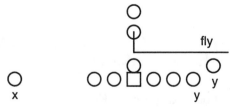

PAIR "Z": The movement is fly to **FLOOD**. **Two TEs** are together to designate strength **LEFT**. There is no change of strength on movement.

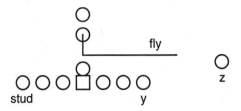

PAIR: Formation is aligned as **SLOT**. The FRONT is aligned on STUD. Fly is to **TIGER** formation. There is no change of strength.

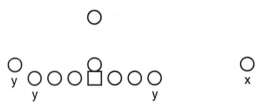

DIAMONDS: Strength in is the side of **two tight ends**. Strength is **LEFT**. If using a two-digit call, the formation above would use the first digit.

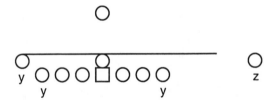

DIAMONDS: Strength is **LEFT**. Movement is a change of strength to the **RIGHT**. In a two-digit call, the second digit would be used.

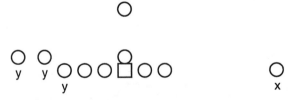

DIAMONDS: Formation strength is **LEFT**.

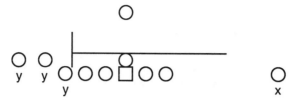

DIAMONDS: Formation strength is **LEFT**. If any of the three TEs moves, the strength remains to the **LEFT**. It is a first-digit call and stays a first-digit call.

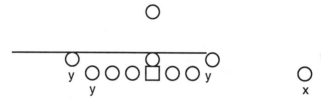

DIAMONDS: Formation strength is **LEFT** (side of two TEs) and remains **LEFT** on movement.

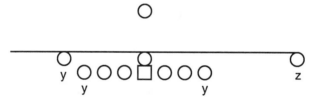

DIAMONDS: Formation is **LEFT** and remains **LEFT** on movement. First-digit call stays.

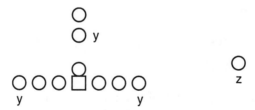

DIAMONDS–PAIR "Z" rule: Strength is **RIGHT** to the side of two receivers. **CP**: By game plan, if STUD rule is applicable, then the strength and front would be aligned on the STUD.

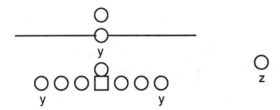

DIAMONDS: Formation strength is **RIGHT**. Movement by either back does not change strength.

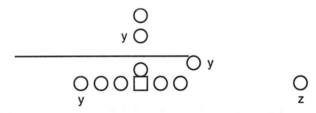

DIAMONDS: Formation strength is **RIGHT**. Movement changes strength to **LEFT**. In a double-digit call, the call goes to the second digit on movement.

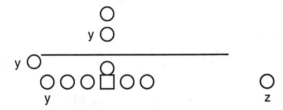

DIAMONDS: Formation strength is **LEFT**. Movement changes the strength to **RIGHT**. First digit goes to the second digit.

SUPPORT ASSIGNMENTS VERSUS END RUN AND RUN–PASS

The secondary and linebackers have the responsibility of stopping the end run and run–pass. This is not a difficult assignment if the players follow the proper pattern of defense. The team defensive pattern has three elements: a **primary support man**, a **cut-back man**, and a **run–pass** or **secondary support man**. If these three elements are properly executed, the end run and run–pass will be defended.

A. Primary Support Man

This term describes the responsibility of meeting the end run in its formative stage, making the tackle, forcing the cut-back, or driving the ball carrier deep so that he is vulnerable to pursuit.

- **Key**: Read the progression and react quickly to meet the lead blocker before he can turn upfield.
- **Technique**:
  1. **React quick and tough** to close the cut-back area. Meet the lead blocker before he can turn the corner.
  2. **Force the lead blocker** to commit himself; cause a decision.
  3. **Cause the ball carrier to cut back**, shrink the cut-back area.
  4. **Drive the ball carrier deep**, make the tackle, or string the play out to the sideline.
  5. To accomplish this, you must **STAY ON YOUR FEET**.

B. Cut-back Man

This term describes the area between the PRIMARY SUPPORT MAN and the first inside pursuit man.

- **Key**: Read the progression. Your key will dictate the sweep, and the type of support dictates cut-back responsibility.
- **Technique**:
  1. Control blocker at the line of scrimmage or at the blocker's depth. TWO-GAP responsibility.
  2. Stay square on the blocker; do not take a side. STAY ON YOUR FEET.
  3. Work out along the line of scrimmage. Be in position to make the tackle inside or outside.

C. Run–Pass or Secondary Support Man

This term defines the type of play we want from our deep players, who are responsible for pass first, run–pass, and play pass. It is the tackling of the ball carrier when the remainder of the team has failed to do so.

- **Key**: SEE "Z" strongside ("X" weakside). If he releases, cover. If he blocks on our PRIMARY SUPPORT MAN, support from outside-in. You must SEE the block.
- **Technique**: When RUN is definite. ALWAYS PLAY THE PASS FIRST.

1. Move to position to cover "Z" strongside ("X" weakside) on run–pass.
2. On block of "Z" ("X") on our primary SUPPORT MAN, support from outside-in.

D. Backer Support: Strongside

SAM (primary support man): On snap, step out and SEE inside, read progression, and determine sweep or off-tackle. Contain sweep, close off-tackle, and force spillage. To accomplish this, you must STAY ON YOUR FEET.

STRONG SAFETY (cut-back man): Read progression. If key blocks, react for run. On sweep, support inside SAM for cut-back responsibility. On off-tackle, adjust to take spillage. Backer = safety.

STRONG CORNER (run–pass or secondary support): Play the pass first; focus on "Z." If he releases, cover; if he blocks on S/S or SAM, SEE block and support from outside-in.

WEAK SAFETY: Revolve to deep middle. Pass first, run second. SEE TE, "Z," SB.

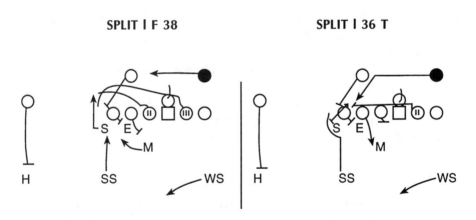

| SPLIT I F 38 | SPLIT I 36 T |

Backer Support: On onside deep pull, the SAM steps out and moves upfield to the depth of the pulling lineman. The SS fills inside SAM to take the cut-back. The corner plays the pass first; if the "Z" cracks on the SAM, he becomes the secondary support defender.

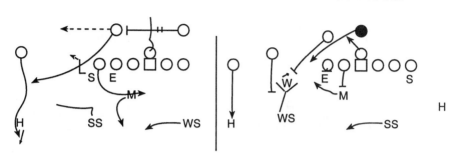

SPLIT I 138   **WEAK SLOT I 18 str.**

On flow, the SS takes the first back. SAM plays the run and finds the second back. MIKE plays the run and gains depth in the middle of the field. **CP:** Look for "Z" first; next look for "X." The corner has the deep outside and the WS rotates to the deep middle. The diagram on the right above shows the SLOT formation. WILL has backer support responsibility. On the action of the backfield triangle, he meets the lead blocker head-up to outside to contain the play and make it cut-back. The DE has the cut-back responsibility. The WS fills on the ball.

E. Safety Support: Strongside

STRONG SAFETY (primary support man): Take alignment that will allow you to beat the crackback block. If pass responsibility will not allow this position, you must call "CORNER" (six yards or under). Read the progression, react to the run, and meet the lead blocker as quickly and as tough as possible. Force the ball carrier to make a sharp cut back to the inside. If the ball carrier continues wide, drive him deep and string it out to the sideline. Always work to shrink the cut-back area. To accomplish this, you must STAY ON YOUR FEET.

SAM (cut-back man): Read the progression, attack the blocker (TE, pulling lineman) at his depth, and control him. TWO-GAP responsibility; do not take a side until the ball carrier commits. **CP:** If the TE blocks on you and releases for run–pass, stay with him man to man. Be alert in short yardage and goal line situations.

STRONG CORNER (run–pass or secondary support): Play the pass first; focus on "Z." If he releases, cover; if he blocks on SS, SEE block. Support from outside-in.

WEAK SAFETY: Revolve to deep middle. Pass first, run second. SEE TE, "Z," SB.

SPLIT I F 38   SPLIT I 36 T

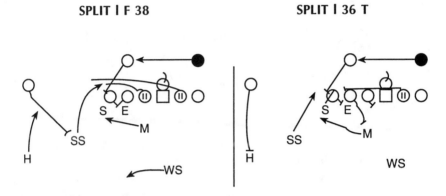

Safety Support: On onside deep pull, the SS moves upfield and meets the lead blocker at the depth of the pulling lineman. The SAM stays square on the blocker to take the cut-back. The corner plays the pass first; if the "Z" cracks on the SS, he becomes the secondary support defender.

SPLIT I 138   SPLIT I 338

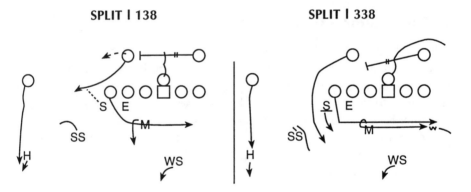

On FLOW, the SS takes the first back. SAM plays the run and finds the second back. MIKE plays the run and gains depth in the middle of the field. **CP:** Look for "Z" first; next look for "X." The corner has the deep outside and the WS rotates to the deep middle.

F. Safety Support: Strongside versus Close "Z"

The close "Z" is primarily a formation used in short yardage situations or at the goal line. Coverage may be either MAN or ZONE. The following description is designed with this in mind.

STRONG SAFETY (primary support man): Take an alignment that will allow you to beat the crackback and to force the "Z" to commit. The purpose of this type of support is to: (1) enable us to play the same support on both sides with the same personnel and (2) make our support a definite assignment for all personnel, which will aid in becoming more aggressive. Read the progression, **from a position where you can see the TE and the backfield triangle.** On the block of the TE, get penetration upfield; force the "Z" to commit quickly if he is going to crackback. If he does not crack, you are in a position to contain the sweep as you would in normal safety support technique. To accomplish this, you must STAY ON YOU FEET! **CP:** Pull of onside lineman will help you determine sweep.

SAM (cut-back man): Take a position that will eliminate the inside release of the TE as much as possible. This is necessary because our strong safety is close to the line of scrimmage and is unable to successfully pick up the TE if allowed to release inside unmolested. The remaining part of your assignment is the same as you would have on normal safety support.

STRONG CORNER (run–pass or secondary support): Take an alignment that will allow you to see the "Z" and the backfield triangle. Play the pass first, from a shade outside position on the "Z." Your assignment will remain the same as prescribed in the defense called. If your assignment is the "Z" man to man, this will still be your assignment. If your assignment is the deep outside zone, this will not change either. See the block, then support for the outside-in as you would in normal safety support.

WEAK SAFETY (revolve): Carry out your assignment as defined by our defense called. Pass first, run second.

G. Corner Support: Strongside

STRONG CORNER (primary support man): Read progression. If "Z" sets to block on you, take the inside and force play at an angle quickly. Shrink the cut-back area. Meet blocker as quickly and as tough as possible. Force the ball carrier to make a sharp cut back to the inside. If the ball carrier continues wide, drive him deep and string it out to the sideline. To accomplish this, you must STAY ON YOUR FEET.

SAM (cut-back man): Read progression. Attack the blocker (TE, pulling lineman) at his depth and control him. TWO-GAP responsibility; do not take a side until the runner commits. **CP:** If the TE blocks on you and releases for run–pass, stay with him man to man.

S/S (run–pass or secondary support): Play the pass first; focus on "Z." If he releases, cover. If he blocks on S/C, SEE block, with support from outside-in.

W/S: Revolve to deep middle, Pass first, run second. SEE TE, "Z," SB.

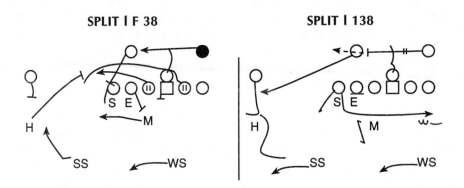

SPLIT I F 38   SPLIT I 138

Corner Support: On onside deep pull, the SC must beat the block of "Z" and move to meet the lead blocker at the depth of the pulling lineman. The SAM stays square on the blocker to take the cut-back. The SS plays the pass first; if the "Z" blocks the SC, he becomes the secondary support defender. The diagram on the right above shows FLOW. On FLOW, the SC takes the first back. SAM plays the run and finds the second back. MIKE plays the run and gains depth in the middle of the field. **CP**: Look for "Z" first; next look for "X." The SC has the deep outside and the WS rotates to the deep middle.

H. Backer Support: Weakside

All coverages are with "X" out in normal position.

WILL (primary support man): Read progression and meet the lead blocker at his depth as quickly and as tough as possible. Shrink the cut-back area. To accomplish this, you must STAY ON YOUR FEET. **CP**: Meet blocker head-up when back-up by coverage.

W/END (cut-back man): Read progression. Attack the blocker and control him. Work out along the line of scrimmage. Do not overrun the ball.

W/C (run–pass or secondary support): Play the pass first; focus on "X." If he releases, cover; if he blocks on WILL, SEE block. Support from the outside-in. **CP**: If "X" blocks, SEE WB for run–pass before secondary support. If "X" runs, take off; SEE path or block of WB before secondary support.

WILL NOTES: Call "LION," "STRAIGHT," "BAM" on BACKER SUPPORT to better define the responsibility between you and your defensive end. LION may be called with any coverage. Use BAM call only on coverage (weakside coverage) when you are backed up. Use STRAIGHT when committed on BLITZ.

- **LION**: Alignment is giant position. On snap, HOLD, read progression, and be in position to fill inside your DE on flow to you. Pursue on flow away. On pass, go to coverage.

- **STRAIGHT and BAM**: Alignment is crackback position. On the snap, with ball and backs to you, close inside the back blocking you; drive the play deep. Cause a decision. On a pass, go to coverage. **CP**: Use BAM call when not committed (coverage). Use STRAIGHT call when committed (BLITZ).

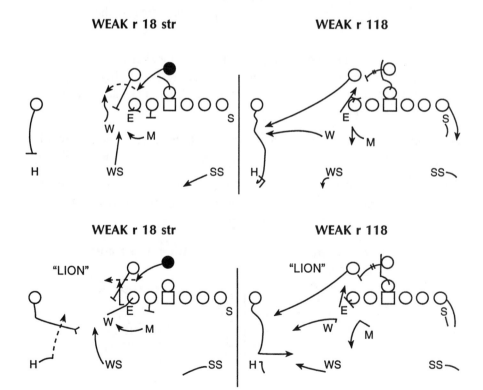

WEAK r 18 str	WEAK r 118

WEAK r 18 str	WEAK r 118

I. Backer Support: Weakside versus "X" Tight or Two TEs

WILL (primary support man): On snap, step out and SEE inside, read progression, and determine sweep or off-tackle. Contain sweep, close off-tackle, and force spillage. To accomplish this, you must STAY ON YOUR FEET. **CP:** TE or "X" blocks and pass shows, engage and cover by coverage. When in strongside coverage and NO NEAR BACK is present, BACKER SUPPORT may be changed to CORNER SUPPORT.

W/C (cut-back man): Read progression; if key blocks, react for run. On sweep, support inside WILL for cut-back. On off-tackle, adjust to take spillage.

W/S (run–pass or secondary support): Pass first; when you read run, revolve and pick up receiver for run–pass. None, secondary support where necessary.

J. Corner Support: Weakside versus "X" Tight or Two TEs

WEAK CORNER (primary support man): Read progression, and meet lead blocker as quickly and as tough as possible. Force the ball carrier to make a sharp cut back to the inside. Shrink the cut-back area. If the ball carrier continues wide, drive him deep and string it out to the sideline.

WILL (cut-back man): Read progression; attack blocker (TE, "X," pulling lineman) at his depth and control him. Two-gap responsibility; do not take a side until the runner commits. **CP:** Near end (TE) blocks and pass shows, engage by coverage.

W/S (run–pass or secondary support): Pass first; when you read run, revolve and pick up receiver for run–pass. None, secondary support where necessary.

WILL NOTES: "GAP" may be called on any coverage versus NEAR (TE) formation to strengthen the B GAP. This gives the DE a TWO-GAP assignment. WILL assignment does not change.

ACE r 18 str   **ACE r 18 str e-flare**

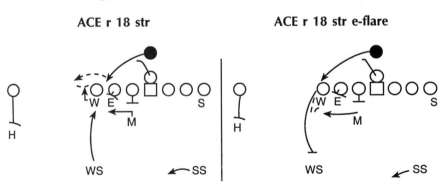

K. Blitz Support: Weakside (Safety and End versus Wes and Wig Blitz; Backer versus Wod Blitz)

WEAK SAFETY (primary support man): Read progression; meet the lead blocker at his depth as quickly and as tough as possible. Shrink the cut-back area. If the ball carrier continues wide, drive him deep and string it out to the sideline. Must SEE block of WB, then support.

WEAK CORNER (run–pass or secondary support): Pass first, focus on "X." If he releases, cover. If he blocks on WILL or WS, SEE block; support from outside-in.

WILL (DE) (cut-back man): Attack blocker head-up on his side of the line of scrimmage. Control him, and be ready to react in or out. Make the play.

STRAIGHT vs 18 str   **WES (LION) vs 18 str**

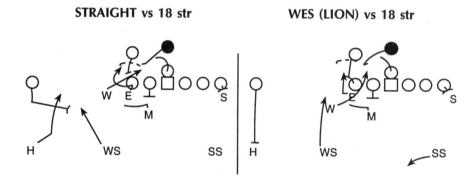

DESTROY TECHNIQUE

This **one-short** and **two-deep** defensive action is used within the defense when three defenders are working together. The defender that is short will be responsible for destroying the pattern and attacking the ball on the gimmick pattern. The defender on each side of the DESTROY MAN is responsible for getting depth to an assigned area (zone) and locating and attacking the ball from that area. In some defensive alignments, it is possible to use the DESTROY TECHNIQUE on both the strongside and the weakside. Most of the time, however, the technique is used on the weakside versus anticipated FRANK ACTION, from the WEAK formation.

The DESTROY TECHNIQUE mostly concerns the linebackers. However, by making this technique part of the basic information, all pass defenders will know what it means and realize the importance of its effective use.

Nothing destroys a pass offense faster than jamming and rerouting receivers. It destroys the timing of the offensive pattern and gives the defense the advantage.

COVER 2: SAM is the destroyer, MIKE and H are on each side to attack the ball

COVER 2: WILL is the destroyer, MIKE and H are on each side to attack the ball

split I

weak I

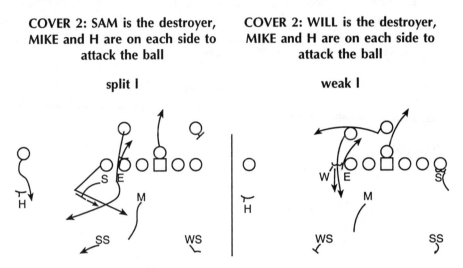

BACKFIELD ALIGNMENTS

Alignments are meaningful. In order to become more aware of various sets, coaches like to give players the following **alert calls** to describe the cheat of the backs: **up, out,** and **in.** The one problem that is created by cheat recognition and alert calls is the failure of the linebacker to play. This is especially true of the inexperienced linebacker. He oftentimes is so intent on looking for and calling the cheat that his play suffers. The coach must be aware of the possible problem and decide how much to stress cheats.

HUNCH: WB is cheated up

weak right

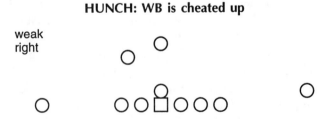

This is a weakside running formation. Strongside the counter is the best play. In the last few years, the tailback has been the deep back and the primary ball carrier. The up back is a blocker. If the fullback is the deep back and the tailback is cheated up, then weakside running can also be expected. The same call will apply to split and strong formation.

FULL: Fullback is cheated up

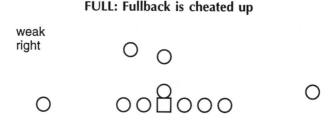

weak
right

This call describes the cheating up of the fullback or back in the fullback position. The more the fullback cheats up, the tougher it is to run weakside. Normally, no frank action will come from this alignment. The lag draw to the tailback is a possibility.

CHIN: A call used to describe the cheat IN of the SB or WB

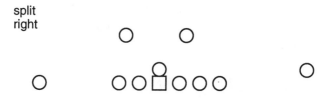

split
right

This type of cheat usually indicates an inside strongside play. The strong back may even be cheated up. The other type of play could be weakside wide.

CHOW: A call used to describe the cheat OUT of the SB or WB

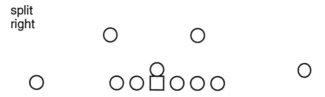

split
right

This type of wide cheat usually indicates a sweep (wide) type of play. The other indication is a pass release by the back that is aligned wide.

The calls displayed above are examples of alignments that indicate the type of play that may be run by the offense. There is usually a counter off of the alignment, but through analysis the staff will learn what the opponent likes best. It is not foolproof, but being conscious of the cheats can be helpful in preparation for the opponent. The same terms—HUNCH, FULL, CHIN, and CHOW—also apply to all two-back formations.

HOLE NUMBERING SYSTEM

The hole numbers are directly over the offensive player. This keeps it simple and very workable. The odd numbers are to the right (left offensively), and the even numbers are to the left (right offensively). Most teams use a similar system. However, when I joined the New York Giants, the numbering system was just the opposite. I decided to keep the same numbering system in use, thinking that the coaches could learn the system a lot faster than asking the players to change.

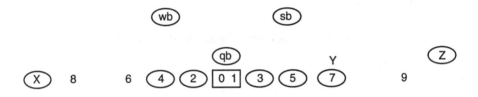

PLAY NUMBERING SYSTEM

The offensive play numbering system is displayed below. It is important that the defense knows and uses the same numbering system. This facilitates communication during practice and ensures that both the offense and the defense are "on the same page" on game day.

There are many different systems, and I do not recommend one over the other. My sole reason for including the example below is to highlight the importance of the play numbering system and to show how it may be handled for the defensive staff.

SPLIT RIGHT

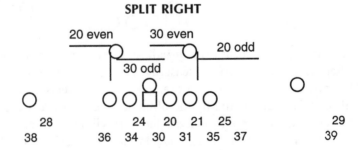

I RIGHT

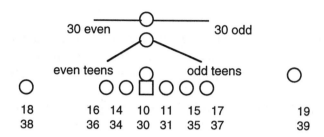

WEAK RIGHT

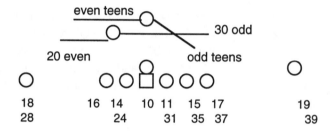

STRONG RIGHT

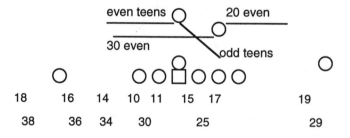

During my more than 40 years of experience, I have been part of many discussions concerning the numbering system, with pros and cons for each one. After all the discussions, I have never found a better system than the one presented above. It is flexible, and by adding a word like *wham, trap,* or *sweep* to define the blocking, the system is very descriptive. I suggest that newer coaches give this system some thought. Experienced coaches have a system they like and probably do not want to consider a change. For the fan, it is an example of how the running play is called.

PASS NUMBERING: PLAY PASS, RUN PASS, BACKUP PASS

In the **play action pass**, when the QB fakes the play and drops back in the pocket, the number one **(1)** is added. (Example: 134 = play 34 is faked and the QB drops back to throw; 118 = play 18 is faked and the QB drops back to throw.)

If the **running back is called to throw the pass**, the number four **(4)** is added. (Example: 439 = play 39 is run and the running back throws the pass; 428 = play 28 is run and the running back throws the pass.)

If the QB **fakes the play and bootlegs away** from the action, the number three **(3)** is added. (Example: 335 = play 35 is faked and the QB bootlegs away from the action.)

If the QB **fakes the play and rolls behind the fake**, the number two **(2)** is added. (Example: 235 = play 35 is faked and the QB rolls behind the fake.)

The blocking and pass pattern will be basic for the numbered play action. If another pattern is needed, a word can be added to describe the pass pattern. As an example, the formation call and the number are called as the offense would make the call.

135

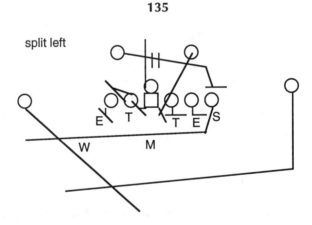

The diagram above shows an example of play pass **135** with the **blocking** and **basic pass pattern**. As the need arises, other patterns may be added by adding a word to describe the pattern.

235

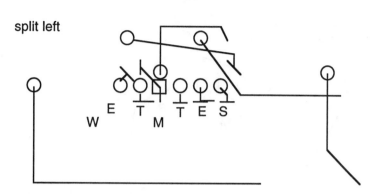

split left

235 would be a similar play action, with the QB rolling behind the play action. The blocking would change slightly because of where the QB will throw. Because of the QB action, the pattern would change and be designated by a word. (Example: **235 Arrow**.)

335

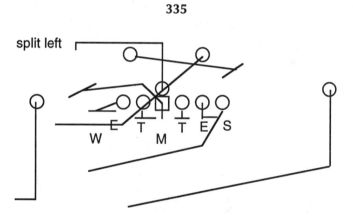

split left

335 would be a similar play action, with the QB bootleg away from the action. The blocking would change because of where the QB will throw. Because of the QB action, the pattern would change and be designated by a word. (Example: **335 Cross**.)

439

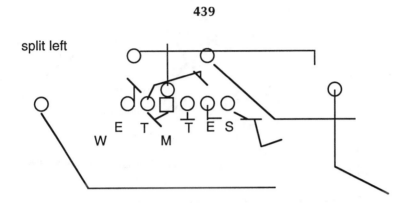

split left

E　T　T　E　S
W　　M

439 would resemble play 39 (a sweep), with the running back throwing the ball. Again, the blocking may be basic to the sweep call, and the number could also contain a basic pass pattern or a word as needed. The **400** pass is normally called a run pass.

The **backup pass** is handled in a similar manner. The number designates a basic pattern and also defines the blocking. The odd number again refers to the offensive left side (right side defensively), and the even number refers to the offensive right side (left side defensively). A left formation would use 1, 3, 5, 7, and 9 as the second number. The right formation would use 0, 2, 4, 6, and 8 as the second number. The sixty and seventy series are used in the following illustrations.

61

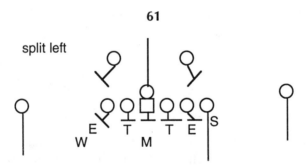

split left

E　T　T　E　S
W　　M

The above diagram shows **61**, the basic backup pass: three receivers releasing, with both backs blocking. The basic pattern may be an all-hook pattern or whatever the staff desires. The blocking for 61 will always be the same. **CP**: If the player the back is blocking does not rush, the back may release in a designated area.

63

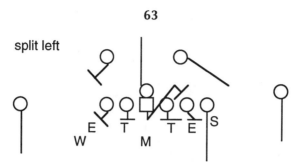

split left

The above diagram shows **63**, the **SB releasing** with the three receivers. It also shows the center, checking the MIKE and releasing for the SAM, and the WB blocking WILL. Again, as above, there is a basic pattern for 63, and additional patterns may be called by adding words. The QB must key the coverage for MIKE and SAM both blitzing and throw hot to the designated receiver.

67

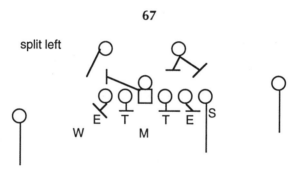

split left

The above diagram shows **67**, the **WB releasing** with the three receivers. It also shows the center releasing for the WILL and the SB double checking MIKE and SAM. Again, as above, there is a basic pattern for 67, and additional patterns may be called by adding words. The QB must key the coverage for MIKE and SAM both blitzing and throw hot to the designated receiver.

The seventy series illustrates the quick **three-step drop-back passing**. This is very effective versus the rush and loose secondary coverage. The offensive line is aggressive, trying to keep the defensive line on the line of scrimmage with their hands down. The backs attack the outside linebackers.

The purpose of these techniques is to create passing lanes for the QB. In the quick passing game, the receivers all run short out and in routes. As above, the offensive left formation uses an odd number as the second number and the right offensive formation uses an even number as the second number.

71

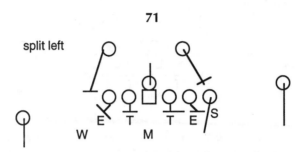

The above illustrations provide examples of the methods used to call the play action pass, the **run pass**, the **backup pass**, and the **quick pass**. They also show the basic protection for the backup pass. Although only the sixty and seventy series are shown in the above examples, a complete offensive pass package would include other series used in various pattern combinations.

As mentioned earlier, it is important that the **defense uses the same terminology** as the offense in referring to running plays and pass plays. This is critical as players on offense and defense work against each other in practice and is also valuable on game day as coaches and players communicate. It is part of the **TEAM** concept, working together to reach a mutual objective: **TO BE THE BEST.**

2

FRONTS

ALIGNMENTS

FRONTS, like all areas, revolve in cycles. These cycles usually revolve around both the EVEN and ODD concepts. In most cases, to some degree, all defensive packages probably use both an EVEN and an ODD alignment.

Although I do not remember our exact alignment in high school, it was an EVEN alignment. In college, it was two platoon, and my position was right offensive tackle. I can recall in detail our calls and the method we used to handle the different defensive line alignments, but to be specific on the defensive fronts we used in college would stretch my memory. However, from that point on, the various defensive fronts are a definite part of my education and training.

Whether EVEN or ODD, all were centered around the concept of an eight-man front. A team would usually use either the EVEN or ODD, but managed within the base to adjust to the other alignment. This was accomplished by moving the line in an overshift or undershift movement before or on the snap. The latter provided a perfect disguise, along with the necessary mixture to be successful.

At this point, it is appropriate to take a quick look at the history of alignments and review some of the early thoughts, some of which remain in action today. Although there is nothing absolutely new in football today, there are new developments in how each staff makes use of the various techniques. Emphasis is placed on teaching and on the talents of the personnel who play the game.

Using the talents of the personnel has always been of primary importance to me. I teach, study the tape, and make sure what I am teaching is being carried out properly in game conditions. Notice that I say *game conditions*. This is important because all too often I have seen the reverse. We spend hours and hours teaching a technique and drilling in practice, but when the whistle blows, the technique we worked so hard to perfect goes down the drain in the added emotion and excitement of the game.

Now let's look at the history and thoughts behind some of the alignments that remain basic today.

A. Even Alignments

The **WIDE TACKLE SIX** was and remains today a favorite of many. It is an eight-man front. The interior lineman must have the ability (strength and agility) to vary the charge, and the ends and linebackers must have the strength and ability to play the run and the agility to be involved in pass defense. The success of the defense depends on the ability of the personnel to vary charges and create blocking problems for the offense. The alignment presents an eight-man front for the run, and by dropping the ends, it allows the team to use a seven-man pass defense.

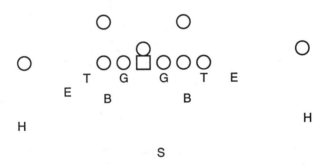

Many teams referred to this defense as "**LETTERS**," where the letters of the alphabet were used to designate various charges. Also, the defense could be divided into two different sections. For example, on the right, the guard, tackle, and end could be involved in a stunt, and the left-side personnel could be involved in a different stunt. The letter "A" usually meant the base, which was either a gap or two-gap responsibility. The above drawing is an example of "A."

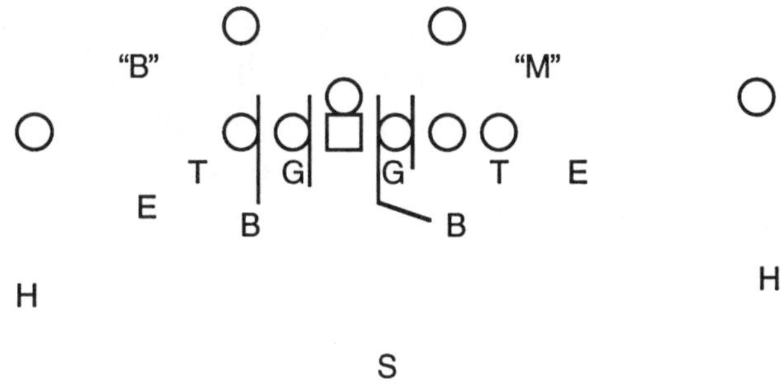

The above drawing is an example of the flexibility of the **WIDE TACKLE SIX**. On the left is the "B" stunt, and on the right is the "M" stunt. However, just a simple "B" stunt or "M" stunt may be called on both sides.

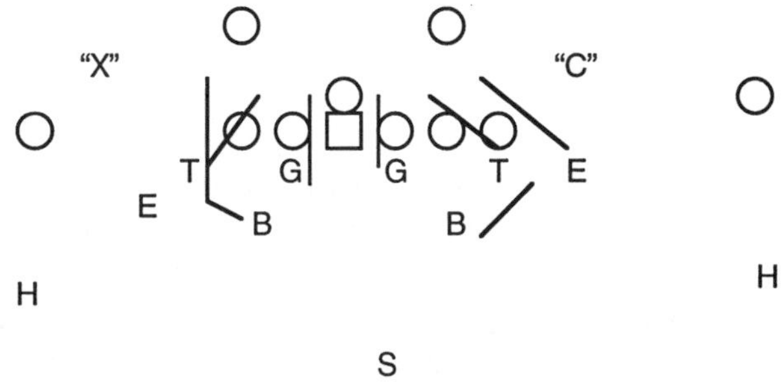

The above example uses "X" as the call on the left and "C" as the call on the right.

These three illustrations (using "A," "B," "M," "X," and "C") show the flexibility of the "LETTERS" concept. Together with the ability to overshift the line to or away from the tight end, this gives the **WIDE SIX** package plenty of variation to create problems for the offense. Instead of moving the line to or away from the tight end, a few teams would substitute a lineman for a linebacker. This would enable the defense to keep the same basic assignments and align the players in a "**seven-diamond**" type of alignment. This made for a great run defense, plus it presented the offense with a pass protection problem, creating one-on-one blocking situations for their line. If not properly recognized, the seven diamond could possibly force a back to block an onrushing defensive lineman. In studying the seven diamond in more detail, something familiar is revealed: shades of the recent popular "**BEAR DEFENSE**" in alignment, assignment, and overall purpose.

During its success and popularity, much was written about this "new innovation." However, as I have mentioned, "there is nothing new under the sun." What is new is the way it is taught and the personnel adjustment so necessary to handle the pro offense and its capabilities.

Seven-Diamond Alignment

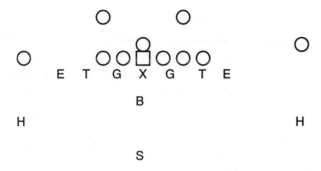

Tennessee and many **WIDE TACKLE SIX** teams used this adjustment with great success in the forties through the sixties. In the diagram above, an "X" appears over the center to note that any position can be used in this alignment. Some teams substituted at this position, others moved their best lineman, and others moved a linebacker in and out to conceal the intent.

Six–One Alignment

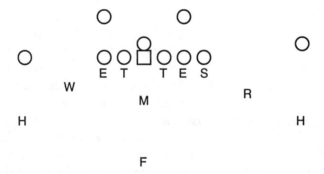

The symbols changed, there were no designated GUARDS, and SAM, MIKE, and WILL became household words. ROVER or "R" was added to still present an eight-man front. ROVER usually aligned to the strongside of the formation, but could be aligned to the wideside of the field regardless of the strongside. This alignment maintains the EVEN concept, but in similar fashion other teams used the same philosophy from an ODD alignment.

B. Odd Alignments

The **OKLAHOMA defense**, a 5–4 alignment:

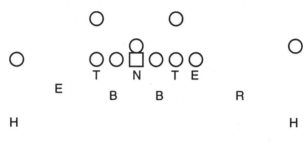

I am not absolutely sure why many referred to this alignment as the Oklahoma defense, but my educated guess is that the Oklahoma coaches under Bud Wilkerson were among the first to use this alignment. It contains many features similar to the old **WIDE TACKLE SIX overshift**: an eight-man front using the ROVER, two linebackers, two ends, two tackles, and a nose. The rover would be the same as the overshifted end that has been dropped for better vision and a more versatile assignment. At one point in the early part of my coaching career, the Oklahoma defense alignment was thought to be a major factor in playing against the "split-T" type of offense. It was another one of those innovations as seen through the evolution of defense.

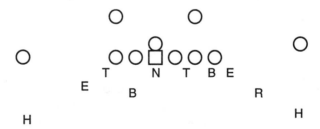

The above diagram shows the adjustment to concentrate more on delaying and jamming the tight end by aligning the linebacker over the tight end. The adjustment is often referred to as "TIGHT" or "**EAGLE**." The adjustment gained popularity because of the success the Philadelphia Eagles experienced in pro football and was quickly picked up by other pro and college teams. In this new concept, the secondary was aligned in more of a four-deep principle than in the collegiate three deep.

In pro football, both sides were often reduced to the "TIGHT" or "EAGLE" adjustment. This alignment also developed the need for more size in the interior line, and the NOSE was backed off the line slightly for better pursuit from tackle to tackle. In some ways, the "EAGLE" adjustment on both sides developed the NOSE as a half linebacker and half lineman, similar to the SIX–ONE mentioned earlier. All of these adjustments gradually brought about the present-day alignments that are used by most teams throughout football.

C. Baltimore Mid-Sixties

My first experience with Baltimore in the mid-sixties consisted of a 4–3, OVER and UNDER. The Colts in the late fifties and early sixties were primarily a 4–3 team, and they had a defensive line capable of playing the alignment successfully. In the mid-sixties, the tackles were smaller, but were very quick and agile. We felt the need to have more variation, and we proceeded to develop an OVER and UNDER concept to go with our 4–3.

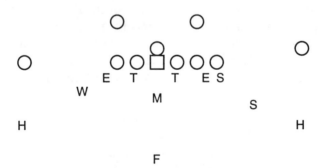

The regular 4–3 as we used it is shown above. The tackles varied their gap responsibilities. Head-on to outside shoulder is shown above. From this, both tackles could have inside gap responsibilities, called **PINCH**. PINCH can be a called alignment or can be a movement on snap.

From the regular alignment, a strongside call was used to move both tackles to the tight end on the snap. This call was called **CROSSED HANDS**.

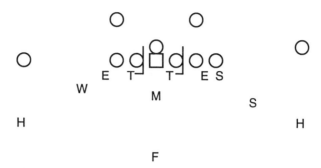

The **CROSSED HANDS** call enabled us to move the tackles strong or weak by formation to better play the run. In pass situations, we liked to keep our ends and tackles normal. The end away from the movement played more of a head-up technique. Our coverage alignment was based on a three-deep concept for zone coverages and a four-deep concept for man coverages and blitz. We stressed movement to disguise and to force the quarterback to hesitate in his read.

The Cowboys under the direction of Tom Landry had an interesting concept of the CROSSED HANDS defense. It was commonly referred to as the **Dallas "FLEX."** The term came from the position of the defensive end away from the direction of the call. The position of the end was off the ball, with a two-gap assignment. In playing against this type of alignment and assignment, the offense had to take particular care to handle the "FLEX." The concept was very effective over the years.

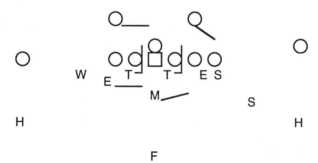

The above drawing shows the Dallas "FLEX." On FLOW away, the tackles take the weakside A and strongside B gaps. The flexed end is two gap, and on FLOW away he pursues, first taking the strongside A gap as MIKE pursues outside the strongside defensive end.

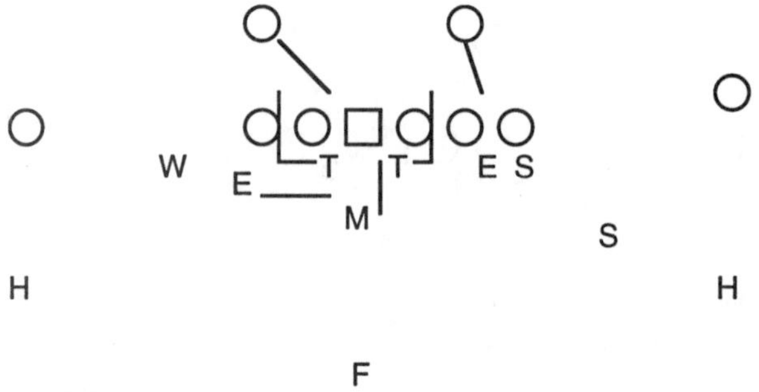

The above drawing shows the weakside tackle in an out charge. This call is the key breaker to the success of the "FLEX." The weakside end is again in the "FLEX" alignment. On FLOW away, he takes the weakside A gap and the MIKE, and on a back and ball read to him takes the strongside A gap.

Shown below is the same call as described, with FLOW to the "FLEX." The end plays off the block and pursues the play from the inside-out. The "FLEX" principle was basic to the Dallas defense for many years. It was so good that at times the Cowboys would show the "FLEX" alignment and play regular.

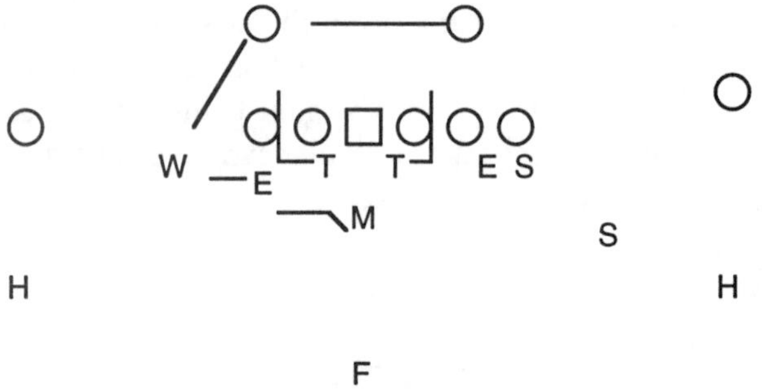

The purpose of these illustrations and the accompanying comments is to help you to better understand the development of FRONTS in the defensive package. Innovations occurred not because they are totally new but because the individual staff adjusted something they saw to their personnel, their thoughts, and what they needed to accomplish.

With this as a background, let's take a look at the adjustments made with the Dolphins and Giants in the seventies, LSU in the mid-eighties, and the Chargers in the early nineties. In the early seventies, we used a form of the OVER and UNDER fronts from a 30 concept. This will be considered in greater detail as part of the discussion of the 30 defense. For now, we'll concentrate on the OVER and UNDER.

OVER AND UNDER

Regarding the OVER and UNDER front, it is my feeling that both four-man alignments, as we used them for many years, and the three-man alignment with the SAM or WILL committed are the same defensive fronts. In fact, this is how we originally began using the three-man line in 1971. We lost a defensive end to injury and needed a replacement. The best player available was Bob Matheson, former middle linebacker for the Browns, who at the time was being used as a defensive end. We traded for Bob and in talking with him saw no reason to line him up with his hand on the ground. Having played middle linebacker at Duke and with the Browns for several years, he no doubt felt more comfortable standing up than aligned in a three-point stance. Thus the Dolphins'-style three-man OVER or UNDER concept began to take shape. This will be discussed in detail as part of the coverage of the 30 front.

When I returned to the sidelines with the Chargers, we discussed the four-man and three-man concepts at great length. In fact, our first defensive book contained the terminology and drawings for both ideas. The more we studied our personnel and their assignments, the more we came to the realization that we needed to concentrate on the four-man front. Our ends were better suited to play the four-man front, which requires an outside tendency in most assignments.

Our linebackers, especially Junior Seau, would have been ideal as rush linebackers, but we did not have the depth necessary to build a successful three-man front. Therefore, we concentrated on the OVER and UNDER four-man front—and made the correct decision.

A. Areas of Responsibility

A GAP: The area from the center's crotch to the crotch of the offensive guard (first man from the center).

B GAP: The area from the crotch of the offensive guard to the crotch of the offensive tackle (second man from the center).

C GAP: The area from the crotch of the offensive tackle to the crotch of the tight end, or the area one yard outside the tackle (third man from the center).

D GAP: The area from the crotch of the tight end to the crotch of the wing back, or the area one yard outside the tight end (fourth man from the center.)

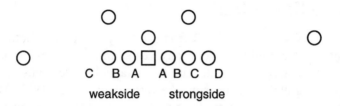

C   B   A   A   B   C   D

weakside   strongside

With these thoughts on the different FRONT concepts as a background, the alignment and assignment of each player should become more meaningful and useful to the student, coach, and fan. The next section covers what I often refer to as "ole faithful," because throughout my career we have always had an alignment that covered the center.

Both the OVER and UNDER have been very successful for me, but if I had to pick just one, it would be the OVER. Having said that, let's begin with the OVER and proceed from that point to describe our FRONT package.

B. Over Front

OVER

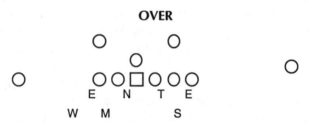

E   N   T   E

W   M   S

- ■ **Position: S/END.**
- ■ **Alignment: Head-on to inside shoulder** of offensive tight end.
- ■ **Key:** Tackle and TE if in normal alignment.
- ■ **Assignment: Ball to**—strongside C GAP, squeeze B. **Ball away**—C-GAP collapse. SEE QB and BALL for bootleg and reverse. **Pass**—rush passer, contain.

- ■ **Position: S/TACKLE.**
- ■ **Alignment: Head-on to outside shoulder** of offensive guard.
- ■ **Key:** Guard and tackle.
- ■ **Assignment: Ball to**—strongside B GAP, squeeze A. **Ball away**—B-GAP collapse. **Pass**—rush passer, break pocket, stay in your lane.

- ■ **Position: NOSE TACKLE.**
- ■ **Alignment: Cocked in weakside gap** on shoulder of center.
- ■ **Key:** Center and guard.

- **Assignment: Ball to**—weakside A GAP. **Ball away**—A-GAP collapse. **Pass**—rush passer, break pocket, stay in your lane.

- **Position: W/END.**
- **Alignment: Head-on to outside shoulder** of offensive tackle.
- **Key:** Tackle and running lane.
- **Assignment: Ball to**—weakside C GAP, squeeze B. **Ball away** C-GAP collapse. SEE QB and BALL for reverse and bootleg. **Pass**—rush passer, contain.

- **Position: SAM** (linebacker on side of overshift). SAM in over and **WILL** in under may be the same player.
- **Alignment: Head-on** the offensive tackle, one to two yards deep (from feet of lineman). Width and depth may vary depending on coverage, formation, and down and distance. Have vision.
- **Key:** Tackle, running lane, and backfield triangle.
- **Assignment: Ball to**—D gap by support pattern.
  1. Back and ball to—Attack blocker at line of scrimmage. Maintain outside leverage.
  2. Back and ball outside—Scrape outside DE, pursue ball from inside-out.
  3. Back and no ball (counter)—HOLD, find ball, pursue.
  Ball away—Strongside A GAP, find ball, pursue from inside-out. **Pass**—play coverage called.

- **Position: MIKE** (linebacker away from overshift).
- **Alignment: Head-on to outside shoulder** of offensive guard, one to two yards (from feet of linemen) deep. Width and depth may vary depending on coverage, formation, and down and distance. Have vision.
- **Key:** Guard, running lane, and backfield triangle.
- **Assignment: Ball to**—weakside B gap.
  1. Back and ball to you—Attack blocker at line of scrimmage. Maintain outside leverage.
  2. Back and ball outside—Fast stack with DE, pursue ball from inside-out.
  3. Back and no ball (counter)—HOLD, find ball, pursue.
  Ball away—strongside A GAP, find ball, pursue from inside-out. **Pass**—play coverage called.

- **Position: WILL.**
- **Alignment: Giant position** is normal. Vary crackback, "I," or out by coverage call—DISGUISE your alignment.

- **Key**: Tackle, running lane, and backfield triangle.
- **Assignment: Ball to**—C GAP, by support pattern (backer, safety, corner). **Ball away**—SEE QB and ball for bootleg and reverse. N/T (no one there)—pursue, weakside B gap to strongside. **Pass**—play coverage called.

Perhaps you wonder why I said I favor the OVER front and started our discussion with that alignment. The answer is simple. First, the alignment places a defender over the **center** or the center–guard gap. That is very important, because the center is usually the poorest blocker on the offensive line. He has to snap the ball first and plays most of the game, or at least the initial movement, with his right arm between his legs. Next, the OVER front places a defender over or slightly inside the **tight end**. This forces the tight end to block a defensive lineman to run wide or off-tackle. Like all fronts, the gaps are assigned, and there are two defenders over the two weakest blockers on most offensive lines.

Next, we will discuss the UNDER front, which from a coverage standpoint is as good as you can call. In addition, you again have all the GAPS covered.

C. Under Front

UNDER

- **Position**: S/END.
- **Alignment: Head-on to outside shoulder** of offensive tackle.
- **Key**: Tackle and tight end, if in normal position.
- **Assignment: Ball to**—strongside C GAP, squeeze B. **Ball away**—C-GAP collapse. SEE QB and BALL for bootleg and reverse. **Pass**—rush passer, contain.

- **Position**: NOSE TACKLE.
- **Alignment: Cocked in strongside gap** on shoulder of center.
- **Key**: Center and guard.
- **Assignment: Ball to**—strongside A GAP. **Ball away**—A-GAP collapse. **Pass**—rush passer, break pocket, stay in your lane.

- **Position**: W/TACKLE.
- **Alignment**: **Head-on to outside shoulder** of offensive guard.
- **Key**: Guard and tackle.
- **Assignment**: **Ball to**—weakside B GAP, squeeze A. **Ball away**—B-GAP collapse. **Pass**—rush passer, break pocket, stay in your lane.

- **Position**: W/END.
- **Alignment**: **One yard** outside the offensive tackle.
- **Key**: Tackle, running lane, and backfield triangle. SEE the ball.
- **Assignment**: **Ball to**—weakside C GAP, squeeze B. **Ball away**—C GAP, pursue. SEE QB and BALL for bootleg and reverse. **Pass**—rush passer, contain.

- **Position**: SAM.
- **Alignment**: By support pattern (backer, safety, corner).
- **Key**: TE, running lane, backfield triangle.
- **Assignment**: **Ball to**—follow support pattern progression, control blocker, locate ball. **Ball away**—contain. SEE QB and BALL for bootleg and reverse. **Pass**—play coverage called.

- **Position**: MIKE (linebacker away from the under).
- **Alignment**: **Head-on to outside shoulder** of offensive guard. One to two yards (from the feet of the linemen) deep. Width and depth may vary depending on coverage, formation, and down and distance. Have vision.
- **Key**: Guard, running lane, and backfield triangle.
- **Assignment**: **Ball to**—strongside B gap.
  1. Back and ball to you—Attack blocker at line of scrimmage. Maintain outside leverage.
  2. Back and ball outside—Fast stack with DE, pursue ball from inside-out.
  3. Back and NO ball (counter)—HOLD, find ball, pursue.
  Ball away—weakside A GAP, find ball, pursue from inside-out. **Pass**—play coverage called.

- **Position**: WILL (linebacker on side of the under). **WILL** in under and SAM in over may be the same player.
- **Alignment**: **Head-on to weakside** offensive tackle. One to two yards deep (from the feet of the linemen). Width and depth may vary depending on coverage, formation, and down and distance. Have vision.
- **Key**: Tackle, running lane, and backfield triangle.
- **Assignment**: **Ball to**—scrape to D GAP.

1. Back and ball outside—Fast stack with DE, pursue ball from inside-out.
2. Back and NO ball (counter)—HOLD, find ball, pursue.

Ball away—weakside A GAP, find ball, pursue from inside-out. **Pass**—play coverage called.

D. The Beginning of the "53" Defense: The Three-Man Line

As a staff, we really stumbled on the three-man front and the blitzing line-backer as used by the Dolphins in the early seventies. Early in the 1971 pre-season, we lost our defensive end Jim Riley to injury, and it was not until later, during the cut-down dates (September 1), that we acquired a replacement. Bob Matheson was the best player available. He had been a #1 draft choice from Duke University and was with the Cleveland Browns in the mid-sixties. The Browns played Bob at middle linebacker, and he was one of the best players in the league at that position. Later, he added weight, to the point that they virtually gave up on him as a linebacker and tried to use him at defensive end. It was at this point that he became available to us. Bob joined us, and I immediately began meeting with him to catch up. Because of his background, and intense desire to succeed, he was a success almost immediately.

To make things simple, we called the defense "53," which was Bob's number. Initially, this meant that he was the blitzing linebacker. As I mentioned, we used the same defense as other teams, except we did not ask Bob to put his hand on the ground. He played the position as a stand-up outside linebacker and was our fourth rusher from either the strongside or weakside. We continued to grow from this point as a beginning. We gradually moved Bob inside and would have him drop or blitz. Offensive blocking schemes were not always set to handle this change-up, and the "53" defense was an immediate success. During the 1971, 1972, and 1973 seasons, the "53" defense was our total package. We got fancy with our terminology and applied numbers to the linebackers. SAM was #9, TED was #7, MIKE #6, and WILL was #8. When no blitzer was called, we kept it simple with the 30 call. When we wanted the ends slightly wider for a better pass rush, we called 31.

With these thoughts as background, I will try to present my thoughts as simply as possible and show how the three- and four-man fronts are interchangeable and very useable in a successful defensive package. Although the three-man front is not used as much as the fronts that we have discussed, it has always been my feeling that the three-man concept is basic to a good defensive package. The **alignment**, **key**, and **assignment** will be discussed in detail position by position. This information, together with what we have already discussed, will give you a solid foundation on which to build and a good understanding of the concept of fronts.

E. 30 Front

30 DEFENSE

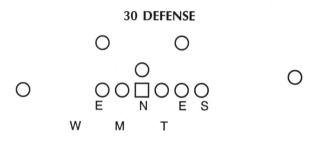

- **Position**: S/END.
- **Alignment**: **Head-on** offensive tackle (toe to toe).
- **Key**: Tackle and both gaps.
- **Assignment**: **Ball to**—strongside B and C gap (two gap). Control the blocker, find the ball. **Ball away**—slide down the line of scrimmage, look for cut-back. **Pass**—rush passer, contain. SEE QB and BALL for bootleg and reverse.

- **Position**: NOSE TACKLE.
- **Alignment**: **Head-on** center (toe to toe).
- **Key**: Center and both gaps.
- **Assignment**: **Ball to**—both A GAPS (two gap). Control the blocker, find the ball. **Ball away**—slide down the line of scrimmage, look for cut-back. **Pass**—take either gap, break pocket, rush passer.

- **Position**: W/END.
- **Alignment**: **Head-on offensive tackle** (toe to toe).
- **Key**: Tackle and both gaps.
- **Assignment**: **Ball to**—weakside B and C gap (two gap). Control the blocker, find the ball. **Ball away**—slide down the line of scrimmage, look for cut-back. **Pass**—rush passer, contain.

- **Position**: SAM.
- **Alignment**: By support pattern (backer, safety, corner).
- **Key**: TE, running lane, and backfield triangle.
- **Assignment**: **Ball to**—by support call (backer, safety, corner). **Ball away**—END is two gap, you have reverse responsibility. **Pass**—play coverage called.

- **Position**: TED.
- **Alignment**: **Head-up to outside** of offensive guard (inside foot splits the crouch of the guard). One to two yards deep (from the feet of the linemen). Width and depth will vary depending on coverage, formation, and down and distance.
- **Key**: Guard and backfield triangle.
- **Assignment**: **Ball to**—B GAP
  1. Back and ball to you—Attack blocker at line of scrimmage. Maintain outside leverage.
  2. Back and ball outside—Fast stack with DE, pursue ball from inside-out.
  3. Back and no ball (counter)—HOLD, find ball, pursue.
  Ball away—A GAP, find ball, pursue from inside-out. **Pass**—play coverage called.

- **Position**: MIKE.
- **Alignment**: **Head-up to outside** of offensive guard (inside foot splits the crouch of the guard). One to two yards (from the feet of the linemen) deep. Width and depth will vary depending on coverage, formation, and down and distance.
- **Key**: Guard and backfield triangle.
- **Assignment**: **Ball to**—B GAP
  1. Back and ball to you—Attack blocker at line of scrimmage. Maintain outside leverage.
  2. Back and ball outside—Fast stack with DE, pursue ball from inside-out.
  3. Back and no ball (counter)—HOLD, find ball, pursue.
  Ball away—A GAP, find ball, pursue from inside-out. **Pass**—play coverage called.

- **Position**: WILL.
- **Alignment**: **Giant position** is normal. Vary crackback, "I," or out by coverage call—DISGUISE alignment.
- **Key**: Tackle, running lane, and backfield triangle.
- **Assignment**: **Ball to**—C gap, by support pattern (backer, safety, corner). **Ball away**—SEE QB and BALL for bootleg and reverse. N/T—pursue, weakside B gap to strongside. **Pass**—play coverage called.

31 FRONT NOTES: The **31** call is used in long yardage pass situations. It is the same as described above, except the **S/END** and **W/END** take an

outside shoulder alignment instead of the head-on alignment in the 30 FRONT. **31** is a three-man front, three-man pass rush front.

The basic **30 FRONT** as described is necessary because of its use in special situations, namely, long yardage in anticipation of the pass. Even then, unless the three-man personnel are capable of hurrying the passer, the pressure is often less than adequate. To aid the rushers, we always emphasized the use of pass rush games. This made the front more useful, and we were better able to take advantage of the variation in coverage that the three-man concept provided.

With this as background, we will discuss in detail the **alignment, keys,** and assignment of the OVER and UNDER version of the three-man line defense. The terms OVER and UNDER refer to the three-man line, with the addition of a called blitzer (SAM, TED, MIKE, or WILL). The number **39** gives the initial front alignment. The first number (3) designates the three-man personnel, and the second number (9) designates the called linebacker blitz.

39 (Over) Defense

SAM (SOD) is the designated blitzer.

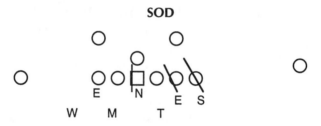

- **Position**: S/END.
- **Alignment**: **Head-on to outside** of offensive tackle.
- **Key**: Guard and tackle.
- **Assignment**: **Ball to**—strongside B GAP. **Ball away**—B-GAP collapse. **Pass**—rush passer, break pocket, stay in your lane.

- **Position**: NOSE TACKLE.
- **Alignment**: **Head-on** the center (toe to toe). **CP**: NOSE may vary alignment from head-on to weakside GAP by game plan.
- **Key**: Center and guard.
- **Assignment**: **Ball to**—weakside A GAP. **Ball away**—A-GAP collapse. **Pass**—rush passer, break pocket, stay in your lane.

- **Position: W/END.**
- **Alignment: Head-on to outside shoulder** of offensive tackle.
- **Key:** Tackle and running lane.
- **Assignment: Ball to**—weakside C GAP, squeeze B. **Ball away**—C-GAP collapse, SEE QB and BALL for bootleg and reverse. **Pass**—rush passer, contain.

- **Position: SAM—SOD** is the term used to tell SAM that he is the designated pass rusher.
- **Alignment: By support call** (safety, corner). **CP:** Backer may be called by game plan.
- **Key:** Follow support pattern progression (TE, running lane, and backfield triangle).
- **Assignment: Ball to**—strongside C GAP, squeeze B, control blocker, locate ball. **Ball away**—C-GAP collapse, contain, SEE QB and BALL for bootleg and reverse. **Pass**—rush passer, contain.

- **Position: TED** (inside linebacker to the side of the call—SAM assignments). As in OVER and UNDER, TED may be the same player to the side of the call. (Example: 38 or 39.)
- **Alignment: Head-on to outside shoulder** of offensive guard. One to two yards (from the feet of the linemen) deep. Width and depth will vary depending on coverage, formation, and down and distance.
- **Key:** Guard and backfield triangle.
- **Assignment: Ball to**—strongside A, C, D GAP by progression.
  1. Back and ball to you—Attack blocker at line of scrimmage. Maintain outside leverage.
  2. Back and ball outside—Fast stack with SAM, pursue ball from inside-out.
  3. Back and no ball (counter)—HOLD, find ball, pursue.
  Ball away—strongside A GAP, find ball, pursue from inside-out. **Pass**—play coverage called.

- **Position: MIKE** (inside linebacker away from the call).
- **Alignment: Head-on to outside shoulder** of offensive guard. One to two yards (from the feet of the linemen) deep. Width and depth will vary depending on coverage, formation, and down and distance.
- **Key:** Guard and backfield triangle.
- **Assignment: Ball to**—weakside B GAP
  1. Back and ball to you—Attack blocker at line of scrimmage. Maintain outside leverage.

2. Back and ball outside—Fast stack with DE, pursue ball from inside-out.

3. Back and no ball (counter)—HOLD, find ball, pursue.

Ball away—strongside A GAP, find ball, pursue from inside-out. **Pass**—play coverage called.

- **Position**: WILL.
- **Alignment**: **Giant position** is normal. Vary crackback, "I," or out by coverage call—DISGUISE alignment.
- **Key**: Tackle, running lane, and backfield triangle.
- **Assignment**: **Ball to**—C GAP, by support pattern (backer, safety, corner). **Ball away**—SEE QB and BALL for bootleg and reverse. N/T—pursue, weakside B gap to strongside. **Pass**—play coverage called.

This covers the defensive line and linebacker run assignments for the 39 (OVER) FRONT in detail. Before going on, it is appropriate to point out the simplicity of using the three-man front within the framework of the principles described above. In the three-man line, as shown above, the SAM would take over the assignments of the S/END. The S/END would take over the assignments of the S/TACKLE, and the TED linebacker would take over the assignments of the SAM. This is the exact concept used with the Dolphins in the early seventies when we replaced our injured DE with the linebacker. It is also the same concept that we were prepared to use with the Chargers in 1992.

It seems to me that many teams are still mixing the three- and four-man fronts with great success today. Although I am not privy to their scheme, I am positive, based on my experience, that the two alignments may be used together successfully. By mixing the two fronts, the three and the four, a team gains a great degree of flexibility, which is needed in today's game. With the freedom the offense possesses, it is mandatory that the defense be flexible and capable of presenting problems to the offense in developing blocking patterns and coverage variations. Mixing the three- and four-man-line fronts allows the defense to create problems for the offense.

One area that is becoming very popular is the **ZONE blitz**. The teams that have had the most success in using the ZONE blitz have been **three-man-line** teams. The reason for this is that there are more qualified pass defenders to drop in coverage in the three-man line. To make the ZONE blitz effective in the four-man line, one or both tackles must normally drop in coverage. In the three-man line, most probably only the NOSE must drop. If for no other reason, more teams will use the three-man line to effectively use the ZONE blitz. The zone blitz is covered in detail in Chapter 3.

It is possible to use the principle used in 39 (OVER) in all the defensive patterns that we will discuss. As I have taught the defense, it is a matter of swapping assignments between players, as illustrated above. This is one of the reasons why I have kept the terms 39 (OVER) and 38 (UNDER) with the defensive call. In the perfect organization, the OVER/UNDER would be used with the four-man-front alignment, and the number 39/38 would be used with the three-man front. Of course, these terms and numbers are not etched in stone. Each team or staff is free to use whatever fits their program. Because these are the terms used by the teams I coached, I feel more comfortable with them in explaining the organization.

37 (Over) Defense

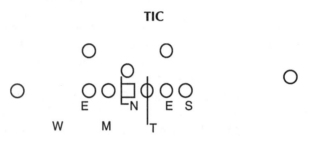

This is a form of the OVER front. The call uses the **TED** linebacker as the **designated rusher**, instead of the SAM as in 39.

- **Position: S/END.**
- **Alignment: Head-on to outside** of offensive tackle.
- **Key**: Tackle and tight end if aligned normal.
- **Assignment: Ball to**—strongside C GAP, squeeze B. **Ball away**—C-GAP collapse, SEE QB and BALL for bootleg and reverse. **Pass**—rush passer, contain, stay in your lane.

- **Position: NOSE TACKLE.**
- **Alignment: Head-on** the center (toe to toe). **CP**: NOSE may vary alignment from head-on to weakside GAP by game plan.
- **Key**: Center and guard.
- **Assignment: Ball to**—weakside A GAP. **Ball away**—A-GAP collapse. **Pass**—rush passer, break pocket, stay in your lane.

- **Position: W/END.**
- **Alignment: Head-on to outside shoulder** of offensive tackle.
- **Key**: Tackle and running lane.

- **Assignment: Ball to**—weakside C GAP, squeeze B. **Ball away**—C-GAP collapse, SEE QB and BALL for bootleg and reverse. **Pass**—rush passer, contain.

- **Position:** SAM.
- **Alignment: By support call** (safety, corner, backer).
- **Key:** Follow support pattern progression (TE, running lane, and backfield triangle).
- **Assignment: Ball to**—strongside C/D GAP, control blocker, locate ball. **Ball away**—C-GAP collapse, contain, SEE QB and BALL for bootleg and reverse. **Pass**—play coverage called.

- **Position:** TED (TIC is the term used to tell TED that he is the designated pass rusher).
- **Alignment:** TIC—**on the snap of the ball** move to a point at the line of scrimmage, **head-up to outside shoulder** of the guard.
- **Key:** Guard and backfield triangle.
- **Assignment:** Time your movement, SEE the BALL. **Ball to**—B GAP, squeeze A, control blocker, maintain outside leverage. **Ball away**—B-GAP collapse, pursue. **Pass**—break pocket, contain.

- **Position:** MIKE (inside linebacker away from the call).
- **Alignment: Head-on to outside shoulder** of offensive guard. One to two yards deep (from the feet of the linemen). Width and depth will vary depending on coverage, formation, and down and distance.
- **Key:** Guard and backfield triangle.
- **Assignment: Ball to**—weakside B GAP.
  1. Back and ball to you—Attack blocker at line of scrimmage. Maintain outside leverage.
  2. Back and ball outside—Fast stack with DE, pursue ball from inside-out.
  3. Back and no ball (counter)—HOLD, find ball, pursue.
  Ball away—strongside A GAP, find ball, pursue from inside-out. **Pass**—play coverage called.

- **Position:** WILL.
- **Alignment: Giant position** is normal. Vary crackback, "I," or out by coverage call—DISGUISE.
- **Key:** Tackle, running lane, and backfield triangle.
- **Assignment: Ball to**—C GAP, by support pattern (backer, safety, corner). **Ball away**—SEE QB and BALL for bootleg and reverse. N/T—pursue, weakside B gap to strongside. **Pass**—play coverage called.

38 (Under) Front

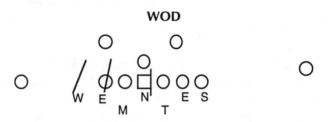

This is a form of the UNDER front. The call uses the WILL as the designated rusher.

- **Position: S/END.**
- **Alignment: Head-on to outside shoulder** of offensive tackle.
- **Key:** Tackle and TE if in normal alignment.
- **Assignment: Ball to**—strongside C GAP, squeeze B. **Ball away**—C-GAP collapse. SEE QB and BALL for bootleg and reverse. **Pass**—rush passer, contain.

- **Position: NOSE TACKLE.**
- **Alignment: Head-on** the center (toe to toe) **CP:** NOSE may vary alignment from head-on to strongside GAP by game plan.
- **Key:** Center and guard.
- **Assignment: Ball to**—strongside A GAP. **Ball away**—A-GAP collapse. **Pass**—rush passer, break pocket, stay in your lane.

- **Position: W/END.**
- **Alignment: Head-on to outside shoulder** of offensive tackle.
- **Key:** Tackle.
- **Assignment: Ball to**—weakside B GAP. **Ball away**—B-GAP collapse. **Pass**—rush passer, break pocket, stay in your lane.

- **Position: SAM**
- **Alignment:** By support call (backer, safety, corner).
- **Key:** TE, running lane, backfield triangle.
- **Assignment:** Follow support pattern progression, control blocker, locate ball. **Ball away**—contain. SEE QB and BALL for bootleg and reverse. **Pass**—play coverage called.

- **Position: TED** (inside linebacker away from the side of the call—MIKE assignments).
- **Alignment: Head-on to outside shoulder** of offensive guard. One to

two yards deep (from the feet of the linemen). Width and depth will vary depending on coverage, formation, and down and distance.

- **Key**: Guard and backfield triangle.
- **Assignment: Ball to**—strongside B GAP
  1. Back and ball to you—Attack blocker at line of scrimmage. Maintain outside leverage.
  2. Back and ball outside—Fast stack with DE, pursue ball from inside-out.
  3. Back and no ball (counter)—HOLD, find ball, pursue.
  Ball away—weakside A GAP, find ball, pursue from outside-in. **Pass**—play coverage called.

- **Position**: MIKE (inside linebacker to the side of the call—WILL assignments).
- **Alignment: Head-on to outside shoulder** of guard. One to two yards deep (from the feet of the linemen). Width and depth will vary depending on coverage, formation, and down and distance.
- **Key**: Guard and backfield triangle.
- **Assignment: Ball to**—scrape to weakside D GAP. **Ball away**—weakside A GAP, pursue. **Pass**—play coverage called.

- **Position**: WILL (**WOD** is the term used to tell WILL that he is the designated rusher.)
- **Alignment: One yard outside** of offensive tackle. See the ball and your key.
- **Key**: Tackle, running lane, and backfield triangle.
- **Assignment: Ball to**—weakside C GAP. **Ball away**—C-GAP collapse, pursue. SEE QB and BALL for bootleg and reverse. **Pass**—rush passer, contain.

36 (Under) Front

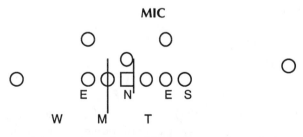

This is a form of the UNDER front. The call uses the MIKE as a designated blitzer.

- **Position**: S/END.
- **Alignment: Head-on to outside shoulder** of offensive tackle.
- **Key**: Tackle and TE if in normal alignment.
- **Assignment: Ball to**—strongside C GAP, squeeze B. **Ball away**—C-GAP collapse. SEE QB and BALL for bootleg and reverse. **Pass**—rush passer, contain.

- **Position**: NOSE TACKLE.
- **Alignment: Head-on** the center (toe to toe). **CP**: NOSE may vary alignment from head-on to strongside GAP by game plan.
- **Key**: Center and guard.
- **Assignment: Ball to**—strongside A GAP. **Ball away**—A-GAP collapse. **Pass**—rush passer, break pocket, stay in your lane.

- **Position**: W/END.
- **Alignment: Head-on to outside shoulder** of offensive tackle.
- **Key**: Tackle and running lane.
- **Assignment: Ball to**—weakside C GAP. **Ball away**—C-GAP collapse, pursue. SEE QB and BALL for bootleg and reverse. **Pass**—rush passer, contain, stay in your lane.

- **Position**: SAM.
- **Alignment**: By support call (backer, safety, corner).
- **Key**: TE, running lane, backfield triangle.
- **Assignment**: Follow support pattern progression, control blocker, locate ball. **Ball away**—contain. SEE QB and BALL for bootleg and reverse. **Pass**—play coverage called.

- **Position**: TED (inside linebacker away from the call).
- **Alignment: Head-on to outside shoulder** of offensive guard. One to two yards deep (from the feet of the linemen). Width and depth will vary depending on coverage, formation, and down and distance.
- **Key**: Guard and backfield triangle.
- **Assignment: Ball to**—strongside B GAP.
  1. Back and ball to you—Attack blocker at line of scrimmage. Maintain outside leverage.
  2. Back and ball outside—Fast stack with DE, pursue ball from inside-out.
  3. Back and no ball (counter)—HOLD, find ball, pursue.
  Ball away—weakside A GAP, find ball, pursue from outside-in. **Pass**—play coverage called.

- **Position**: MIKE (MIC is the term used to tell MIKE that he is the designated pass rusher).
- **Alignment**: MIC—**on the snap of the ball** move to a point at the line of scrimmage, **head-up to outside shoulder** of the guard.
- **Key**: Guard and backfield triangle.
- **Assignment**: Time your movement, SEE the BALL. **Ball to**—weakside B GAP, squeeze A, control blocker, maintain outside leverage. **Ball away**—B-GAP collapse, pursue. **Pass**—rush passer, break pocket, contain.

- **Position**: WILL.
- **Alignment**: **Giant position** is normal. Vary crackback, "I," or out by coverage call—DISGUISE.
- **Key**: Tackle, running lane, and backfield triangle.
- **Assignment**: **Ball to**—weakside C GAP, by support pattern (backer, safety, corner). **Ball away**—SEE QB and BALL for bootleg and reverse. N/T—pursue, weakside B gap to strongside. **Pass**—play coverage called.

F. Even Front: "Roger" Call

ROGER

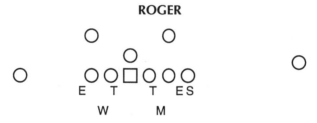

Tackles will move to the RIGHT. Tackles move to the tight end or in the **direction where the RUN threat is greater**. EVEN is a good mixture to go with OVER and UNDER, especially in long yardage situations to rush the passer and maintain GAP run responsibility.

- **Position**: S/END.
- **Alignment**: **Head-on to outside shoulder** of offensive tackle.
- **Key**: Tackle and tight end if in normal alignment.
- **Assignment**: **Ball to**—strongside C GAP, squeeze B. **Ball away**—C-GAP collapse. SEE QB and BALL for bootleg and reverse. **Pass**—rush passer, contain.

- **Position**: S/TACKLE (tackle in direction of call: ROGER = right, LOU = left).
- **Alignment**: **Head-on to outside shoulder** of offensive guard.

- **Key**: Guard and tackle.
- **Assignment: Ball to**—strongside B GAP, squeeze A. **Ball away**—B-GAP collapse. **Pass**—rush passer, break pocket, stay in your lane.

- **Position**: NOSE TACKLE or W/TACKLE (tackle away from direction of call).
- **Alignment: Head-on to inside shoulder** of offensive guard. **CP**: May vary alignment from cocked on center to inside shoulder of offensive guard by game plan.
- **Key**: Center and guard.
- **Assignment: Ball to**—weakside A GAP. **Ball away**—A-GAP collapse. **Pass**—rush passer, break pocket, stay in your lane.

- **Position**: W/END.
- **Alignment: Head-on to outside shoulder** of offensive tackle.
- **Key**: Tackle and running lane.
- **Assignment: Ball to**—weakside C GAP, squeeze B. **Ball away**—C-GAP collapse. SEE QB and BALL for reverse and bootleg. **Pass**—rush passer, contain.

- **Position**: SAM.
- **Alignment**: By support call (backer, safety, corner).
- **Key**: TE, running lane, backfield triangle
- **Assignment**: Follow support pattern progression, control blocker, locate ball. **Ball away**—contain. SEE QB and BALL for bootleg and reverse. **Pass**—play coverage called.

- **Position**: MIKE (inside linebacker to side of overshift).
- **Alignment: Inside shoulder** of strongside offensive tackle. One to two yards deep (from the feet of the linemen). Width and depth may vary depending on coverage, formation, and down and distance. Have vision.
- **Key**: Tackle, guard, and backfield triangle.
- **Assignment: Ball to**—strongside A GAP.
  1. Back and ball to you—Attack blocker at line of scrimmage. Maintain outside leverage.
  2. Back and ball outside—Fast stack with DE, pursue ball from inside-out.
  3. Back and no ball (counter)—HOLD, find ball, pursue.
  Ball away—strongside A GAP, find ball, pursue from inside-out. **Pass**—play coverage called.

- **Position**: WILL (inside linebacker away from overshift).
- **Alignment**: **Outside shoulder** of weakside offensive tackle. One to two yards deep (from the feet of the linemen). Width and depth may vary depending on coverage, formation, and down and distance. Have vision.
- **Key**: Tackle, running lane, and backfield triangle.
- **Assignment**: **Ball to**—step up and fill B GAP.
  1. Back and ball outside—Fast stack with DE, pursue ball from inside-out.
  2. Back and no ball (counter)—HOLD, find ball, pursue.
  Ball away—strongside A GAP, find ball, pursue from inside-out. **Pass**—play coverage called.

G. Even Front: "Lou" Call

Tackles will move to the left. Tackles move to the tight end or in the **direction where the RUN threat is greater**. EVEN is a good mixture to go with OVER and UNDER, especially in long yardage situations to rush the passer and maintain GAP run responsibility.

The alignment, key, and assignment are the same as described above for the S/END, W/END, SAM, MIKE, and WILL. The two tackles are different because it is a **LOU** call and they are moved to the left.

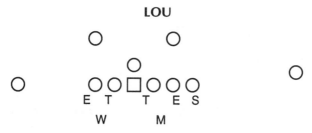

- **Position**: W/TACKLE (tackle in the direction of the call).
- **Alignment**: **Head-on to outside shoulder** of offensive guard.
- **Key**: Guard and tackle.
- **Assignment**: **Ball to**—weakside B GAP, squeeze A. **Ball away**—B-GAP collapse. **Pass**—rush passer, break pocket, stay in your lane.

- **Position**: S/TACKLE or NOSE TACKLE (tackle away from direction of the call).
- **Alignment**: **Head-on to inside shoulder** of offensive guard. CP: May vary alignment from cocked on center to inside shoulder of offensive guard by game plan.

- **Key**: Center and guard.
- **Assignment**: **Ball to**—strongside A GAP. **Ball away**—A-GAP collapse. **Pass**—rush passer, break pocket, stay in your lane.

To close our discussion on fronts, let me add one thought that has been important in my career. Whatever you are teaching, you must create a learning atmosphere. Learn all you can about the personnel you are teaching, and spend the time necessary to teach, drill, and practice the techniques and defensive patterns. Each individual must learn and know as much about his position as possible. The player must also understand the TEAM concept, including where he fits and that he must depend on others to be successful. Equally important, he must realize that others are depending on him to carry out his assignment. This one factor has more to do with winning than anything else we might discuss.

Coach Shula often talked about "gaining the edge." To me, being a TEAM, playing as a TEAM, and understanding the TEAM concept truly are the "winning edge." Most players have to learn the TEAM concept, because they have never experienced what it means or how it truly feels. Whether as an individual or as a member of a team, it is important to fully understand that the TEAM concept is the first step toward success and winning a championship.

DEFENSIVE LINE FUNDAMENTALS

Having discussed FRONTS and their alignment, keys, and assignment, it is important that we now review the fundamentals and techniques necessary for success. First, we will discuss the fundamentals and techniques of the defensive line, followed by the linebackers and the defensive backs. Each group will be discussed in detail.

Like everything else in the game of football, there are different methods and ideas regarding the fundamentals and the techniques used by the three groups. The variation ranges from the very technique-minded coach to the execution-minded coach with little emphasis on technique. I am probably somewhere in between the two. To be successful in the execution of an assignment, certain fundamentals and techniques are important and necessary. The ones that fall into that category must be taught by the coach and followed by the player. However, the key to success is still execution, although I realize that there are players who have the innate ability to overcome an error and execute effectively.

Keep in mind that our discussion centers around methods used by the coach in relation to the needs of the player. In many cases, it may seem like

I am referring to the coach, to the player, or at times to both. In a true "playbook" approach, any one or all three could be true.

A. Running

1. This is the most important fundamental in football. From it, we get movement, balance, and quickness. Football is a game of movement. Improving your speed and quickness will help you become a better athlete.
2. Run with good form in all of your work. Start when you are loosening up and jogging during the warm-up. Keep your thumbs up. Use your arms to help you drive. Run off of the balls of you feet. Work for balance and control of your body.
3. We will run backwards in our drills. You must work to keep your shoulders over your feet and to have a good bend in the knees. This will put you in a good fundamental position to react off of either foot. It will help your balance and control.
4. For lateral movement, we will run a 60-yard shuttle to continue the development of quickness, reaction, and body control. The 60-yard shuttle is up 5 yards and back, up 10 yards and back, and up 15 yards and back. This drill contains all the important elements of playing the game: a short burst of speed, quickness in turning, and the mental alertness necessary in competition.

B. Stance

1. Your stance must be like a spring, ready to explode and react.
2. Take a good fundamental position, with your feet under your shoulders and with your forearms resting on your thighs.
3. To take your stance, reach out with your most natural hand and arm so that your tail will be slightly higher than your head. Your feet will be slightly staggered (toe to instep) and your weight will be slightly forward. Your weight will be on your fingertips and the balls of your feet.

C. Alignment: The Defensive Progression

1. Your position on the line will vary as to your responsibility in each front.
   a. **Head-up**: A **two-gap** responsibility. You must control the blocker at the line of scrimmage and protect both gaps of the blocker.
   b. **Head-up to outside**: You have a **one-gap** assignment. You must control the blocker from outside-in. Keep the inside gap small, and

take the angle away from the blocker on his down block or his release through the line.

 c. **Outside shoulder**: You have a **one-gap** responsibility. You must control the blocker from the outside-in. Keep the inside gap small. You will be slightly wider than above and will be of no help to protect the down block or the release through the line.

 d. **Inside shoulder**: You have a **one-gap** responsibility.

2. Your distance off the ball will vary based on your assignment, down and distance, and your quickness to react.

 a. **Tackles**: two-gap assignment—12″ is basic.
   Tackles: one-gap assignment—6″ is basic.

 b. **Ends**: two-gap assignment—12″ is basic.
   Ends: one-gap assignment—6″ is basic.

 c. **Short yardage** and **goal line**: Take as much of the ball as possible.

Let's discuss a fundamental before leaving this area. The above is a guide concerning distance off the ball for tackles and ends. This is a starting point. Having worked with many players, it is my opinion that this distance must be adjusted for some players. If a player is having a problem controlling the blocker, finding the ball, or releasing from the block, he may be too close or too far off the ball. If he reacts a little slowly, you may want to experiment and move him back a little. Give him more time to read and react. If he is extremely quick, you may want to move him closer to the ball to take advantage of his speed. No technique is etched in stone. Remember that, as the coach, you want the player to be successful, and that may at times mean fitting the technique to the player.

3. Your assignment will consist of one of the following in each front.

 a. You will be given a **key**. React to your key. Your key will determine your defensive point (two-gap assignment).

 b. You will be given a definite **gap**. Charge to your point and react to the blocker in that area. Find the ball and react to it (one-gap assignment).

CP: **Focus your eyes** on your key or keys or on the area where you are going. Broaden your vision to SEE as much as possible. Recognize the blocking pattern and react to it. The faster you react, the more you will improve as a player. That is the key to defensive line play.

D. Charge

1. On the **snap of the ball** or **movement** of your key, be ready to explode into your man. React to movement of the ball or your key, *not* the sound of the QB's cadence.
2. **Drive hard and low**, rolling off your front foot as you bring up the back foot in short driving steps. This movement will enable you to reach as close to a parallel position as possible. Maintain a good bend in your knees and keep your back at an angle that gives you a sound fundamental position on contact.
3. **Continue to drive** as you strike the blow. Use the weight of your body and the power of your legs to strike a blow. Neutralize the blocker. Keep driving and locate the ball as you react to the pressure of the blocker. Fight the pressure until you locate the ball. Move to the ball, and make the tackle.
4. **Versus the pass set**, drive hard and low toward the blocker. Use the hand shiver. Keep moving and driving as you work toward the passer. **Tackles** must break the pocket and penetrate. **Ends** must contain the passer. Keep your lanes tight and get the QB.
5. Should a **screen or draw** show, we must force the **screen** before it forms. The lead rusher must make the QB throw quickly. The delayed rushers (at least two) must get into the screen and destroy the blocking pattern. If a **draw** shows (back and QB mesh on a draw), keep your area small and react. Ends must be alert for the bounce-out.

E. Control the Blocker

1. **Hand shiver**: The basic charge is the same as far as the feet, knees, and body are concerned. Drive the hands to strike a blow on the upper arms, just under the shoulder pads of the blocker. Keep the knees bent. As soon as you make contact, grab the jersey for balance and leverage. As you strike the blow, the thumbs should be up, which will allow you to use the meaty part of the hand to add strength to the blow. If possible, lock the elbows. This allows you to keep distance between you and the blocker.

Keep your distance, keep the knees bent, and keep your back at a good 45-degree angle. Throw off, and move to the ball.

2. **Forearm–shoulder**: Strike a blow up under the chest of the blocker. The basic charge is the same as the hand shiver for the feet and knees. Use the free hand to help you maintain balance and leverage. To the side of the forearm, use the flip technique to release through the block. The one problem with this technique is that it is easier for the blocker to lock on and hold you.

3. **Shoulder drive**: Drive the shoulder to the chest of the blocker. Grab the upper arms with the free hand, control the blocker, play pressure, twist, and throw off. This is a good short yardage technique and a good mixture on other downs.

F. Fundamental Position

Maintain a good fundamental position and **keep the blocker's head from going by your shoulder**. Win the battle of the heads. If the blocker's head goes past your head or shoulder, you are cut off from that area. Keep your head to the side of your responsibility. In a two-gap situation, fight to stay head-up.

Several years ago, we stressed keeping the blocker's head from going past the hip, but the technique is much higher now. Therefore, our objective is higher. We now strive to **win the battle of the heads**. Our objective is to keep the blocker's head from going past the head or shoulder. Using the **EYES** to focus and concentrate on the objective will help the lineman achieve his objective.

1. **Shoulders** and **feet** parallel (toe to instep) to the line of scrimmage.
2. Keep **arms** and **hands** between you and the blocker. Maintain your back at a 45-degree angle.

G. Find the Ball

Generally, **look inside first**. There is only one offensive play in which the ball is outside quickly, and that is the quick pitch to the near back.

1. **SEE**—use your eyes. The depth of your charge is determined by the ball and how quickly you locate the ball.
2. Read the action of your key and the blockers in your area.
   a. **SEE** the flow of the backs. Make sure you don't guess.
   b. Sort out the ball carrier.

3. **Protect your area**. If you cannot deliver a blow, **HOLD** until you locate the ball. The quicker you can find the ball, the better football player you will become.
4. Recognizing screens and draws is important. The line will usually set more on the line of scrimmage and invite you away quickly. On **draws**, the QB and back will **mesh at the handoff**. This action usually does not happen on pass action. On a **screen**, the QB will usually set and quickly **reset** at a **greater depth**. Don't be the second defender to chase a retreating QB; look for the screen.

H. Pursuit

Running to the ball is a matter of individual and team pride. Don't follow a teammate. Stay in your lane. **Never allow our defense to be split**.

1. Work **through the blocker**. Play pressure. Don't run around or spin out.
2. **Throw off** the blocker. Clean yourself; never stay blocked.
3. Move **lateral** with the ball in your area.
4. **Ball away**: Take the pursuit angle to the ball that will put you in position for the cut-back. You should want the ball carrier to cut back. Keep the ball in front of you.
5. **Desire**: There is always a path to the ball carrier. Run to the ball on every play. Make the tackle. Strip the ball. Look for the fumble. Be involved.

I. Tackling: Eyes at the Numbers—Knock Him Back

1. **Fundamental position**: Step on his toes. Most of the time you miss, it's because you are too far away.
   a. **EYES at the numbers**. Make the ball carrier run through your body. No arm tackling.
   b. Explode into the ball carrier. Drive him back; don't let him fall forward. Many first downs are made as a result of the ball carrier falling forward.
   c. **Grab cloth** or club arms around him. Drive the legs hard and through the ball carrier.
2. **Gang tackle**: First man hit through the ball carrier; second and third search and strip. Cause the fumble.
3. Have the desire to make the tackle. Never assume someone else will. Think **"I must."**

J. Line Splits and Back's Feet

Learn to look for things that will help you carry out your assignment. Players form habits. Look for the careless player. Don't guess; make sure your information is accurate. As an example, **wider line splits** may indicate an inside running play. **Tighter splits** may indicate a wide running play. **More weight** on the hand is an indication the blocker will be moving forward. **Less weight** on the hand may indicate the lineman will pull. A lineman **sitting back** in his stance may indicate a pass. This is particularly true of the offensive tackle who is assigned to block a quick outside rushing defensive end.

K. Short Yardage and Goal Line

1. **Three-point stance** (more than one yard): Take your normal alignment by the front called. Charge on the snap of the ball, low and hard. Do not lunge; keep your feet driving and penetrate the running lane. In a **two-gap** assignment, drive into your man and drive him into the running lane. **On a pass,** keep scrambling and be a factor in the pass rush. Force offensive errors.
2. **Four-point stance** (one yard or less): Crowd the ball as much as possible. Be alert for the broken cadence or long count to force you to jump. **Concentrate on the ball.** Charge under and up through the man, or take the outside or inside leg by assignment as you drive to the running lane. Force errors. **On a pass,** keep moving until you find the ball (QB). **CP:** Ends to the side of no TE or TE flex, take a three-point stance.

L. Pass Rush

Rushing the passer is an art. A player must work at the techniques every day. Hard work and study will help you develop the fundamentals that are necessary to defeat the blocker. Be determined to win every time. Know the down and distance. This is your responsibility. Teams will vary, so know the situation and the tendencies of the opponent.

The general rule is:

Second and long	Seven yards or more
Third and medium	Three to five yards
Third and long	Six yards or more

In the above situations, your **first thought is to rush the passer**. Be sure of your **alignment**. Narrow your **stance** so that it will enable you to move on the ball as quickly and as hard as possible. **Sprint** to your man. SEE and concentrate on the blocker's set (be alert for the quick stab). **Beat his set,** strike a blow with your hands, and drive hard. Keep your **knees bent** as you drive and make your hands **work for leverage.** Work to get the blocker off balance, keep driving, and bear in hard. **Stay in your lane,** and maintain your angle to the passer.

Inside rushers must get penetration and break the pocket. Stay in your rush lane. Get your hands up, keep coming, and make the passer throw through you or over you. Keep the pressure on the passer. Get in all screens and keep the draw lanes tight.

Outside rushers must contain. Your **leg drive** and **leverage** will get you to the passer, so drive hard and bear in on the blocker to win. Keep the passer in the pocket, and keep the pocket tight. On bootlegs and rollouts, SEE the action and contain. Your angle to the passer is important. If you are rushing on the side of the throwing arm, aim your rush at the throwing arm. This angle will give you a good rush, plus it will ensure your contain. Force the screen; make the passer throw faster than he wants. On draws, react back, and keep the play from bouncing outside.

Techniques: Pass Rush

1. **Arm over**: This is the best technique. **Drive off the ball** hard and **strike a hard blow** outside on the upper arm of the blocker. Continue to **drive and pull hard** to turn the blocker's shoulders. When you feel the pull, throw the arm away from the pull, **over the head and shoulders** of the blocker. Continue to drive hard and sprint to the passer. Keep your feet moving as you throw your arm over. Ends must get the inside arm over. Tackles may go to either side.

   The pull-down may come early or late. You must feel the leverage and make your move quickly. Keep in mind that your legs will get you to the QB. Never let up—keep driving, and don't stop or slow down. The **arm-over** technique may be used on the outside or inside rush.

2. **Arm under**: This is a **countermove** to the arm-over technique. Everything is the same as in the arm-over technique. If you are **unable to get the pull-down** because the opponent's arms are high or outside, continue your drive and **throw your arm under** the blocker's armpit and **lift and bear in** as you drive to the QB.

3. **Quick arm over**: **Sprint off the ball** and drive hard at the blocker. Convince him that you are going to run over him (get close enough to step on his toes); **make him commit.** In one quick motion, **grab or slap the outside arm** and throw the other **arm over** quickly. Drive to the QB. This technique may be used on the outside or inside rush.

4. **Upfield move** (ends only): Make sure you have a good alignment. Pick out a spot about **four yards deep** outside the offensive tackle. Sprint off the ball, stay low, and drive for your spot. SEE the blocker, and drive to beat him on his outside shoulder. Keep your inside shoulder low and bear in hard. **Make the opponent move.** If he is slow, you can **beat him to the spot**; keep moving low and hard for the QB. If he overcommits and beats you to the spot, then drive your **outside arm under his inside armpit**, lift, and drive hard inside. **CP:** Make sure you have enough depth to contain the QB when you make the inside move.

The best pass rushes occur with very little contact with the blocker. The greater the contact, the more the blocker will hold or stop the rusher and make him slow down or stop. When the rusher slows down or stops, he violates the **law of inertia**, which states that matter at rest has a tendency to remain at rest and matter in motion has a tendency to keep moving. Starting and stopping takes time, and it is difficult for the rusher to start over. Timing is such in the passing game that if the rusher stops or slows down, he will be late and never hurry the passer.

Because the blocker may use his hands, he has the advantage. This is by design. The Rules Committee wants the offensive blocker to have the advantage to protect the QB. This means that the rusher must take the **proper alignment, move on the ball** or movement, have good **leg drive**, and **gain leverage** with his hands. Working hard and studying a blocker's technique will help a rusher be the best.

In most games, 50% of the time will be devoted to rushing the passer. It is extremely important that you work on your techniques daily. You must be quick off the ball and sprint to the spot. You must perfect your technique and be aggressive with your hands. Gain leverage, throw, and get rid of the blocker. Keep moving. NEVER stop.

M. Study Your Opponent

1. SEE the huddle, and SEE your opponent as he breaks the huddle.
2. Observe his approach to the line of scrimmage.
3. SEE him set, two-point stance to three-point stance or line up in a three-point stance.
4. Be alert for the quick count or broken cadence. SEE the ball or movement.
5. SEE his line split.
6. Check his stance (weight forward or weight back for pulling or pass set).
7. Does he stab or cut on his quick pass set?
8. Does he set at the line of scrimmage or set deep (false stepper)?

9. SEE the back's alignment (cheat out, up, deep). **CP:** The linebacker will help you with this alignment by the back.
10. Know down and distance, hash tendencies, and the best blocker.
11. Any information that will help you be successful is important. Study the tapes, and get to know your opponent. Be prepared. WIN the battle.

DEFENSIVE LINE GAMES

Let's begin our discussion by considering the purpose of LINE GAMES within the framework of a defensive package. The purpose is to keep the offense from teeing off on an individual or group. Games are important and should be mixed with the "A" technique or what we will refer to as normal. They are necessary versus the run, and they are very important versus the pass. They serve a very definite purpose in keeping the offense honest and making them respect the defensive capabilities.

Pass rush games are used in a passing situation to improve the pass rush. They are also effective against teams that like to feature draw, lag, or delay type of plays and screens. Games are determined by the game plan, the defense, and the formation. Defensive linemen can and must use these games at the line of scrimmage or in "check-it" situations. More importantly, I have always felt that the lineman must be the one to call the game. As coaches, we can guide and prepare a player in terms of what we like and why, but in the final analysis the lineman is the only person who actually knows what is needed and when. Experience has taught me that he should be encouraged to call the appropriate game within the framework of the plan and preparation.

Players must always be aware of the offensive pass-blocking pattern. As a rule, it is usually man to man or area. Some teams use what is called slide blocking, which falls into the area category. At times, it is more difficult to use the game needed versus this protection because the tackle, guard, and center are responsible for the DE, DT, and MIKE. If MIKE is in coverage, then the three offensive linemen are responsible for the defensive tackle and end. A three-on-two situation is not the type of blocking pattern we want. If this protection is standard, we may have to concentrate more on the other side, away from the slide. Our objective is to destroy the protection area and force the QB to hurry, move, or be sacked.

Games may be used in all fronts. More are probably used in the 30 FRONT because of the personnel involved, but many of the games we will discuss can be used in all alignments.

To begin, we will discuss the games used in the pass rush. The first game that comes to mind is what is referred to as the **ME** game. The ME is used by the defensive END to keep the offensive TACKLE honest. Versus a good outside rusher, the offensive blocker has a tendency to set wider and deeper. This is excellent technique and is used effectively versus the defensive END. The DE is responsible for the call.

To counter the offensive move, the defensive END must employ the ME game. There are a couple of different ways to run the ME game: (1) quick and (2) delay. Which method is used depends entirely on the offensive tackle and the way he sets up to block the rushing end.

Versus man-to-man pass protection, the tackle will try to stay with the DE that is driving inside. It is important that the DE continue driving hard inside and prevent the offensive guard from picking up the engaged tackle as he comes around. The DE must break the pocket with his drive inside.

Versus area blocking, the DE must go at an angle inside to make it difficult for the offensive guard to adjust. A better adjustment versus area blocking is probably the DELAY ME. This technique doesn't show as quickly, and the DE has a better chance by hitting straight into the OT and then driving hard inside. The DT uses the same DELAY technique, driving first into the OG and then coming around as the DE drives inside. Using both the QUICK and DELAY ME gives the DE and DT the tools needed to keep the offensive linemen honest in their protection pickups.

CP: Versus the run, it is important that both the DE and DT execute the game on the QUICK ME. The same is true in the beginning of the DELAY ME. However, if the play is away, both experienced linemen may HOLD and pursue the play in their natural lanes. If the play is to you, both the DE and DT should execute the game. Like anything else, working together and understanding the objective make for a better ME game and a better pass rush.

A. Me Game

<table>
<tr>
<td align="center">QUICK ME:
The DE drives quick inside
and the DT comes around
to contain</td>
<td align="center">DELAY ME:
Both the DE and DT drive
straight into blockers; the DT
drives outside to contain</td>
</tr>
<tr>
<td align="center"></td>
<td align="center"></td>
</tr>
</table>

The ME game, whether quick or delay, should be called by the DE, because he is the one who knows what he needs to keep the tackle honest in his set.

Quick ME is more useful versus an offensive tackle that is setting deep and wide. The tackle cannot prevent the DE from taking the inside quick when he sets in that manner. If the offensive tackle is setting more on the line, then the **delay ME** should be better. With this technique, the DE must make the offensive blocker believe that he is going to run over him; when he creates that illusion, then he drives inside hard to break the pocket.

In the ME game, the **end** will be the gap player and goes first. The **tackle** will be the engage player and goes second. The **end is the penetrator** and the **tackle is the contain** player. Moving on the snap and your alignment are very important. Also, it is important to **know the offensive pickup**: man to man or area blocking. **CP**: The tackle must know the technique to be used: quick or delay.

- **Man to man** versus the ME game: The offensive tackle will stay with the end. The end must continue to penetrate and pick the offensive guard that is trying to pick up the tackle coming around. If the end is double-teamed, continue to fight through the block, penetrate, and break the pocket.
- **Area blocking** versus the ME game: The end must penetrate before the offensive guard can pick up. If he is in your path, take the blocker on and win. The **delay** game is best versus area blocking. Both the DE and DT hit into the offensive linemen. The DE then hits the inside gap and the DT comes around. The delay is a type of disguise for the game. **CP**: DE—run away or QB roll away; you have contain. Find QB and ball, and be alert for gimmick.
- **Tackle**: Engage man, then come around and contain. **Man to man** you have an opportunity to come around free. The end will pick the offensive guard.
- **Area blocking**: HOLD your engage long enough to let the DE clear; then come around quickly. **CP**: DT—run away HOLD. Run to your side, then come around and react. You must come around on all plays to your side.

To review, the **quick ME** game works best when the offensive blocker is setting deep, and the END can take the inside quick. If the blocker is setting on the line, the **delay ME** is much better. The reverse is true for the DT.

B. U Game

The next change-up for the DE is the U game. U tells the DT that he is going first and the DE will come around to break the pocket. As in the ME game, there is a **quick U** and a **delay U**. The **end is responsible for the call.** The tackle is the **gap** man and goes first. The end is the **engage** man and comes around second.

QUICK U:
DT will drive to outside gap. DE will drive into blocker,
then come around DT and break pocket. DT will contain.

The **tackle** is the gap man. Move on the snap, and hit the gap quickly and beat the offensive guard outside. You must beat the blocker quickly, because you have contain. You cannot be picked off by the offensive tackle.

DELAY U:
Both DE and DT drive into blockers. DT drives outside
and DE comes around DT and drives to break pocket.

The **quick U** works best when the offensive guard is setting deep, which allows the DT to drive outside quick, allowing the DE to come around and drive for the pocket. The **delay U** is best when the offensive blocker is setting on the line. If this is the case, the DE and DT must drive straight into the blockers; make them think you are going to run over them. Then the DT drives to the outside, and the DE comes around and drives for the pocket.

- Versus **man to man**: Your charge should pick the offensive tackle, and our DE should come around free.
- Versus **area blocking**: You must drive through the gap quickly and pick the offensive tackle. You have the best opportunity to come free versus area blocking. If you are double-teamed, continue to penetrate and break the pocket.

The **end** is the engage man. Move on the ball and engage the offensive tackle with your hands. Step around the DT as quickly as possible. Stay in your rush lane, penetrate, and break the pocket. **CP**: Be alert for inside runs.

These two combinations force the offensive blockers to stay honest and not set to block any particular type of rush. Very few ENDS or TACKLES can be the best without using the **ME** and **U** games. It's as if you must use them to survive as an effective pass rusher.

C. Tom and Tomy

The next games that are important for a good pass rush are the **TOM** and **TOMY**. Both are used as quick or delayed. **CP**: Before calling the TOM or TOMY, make sure your DE is not thinking of a ME or U. The TOM or TOMY is usually called at the line of scrimmage, because the offensive backfield set is of importance as to which tackle goes first.

QUICK TOM:
RT drives inside and upfield to break pocket. NOSE drives straight into blocker and comes around RT into pocket.

DELAY TOM:
Both RT and NOSE drive into blockers. RT drives inside and NOSE comes around the pocket.

Q

Q

Quick TOMY and **delay TOMY** are the same techniques as described above, except the LT or NOSE is the initial penetrator, and the LT is the tackle that comes around. The ME and U games as described are called the same on both sides. In most cases, the ME and U games will take precedence over the TOM or TOMY. If the ME or U is not called, then the tackles may use a TOM or TOMY. **CP**: Communication is important before the snap to ensure all lineman are "on the same page."

D. Double Me and Double U

Q

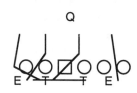

The diagram above is an example of the **DOUBLE ME**. Both the DE and DT drive inside QUICK. The offside tackle HOLDS and then comes around to contain. This type of three-man game must be used only in definite pass-only situations.

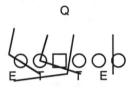

The diagram above is an example of the **DOUBLE U**. Both defensive tackles drive to the outside, and the DE HOLDS and then comes around to break the pocket. As stated above, all three-man games must be used only in definite pass-only situations.

Many different combinations of rushes can be used. I have presented the ones that have been most effective for me. As you go along, depending on the protection pattern of the opponent, changes can be made or new combinations developed to meet the need to improve the pass rush. Working together is again the key to success. There is always an answer. You must keep studying and working hard on your techniques to win.

It is important to emphasize the importance of the players making the calls on the field. They and they alone know what they need to use to keep the offensive blockers honest. That is what I always liked about the ME/YOU call. The DE is in control and can immediately call ME to take advantage of the offensive lineman. What each lineman needs may be discussed between downs or on the sideline, but the call is made on the field. When you have linemen who are hesitant to make calls, one or two things are usually the cause. First, they don't understand the purpose, or they are selfish and hesitate to charge in a manner to help one another. Another reason that also may be a factor is that a lineman may be concerned about a leg injury and therefore may not want to drive inside, where he is more susceptible to blockers throwing at the legs. Either of these reasons prevents the defensive line from being the best, and the pass rush as a group will be only average. Great lines have always used pass rush games, and as long as they continue to keep score, the defensive line on those teams will be the winner.

Probably the worst thing that can happen to the LINE GAMES is for the penetrator or gap player to be stabbed at the line and not allowed to penetrate. This is important to consider in the game plan. However, if, for example, the OT is a stabber, then the U game would be a better call on that side. Because there is no way the offensive blocker pattern can pick up all possible games, defensive linemen must mix it up, study the opponent, and be smart.

LINEBACKERS

A. Individual

The success of the defense depends on how effectively the linebackers carry our their defensive responsibility. The linebacker must make a split-second decision to determine RUN or PASS. Several factors will aid him in making this quick decision: **down and distance, position on the field, time remaining,** and the **score.** Together, all of this information will help the linebacker anticipate, but the most important factor will be his KEY or KEYS on each play.

Whatever the play, run or pass, the linebacker must know his assignment and alignment. By knowing this, he puts himself in position to be successful. Not knowing gives him no opportunity to prove how good he is, and he fails before the play begins. Experience has taught me over and over the importance of **knowing the assignment** and taking the **proper alignment** to execute the assignment. The two go together. They are a *must* for a defense to be successful. As coaches, we often get hung up on technique and overlook the obvious. Know the assignment and take the proper alignment. It is so simple that knowing the assignment and taking the proper alignment are often put on the back burner.

Returning to the linebacker KEYS, on a RUN, the linebacker must control the blocker, find the ball, and react to the ball in the same manner as a defensive lineman. On a PASS, he must react with quickness and speed in his coverage responsibility in the same manner as a defensive back. Both must be practiced and developed to coordinate the linebacker's action with the lineman on a run and with the secondary on a pass. The success of the total defensive package depends on this coordination among the line, linebackers, and secondary.

Strongside Alignment

For **strongside** alignment by SAM on the TE, the alignment will be determined by the defense called and the required support pattern.

1. **Head-on** (toe to toe)*:* This alignment on the TE will enable SAM to jam and control the opponent. With the head-on position on a run, the player

is in a position to play a TWO-GAP assignment and take the **cut-back** responsibility in the support pattern. This position is also ideal on the pass, as it places the defender in an alignment to effectively JAM the TE as he plays his coverage responsibility.

2. **Outside shoulder** (inside foot splits the TE's stance): This alignment will enable SAM to work out quickly to the outside. This position will allow the linebacker to take the **primary support** responsibility on the run, while on the pass, he will most likely have an **outside zone** responsibility or **man** coverage on the back aligned to his side.

3. **Outside** (inside foot even with the TE's outside foot): This is a wider alignment than above and is often used to help the player to play his run or pass responsibility better. The wider alignment is also used to carry out a blitz assignment. To be successful and not give away his assignment responsibility to the opponent, the linebacker **must** move around. Example: Take a head-on position and move out, or line up outside and move in.

    Developing good movement not only gives the linebacker flexibility within the framework of the system, but also enables him to successfully "**play the game**" with the QB. This only comes with study and a thorough understanding of the assignment, plus daily practice. **Disguise** is a great word, and movement by the player will disguise the intended defensive assignment. However, **being the best** takes preparation and thought regarding what needs to be accomplished, along with practice and the patience to make it happen. The player must be set and ready to play on the snap.

    One of the best at moving around was Doug Swift, who played his college football at Amherst College. He came to the Dolphins after being released in Canada. When he was released, his coach called and said, "I think he has a chance." He did; it was the strike year (1970) and we needed bodies. Doug arrived and received plenty of work. He learned, he had ability, and he became the best. He left in 1975 to return to medical school and today is an anesthesiologist at a hospital in Philadelphia.

4. **Inside shoulder** (outside foot splits the TE's stance): An alignment that may develop when the TE flexes. On the flex, as this position is taken, it is also suggested that the player line up deeper in order to SEE the TE, the backfield triangle, and the running lane. This alignment may also be used in short yardage or goal line situations as the defense called dictates.

5. **Inside** (outside foot even with TE's inside foot or more, depending on the position of the TE): A blitz, short yardage, or goal line alignment dictated by the defense called.

6. **Loose**: An alignment off the line of scrimmage, inside the DE, and shading the outside shoulder of the offensive tackle. The distance off the ball will vary according to the situation (down and distance) and the assignment. Normal will be approximately one to two yards off the feet of the linemen.
7. **Stack**: An alignment off the line of scrimmage, inside the DE and shading the outside shoulder of the offensive guard. The distance off the ball will vary according to the situation (down and distance) and the assignment. Normal will be approximately one to two yards off the feet of the linemen.

Weakside Alignment by Will on the Side Away from the TE

With the NEAR END present or two TEs, the alignment will be the same as described for SAM. On the side away **versus "X,"** there are **four basic positions**. This flexibility will help the player align himself in the best possible position to carry out the assignment in the defense called.

1. **Crackback**: An alignment on the line of scrimmage, approximately one yard outside your DE, seeing inside to the **backfield triangle** and the **running lane**. If this type of block remains a problem, I suggest that the player **turn and face inside**, turning his back on the "**X**." From this alignment, the linebacker is in a position to get upfield on the initial action and beat the block.
2. **Giant**: The normal alignment, one to two yards outside the DE and one to two yards off the feet of the DE. The outside foot is back. SEE inside to the backfield triangle and running lane.
3. **"i"**: A deeper alignment than normal, splitting the difference between the WB and "X." The depth will be determined by the distance "X" is from the ball. The player must be in a position to SEE both the backfield triangle and "X." The alignment may vary based on down and distance and the backfield formation.
4. **Out**: An alignment designed to JAM and DELAY the "X." It is best used in a pass situation to enable the player to carry out the assignment better. Focus on "X"; take away the inside release, and force him to reroute. Down and distance and the formation tendencies will aid the player in carrying out the defensive assignment.

Alignment for Ted and Mike

The alignment for each player will be determined by the defense called. First, we will discuss the alignment of **MIKE**, because he will be involved in all normal **four-man-line** calls. **Three-man-line** calls which involve **TED** will be discussed in that context.

The basic **STACK** position is normal for MIKE in both the three- and four-man-line calls. The STACK position is also basic for TED in the three-man-line call. Alignment will be one to two yards off the feet of the defensive line or deeper, depending on down and distance.

1. **Head-on** (toe to toe): This alignment on the offensive guard will enable the player to SEE through the guard to the backfield triangle and the back and ball keys. With the head-on position, the player is in a position to play a TWO-GAP assignment on a run and make the play in either gap. As the charges of the defensive line change, MIKE/TED will adjust to a ONE-GAP assignment.
2. **Outside shoulder** (inside foot splits the offensive guard's stance): This alignment is normal and will give the player an opportunity to SEE through the guard to the backfield triangle for back and ball keys.

The basic **LOOSE** position is taken by **MIKE** or **TED** when an adjustment is required by the defense called or when it is necessary to adjust because of the offensive formation.

1. **Outside shoulder** (inside foot splits the offensive tackle's stance): This alignment is normal and gives the player an opportunity to SEE through the tackle to the backfield triangle for back and ball keys.
2. **Outside** (inside foot even with tackle's outside foot): A wider alignment that is necessary because of the defense called or when it is necessary to adjust because of the offensive formation.
3. **Inside** (outside foot even with tackle's inside foot): A closer alignment that is necessary because of the defense called and when it is necessary to adjust because of the offensive formation.

The positions outlined above are basic guides. As previously mentioned, linebackers need the flexibility to adjust their alignments based on the offensive formation and their assignments. With the ever-increasing number of offensive formations that defenses face today, this ability to adjust becomes more and more important. Also, it is important that these adjustments be reviewed by the staff and taught to the players. The point is that in many cases the alignment of the linebacker is dependent on the offensive formation. The player must understand this philosophy and be given the latitude to react properly. In addition, as the linebacker adjusts his alignment, he must coordinate his move with the defensive lineman in front of him. As an example, if the linebacker moves wider, he may need to move the lineman more inside by either a call or a change in the lineman's charge. The linebacker and the lineman are changing GAP responsibilities.

Stance

Take a good fundamental position; be cocked and ready to move.

1. **Feet** comfortably spread (shoulder width), even to staggered (toe to instep), with the outside foot back.
2. **Knees** flexed, hips dropped, with weight evenly distributed over the balls of the feet.
3. **Shoulders** parallel to the line of scrimmage.
4. **Arms/hands** in front of the knees in the "ready position."

Focus your eyes, first on your main key, and then see as much as possible (peripheral vision).

1. SAM: When aligned over the TE/NEAR, you must concentrate on the TE/NEAR, and *not* on the backfield. SEE the man that can attack you, and then develop the ability to SEE through the TE/NEAR to the backfield triangle and the running lane.
2. MIKE and TED: Develop the ability to SEE through the man you are aligned over (offensive guard/tackle) to the backfield triangle. The backfield triangle will give you the back and ball keys necessary to play your position.
3. WILL: Versus NEAR, same as SAM. When aligned away from the TE, SEE through the offensive tackle to the backfield triangle and running lane. The offensive tackle will usually be the first to give you a run/pass read.

Proper use of the **EYES** may be the **most important fundamental** in developing into an outstanding football player. Speed, strength, quickness, and agility are all important, but they all become virtually useless without proper use of the EYES. Using the EYES—seeing—enables you to pick out the target (bull's-eye). Proper focus of the EYES enables you to pick out a spot in the bull's-eye The **EYES** lead and control the function of the body.

Proper use of the **EYES** will help prevent obvious errors—from **falling over a blocker,** being **blocked in when aligned to the outside,** and being faked and **missing the tackle.** As a coach, during practice I always like to stand where I can SEE a player's EYES. Why? To make sure that he is looking at the correct things, his keys—the man over, the backfield triangle, the running lane, the ball carrier, the receiver, and when the ball is thrown.

I am convinced that the EYES will help you to do whatever your assignment requires, IF YOU ARE LOOKING AT THE PROPER THINGS AND HAVE THE PROPER FOCUS.

B. Keys versus the Run

The player's KEY and his reaction to that key are described with each defense. The quicker a player learns to READ the KEY, **control the block**, react, and **find the ball**, the better defensive player he will become. Although there are a few general keys that will help a player distinguish between the run and pass, they are an indication and **not a definite answer**. A good offense will have what is referred to as a key-breaker—make the player believe one thing and do the other. (Example: Show a run fake and pass, or show a pass fake and run.)

Sam: TE Blocks on You—Control Block, Find Ball = Run

- **TE drives to inside to block the DE or MIKE**: SEE the running lane. Offside lineman pull = RUN inside. Onside lineman pull deep = RUN outside. SEE the backfield triangle, find ball. The running lane and the backfield triangle will indicate sweep (deep pull) or off-tackle (offside pull) and tell you how to react.
- **TE releases**: Indication is PASS. Follow key progression (running lane, backfield triangle, find ball). Execute coverage called (zone, man, or blitz).
- **TE releases or flexed**: SEE the running lane and backfield triangle (back your side) will give you the information. Lineman pulling deep and the back blocks on you = RUN (sweep). Lineman setting, back avoiding you (wider course) = PASS.

Mike and Ted: See as Much as Possible Before the Snap

- **Offensive lineman**: Weight distribution in stance—forward lean = RUN, backward lean = PASS.
- **Backfield triangle**: Backs cheat up, cheat wide, deeper alignment.
- **On the SNAP**—lineman in front: The backfield triangle will give you the back and ball keys.

Study your **KEYS** and learn what they mean. Visualize a situation happening and visualize how to react. Practice the proper reads in practice. Study the tape to SEE if you reacted properly. The key word is *repetition.*

Will: Versus TE/Near (Same as Described Above for Sam)

- **Away from TE:** The running lane and the backfield triangle (**back your side**) will give you the information you need. Lineman pulling deep and the back blocks on you = RUN (sweep). Lineman setting and the back avoiding you (wider course) = PASS.

C. Keys versus the Pass: Individual Pass Defense Technique

- **SAM:** LB to TE. S/O—slot/opposite formation.
  MIKE: MLB—over/under front. MLB away from TE in 30 defense.
  TED: Inside LB on TE side in 30 defense.
  WILL: LB away from TE. W/O—slot/opposite formation.
  1. **Alignment:** By defense called and support pattern.
  2. **Key:** Defined by defense called and support pattern. SEE as much as possible.
  3. **Jam:** By defense called, plus position on the field and the location of the receiver ("Z," "X," TE, SB, WB). If possible, each receiver must be delayed and rerouted. SEE as much as possible.
- **Proper jam technique:**
  1. **Be patient.** HOLD your position; be a knee bender. Focus on the **inside of the numbers** to force the receiver outside. Focus on the **outside of the numbers** to funnel the receiver inside. Do not attack or extend yourself.
  2. **Drive hands** up and under to the inside/outside of the numbers.
     a. **Back/slap technique:** Used best versus the TE or NEAR. As the TE/NEAR releases, push both hands on the back of the receiver, pushing back and down. This is a good change-up to knock the receiver off balance in his attempt to avoid the defender.
  3. Good fundamental position: Move with "cat-like quickness." You must have good knee bend.

I mentioned linebacker Doug Swift earlier as a player who moved and disguised his alignment. He also mastered the back/slap technique. He mixed it with the JAM and was very effective.

Before leaving our discussion on the importance and technique of the JAM, let's go back in history for a moment. It is my opinion that the NFL Rules Committee has tried to deliberately restrict the defense and give the offense more of an opportunity to be successful and to score. Greater media and fan interest is the generally accepted reason.

At one time, in the middle sixties through the early seventies, the defense could JAM the receiver until the ball was in the air, or it was possible to CUT the receiver at the line of scrimmage. Good defenses perfected the JAM or the CUT, and it was very effective. It destroyed the timing of the passing game. Players on defense have always been allowed to use their hands to protect themselves from blockers. Jamming the receiver was a part of good defense. Maybe cutting the receiver took advantage of the rule, but it was allowed and was effective. As the defense perfected the JAM technique, the pass offense suffered. Each year, the Rules Committee placed additional restrictions on the defense to free up the receiver. Now the JAM is restricted to a five-yard area, and it is almost to the point that you can't even look at the receiver hard. Increased scoring is the intent. The media like it, the fans like it, and the defensive coaches continue to work hard to stop the score. When I was coaching, I sometimes felt that the defense would eventually only be allowed to have ten men on the field.

College and high school rules are less restrictive. Every time I discuss pass defense with those groups, I begin by emphasizing the JAM and the importance of rerouting the receiver. To be successful, the timing in the passing game must be destroyed by a JAM and by a PASS RUSH. The defense must make the quarterback hesitate. The JAM accomplishes this, and then the RUSH has time to be effective. It is important to remember that football is a TEAM game. Every successful player depends on another player.

- **DROP**: Called by the defense and offensive pass pattern. The assignment will consist of one of two possibilities:
  1. **Drop to a definite area**: Locate the receiver or receivers in the area through which you will drop. Locate and work through (jam if possible) the receiver as you move into the area. SEE the QB! Destroy the pattern; cause the route to be altered.
     a. **SAM/WILL**: Your route progression as you go to the **outside zone** area will be "i," quick out, oh and curl.
     b. **SAM/WILL**: As you go to the **inside zone** area, SAM must keep vision on TE/SB for hook, circle, and inside route of "Z." WILL must keep vision on WD for circle and inside route of "X" or crossing pattern by TE, SB.
     c. **MIKE**: On your drop strongside, locate TE, SB, and "Z." On drop weakside, locate (NEAR) WB and "X."
  2. **A definite man** (back/TE) **to cover**: SEE him, concentrate on him, and focus the **EYES at the numbers** (inside/outside), depending on coverage definition (where help is). As you begin your movement, get in

position to cover (inside-out or outside-in), backpedal, shuffle, slide, and hold. Position yourself to JAM (know the position of your help, inside or outside). When you have **definite** help, it is important to JAM, destroy the pattern, and then go with your man. When you have **no help**, maintain your man-to-man coverage technique (JAM if possible), and be prepared to run with the receiver all the way.

- **SQUARE AWAY**: Zone coverage. When the quarterback stops, bring yourself under control and get in position to locate the QB, SEE the pattern, find the ball, and attack the ball and receiver. **INTERCEPT!** As you square away, move lateral to the reception area. Don't round it off. Weight should be over your knees. Break on the ball. When you are free, with no receivers in your area, continue to get depth, SEE QB/RECEIVERS, and attack the ball.

  If the **quarterback scrambles** and it is a **zone coverage**, stay in your area of responsibility, and make him cross the line of scrimmage. If he scrambles away from you, close down your area toward the QB. SEE the receivers. In **man coverage**, stay with your man until he crosses the line of scrimmage. **This is your scramble rule**.

- **INTERCEPT**: Get the ball! Move lateral to the reception area, and attack the ball. Go after the ball at the highest point with both hands. It is very important in covering deep routes that you RUN first. Then, when you hear the "BALL" call or recognize "BALL," attack at that point. Play through the receiver (**cradle technique**). (Example: Going to your left, use the right arm to play the ball. The left arm is behind the receiver.) On the high pass, play up and over. NEVER GO AROUND. Look the ball into your hands (**pop the head down**), put it away, and hand over the point. Your attitude must be, "When the ball is in the air, it belongs to us."

- **TACKLE**: EYES at the NUMBERS. As a linebacker, you must SET THE TEMPO. As a TEAM, it is important that we HIT and GANG TACKLE. First man hit through ball carrier; second and third man SEARCH and STRIP. GET THE BALL—take it away. WIN!

  1. **Strip technique**: If the ball carrier is stopped, force the elbow up and away from the ball or tackle the ball arm. If you are the lone tackler, tackle from the **ball side** or from **behind** to the ball side. Come under and up on the ball with the inside arm (cradle technique), as the outside arm wraps around the ball carrier to make the tackle. If you are approaching the ball carrier **away from the ball side**, the same cradle technique is possible. Come under and up on the ball with the inside arm; the outside arm wraps around to make the tackle.

Like anything else, this technique must be stressed and practiced. Using this technique in practice will not only help the defense improve, but will also make the offense aware of protecting the ball.

Sam Linebacker: Backer Support

- **Alignment**: Outside shoulder of TE (inside foot splits stance of TE).
- **Responsibility**: Primary support man—contain sweep or close off-tackle (C gap).
- **Key**: SEE through TE for backfield action (near back and onside pull of lineman).
  1. **TIGHT END STAND or STRAIGHT BLOCK**: Step out and work upfield to a depth of the lead blocker (pulling lineman, near back). **CP**: TE versus sweep flex—make a LION call—control TE and stay square. Be prepared to fill inside-outside on ball.

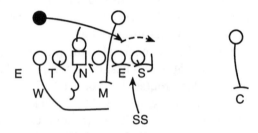

  2. **HOOK BLOCK**: Step out and drive through his head with inside arm. Work upfield to a position of containment (outside and as deep as lead blocker).

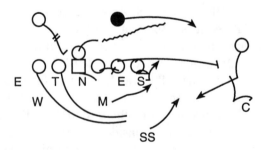

  3. **TURN OUT BLOCK**: Control blocker, and close the C GAP with the blocker's body. You are responsible for the ball carrier bouncing outside and keeping the inside small.

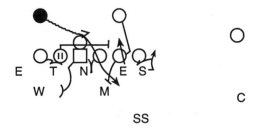

4. **FLOW BLOCK**: Step out, SEE inside, and determine if the play is sweep or off-tackle. Deep pull of onside guard—tackle will indicate sweep. Contain, work out and upfield. No onside pull will indicate off-tackle. Close the C GAP, drive into off-tackle running lane, force spillage, and strip off-guard. Shallow pull—attack onside guard, tackle at his depth.

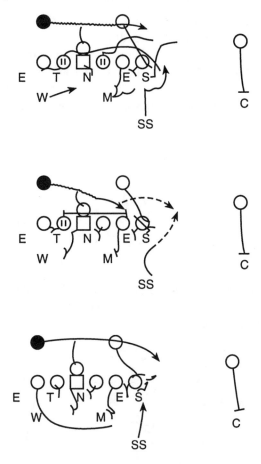

5. **CRACKBACK BLOCK**: By position of close "Z," expect change in support call—corner or safety. On sweep read, turn, SEE blocker, and attack. Control and square up to play cut-back responsibility.

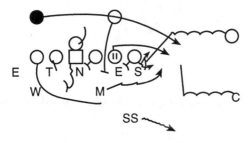

6. **PASS and TE SETS UP or DELAYS**: Go to coverage call.

Sam Linebacker: Corner, Safety Support

- **Alignment**: Head-on TE (toe to toe).
- **Responsibility**: Cut-back (TWO GAP).
- **Key**: Tight end, onside pull of lineman, backfield triangle.
  1. **TIGHT END STAND UP or STRAIGHT BLOCK**: Attack and control blocker. Drive him back, and be prepared to make play inside or out. **CP**: If TE releases for RUN/PASS option, he is your man to man. Be alert in short yardage and goal line situations.

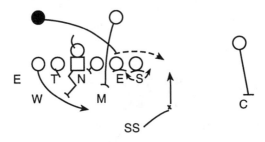

2. **HOOK BLOCK**: Drive through his head with outside arm. Keep head from going past shoulder. Stay square, control blocker, drive him back, and make play inside or out.

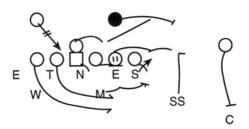

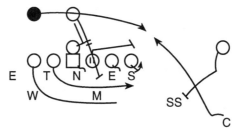

3. **TURN OUT BLOCK**: Control blocker; close the C GAP with the blocker's body. Stay square, and be prepared for ball carrier inside or outside.

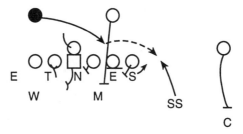

4. **FLOW BLOCK**: Jam TE, and knock blocker off balance. Look for pull of onside guard and tackle. Meet blocker (pulling lineman, near back), head-up at his depth. Control blocker, keep square, and work out along line of scrimmage. Be prepared to make play in or out. **CP**: No onside pull—drive into off-tackle (C GAP), running lane, force spillage, and strip off-guard.

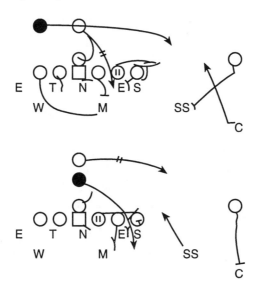

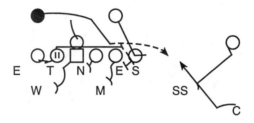

5. **PASS and TE SETS UP or DELAYS**: Go to coverage.

Will Linebacker: Backer Support (Away from TE)

- **Alignment**:
  1. **Giant position**: Normally one yard outside DE and one yard deep.
  2. **Crackback position**: One yard outside DE and on the LOS, facing in. If this position will not allow you to beat the crackback, move to a head-up position on "X" and call corner or backer support by coverage.
  3. **"i" position**: Position splitting the distance between "X" and the WB, OT. Your distance off the ball will be determined by down and distance and the split of "X."
  4. **Out position**: A position to jam and reroute "X" in a passing situation or to carry out your assignment by the defense called. **CP**: Eliminate inside release of "X."

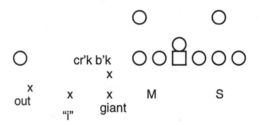

- **Responsibility**: Primary support man—contain the sweep.
- **Key**:
  1. **Giant and crackback**: SEE through the onside lineman (guard, tackle) to backfield triangle. You must SEE the QB.
  2. **"i" and out**: SEE as much as possible. In the "i" position, have depth, SEE from inside-out (backfield triangle to "X"). In the **out position**, focus on "X" and then read the progression ("X" to backfield triangle). **CP**: On sweep, read force as quickly as possible. Your responsibility is the same as shown in giant and crackback position. **On**

PASS, in both positions, work through "X" and force the receiver outside. Never let the receiver come under to the inside.

a. **BACK and BALL TO** and straight block by near back: Meet blocker one yard in backfield. Control block from outside-in, keep square, and be prepared to make the tackle or string the play out to the sideline if ball carrier continues wide. **CP**: QB and near back will tell you play pass. SEE QB on play pass, Near back will run a path to avoid you. On RUN, he will attack you. On PLAY PASS, sprint to your coverage responsibility.

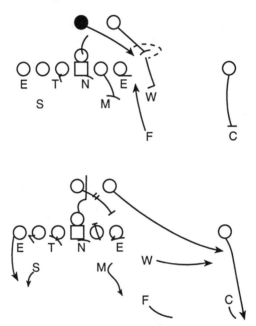

b. **FLOW AWAY**: HOLD—find ball. SEE QB and backfield triangle, RUN (reverse) or PASS (bootleg). RUN shows—pursue and take the proper angle to get to the ball. **CP**: On reverse, get depth upfield and drive the ball carrier deep.

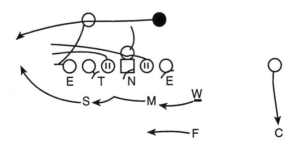

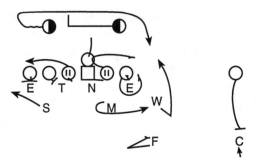

c. **"LION" CALL**: A change in assignment between you and your DE. DE has contain and reverse responsibility. WILL has B-GAP responsibility and pursuit on FLOW AWAY. FLOW TO—HOLD and be ready to fill inside or outside DE. Back and ball—attack B GAP, fill tough. FLOW AWAY—crossover pursue. PASS—go to coverage.

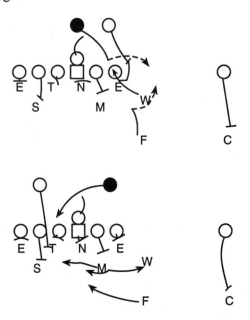

d. **BAM or STRAIGHT CALL**: A change-up in assignment to defend the weakside run better. Use on "I" and WEAK formation when backed up with coverage. (Example: 8, 2, WZ.) On snap, with ball and backs to you, close inside back that is blocking you, drive play deep, and cause a decision. On **PASS**, continue inside back blocking on you, break pocket, DE will contain. **CP**: Use "**STRAIGHT**" only when WILL is committed (blitz in a four-man alignment or three-man line with WILL committed). DE has contain. On "**BAM**," if PASS develops, jam back and go to coverage. DE has contain on PASS.

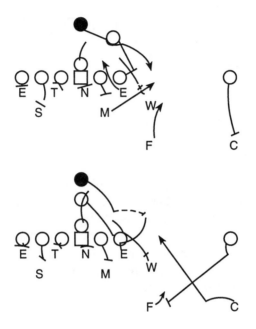

Will Linebacker (Away from TE versus "X" Tight or Two TEs)

- **BACKER SUPPORT**: On snap, step out and SEE inside. Same as SAM assignments, contain sweep, close C GAP.
- **CORNER SUPPORT**: Cut-back responsibility, TWO GAP. Same as SAM assignments.

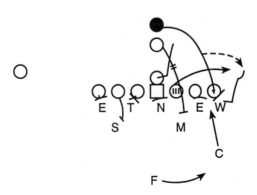

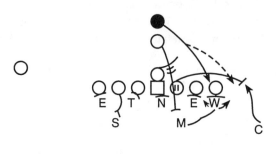

D. Blitz Paths

The linebacker's path and calls for SAM, MIKE, and WILL in the 4–3, OVER, and UNDER fronts are shown below. Also included are the calls for the 30 defensive front. The linebacker names are listed as SAM, TED, MIKE, and WILL. Their paths are drawn with the name of the path at the top. This section shows the linebacker blitz paths and the various possibilities available from both the four-man and three-man line. The actual blitz is shown in the FRONT and COVERAGE sections.

4–3

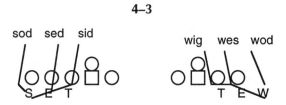

The blitz paths for **SAM** are shown on the left above: **SOD** is outside, **SED** is inside the DE, and **SID** is inside the DT. The paths for **WILL** are shown on the right. **WOD** is outside, **WES** is inside the DE, and **WIG** is inside the DT.

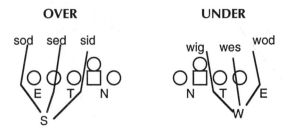

The diagram on the left above shows the blitz paths for **SAM** and **WILL** from the **LOOSE** position. The names of the blitz paths remain the same.

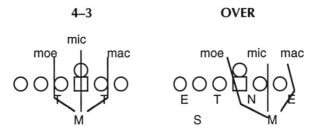

The drawing above on the left shows the blitz paths for **MIKE** in the 4–3 alignment. **MIC** is straight ahead, **MOE** is to the TE around the DT, and **MAC** is away from the TE around the DT. The drawing on the right above shows the blitz paths for **MIKE** in the OVER front (UNDER would be the same). **MOE** is to the TE around the DT, **MIC** is straight ahead, and **MAC** is away from the TE around the DE.

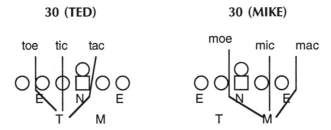

The drawing above on the left shows the blitz paths for **TED** in the 30 front. **TIC** is straight ahead, **TOE** is to the TE around the DE, and **TAC** is away from the TE around the NOSE. On the right are the blitz paths for **MIKE** in the 30 front. **MOE** is to the TE around the NOSE, **MIC** is straight ahead, and **MAC** is away from the TE around the DE.

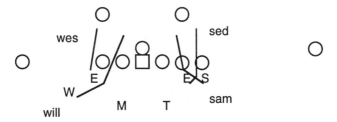

WES and **SED** are inside games involving the DE on their side for WILL and SAM. Both of these games can be called at the same time in an actual blitz.

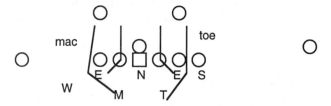

MAC and TOE are outside games involving the DE on their side for MIKE and TED (30 defense). The original terminology was meant for MIKE and TED. MAC means MIKE in a game **away from the TE**. TOE means TED in a **game to the TE**.

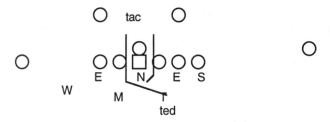

TAC is a game for TED with the NOSE, **away from the TE**.

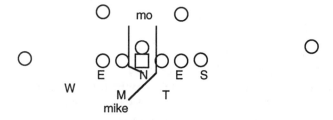

MOE is a game for MIKE with the NOSE, **to the TE**.

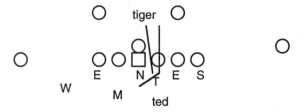

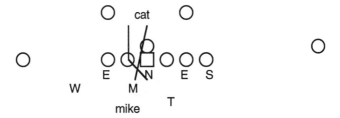

TIGER and CAT are games where TED and MIKE move up and hit the A GAP on the snap, with the NOSE coming around.

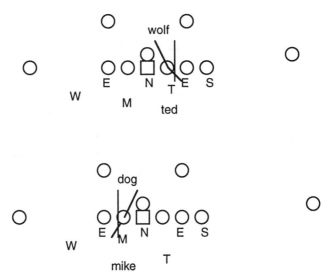

WOLF and DOG are games where TED and MIKE move up and hit the B GAP on the snap, with the END coming around.

The games shown above are examples of some I have used. However, there are many other combinations that may be used. The point is that in preparation, the opponent's blitz pickup is studied and the game plan tries to take advantage of the pickup. If it is a **man-to-man** pattern, then we try to pick the protector and break a man free in the pocket, as in basketball. If it is a **zone** pattern, we want to use a game that will defeat the switch that occurs in the zone pattern. This is the concept, and the idea involves a good rush package.

Other Blitz Paths

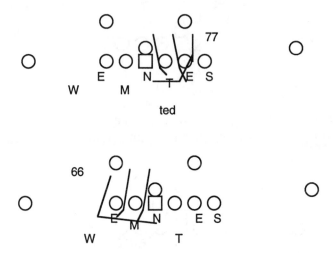

In the 30 defense, TED is #7 by call and MIKE is #6. Carrying this over, the games shown above are **#77** for TED and **#66** for MIKE. On **77**, TED moves up and hits the **A GAP**, the DE drives inside through the **B GAP**, and the NOSE comes around the DE to the strongside.

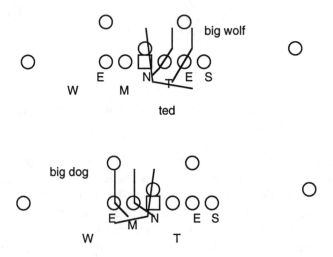

When you finally run out of numbers, words can replace them with the same effectiveness. Earlier, WOLF was a game between TED and the DE on his side. **BIG WOLF** involves TED in the **C GAP**, NOSE in the **B GAP**, and the DE comes around in the strongside **A GAP**. BIG DOG involves MIKE in the **C GAP**, NOSE in the **B GAP**, and the DE comes around in the weakside **A GAP**.

In concluding our discussion of terms and blitz paths, it is appropriate to mention that the most important point is to **study the opponent's blocking pattern** and develop a game that will take advantage of the blocking. Sometimes the movement of personnel will accomplish this; other times it means changing the charge from outside to inside or inside to outside. There is always a weakness, and if your opponent has not seen you use a particular game or a particular alignment, then you have the advantage. Make the most of the opportunity, and call it at the right time to make a big play.

I remember a similar situation in Super Bowl VII versus the Washington Redskins. The game was and remains the only defensive shutout in Super Bowl history. If Garo Yepremian had not tried a pass in order to market and sell more ties, it would have been the only shutout. But he had to give it a try. The pass was intercepted for a touchdown. The defense continued to play well in the final minutes, and the Dolphins won 14–7. Our alignment most of the year and in this game had been normal, with #59 Doug Swift playing SAM. Doug was one of the best SAM linebackers I ever had the privilege of coaching. #53 Bob Matheson was playing his usual position as WILL, MIKE, or TED. We needed a big play, so we moved Bob to SAM and Doug to TED. The Washington offensive line recognized #53 Matheson at SAM and used slide protection to Bob. This change-up allowed Matheson to drop in coverage and left #59 Swift free in the pocket, with a possible back pickup. I don't know if the back missed the pickup or failed to make the adjustment, but the result of the change in alignment was a *sack* at a critical point in the game. The change I refer to is shown below.

REGULAR DOLPHIN ALIGNMENT

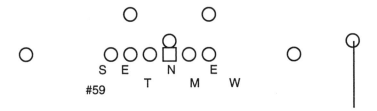

#53 is one of the three spots, usually WILL

CHANGE-UP ALIGNMENT

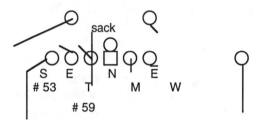

**The change in alignment allows #59
to be free in the pocket for a SACK!**

Moving #53 Bob Matheson was a major part of the 53 defense, but we liked Doug Swift over the TE most of the time, because of his ability to jam the TE and cover. We had shown the change-up alignment during the year, but it had not been a major adjustment. Normally, Matheson was the WILL, and at times he was MIKE and TED. He was an excellent pass rusher, and we counted him as our fourth rusher most of the time. This change-up is an example of a change in alignment to create a problem for the offense. It worked, and I mention it as a possible way for the defense to gain an advantage.

3

COVERAGE: ZONE, MAN, AND BLITZ

Coverage has been an area of interest to me throughout my coaching career. There are many different ideas and many different thoughts about how to play and teach the techniques. This is true in zone, man to man, and blitz. The common thread among all the ideas is this: Does it meet your needs in terms of what you want to accomplish? And most importantly, are the players capable of executing what you are teaching? In other words, does it work in game situations? That is the final test. I have sat in many a clinic and listened intently to some guru explain his ideas about coverage. The discussion may have been excellent, even exciting, as he described techniques that enabled his team to be successful. But when I had an opportunity to view the films, it was a different story.

I say this because it is important to make sure that the players are actually doing what you, as the coach, are teaching. And they must do it in actual game situations. Many of the things we teach and demand may be carried out in practice, which is good, but to be totally effective, they must be good enough to pass the game test.

The other key is to make sure that you have a good mixture of man, zone, and blitz. Work on them. Perfect them. Develop the package that is needed to play your schedule. From time to time, individual calls may be added to make an adjustment that is needed to handle a potential problem. Anticipate, adjust, prepare, and play the game.

Another interesting aspect of pass coverage is deciding on the exact assignment of players, within the scheme, when studying the coverage of another team. For example, in several types of man coverage, a particular player may have a drop that resembles zone, and if no receiver threatens, the assignment will be recorded as zone. The reverse may also be true; in a zone coverage, the assignment may resemble a man-to-man technique but may actually be zone because the route is within the player's zone area.

Through the years, I have heard many interesting discussions among the staff as they described what they thought they saw in a tape. I quickly learned that sometimes you cannot be sure of the actual assignment until you observe the coverage versus all pattern combinations. This is one reason why I like to draw the coverage versus all patterns. Only through this process can you be absolutely sure that you have properly defined the coverage. We have discussed the importance of step-by-step teaching, and this is another example of that principle.

This chapter presents what has been the base during my career. While everyone may not agree with what I say, it accomplished what I was interested in achieving. Yes, we were beaten at times, but overall we were successful. I give credit to our coaches and players for developing and perfecting the details.

Before continuing, let's review the proper alignment of the linebackers and secondary as we discuss their assignments for zone, man, and blitz coverage in both the **regular** and **slot** formation.

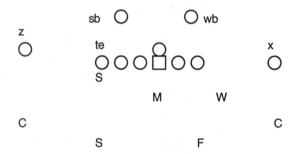

The drawing above will be referred to as **regular formation**. In regular formation, the "**Z**" and **TE** are the two receivers on one side and the "**X**" is the receiver on the other side. The two backs may be aligned in a **split, strong, weak, I, flood,** or **double** alignment.

Versus a regular formation, the linebackers and secondary are aligned as shown above. The linebackers: **SAM** (S) is on the side of the TE, the **WILL** (W) is aligned on the side away from the TE, and the **MIKE** (M) is aligned between SAM and WILL.

The secondary: the **STRONG CORNER** (C) is on the side of the two receivers (strongside) aligned over the "Z." The **STRONG SAFETY** (S) is on the side of the two receivers aligned over or in the area of the TE. The **WEAK SAFETY** (F) is aligned on the weakside away from the side of the two receivers. The **WEAK CORNER** (C) is aligned on the weakside over the "X" away from the side of the two receivers.

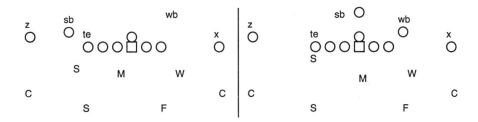

The two drawings above are variations of the regular formation. **FLOOD** formation is on the left, and **DOUBLE** formation is on the right. **FLOOD** is a strong formation, and **DOUBLE** is a weak formation. The linebackers and secondary will vary their position based on the offensive formation, but their basic positions will remain as described above.

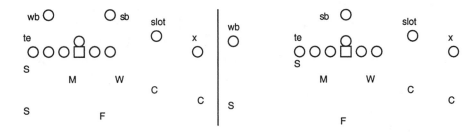

The drawing on the left above is referred to as **SLOT** formation. In **SLOT** formation, the "Z" usually comes across and aligns in the **slot**, with the "X" remaining on the outside. The **TE** is aligned on the weakside. The two backs may be aligned in a **split, strong, weak, I, tiger,** or **doc** alignment. The change in alignment of "Z" to the side of "X" changes the strength of the formation (strongside) and places the two wide receivers to the same side. To properly defend this alignment in zone, man, and blitz, the **CORNER** normally aligned on "Z" comes across and aligns on "Z" now in the **slot**.

The drawing on the right above is referred to as **DOC** formation. **DOC** is a form of the **SLOT** formation, but there is only one back in the backfield. The other back is removed from the base formation and aligned away from the side of the two receivers (strongside) to the side of the TE (weakside).

The two **CORNERS** (C) will remain on the side of the slot. The **STRONG SAFETY** (S) will adjust his position and align over the **WB**. The linebackers **SAM**, **MIKE**, and **WILL** and the **WEAK SAFETY** (F) will adjust their alignment based on the formation and their assignment.

These drawings and the accompanying descriptions are provided to help you to better understand the two basic formations (**regular** and **slot**) and the alignment of the linebackers and secondary in each. Defensively, we must meet strength with strength. When offensive personnel change alignment, the defense must adjust the defensive alignment to properly defend the offensive formation. This is a part of the game that is both intriguing and exciting to the coach and to the fan. It is often the winning edge.

ZONE COVERAGE

A. Cover 2

For **COVER 2** to be effective, it is important for all receivers to be jammed and rerouted. The outside receivers must be funneled inside. The TE must be jammed and delayed from entering the deep middle of the field. Either the SAM or MIKE will have the responsibility of keeping this from happening. In professional football, the rule change several years ago to restrict the jamming of receivers has hurt the defense in this respect. However, proper focus and stress by the defense can still make it happen. Many teams still use COVER 2 as their major defense versus both the pass and the run. If played properly, COVER 2 along with a mixture of TWO MAN will cause problems for the offense. High school and college rules allow defenders to "jam" receivers at any depth, and this is a tremendous advantage. High school and college coaches should take advantage of the "jam" opportunity that their rules permit.

UNDER TWO

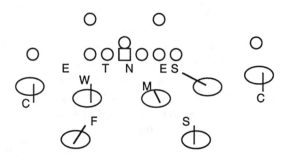

- **Position**: SAM.
- **Alignment**: Take a position head-on the TE. If TE flexes, drop off line of scrimmage and inside.
- **Key**: Corner support—TE, running lane, and backfield triangle.
- **Assignment**: **On pass with strong back present**—jam #2 and SEE SB and work to "M" zone; destroy pattern. No gimmick—get depth with outside receiver #2, #3, and #1. **No strong back present**—jam #2, allow no inside release. Do not attack; build a wall with #2 back through the hook area.
- **Slot**: WILL assignments, short inside zone on weakside. Build wall on #4, read and locate #4 and #5 by release.

- **Position**: MIKE.
- **Alignment**: By alignment called (UNDER, OVER, 30).
- **Key**: Guard and backfield triangle (strong back).
- **Assignment**: **Strong back present**—favor strongside hash and SEE receivers #2, #3, and #1. Get depth with inside receiver. Square up and attack ball. With #2 and #3 both outside, get depth in middle of field. SEE QB play the ball. **No strong back present—frank action**. Favor weak hash, and SEE receivers #4, #3, and #1. Get depth, square up, and attack ball.
- **Slot**: Pass responsibility is the same. **CP**: Strongside is the side of the **slot**.

- **Position**: WILL.
- **Alignment**: By alignment called (UNDER, OVER, 30).
- **Key**: Corner support—weak back, "X" (SB, TE). Versus NEAR—near, WB.
- **Assignment**: **On pass—short inside zone on weakside**. SEE #4 and #5—drop straight back, SEE the pattern as you go, get depth. **#4 on inside route**—force him to outside, work to zone. **#4 outside**—work back to zone, get depth, square up, locate #5, #2, and #3 on crossing pattern. **Frank action**—HOLD, destroy circle, be ready to attack gimmick, No gimmick—get depth, square up, and attack ball.
- **Slot**: SAM assignments, short inside "M" zone strongside, jam #2, locate #3 and #1 by release of #2.

- **Position**: STRONG CORNER.
- **Alignment**: Take a position head-on "Z," no more than five yards deep. You **must be within the five-yard area** to **JAM** and **reroute** the receiver. This is very important in **COVER 2**. High school and college rules are different, and the corner may line up deeper if the coach desires.
- **Key**: **Corner support**—"Z," TE, SB, SEE QB and ball.

- **Assignment: On pass—short outside zone on strongside.** Before snap, move to an outside technique. **HOLD** at five yards, **jam and FUNNEL #1** inside, take away the "oh" and fade, SEE #3 and #2, **N/T** (no one there)— **cushion** with depth, square away, react to ball.
- **Slot:** Pass responsibility is the same.

- **Position: STRONG SAFETY.**
- **Alignment:** Take a position a shade outside of TE, at least seven yards deep. Your distance may vary depending on the split of "Z."
- **Key:** Corner support—"Z," TE, SB, QB, and ball.
- **Assignment: On pass—deep half of field strongside.** Gain depth to three yards inside the numbers. This may vary in high school and college, as the numbers are located in a different position. Read receivers on your side, SEE BALL. Play deep to short, react to ball.
- **Slot:** Pass responsibility is the same.

- **Position: WEAK SAFETY.**
- **Alignment:** Take a position ten yards deep on the weakside offensive tackle. The offensive formation may alter your alignment and depth.
- **Key:** Corner support—"X," WB, QB, and ball.
- **Assignment: On pass—deep half of field weakside.** Gain depth to three yards inside the numbers. (High school and college numbers are different as noted above.) Read receivers on your side, SEE BALL. Play deep to short, react to ball.
- **Slot:** Pass responsibility is the same.

- **Position: WEAK CORNER.**
- **Alignment:** Take a position head-on "X," no more than five yards deep. You **must be within the five-yard area** to JAM and **reroute** the receiver. This is very important in **COVER 2.** (Alignment may vary as noted above in high school and college.)
- **Key: Corner support**—"X," WB, SEE QB and ball.
- **Assignment: On pass—short outside zone on weakside.** Before snap, move to an outside technique. **HOLD** at five yards, **jam and FUNNEL #5** inside, take away the "oh" and fade, SEE #4 and crossing receivers. N/T—cushion with depth, square away, react to ball.
- **Slot:** Pass responsibility is the same.

Front Notes

The **alignment, key, and assignment** have been written for the **UNDER** and **OVER** front. If the **30** front is used, all coverage responsibilities remain the same. To keep it simple, WILL, MIKE, or TED should be called as the **designated blitzer**. The linebackers not designated would assume the assignment as indicated. (Example: If MIKE is the designated blitzer, then TED would have MIKE assignments. WILL and SAM would have the same assignments as described above.)

I personally like to have SAM aligned on the line of scrimmage to JAM the tight end, as in the UNDER front. However, I have used OVER and, with hard work and SAM's understanding of his responsibility, the pass coverage can be effective. Both are good versus the run.

Adjustment Notes

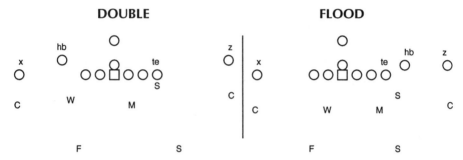

Regardless of the front (**UNDER** is shown above), the outside linebacker must adjust his position to jam and delay receivers. The diagram above is **DOUBLE** formation, and **WILL** adjusts to the outside, to carry out the assignment of the defense. The diagram on the right above shows **FLOOD** formation, and **SAM** adjusts to carry out the assignment of the defense. **CP:** As the linebacker adjusts, he must keep in mind his responsibility, get depth, and maintain vision for the run or pass.

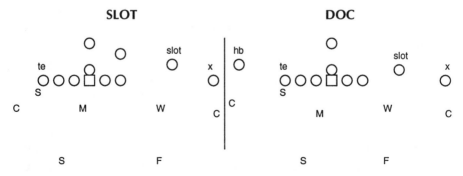

The diagram on the left above shows **SLOT** formation, with **WILL** adjusting to carry out the assignment of the defense. The diagram on the right above shows **DOC** formation, with the alignments necessary to carry out the assignment of the defense. In both drawings, SAM may align deeper for better vision.

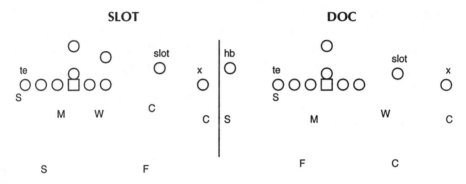

There is an alternative to **SLOT** and **DOC** formations. This alignment uses a double-digit call **(27)** to properly identify the variation of alignments and assignments. TWO identifies the coverage for **regular** formations, and SEVEN identifies the coverage for **SLOT** formations.

The **CORNER** will come across with the wide receiver and play the assignment of the defense. This works well because it ties in with other looks and keeps the linebackers inside to better play the run. However, in **DOC**, **WILL** must realign in position to carry out the assignment of the defense. CP: Notice in the diagram on the left above that **SAM** must take a backer support alignment for the run and the short outside zone assignment for the pass weakside.

B. Cover 3

The **THREE-DEEP ZONES** have been the base coverage for most teams. There are two concepts of the **three-deep zones**. In one concept, the underneath coverage drops to **specific spots**, then square away in a position to react to routes in the area. The other concept has the underneath coverage begin their drop, but the **pattern dictates the path and action of the defender**. This is more of a zone-defined man-to-man technique, based on the pattern.

Actually, we used both concepts with the Miami Dolphins. When we used the **three-deep zone** with **four underneath** in coverage, we used what we called a "slot" or **pattern technique**. We started our drop, but we read the pattern and reacted accordingly. When we used the **three-deep zone** with **five underneath** in coverage, we used the regular "**zone**" or **spot drop**

technique. We felt that the addition of the fifth player underneath helped us to better cover the field, and dropping to spots was more effective. One of the factors that brought about this adjustment was movement of the hash marks to basically the middle of the field or in line with the goalposts, as used today. When the hash marks were moved (in pro football), the fifth underneath defender was needed to cover the field. However, without the fifth defender, we felt it was necessary to use the pattern read as described above. The discussion here follows the two concepts as used by the Dolphins and later by the San Diego Chargers when I was a part of those programs.

Cover 3 Sky

COVER 3 SKY is three-deep strongside zone coverage with four underneath and safety support.

- **Position:** SAM.
- **Alignment: Head-on** the TE. Alignment will vary based on the front, formation, and position of the TE.
- **Key:** Safety support—TE, running lane, backfield triangle, "Z."
- **Assignment: On pass—short inside zone on strongside,** force the #2 outside and see the #3. Work back with inside receiver (#2, #3, or #1) man to man in your zone. **#2 inside**—jam, drive #2 inside and destroy outside route, cover #2 man to man in your zone (to middle of formation). **#2 outside**—jam #2 and read release of #3. **#3 inside**—stay in your zone. **#3 outside**—get width with #2, locate #1. **Frank action**—work weakside with depth to the middle of the formation, SEE inside receivers #3 and #2 (#1) in your zone.
- **Slot:** WILL assignments, short outside zone on weakside, read #4 and #5.

- **Position:** MIKE.
- **Alignment:** By alignment called (OVER, EVEN, 30).

- **Key**: Guard and backfield triangle.
- **Assignment: On pass—short inside zone on weakside**, SEE #4 and #5. **#4 on inside route**—force outside and work back with him man to man in your zone. **#4 on outside route**—work back and look for #5 on inside route in your zone. **Frank action**—move laterally, destroy circle route, get depth in zone (middle of field).
- **Slot**: Pass responsibility is the same.

- **Position: WILL.**
- **Alignment**: By alignment called (OVER, EVEN, 30).
- **Key: Backer support**, backfield triangle, "X."
- **Assignment: On pass—short outside slot on weakside**, SEE #4 and #5. **#4 on inside route**—locate #5 and work back with him man to man on inside routes in your zone. Locate #4 in "fan area," react to "oh." **#4 on outside route**—HOLD with depth and delay inside route of #5, attack #4 on ball. **CP**: Run with second man through your zone.
- **Slot**: SAM assignments, short inside zone strongside, force #2 outside man to man in your zone. Read #3 and #1.

- **Position: STRONG CORNER.**
- **Alignment**: Outside technique on "Z," five to seven yards deep.
- **Key: Safety support**—"Z," TE, SB. SEE QB to ball.
- **Assignment: On pass—deep outside zone on strongside**, you have inside help shallow and deep middle on strongside. Play outside routes of #1, #2, and #3 man to man. React and play through receiver from outside-in on inside routes of #1, #2, and #3. **CP**: Stay as deep as the deepest receiver on your side.
- **Slot**: STRONG SAFETY assignments, short outside slot on strongside. See #2, #3, and #1.

- **Position: STRONG SAFETY.**
- **Alignment**: A **shade outside** of TE, five to seven yards deep.
- **Key: Safety support**—TE, SB, "Z" to QB and ball.
- **Assignment: On pass—short outside slot on strongside**, SEE #2, #3, and #1. **#2 releases outside** (vertical)—HOLD, jam at five yards, work back with #2 through your zone. **#2 diagonal** (outside)—HOLD with depth and delay inside route of #1, attack #2 on ball. **#2 blocks or #3 on outside route**—HOLD with depth and delay inside route of #1, attack #2 and #3 on ball. **#2 inside and #3 blocks or outside**—HOLD with depth, SEE #1 and #3 and ensure #2 in bow-out area.
- **Slot**: WEAK CORNER assignments, deep third of outside zone on weakside.

- **Position: WEAK SAFETY.**
- **Alignment: Take a position ten yards deep** on the weakside offensive tackle. The offensive formation may alter your alignment and depth.
- **Key:** Backfield triangle, QB and BALL.
- **Assignment: On pass—deep middle zone.** SEE QB and all receivers, play from deep to short. Take **deep inside route of #1, #2, and #3** strongside or **deep inside route of #5 and #4** weakside.
- **Slot:** Pass responsibility is the same.

- **Position: WEAK CORNER.**
- **Alignment:** Outside technique on "X," five to seven yards deep.
- **Key:** Backer support—"X," WB. SEE QB to ball.
- **Assignment: On pass—deep outside zone on weakside,** you have inside help shallow and deep middle on weakside. Play outside routes of #5 and #4 man to man. React and play through receiver from outside-in on inside routes of #5 and #4.
- **Slot: STRONG CORNER** assignments, deep third of zone on strongside.

Front Notes

The alignment shown is for OVER. The three-deep strongside zone can be played from this alignment or from an alignment where the SAM lines up over the TE. Both are productive. However, if your goal is to JAM and disrupt the TE pattern, then it is better for SAM to align over the TE.

A similar situation develops weakside with WILL. In terms of coverage, it is better if WILL is aligned outside in the **giant, I,** or **out** position. WILL can align inside as in UNDER and EVEN, but you give up a little in the short outside slot weakside. WILL may be unable to get as wide as necessary from the inside position. Like everything else, it is usually fine as a mixture, but as a steady diet, WILL needs to be aligned outside.

Adjustment Notes

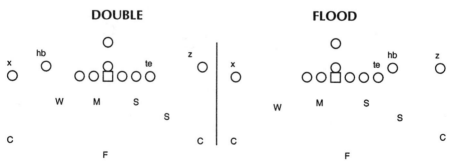

The adjustments shown in the diagram on the left above are for **DOUBLE** formation from the **OVER** front. **UNDER** is good, but **OVER** allows for WILL and the **SS** to have better alignments, while keeping two linebackers in the box for the run. Vision and depth are important for both **WILL** and the **SS**. **FLOOD** formation is shown in the diagram on the right above.

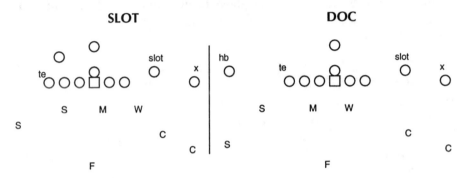

SLOT formation is shown in the diagram on the left above. **DOC** formation is shown in the diagram on the right, with the adjustments. In both examples, notice that the **CORNER** comes across and plays the **SS** zone assignments. The SS goes weakside and plays the **WEAK CORNER** zone assignments. In DOC formation, take note of the alignment adjustment of SAM, MIKE, and WILL.

Cover 3 Cloud

COVER 3 CLOUD is three-deep strongside zone coverage with four underneath and corner support. The assignments are the same with the exception of the STRONG CORNER and STRONG SAFETY. These two positions change assignments. The STRONG CORNER becomes the short defender in the short outside slot strongside, and the STRONG SAFETY becomes the deep defender in the deep outside zone strongside.

- **Position:** STRONG CORNER.
- **Alignment:** Inside technique on "Z," five to seven yards deep.
- **Key: Corner support**—"Z," TE, SB. SEE QB to ball.
- **Assignment: On pass**—**short outside slot on strongside,** HOLD, jam and FORCE #1 outside, work back to short outside slot (no wider than numbers). SEE #2 and #3. **Shallow outside route**—get depth and delay inside route of #1. Attack #2 and #3 on BALL. **#2 blocks or #3 on outside route**—HOLD with depth and delay inside route of #1. Attack #2 and #3 on BALL. **#2 inside and #3 blocks or outside**—HOLD with depth, SEE #1 and #3 and ensure #2 in bow-out area.
- **Slot:** NO CLOUD CALL on **SLOT** FORMATIONS. Stay SKY. **CP:** If there were a need by the game plan, the STRONG CORNER would have the same assignment as on regular formation. In that case, the next inside defender (SAM or WILL) must adjust to the **slot** receiver.

- **Position:** STRONG SAFETY.
- **Alignment: A shade outside** of TE, five to seven yards deep. **CP:** Make sure you align deeper and wider, if formation dictates.
- **Key:** Corner support—TE, SB, "Z" to QB and ball.
- **Assignment: On pass**—**deep outside zone on strongside.** You have inside help shallow and deep on strongside. Play outside routes of #1, #2, and #3. React and play through receiver from outside-in on inside routes of #1, #2, and #3.
- **Slot:** WEAK CORNER assignments, deep third of zone weakside.

Front Notes

Either OVER, EVEN, UNDER, or 30 may be called for 3 CLOUD. 3 CLOUD affects only the S/CORNER and the S/SAFETY. The other positions can effectively carry out their assignments from their basic alignments.

Cover 3 Sam

COVER 3 SAM is three-deep strongside zone coverage with four underneath and SAM aligned in the backer support position. The assignments are the same with the exception of SAM and the STRONG SAFETY. These two positions change assignments. SAM becomes the short defender in the short outside slot strongside, and the STRONG SAFETY becomes the short inside zone defender on the strongside. 3 SAM is similar to 3 CLOUD in that only the SAM and S/SAFETY are involved in the change of assignments.

As mentioned earlier, 3 SAM fits very well in the UNDER package with ZERO and ONE (man coverage). This allows the STRONG SAFETY the flexibility needed to disguise his alignment for MAN coverage and BLITZ. It also places him in a position to create an eight-man front versus the run.

UNDER 3 SAM

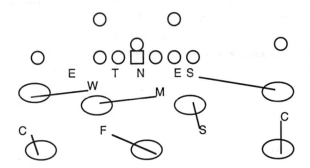

- **Position**: SAM.
- **Alignment: Backer support—outside shoulder** of TE. If TE is flexed, drop off the line of scrimmage at a depth to see the both the TE and offensive tackle and the backfield triangle.
- **Key**: TE, running lane, backfield triangle, and "Z."
- **Assignment: On pass—short outside slot on strongside.** SEE TE, SB, and "Z." **TE outside releases**—jam at five yards, work back with TE through your zone. **TE diagonal** (outside)—drop with depth to slot and delay inside route of "Z," attack TE on ball. **TE blocks or SB on outside route**—drop with depth and delay inside route of "Z," and attack TE and SB on ball. **TE inside and SB blocks or outside**—drop with depth, SEE "Z" and SB, and ensure TE in bow-out area.
- **Slot: NO SAM CALL on slot.** SKY is best. CLOUD may be used by game plan.

- **Position**: STRONG SAFETY.
- **Alignment: Head-on** the TE. Alignment will vary based on the formation and the position of the TE.
- **Key**: Backer support—TE, running lane and backfield triangle, "Z."
- **Assignment: On pass—short inside zone on strongside.** Force #2 outside and see #3. Work back with inside receiver (#2 or #3) or #1 man to

man in your zone. **#2 inside**—jam, drive #2 inside and destroy outside route, cover #2 man to man in your zone (middle of formation).

- **Slot: NO SAM CALL on slot.** SKY is best. CLOUD may be used by game plan.

Front Notes

SAM must be aligned on the line of scrimmage in a backer support position to successfully play **COVER 3 SAM**. The UNDER front is a perfect call for cover 3 SAM. It is the same FRONT that was recommended for ZERO and ONE (man coverage). Along with 3 SAM, this makes for a good ZONE, MAN, and BLITZ package.

Adjustment Notes

The adjustments for **3 CLOUD** are the same as shown in the **3 SKY** diagrams. **3 SAM** adjustments must come from the **UNDER** front, to allow **SAM** to take the short outside zone strongside. **CP**: Versus **FLOOD** and **SLOT** formations, 3 SAM should revert to 3 SKY.

C. Cover 6

Cover 6 Sky

UNDER 6 SKY

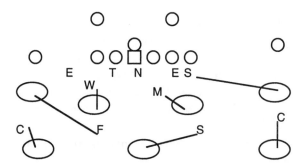

COVER 6 SKY is three-deep weakside zone coverage with four underneath and safety support weakside. This coverage has proved to be a good mixer, particularly with TEN (man coverage), as the WEAK SAFETY alignment is similar to his alignment taken on ZERO.

- **Position**: SAM.
- **Alignment: Backer support—outside shoulder** of TE. If TE is flexed, drop off the line of scrimmage at a depth to see both the TE and offensive tackle and the running lane and backfield triangle.
- **Key**: TE, running lane, backfield triangle, and "Z."
- **Assignment: On pass—short outside slot on strongside**, SEE #2, #3, and #1. **#2 outside releases**—jam, work through the #2 to your zone. **#2 diagonal** (shallow outside)—drop with depth to slot and delay inside route of #1, attack #2 on ball. **#2 blocks or #3 on outside route**—drop with depth and delay inside route of #1, attack #2 and #3 on BALL. **#2 inside and #3 blocks or outside**—drop with depth, SEE #1 and #3, and ensure #2 in bow-out area.
- **Slot**: WILL assignments, short inside zone on weakside.

- **Position**: MIKE.
- **Alignment**: By defense called.
- **Key**: Guard and backfield triangle.
- **Assignment: On pass—short inside zone on strongside**, force #2 outside, SEE #3. Work back with inside receiver (#2, #3, #1) in your zone. **#2 inside**—jam and destroy #2 on inside route. **#2 outside**—read #3 release. **#3 inside**—stay in your zone. **#3 outside**—gain width, SEE #2 and #1. **Frank action**—work strongside with depth in middle of formation, look for inside receivers #4, #3, and #5 in your zone.
- **Slot**: Pass responsibility is the same.

- **Position**: WILL.
- **Alignment**: By front called.
- **Key**: Weak safety support, backfield triangle, "X."
- **Assignment: On pass—short inside zone on weakside**. SEE #4 and #5. **#4 on inside route**—force outside and work back with him man to man in your zone. **#4 on outside route**—work back and look for #5 on inside route in your zone. **Frank action**—HOLD, destroy circle, get depth in your zone.
- **Slot**: SAM assignments, short outside slot on strongside. **CP**: "I" position is the best position.

- **Position**: STRONG CORNER.
- **Alignment**: Outside technique on "Z," five to seven yards deep.
- **Key**: Backer support—"Z," TE, SB. SEE QB to ball.
- **Assignment: On pass—deep outside zone on strongside**. You have inside help shallow and deep on strongside. Play outside routes of #1, #2,

and #3 man to man. React and play through receiver from outside-in on inside routes of #1, #2, and #3.

- **Slot:** Deep middle zone, middle of field.

- **Position: STRONG SAFETY.**
- **Alignment:** A shade outside of TE, five to seven yards deep.
- **Key:** Backer support—TE, backfield triangle to QB and ball.
- **Assignment: On pass**—move to the **deep middle zone.** SEE QB and all receivers, play from deep to short. Take **deep inside route of #1, #2,** and **#3** strongside or **deep inside route of #5** and #4 weakside.
- **Slot:** WEAK SAFETY assignments, short zone area weakside. **CP:** Use SKY call only on DOC.

- **Position: WEAK SAFETY.**
- **Alignment: Take a position eight to ten yards deep** on the weakside offensive **tackle.** The offensive formation may alter your alignment and depth.
- **Key: Weak safety** support—backfield triangle, QB, and ball.
- **Assignment: On pass**—**short outside slot on weakside.** SEE #4 and #5. **#4 on inside route**—locate #5 and work back with him man to man on inside routes in your zone. Locate #4 in fan area, react to "oh." **#4 on outside route**—HOLD with depth and delay inside route of #5, attack #4 on BALL.
- **Slot:** Deep third of outside zone weakside.

- **Position: WEAK CORNER.**
- **Alignment:** Outside technique on "X," five to seven yards deep.
- **Key:** Weak safety support—"X," WB. SEE QB to ball.
- **Assignment: On pass**—**deep outside zone on weakside.** You have inside help shallow and deep on weakside. Play outside routes of #5 and #4 man to man. React and play through receiver from outside-in on inside routes of #5 and #4.
- **Slot:** STRONG CORNER assignments, deep third of outside zone strongside.

Front Notes

COVER 6 SKY works well with UNDER, EVEN, and 30. If 30 is the call, the MIKE is in the best position to become the designated blitzer. This leaves WILL, TED, and SAM free to play the coverage called. TED could be used as the designated blitzer. MIKE would need to make a slight alignment adjustment to reach his short inside zone strongside.

Adjustment Notes

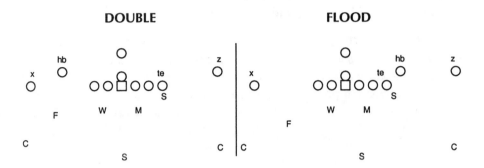

DOUBLE	FLOOD

SLOT	DOC

The diagram on the left above shows **6 SKY** alignment versus **DOUBLE**. The diagram on the right shows **6 SKY** versus **FLOOD**. CP: Normally, the WEAK SAFETY probably would not cheat as much as shown in the drawing.

Notice in the diagram on the left above that SKY reverts to CLOUD versus **slot**. WILL is in a poor position to carry out his assignment. He may cheat a little, but not much because of the run threat. The diagram on the right shows 6 SKY versus DOC. This is a good mixture. The deep defenders, except the STRONG SAFETY and WEAK SAFETY, have the same responsibilities as shown on the left.

Cover 6 Cloud

COVER 6 CLOUD is three-deep weakside zone coverage with four underneath and corner support. The assignments are the same with the exception of the WEAK CORNER and WEAK SAFETY. These two positions change assignments. The WEAK CORNER becomes the short defender in the short outside zone weakside, and the WEAK SAFETY becomes the deep defender in the deep outside zone weakside.

UNDER 6 CLOUD

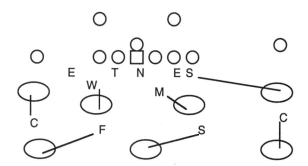

- **Position**: WEAK SAFETY.
- **Alignment**: Take a position **ten yards deep** on the weakside offensive tackle. The offensive formation may alter your alignment and depth.
- **Key**: Weak corner support, QB, and backfield triangle.
- **Assignment**: **On pass—deep outside zone on weakside.** You have inside help shallow and deep middle on weakside. Play outside routes of #5 and #4 man to man. React and play through receiver from outside-in on inside routes of #5 and #4.
- **Slot**: Pass responsibility is the same.

- **Position**: WEAK CORNER.
- **Alignment**: Inside technique on "X," five to seven yards deep.
- **Key**: **Weak corner support**—"X," WB, backfield triangle. SEE QB to BALL.
- **Assignment**: **On pass—short outside slot on weakside.** HOLD, jam and FORCE #5 outside, work back to short outside slot (no wider than numbers; numbers are in a different location in high school and college). SEE #5 and #4. **Shallow outside route**—get depth and delay inside route of #5. Attack #5 and #4 on BALL. **#4 inside**—HOLD with depth, SEE #5 and #4 and ensure #4 in fan area.
- **Slot**: STRONG CORNER assignments, deep third of outside zone strongside.

Front Notes

The **FRONTS** that go with **COVER 6 SKY** will fit comfortably with **6 CLOUD**.

Cover 6 Will

COVER 6 WILL is three-deep weakside zone coverage with four underneath and backer support. The assignments are the same with the exception of WILL and the WEAK SAFETY. These two positions change assignments. WILL becomes the short defender in the short outside slot weakside, and the WEAK SAFETY becomes the short inside zone defender on the weakside.

UNDER 6 WILL

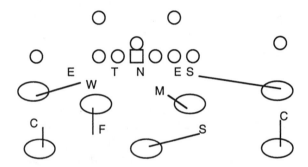

- **Position: WILL.**
- **Alignment:** By front called (UNDER, EVEN, 30).
- **Key: Backer support**—backfield triangle, "X."
- **Assignment: On pass**—**short outside slot on weakside.** SEE #4 and #5. **#4 on inside route**—locate #5 and work back with him man to man on inside routes in your zone. Locate #4 in fan area, react to "oh." **#4 on outside route**—HOLD with depth and delay inside route on #5, attack #4 on BALL. **Frank action**—gain width and depth, SEE and react on BALL.
- **Slot:** No WILL call on **slot.** SKY or CLOUD may be used by game plan.

- **Position: WEAK SAFETY.**
- **Alignment:** Take a position **eight to ten yards deep** on the weakside offensive tackle. The offensive formation may alter your alignment and depth.
- **Key: Backer support**—QB and backfield triangle.
- **Assignment: On pass**—**short inside zone on weakside.** SEE #4 and #5. **#4 on inside route**—force outside and work back through with him man

to man in your zone. **#4 on outside route**—work back and look for #5 on inside route in your zone. **Frank action**—HOLD, destroy "circle," get depth in zone.

- **Slot**: Pass responsibility is the same as 6 CLOUD or 6 SKY by call.

Front Notes

OVER front would be a better call for WILL, because it would allow him to take the "I" position. This would place WILL in a better position to carry out his assignment. However, if **6 WILL** is only used as a mixer in passing situations, UNDER or EVEN will prove effective.

Adjustment Notes

The adjustments for **6 CLOUD** are the same as shown in the diagrams for **6 SKY**. **6 WILL** adjustments must come from the **UNDER** front, to allow **SAM** to take the short outside zone strongside.

There is one problem with **COVER 6** that must be pointed out before moving on. **COVER 6** is a weak coverage, and a decision must be made on how to handle FLOW (both backs to the strongside). Again, there are two distinct positions: (1) stay in the coverage and let the linebackers SAM, MIKE, and WILL adjust or (2) have the safeties come out of the coverage and go to what is described here as **3 SKY**. This enables SAM and MIKE to play the run first, without having to worry about vacating their area with the ball coming toward them. Experience has shown that this is best versus the run and sound versus the pass. The first option is easier to teach, and many coordinators and secondary coaches make their decisions based on this one factor. Using **COVER 6** as a mixer is probably a good decision, because the players do not get enough work on seeing FLOW and adjusting to 3 SKY. With the other coverages, **COVER 6** in all probability is only a mixer, and there is no sense creating problems for the player. KEEP IT SIMPLE and EXECUTE.

D. Cover 7

COVER 7 is a TWO-DEEP coverage that is only used as a second-digit call with cover 2. As discussed earlier, COVER 2 may be called individually or may be used as a double-digit call with COVER 7. When used as a double-digit call, **COVER 7 is used only versus the slot formation**. The alignment, key, and assignment for COVER 7 are discussed in their entirety in this section.

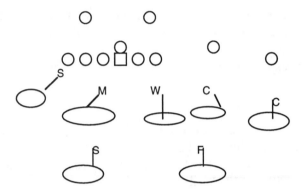

- **Position:** SAM.
- **Alignment:** Take a position **head-on** to outside of TE. If TE flexes, drop off line of scrimmage and inside.
- **Key: Backer support**—TE, running lane, and backfield triangle.
- **Assignment: On pass, weak back present**—jam #5 and SEE WB, work to short outside zone on the weakside. **No weak back present**—jam #5, do not attack. Build a wall on #5 from the outside-in, as you work back and out to area.

- **Position:** MIKE.
- **Alignment:** By alignment called (UNDER, OVER, 30).
- **Key:** Guard and backfield triangle.
- **Assignment: Weak back present**—favor weakside and SEE receivers #4 and #5. Get depth with inside receiver, square up and attack ball. **#4 and #5 both outside**—get depth in middle of field. SEE QB play the ball. **No weak back present**—favor strongside and SEE receivers #4, #3, and #2. Get depth, square up, and attack ball. **Frank action**—HOLD, destroy circle, be ready to attack gimmick. If no gimmick, get depth, square up, and attack ball.

- **Position:** WILL.
- **Alignment:** By alignment called (UNDER, OVER, 30).
- **Key:** Corner support—strong back, "Z" (SB, **slot**).
- **Assignment: On pass—short inside zone on strongside.** SEE #2 and #3—drop straight back. SEE the pattern as you go, get depth. **#3 on inside route**—force him to outside, work to zone. **#3 outside**—work back to zone, get depth, square up, locate #1, #2, and #4 on crossing pattern. **Frank action**—favor weak hash, see receivers #4, #3, and #2. Get depth, square up, and attack ball.

- **Position**: SLOT CORNER.
- **Alignment**: Take a position **head-up to inside** of slot. Have enough depth to SEE **slot** and next inside BACK.
- **Key**: Corner support—**slot**, running lane, and backfield triangle.
- **Assignment**: **On pass, strong back present**—jam #2 and SEE SB, and work to "M" zone; destroy pattern. If no gimmick, get depth with outside receiver #2, #3, and #1. **No strong back present**—jam #2, allow no inside release. Do not attack, build a wall with #2 back through the hook area.

- **Position**: STRONG CORNER.
- **Alignment**: Take a position head-on "Z," no more than five yards deep. You **must be within the five-yard area** to JAM and **reroute** the receiver (this rule is different in high school and college). This is very important in **COVER 2**.
- **Key**: **Corner support**—"Z," slot, SB, SEE QB and ball. **CP**: Support will be by game plan.
- **Assignment**: **On pass—short outside zone on strongside**. Before snap, move to an outside technique. **HOLD** at five yards, **jam and FUNNEL #1** inside, take away the "oh" and fade, SEE #3 and #2, N/T—cushion with depth, square away, react to ball.

- **Position**: STRONG SAFETY.
- **Alignment**: Take a position a **shade outside** of TE, at least seven yards deep. Your distance may vary depending on the alignment of the TE.
- **Key**: Backer support—TE, WB, QB, and ball.
- **Assignment**: **On pass—deep half of field weakside**. Gain depth to three yards inside the numbers. Read receivers on your side, SEE BALL. Play deep to short, react to ball.

- **Position**: WEAK SAFETY.
- **Alignment**: Take a position ten yards deep on the strongside offensive tackle. The offensive formation may alter your alignment and depth.
- **Key**: Corner support—"Z," SB, QB, and ball.
- **Assignment**: **On pass—deep half of field strongside**. Gain depth to three yards inside the numbers. Read receivers on your side, SEE BALL. Play deep to short, react to ball. (Remember, the numbers are different in high school and college.)

Adjustment Notes

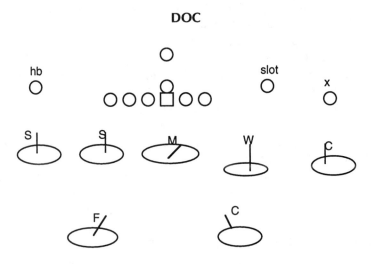

The adjustment shown above is for **COVER 7** versus **DOC** formation. The adjustment returns the coverage call to **COVER 2** assignments.

E. Cover 8

COVER 8 is a basic FOUR-DEEP call that can successfully be used with either man-to-man or zone principles. I first became acquainted with this coverage when I went to the Baltimore Colts in 1964. At that time, as coached by Charley Winner, it was one of two or three basic man coverages. Through the years, revisions were made by adding weakside or strongside calls. This can be done very easily because of the balanced structure. These additional calls were very successful both in Baltimore and later in Miami. We also used the coverage very successfully at LSU in the mid-eighties. Upon returning to the sideline with the San Diego Chargers in 1992, two of our defensive coaches, Dale Lindsey and John Fox, were familiar with cover 8 principles. After much discussion, we incorporated their ideas, and the coverage continued to be a reliable mixture in our package. Although their experience with cover 8 was more of a zone concept, it was nevertheless just as effective.

Through our discussions and by looking at tapes of other teams, it became obvious to me that the basic four-deep principle of cover 8 is necessary to all defensive packages. It grew as many coaches contributed changes to fit their needs. This is usually the case; there really are not many entirely new defenses or offenses in the game. We have all used something that impressed us from another coach or another team. Then, as innovators, we proceeded to adapt it to our program. Sometimes the result is instant success, and other times the innovation winds up in the recycle bin.

Both zone and man-to-man principles, and the calls used as the situation demands, will be discussed. Then it is up to you to decide which best fits your need. You might even be brave enough to use both, which will probably come in handy at some time during the year. Because we are discussing ZONE coverage in this section, COVER 8 ZONE is described first. COVER 8 MAN is discussed in the section on MAN coverage.

Cover 8 Zone

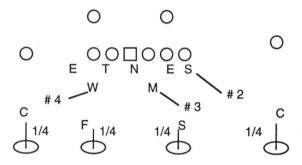

- **Position: SAM.**
- **Alignment: Backer support—outside shoulder of TE.** If TE is flexed, drop off the line of scrimmage at a depth to see both the TE and offensive tackle and the backfield triangle.
- **Key: TE, strong back, "Z."**
- **Assignment: On pass—drop to slot strongside,** SEE #2 and #3. **#2 is vertical—**locate #1. **#2 on diagonal—**take man to man with depth. N/T—get depth, locate crossing receivers.
- **Slot:** WILL assignments, shortest of #4 and #5 inside.

- **Position: MIKE.**
- **Alignment:** By front called (UNDER, EVEN, 30).
- **Key:** Strong back, TE, backfield triangle.
- **Assignment: On pass—short inside zone strongside.** SEE #2 and #3. **Inside receiver is vertical—**get depth and locate outside receiver crossing in your area. **Inside receiver (#2 and #3) is short—**cover man to man. **#2 and #3 both outside—**cover inside receiver man to man.
- **Slot:** Pass responsibility is the same.

- **Position: WILL.**
- **Alignment:** By front called (UNDER, EVEN, 30).
- **Key: Backer support** is normal, with "X" in normal split position. **Corner support** versus NEAR or TE.
- **Assignment: On pass—short inside zone weakside.** SEE #4. **#4 is vertical**—work through #4 and locate #5. **#4 is short**—cover man to man from depth.
- **Slot:** SAM assignments, match #2 and #3 from depth, drop vertical.

- **Position: STRONG CORNER.**
- **Alignment: Head-on "Z,"** five to seven yards deep. **CP:** Alignment will vary by position of "Z."
- **Key:** Backer support, "Z," TE, SB to QB.
- **Assignment: On pass—deep quarter of outside zone** on strongside. You have inside help shallow and deep.
- **Slot:** STRONG SAFETY assignments, deep quarter of zone inside strongside.

- **Position: STRONG SAFETY.**
- **Alignment:** Take a position a **shade outside** of TE, five to seven yards deep. TE flex, shade inside.
- **Key:** Backer support, **TE, SB, "Z,"** SEE QB and backfield action.
- **Assignment: On pass—deep quarter of inside zone** on strongside. SEE all strongside receivers—**responsible for #1, #2, and #3** through post area.
- **Slot:** WEAK CORNER assignments, deep quarter of zone outside weakside.

- **Position: WEAK SAFETY.**
- **Alignment:** Take a position by **field position,** favor the **formation** and **wide side.** Ten yards deep.
- **Key:** SEE backfield triangle and "X."
- **Assignment: On pass—deep quarter of inside zone** on weakside. SEE all weakside receivers—**responsible for #4 and #5** through post area. **Read #4.** If #4 short, play #5 inside, deep to short.
- **Slot:** Pass responsibility is the same.

- **Position: WEAK CORNER.**
- **Alignment: Head-on "X,"** five to seven yards deep.
- **Key:** Backer support, SEE "X" and WB to QB.
- **Assignment: On pass—deep quarter of outside zone** on weakside. You have inside help shallow and deep. SEE #4 and #5, play widest and deepest from outside-in.

- **Slot**: STRONG CORNER assignments, deep quarter of outside zone on strongside.

Adjustment Notes

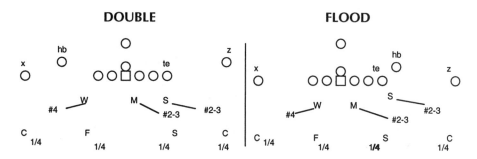

The diagram on the left above shows the adjustments for cover **8 ZONE** on **DOUBLE**. The **UNDER** front is shown, because it ties in better with the linebacker assignments. The diagram on the right is for **FLOOD**. **SAM** and **MIKE** need to cheat to their position, depending on the position of #2 and #3. **CP**: If #3 blocks or releases weakside, MIKE needs to be aware.

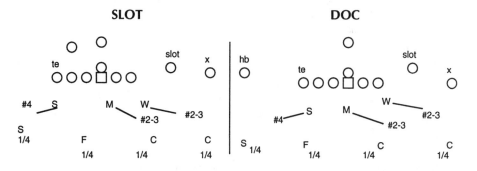

The above **SLOT** and **DOC** formations are shown with the adjustments for cover **8 ZONE**. Again, the linebackers must adjust their alignment based on the position and release of #2, #3, and #4.

F. 31

31 Zeke

31 ZEKE is a THREE-DEEP strongside zone coverage with five underneath and corner support.

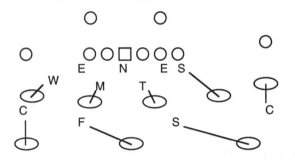

- **Position:** SAM.
- **Alignment: Head-on TE.** Alignment will vary based on formation and the position of the TE.
- **Key:** Corner support, TE, running lane and backfield triangle, "Z."
- **Assignment: On pass, short "M" zone on strongside**—JAM #2 and work to "M" zone, SEE #3. **#3 out**—destroy gimmick pattern. If no gimmick, get depth in "M" zone, square away, locate and attack BALL. **No #3**—allow no inside release. Do not attack, build wall, back through TE to inside hook zone.
- **Slot:** WILL assignments, short outside zone on weakside.

- **Position: TED.**
- **Alignment:** 31 front alignment.
- **Key:** Guard and backfield triangle.
- **Assignment:** Be aware of field position and formation. **#3 strongside**—favor SS hash and SEE inside receiver of #2 and #3. Get depth and square up. **No #3 strongside**—**frank action,** favor WS hash and SEE inside receiver #3 and #4. Get depth and square up, locate and attack BALL.
- **Slot:** MIKE assignments, short inside zone on weakside.

- **Position: MIKE.**
- **Alignment:** 31 front alignment.
- **Key:** Guard and backfield triangle.
- **Assignment: On pass—short "M" zone on weakside,** Be aware of field position and formation. SEE #4 and #5. **#4 on inside route**—force outside and work back to area. Get depth and square up. **#4 on outside route**—work back and look for #5 on inside route in your zone. **Frank**

action—move laterally, destroy gimmick, get depth in zone. If no gimmick, get depth in curl area, square away, locate and attack BALL.

- **Slot:** TED assignments, short inside zone on strongside.

- **Position: WILL.**
- **Alignment:** 31 front—vary alignment, **giant, "I," and out** by formation and down and distance.
- **Key:** Backfield triangle, "X."
- **Assignment: On pass**—**short outside zone on weakside.** On drop, get depth and SEE #4 and #5. **#4 on inside route**—locate #5, take away "I," quick out, "oh" as you work to zone. Locate #4 in fan area, react to "oh." **#4 on outside route**—HOLD with depth and delay inside route of #5, attack #4 on BALL. RUN WITH second BACK THROUGH ZONE. **CP:** Versus NEAR and NO #4 present—head-on alignment. Near block—engage.
- **Slot:** SAM assignments, short inside slot on strongside. **CP:** Take "i" position.

- **Position: STRONG CORNER.**
- **Alignment: Inside technique** on "Z," five to seven yards deep.
- **Key: Corner support,** "Z," TE, SB. SEE QB to ball.
- **Assignment:** Be aware of field position. **On pass**—**short outside zone on strongside.** HOLD at five yards, jam and FORCE #1 outside, work back to short outside zone, take away "oh." SEE #2 and #3. **Shallow outside route**—get depth and delay inside route of #1. Attack #2 and #3 on BALL. **#2 blocks or #3 on outside route**—HOLD with depth and delay inside route of #1. Attack #2 and #3 on BALL. **#2 inside and #3 blocks or outside**—HOLD with depth, SEE #1 and #3 and ensure #2 in bow-out area.
- **Slot:** STRONG SAFETY assignments, deep outside third of zone on strongside.

- **Position: STRONG SAFETY.**
- **Alignment: A shade outside** of TE, five to seven yards deep.
- **Key:** Corner support, TE, SB, "Z" to QB and ball.
- **Assignment: On pass**—**deep outside zone on strongside.** You have inside help shallow and deep on strongside. Play outside routes of #1, #2, and #3. React and play through receiver from outside-in on inside routes of #1, #2, and #3.

- **Slot**: WEAK CORNER assignments, deep outside third of zone on weakside.

- **Position**: WEAK SAFETY.
- **Alignment**: Take a position **ten yards deep** on the weakside offensive tackle. The offensive formation may alter your alignment and depth.
- **Key**: Backfield triangle, QB, and BALL.
- **Assignment**: **On pass—deep middle zone**. SEE QB and all receivers, play from deep to short. Take **deep inside route of #1, #2, and #3** strongside or **deep inside route of #5 and #4** weakside.
- **Slot**: Pass responsibility is the same.

- **Position**: WEAK CORNER.
- **Alignment**: **Outside technique** on "X," five to seven yards deep.
- **Key**: Backer support, "X," WB. SEE QB to ball.
- **Assignment**: **On pass—deep outside zone on weakside**. You have inside help shallow and deep on weakside. Play outside routes of #5 and #4 man to man. React and play through receiver from outside-in on inside routes of #5 and # 4.
- **Slot**: STRONG CORNER assignments, short outside zone on strongside.

31 Safety Zeke

31 SAFETY ZEKE may be called by game plan or by formation. SAFETY ZEKE is a change in assignments between the STRONG CORNER and STRONG SAFETY.

- **Position**: STRONG CORNER.
- **Key**: Safety support, "Z," TE, SB to QB and ball.
- **Assignment**: **On pass—deep outside zone on strongside**. You have inside help shallow and deep on strongside. Play outside routes of #1, #2, and #3 man to man. React and play through receiver from outside-in on inside routes of #1, #2, and #3.
- **Slot**: NOT A CALL THAT YOU WOULD USE ON SLOT. STAY ZEKE.

- **Position**: STRONG SAFETY.
- **Assignment**: **On pass—short outside zone on strongside**. SEE #2, #3, and #1. **#2 releases outside**—HOLD, jam at five yards, work back with #2 through your zone. **#2 diagonal**—HOLD with depth and delay inside route of #1, attack #2 on ball. **#2 blocks or #3 on outside route**—HOLD with depth and delay inside route of #1, attack #2 and #3 on ball. **#2**

inside and #3 blocks or outside—HOLD with depth, SEE #1 and #3 and ensure #2 in bow-out area.

31 Zorro

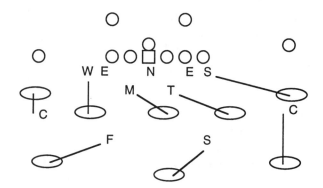

- **Position**: SAM.
- **Alignment**: **Backer support—outside shoulder of TE.** If TE is flexed, drop off the line of scrimmage at a depth to see both the TE and offensive tackle and the running lane and backfield triangle.
- **Key**: TE, running lane, backfield triangle, and "Z."
- **Assignment**: **On pass—short outside zone on strongside.** SEE #2, #3, and #1. **#2 outside releases**—jam, work through #2 to your zone. **#2 diagonal**—drop with depth to zone and delay inside route of #1, attack #2 on ball. **#2 blocks or #3 on outside route**—drop with depth and delay inside route of #1, attack #2 and #3 on BALL. **#2 inside and #3 blocks or outside**—drop with depth, SEE #1 and #3, and ensure #2 in bow-out area. RUN WITH second RECEIVER THROUGH ZONE.
- **Slot**: WILL assignments, short inside zone on weakside.

- **Position**: TED.
- **Alignment**: 31 front alignment.
- **Key**: Guard and backfield triangle.
- **Assignment**: **On pass—short inside zone on strongside.** Be conscious of field position, force #2 outside, SEE #3. Work back with inside receiver (#2, #3, #1) in your zone. **#2 and #3 inside**—jam and destroy and work through #2 and #3 as you go to your zone. **#2 and #3 outside**—gain width, SEE #1. **Frank action**—SEE #2 and #1 in your zone. React to draw and screen.
- **Slot**: MIKE assignments, short inside zone in middle of field.

- **Position**: MIKE.
- **Alignment**: 31 front alignment.
- **Key**: Guard and backfield triangle.
- **Assignment**: Be conscious of field position. **On pass—short inside zone in middle of field,** force #2 outside, SEE #3. Work back with inside receiver (#2, #3, #1) in your zone. **#2 inside**—jam and destroy #2 on inside route. **#2 outside**—read #3 release. **#3 inside**—stay in your zone. **#3 outside**—SEE #2 and #1. **Frank action**—favor WS hash, SEE inside receivers #4, #3, and #5 in your zone.
- **Slot**: TED assignments, short inside slot strongside.

- **Position**: WILL.
- **Alignment**: 31 front called.
- **Key**: Weak corner support, backfield triangle, "X."
- **Assignment: On pass—short inside zone on weakside.** Drop straight back, SEE #4 and #5. **#4 on inside route**—force outside and work back with him in your zone. **#4 on outside route**—work back and look for #5 on inside route in your zone. N/T—locate #2 and #3 on crossing route. **Frank action**—HOLD, destroy circle, get depth in your zone.
- **Slot**: SAM assignments, short outside zone on strongside. **CP**: "I" position is best to carry out assignment.

- **Position**: STRONG CORNER.
- **Alignment: Outside technique** on "Z," five to seven yards deep.
- **Key**: Backer support, "Z," TE, SB. SEE QB to ball.
- **Assignment: On pass—deep outside zone on strongside.** You have inside help shallow and deep on strongside. Play outside routes of #1, #2, and #3 man to man. React and play through receiver from outside-in on inside routes of #1, #2, and #3.
- **Slot**: STRONG SAFETY assignments, deep middle third of field.

- **Position**: STRONG SAFETY.
- **Alignment**: A **shade outside of TE**, five to seven yards deep.
- **Key**: Backer support, TE, backfield triangle to QB and ball.
- **Assignment: On pass**—move to the **deep middle zone.** SEE QB and all receivers, play from deep to short. Take **deep inside route of #1**, #2, and #3 strongside or **deep inside route of #5** and #4 weakside.
- **Slot**: WEAK CORNER assignments, short outside zone on weakside.

- **Position**: WEAK SAFETY.
- **Alignment**: Take a position **ten yards deep on the weakside offensive tackle**. The offensive formation may alter your alignment and depth.

- **Key:** Weak corner support, QB and backfield triangle.
- **Assignment: On pass—deep outside zone on weakside.** You have inside help shallow and deep on weakside. Play outside routes of #5 and #4 man to man. React and play through receiver from outside-in on inside routes of #5 and #4.
- **Slot:** Pass responsibility is the same.

- **Position:** WEAK CORNER.
- **Alignment: Inside technique** on "X," five to seven yards deep.
- **Key: Weak corner support,** "X," WB, backfield triangle. SEE QB to BALL.
- **Assignment: On pass—short outside zone on weakside.** HOLD at five yards, jam and FORCE #5 outside, work back to short outside zone. SEE #5 and #4. **Shallow outside route**—get depth and delay inside route of #5. Attack #5 and #4 on BALL. **#4 inside**—HOLD with depth, SEE #5 and #4 and ensure #4 in fan area.
- **Slot:** STRONG CORNER assignments, deep outside third of zone strongside.

31 W/Safety Zorro

31 W/SAFETY ZORRO may be called by game plan or by formation. WEAK SAFETY ZORRO is a change in assignments between the WEAK CORNER and WEAK SAFETY.

- **Position:** WEAK CORNER.
- **Key:** Weak safety support, QB and backfield triangle.
- **Assignment: On pass—deep outside zone on weakside.** You have inside help shallow and deep on strongside. Play outside routes of #4 and #5 man to man. React and play through receiver from outside-in on inside routes of #4 and #5.
- **Slot:** NOT A CALL THAT YOU WOULD USE ON **SLOT**. STAY ZORRO.

- **Position:** WEAK SAFETY.
- **Assignment: On pass—short outside zone on weakside.** SEE #4 and #5. **#4 releases outside**—HOLD, jam at five yards, work back with #4 through your zone. **#4 diagonal**—HOLD with depth and delay inside route of #5, attack #4 on ball. **#4 blocks**—HOLD with depth and delay inside route of #5, attack short receivers on ball. SEE short receivers and ensure #4 in bow-out area.

31 Zelda

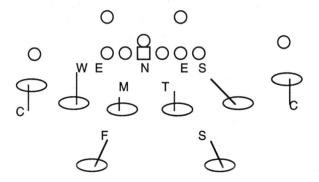

- **Position**: SAM.
- **Alignment**: Take a position **head-on TE**. If TE flexes, drop off line of scrimmage and inside.
- **Key**: Corner support, TE, running lane, and backfield triangle.
- **Assignment**: **On pass, strong back present**—jam #2 and SEE SB and work to "M" zone; destroy pattern. If no gimmick, get depth with outside receiver #2, #3, and #1. **No strong back present**—jam #2, allow no inside release. Do not attack, build a wall with #2 back through the hook area.
- **Slot**: WILL assignments, short inside zone on weakside.

- **Position**: TED.
- **Alignment**: 31 front alignment.
- **Key**: Guard and backfield triangle (strong back).
- **Assignment**: **Strong back present**—favor strongside hash and SEE receivers #2, #3, and #1. Get depth with inside receiver, square up, and attack ball. If #2 and #3 both outside, get depth in middle of field. SEE QB play the ball. **No strong back present—frank action**, favor weak hash, and SEE receivers #4, #3, and #1. Get depth, square up, and attack ball.
- **Slot**: MIKE assignments, short middle zone on weakside.

- **Position**: MIKE.
- **Alignment**: 31 front alignment.
- **Key**: Guard and backfield triangle
- **Assignment**: **On pass—short inside zone on weakside**. Favor weakside hash, SEE #4 and #5. SEE the pattern as you go, get depth. **#4 on inside route**—force him to outside, work to zone. **#4 outside**—work back to zone, get depth, square up, locate #5, #2, and #3 on crossing pattern.

Frank action—HOLD, destroy circle, be ready to attack gimmick. If no gimmick, get depth, square up, and attack ball.

- **Slot**: TED assignments, short middle zone strongside.

- **Position**: WILL.
- **Alignment**: 31 front alignment (giant, crackback, I).
- **Key**: **Corner support**, weak back, "X" (SB, TE). Versus NEAR—near, WB.
- **Assignment**: **On pass—short inside zone on weakside**. HOLD, SEE #4. **#4 out**—JAM #4 and force outside, destroy pattern as you drop to slot zone. If no gimmick, get depth with receiver through zone. Square away, locate and attack BALL.
- **Slot**: SAM assignments, short outside slot on strongside.

- **Position**: STRONG CORNER.
- **Alignment**: **Take a position head-on** "Z," no more than five yards deep. You **must be within the five-yard area** to JAM and **reroute** the receiver. This is very important in **COVER 2**.
- **Key**: **Corner support**, "Z," TE, SB. SEE QB and ball.
- **Assignment**: **On pass—short outside zone on strongside**. Before snap, move to an outside technique. **HOLD at five yards, jam and FUNNEL #1** inside, take away the "oh" and fade, SEE #3 and #2, **N/T—cushion** with depth, square away, react to ball.
- **Slot**: STRONG SAFETY assignments, deep half of zone strongside.

- **Position**: STRONG SAFETY.
- **Alignment**: Take a position a shade outside of TE, at least seven yards deep. Your distance may vary depending on the split of "Z."
- **Key**: Corner support, "Z," TE, SB, QB, and ball.
- **Assignment**: **On pass—deep half of field strongside**. Gain depth to three yards inside the numbers. Read receivers on your side, SEE BALL. Play deep to short, react to ball.
- **Slot**: WEAK CORNER assignments, short outside zone weakside.

- **Position**: WEAK SAFETY.
- **Alignment**: Take a position ten yards deep on the weakside offensive tackle. The offensive formation may alter your alignment and depth.
- **Key**: Corner support, X," WB, QB, and ball.
- **Assignment**: **On pass—deep half of field weakside**. Gain depth to three yards inside the numbers. Read receivers on your side, SEE BALL. Play deep to short, react to ball.
- **Slot**: Pass responsibility is the same.

- **Position**: WEAK CORNER.
- **Alignment**: Take a position head-on "X," no more than five yards deep. You **must be within the five-yard area** to JAM and **reroute** the receiver. This is very important in COVER 2.
- **Key**: Corner support, "X," WB. See QB and ball.
- **Assignment**: On pass—**short outside zone on weakside**. Before snap, move to an outside technique. HOLD at five yards, **jam and FUNNEL** #5 inside, take away the "oh" and fade, SEE #4 and crossing receivers. N/T—cushion with depth, square away, react to ball.
- **Slot**: STRONG CORNER assignments, short outside zone on strongside.

As described above in **31 ZEKE, ZORRO,** and **ZELDA,** when you can use five underneath in coverage, there are not a lot of holes or creases available to teams that throw short. If you properly JAM the eligible receivers, that will help to destroy the deep route. The JAM plus the RUSH go hand in hand. To get the maximum from the three-man rush, the rush games must be used. If the quarterback is a scrambler, an added burden is placed on the front, and this becomes quite a concern to you as the coach. Sometimes the scrambler may prevent the use of the three-man line, except in special situations. It is a coaching decision. The merits need to be considered, but the problems presented by the offense must be the deciding factor.

ZONE BLITZ

The **ZONE BLITZ** has become popular in the last couple of years. It is a way to take advantage of the offense. It forces the offensive team to pick up the blitz, but instead of the defensive back being in man-to-man blitz coverage, the coverage is ZONE. A brief discussion of the ZONE BLITZ is presented in this section, but the exact details will be covered later in Chapter 4 on the BLITZ.

In recent years, the Pittsburgh Steelers have had success with the concept, and, like everything else, it has been copied. Each team views the tapes of all teams in the league, and anything that is worthwhile is copied, improved upon, and used very successfully by others. At the present time, all defenses in the NFL probably use some type of ZONE BLITZ. Some college and high school teams have adapted the concept to their programs. A Pop Warner League coach was recently overheard talking about the zone blitz that he planned to use. It has become the "in thing" to do.

What makes the ZONE BLITZ successful is that it allows the defense to bring outside linebackers and safeties to one side or both sides without using man-to-man blitz coverage. Normal blitzes use man-to-man blitz coverage. The ZONE BLITZ uses **ZONE** coverage, but presents protection problems to the offense. The offensive line and one or two backs are assigned to block the defensive line and linebackers. In the ZONE BLITZ, the linebacker blitzes along with a secondary player, but the offensive pickup is different. It is different because **defensive linemen** who usually rush are now dropping out to **short inside zones** to replace the linebacker and secondary player that blitz. Because of the blitzer's path, it is difficult for the offensive lineman to adjust. It is indeed a good concept and has proved helpful to many teams.

The Miami Dolphins used a form of the ZONE BLITZ in the early eighties. It wasn't nearly as sophisticated as the present-day version, but it was successful, and it helped our defense to be the best. We were fortunate to have a defensive end by the name of Kim Bokamper who had been trained earlier as an outside linebacker. Because of his training, he was aware of the short inside zones and his responsibility on the drop. Today, defensive tackles or ends drop to those zones, and in most cases, it is a new experience for them. With the Dolphins, we liked the ZONE BLITZ so much that we called the coverage to Bokamper. This enabled him to drop to the **short inside zone** with the rotation strong and weak.

Like many other supposedly new techniques and schemes, we all take existing ideas, build them into separate defensive packages, and work hard to gain the edge. At present, the ZONE BLITZ offers that edge, and most teams are clamoring to hire defensive coaches who are familiar with the concept. It is a "hot" ticket to a new job and more compensation.

31 ZONE TO BO (6 SKY)

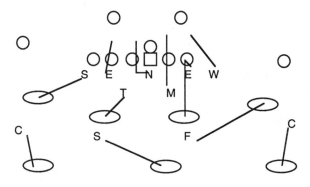

The diagram above shows the ZONE BLITZ that we used with the Dolphins and the call we used. It is drawn to the weakside and was probably most effective weakside. However, at times we used the call strongside. With experience, we adopted the double-zone concept, which proved equally effective.

At the time, I felt that the "**zone to BO**" scheme was most valuable from the 31 alignment. In view of the recent return of the ZONE BLITZ, I still feel it is best accomplished by using the 31 FRONT, because you have more linebackers, to drop or rush, and fewer linemen to drop into coverage. Then, as now, it created a problem for offensive pass protection, and it has proved valuable in hurrying or sacking the QB. Other ZONE BLITZ ideas that are in use today are presented in Chapter 4 on blitz coverage. Many new ideas and change-ups are being used. The pickup remains an offensive problem.

I am indebted to Dick LeBeau, defensive coordinator of the Cincinnati Bengals and previously coordinator of the Pittsburgh Steelers' defense, for giving me credit for providing him with the idea of the "**zone blitz.**" In the September 1, 1997 issue of *Sports Illustrated,* Peter King tells the story of Dick LeBeau visiting with me on a scouting trip in the mid-eighties. During a conversation, I casually expressed a thought about trying to get pressure on the quarterback without exposing the secondary. It was the same "**zone to BO**" scheme described above.

On a vacation in Kentucky in July 1997, I visited the new Bengals' training camp at Georgetown College. I watched a practice, and afterward Dick and I chatted. I thanked him for his kindness and congratulated him on developing the zone blitz to the point where it is today. We also agreed that it was much more effective in the three-man-line package. The scheme has grown a great deal since its beginning. Like everything in football, when you see something good, you add your ideas and make it better—and the zone blitz is no exception. It has definitely improved and is now a threat to all offensive coaches.

MAN COVERAGE

MAN coverage is an important part of the defensive coverage package. I use the word "package" to emphasize the importance of a good mixture. Why do I continue to talk about a mixture? The answer is simple. If as a defense you play mostly ZONE or mostly MAN, the offense can prepare the game plan to take advantage of your preference. In preparing a plan for the ZONE, the offense can concentrate on the seams and throwing underneath. In preparing for MAN, the offense can concentrate on crossing patterns or "take-off" patterns, isolating a defender. By using a mixture, the offense is forced to prepare for both, and the result is a guessing game. You can also force the quarterback and receiver to read the coverage, in which case both must make the proper adjustment. This combination, plus selected blitzes, gives the defense an excellent package.

A. Cover 0

COVER 0 is a man coverage that has historically been used in combination with ONE. As an example, the call would be TEN. It is used primarily when #4 is a good receiver and good run support is needed weakside.

The combination call **TEN** gives the defense the best coverage and the best run support on all formations. Versus the run, there is an extra man in the box. It affords the defense the best coverage possible on both the #2 and #4 receivers. ONE coverage may be a single call, but ZERO must always be used in combination with ONE.

UNDER is the best FRONT to use with ZERO and ONE. It places the linebackers and secondary in the best possible position to cover, and it easily places eight players in the box to play the run.

UNDER 0

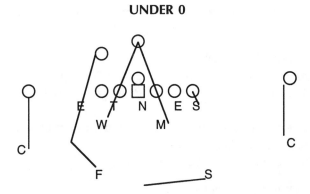

ZERO when used with the double-digit call TEN is a formation call. ZERO coverage is used on WEAK, DOUBLE, and TIGER formations.

- **Position**: SAM.
- **Alignment**: A shade outside shoulder of TE.

- **Key: Backer support**—TE, running lane, and the backfield triangle.
- **Assignment: Cover #2 man to man** (outside–in). You have inside help shallow by MIKE or WILL. **CP**: Stay with #2 on all routes unless called off by MIKE or WILL. The call will be "I got him" by MIKE or WILL if they are free to help.
- **Slot**: Backer support. Pass responsibility is the same.

- **Position: MIKE.**
- **Alignment**: Under alignment. Position may vary because of the formation and coverage responsibility.
- **Key**: Strong back with WILL, backfield triangle.
- **Assignment: Read #3 with** WILL. **#3 blocks strong**—HOLD for draw, screen, checkdown. **#3 releases strong**—cover man to man. **#3 releases weak**—HELP SAM with #2 on inside route. N/T—FREE help in middle on crossing routes.
- **Slot**: Pass responsibility is the same.

- **Position: WILL.**
- **Alignment**: Under alignment. Position may vary because of formation and coverage responsibility.
- **Key**: Strong back with MIKE, backfield triangle.
- **Assignment: Read #3 with** MIKE. **#3 blocks or releases strong**—HELP SAM on all crossing routes. **#3 blocks weak**—HOLD for draw, screen, checkdown. **#3 releases weak**—cover man to man.
- **Slot**: Pass responsibility is the same.

- **Position: STRONG CORNER.**
- **Alignment**: Head-on "Z," five to seven yards deep.
- **Key**: Backer support—"Z" and QB. **CP**: Alignment will vary by position of "Z."
- **Assignment: On pass**—outside technique, **man to man on #1.** You have help in the deep middle.
- **Slot**: Man to man on **slot**, #2. You have post help.

- **Position: STRONG SAFETY.**
- **Alignment**: Take a position a shade outside of TE, five to seven yards deep. TE flex—a shade inside.
- **Key**: Backer support—TE, SEE QB and backfield action.
- **Assignment: Deep middle**—FREE. Play from deep to short. You are the center fielder. SEE QB. Play the ball.
- **Slot**: Deep middle.

- **Position:** WEAK SAFETY.
- **Alignment:** Head-on the weakside tackle, ten yards deep. **CP:** Alignment may vary by formation and position on the field.
- **Key: W/safety support**—weakside offensive tackle, running lane, and backfield triangle.
- **Assignment: On pass**—outside technique, **man to man on #4.**
- **Slot:** Man to man on #3.

- **Position:** WEAK CORNER.
- **Alignment:** Take a position head-on "X," five to seven yards deep.
- **Key:** Backer support—"X" and QB. **CP:** Alignment will vary by position of "X."
- **Assignment: On pass**—outside technique, **man to man on #5.** You have help in the deep middle.
- **Slot:** Man to man on #1.

30 Front Notes

The alignment, key, and assignment have been written for the **UNDER** front. If the **30** front is used, all coverage responsibilities remain the same. To keep it simple, **WILL** should be called as the **designated blitzer.** MIKE would have WILL assignments. TED would have MIKE assignments. SAM assignments would remain the same.

Adjustment Notes

MO TO DOUBLE   FLY TO FLOOD   DOUBLE

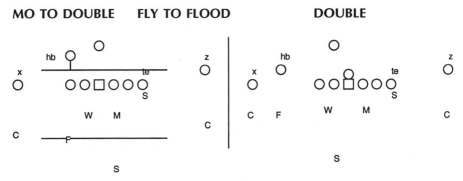

On **ZERO,** the **WEAK SAFETY** moves up in a position to cover the HB (weak back). Any movement by the back, MOTION to **DOUBLE,** or FLY to **FLOOD** is handled by the WEAK SAFETY. The diagram on the right above shows **DOUBLE,** with the WEAK SAFETY in an alignment to cover the back.

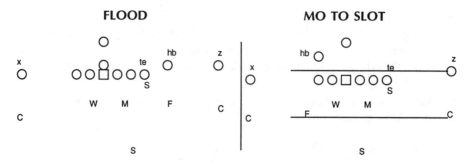

FLOOD   **MO TO SLOT**

The diagram on the left above shows **FLOOD**, with the WEAK SAFETY in an alignment to cover the back. The diagram on the right shows movement by "**Z**" to form a **SLOT** formation. The CORNER comes across with "Z" to cover.

MO TO DOC   **DOC**

The **WEAK SAFETY** takes all movement by the back. The drawing on the right above shows the **DOC** formation and the alignments.

TIGER   **MO TO SPREAD**

The drawing on the left above shows the **TIGER** formation. The drawing on the right shows movement to **SPREAD**. This formation is also referred to as EMPTY.

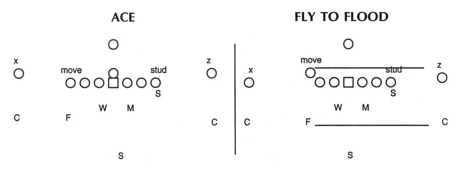

The drawing on the left above shows the **ACE**. Alignment is designed by the **STUD TE**. The drawing on the right shows movement to **FLOOD**.

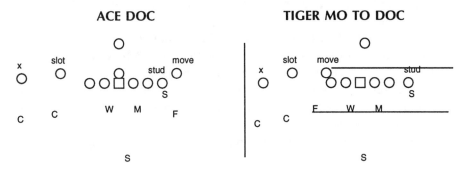

The drawing on the left above shows the **ACE DOC** formation. The drawing on the right shows **TIGER** formation, with movement back to **DOC**. The WEAK SAFETY takes all movement by the **MOVE TE**.

B. Cover 1

When used with the double-digit call TEN, **COVER 1** is a formation call. ONE coverage is used on SPLIT, STRONG, I, and FLOOD formations.

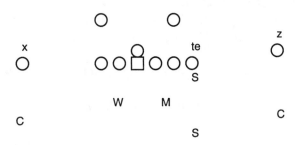

- **Position**: SAM.
- **Alignment**: **Backer support**—outside shoulder of TE. If TE is flexed, drop off the line of scrimmage at a depth to see both the TE and offensive tackle and the backfield triangle.
- **Key**: TE, running lane, and backfield triangle.
- **Assignment**: **On pass—in/out on #3 with MIKE. #3 blocks or close circle**—work out to slot area. SEE #3 and #1. **#3 releases wide**—cover man to man. **Frank action**—drop with depth to inside, look for inside breaking receivers. **CP: Counteraction**—in/out on first back with MIKE.
- **Slot**: Pass responsibility is the same. In/out on back to side of "Y."

- **Position**: MIKE.
- **Alignment**: Under alignment. Position may vary because of formation and coverage responsibility.
- **Key**: Strong back with SAM and backfield triangle.
- **Assignment**: **On pass—in/out on #3 with SAM. #3 blocks**—HOLD for draw, screen, checkdown. **#3 releases close inside**—cover man to man. **#3 releases outside**—destroy #2 on inside route and work through #2 to slot area (SEE all receivers). **Frank action**—destroy route, look for gimmick (wide) route of #3.
- **Slot**: Pass responsibility is the same. In/out on back to side of "Y."

- **Position**: WILL.
- **Alignment**: Under alignment. Position may vary because of formation and coverage responsibility.
- **Key**: **Backer support** is normal with "X" in normal split position.
- **Assignment**: **On pass—#4 releases weakside, cover man to man. #4 blocks**—HOLD for draw, screen, checkdown. **Frank action**—gain depth and outside position to cover first back on route outside and upfield.
- **Slot**: Man to man on #3.

- **Position**: STRONG CORNER.
- **Alignment**: Take a position head-on "Z," five to seven yards deep.
- **Key**: Backer support—"Z" and QB. **CP**: Alignment will vary by position of "Z."
- **Assignment**: **On pass**—outside technique, **man to man on #1**. You have help in the deep middle.
- **Slot**: Man to man on #2. You have post help.

- **Position**: STRONG SAFETY.
- **Alignment**: Take a position one yard outside of TE, five to seven yards deep.

- **Key:** Backer support—TE and backfield triangle.
- **Assignment: On pass—cover #2 man to man,** outside technique.
- **Slot:** Man to man on #5 (TE).

- **Position:** WEAK SAFETY.
- **Alignment:** Head-on the weakside tackle, ten yards deep. **CP:** Alignment may vary by formation and position on field.
- **Key:** SEE QB and ball.
- **Assignment: On pass—**the **deep middle,** you are **FREE,** play from deep to short. Be in position to make a play on the deep pass. You are the center fielder.
- **Slot:** Pass responsibility is the same.

- **Position:** WEAK CORNER.
- **Alignment:** Take a position head-on "X," five to seven yards deep.
- **Key:** Backer support—"X" and QB. **CP:** Alignment will vary by position of "X."
- **Assignment: On pass—**outside technique, man to man on #5. You have help in the deep middle.
- **Slot:** Man to man on #1. You have post help.

Adjustments Used with Cover 0 and Cover 1

PINCH: A term used with cover 1 to double the WEAK BACK by WILL and MIKE.

- **Assignment:**
  MIKE—in/out with WILL on WEAK BACK. **WB blocks**—HOLD for draw, screen, checkdown. **WB releases outside** (wide)—work outside to curl, SEE WB and "X." **WB releases close**—cover man to man. **Frank action**—stay in/out with WILL on WB. **Counteraction**—cover first back weakside with WILL.

  WILL—in/out with MIKE on WEAK BACK. **WB blocks** or **releases close**—work outside to curl, SEE WB and "X." **WB releases outside** (wide)—cover man to man. **Frank action**—stay in/out with MIKE on WB. **Counteraction**—cover first back weakside with WILL.

CP: This call is not needed on ZERO, because the WEAK SAFETY is responsible for the WEAK BACK and should not need help. Use only with two backs in the game.

Other calls may be added, as the need arises, by adding terms that are descriptive of the system. ZERO and ONE work well together; however, if ONE is used alone, there may be a need for **pinch** on the weak back.

30 Front Notes

The **alignment, key, and assignment** have been written for the **UNDER** front. If the **30** front is used, all coverage responsibilities remain the same. To keep it simple, **WILL** should be called as the **designated blitzer**. MIKE would have WILL assignments. TED would have MIKE assignments. SAM assignments would remain the same.

Adjustment Notes

The adjustments for **TEN** coverage are shown here, rather than **ONE** as a single call, in order to provide a complete description of the adjustments for both **ZERO** and **ONE**, plus **TEN**.

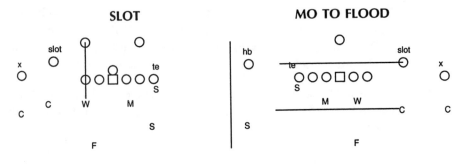

FLY TO FLOOD   **DOUBLE**

The **STRONG SAFETY** takes movement by the strong back on **TEN**. If it were **ONE** as a single call, the **SAM** or **SS** would take the movement by plan. The diagram on the right above shows the **WEAK SAFETY** moving to cover the **WEAK BACK** on **DOUBLE**. CP: SAM could take the coverage on the back, but it is better to keep SAM inside and let the SS adjust.

SLOT   **MO TO FLOOD**

In the diagram on the left above, **slot** is the formation. **WILL** has coverage on the back. **SS** has the **TE**. The diagram on the right above shows **DOC** formation and movement to **FLOOD**.

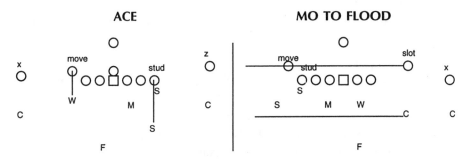

ACE

MO TO FLOOD

The diagram on the left above shows **ONE** as a single call. **WILL** has the **MOVE TE**, and the **SS** has the **STUD TE**. In the diagram on the right above, **ACE DOC**, the **SS**, has the **MOVE TE**, and the **CORNER** takes movement of the **slot** to **ACE FLOOD**.

The **double-digit call TEN** takes care of more formation adjustments, plus it always gives the defense the maximum personnel in the box for the run.

C. Cover 2 Man

UNDER 2 MAN

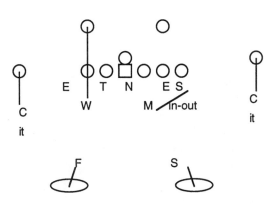

- **Position**: SAM.
- **Alignment**: Take a position head-on the TE.
- **Key**: Corner or safety by game plan, TE and SB.
- **Assignment**: **On pass, strong back present**—in/out on #2 and #3 with MIKE. **#2 outside releases**—cover man to man. **#2 and #3 both outside release**—hold off #2, SEE #3, cover #2 man to man. **#2 inside releases**

and **#3 outside**—cover #3 man to man. **#2 inside releases and #3 blocks**—JAM #2, SEE #3, HOLD for draw, screen, and checkdown. **#2 and #3 both release inside**—cover #2 man to man. **No strong back present**—lock TE, cover man to man.

- **Slot:** Pass responsibility is the same. In/out with MIKE on TE and strong back (#4 and #5).

- **Position: MIKE.**
- **Alignment:** By alignment called (UNDER, EVEN, 30).
- **Key:** SB and TE.
- **Assignment: On pass, strong back present**—in/out on #2 and #3 with SAM. **#2 outside releases and #3 blocks**—HOLD for draw, screen, and checkdown. **#2 and #3 both outside release**—cover #3 man to man. **#2 inside releases and #3 outside**—cover #2 man to man. **#2 inside releases and #3 blocks**—cover #2 man to man. **#2 and #3 both release inside**—cover SB man to man. **No strong back present**—cover #3 man to man.
- **Slot:** Pass responsibility is the same. In/out with SAM on TE and strong back (#4 and #5).

- **Position: WILL.**
- **Alignment:** By alignment called (UNDER, EVEN, 30).
- **Key:** Corner support—weak back.
- **Assignment: On pass—#4 man to man.**
- **Slot:** Man to man on #3.

- **Position: STRONG CORNER.**
- **Alignment:** Take a position head-on "Z," no more than five yards deep. You must be within the five-yard area to JAM and reroute the receiver. This is very important in **COVER 2 MAN. CP:** Remember that the high school and college "jam" rule is different.
- **Key: Corner support**—Z," TE, SB, SEE QB and ball. **CP:** Support will be by game plan (corner or safety).
- **Assignment: On pass**—before snap, move to an inside (kick) technique. HOLD, jam and FORCE #1 outside, take away the inside route, **cover #1 man to man. CP:** Be aware of your alignment and the line of scrimmage.
- **Slot:** Kick technique on #2.

- **Position: STRONG SAFETY.**
- **Alignment:** Take a position a **shade outside** the TE, at least seven yards deep. Your distance may vary depending on the split of Z."
- **Key:** Corner support—Z," TE, SB, QB, and ball. **CP:** Support will be by game plan (corner or safety).

- **Assignment: On pass—deep half of field strongside.** Gain depth to three yards inside the numbers. Read receivers on your side, SEE BALL. Play deep to short, react to ball. **CP:** Again, the high school and college rule is different.
- **Slot:** Deep half of field weakside.

- **Position: WEAK SAFETY.**
- **Alignment:** Take a position **ten yards deep** on the weakside offensive tackle. The offensive formation may alter your alignment and depth.
- **Key:** Corner support—X," WB, QB, and ball. **CP:** Support will be by game plan (corner or safety).
- **Assignment: On pass—deep half of field weakside.** Gain depth to three yards inside the numbers. Read receivers on your side, SEE BALL. Play deep to short, react to ball.
- **Slot:** Deep half of field strongside.

- **Position: WEAK CORNER.**
- **Alignment:** Take a position head-on X," no more than five yards deep. You must be within the five-yard area to JAM and reroute the receiver. This is very important in **COVER 2 MAN.**
- **Key: Corner support,** "X," WB, SEE QB and ball. **CP:** Support will be by game plan (corner or safety).
- **Assignment: On pass**—before snap, move to an inside (kick) technique. HOLD, jam and FORCE #5 outside, take away the inside route, **cover #5 man to man.**
- **Slot:** Kick technique on #1.

Adjustments for Two Man

The calls are as follows. **KICK,** as described, is regular. **VISE** may be called as a variation on #1 or #5. VISE is an in-and-out technique on the receiver, involving the S/CORNER and S/SAFETY or the F/SAFETY and W/CORNER. **CP:** VISE should be played with CORNER support.

I have indicated that the support on **TWO MAN** is to be decided by the game plan. This is an area of debate among secondary coaches and defensive coordinators. It is my feeling that if you want good coverage on "Z" and "X" by the corners, then run support should be handled by the strong safety on the strongside and the weak safety on the weakside. To have good coverage, the corners must focus on the receiver, and this is very difficult if you ask them to have primary run support. I personally have always favored the safety as the primary support player in **COVER 2 MAN.** I understand that the safety may be a fraction late, but the purpose of the coverage is good tight coverage in a passing situation. This can be accomplished by having safety support on the coverage as described.

The other side of the argument believes that the corner can successfully do both jobs. There is no doubt in my mind that he can, but you give up coverage efficiency on the quick inside route. In my opinion, it is very difficult for the corner to take away the inside route from an inside position and see the blocking pattern as the primary run support defender. I raise this issue so that you will better understand the controversy and thus make a decision based on what you want to accomplish and expect in the coverage. Although I have at times used both methods, it is my personal feeling that the safety as the primary run support player is best for what I wanted and expected from the coverage.

Front Notes

The **alignment, key, and assignment** have been written for the **UNDER** and **EVEN** front. If the **30** front is used, all coverage responsibilities remain the same. To keep it simple, WILL, MIKE, or TED should be called as the **designated blitzer**. The linebackers not designated would assume the assignment as indicated. (Example: If MIKE is the designated blitzer, TED would have MIKE assignments, and WILL and SAM would have the same assignments as described above.) In **TWO MAN**, SAM must be aligned on the line of scrimmage to play in/out with MIKE on the strong back and TE. You want the best blitzer among WILL, MIKE, and TED be the designated blitzer. The two of those three linebackers that offer the best coverage should be involved in coverage. If the best cover linebacker is also the best blitzer, you have a decision to make. Score, time remaining, and what you are trying to accomplish versus the opponent's personnel will usually give you the answer.

Alignment Notes

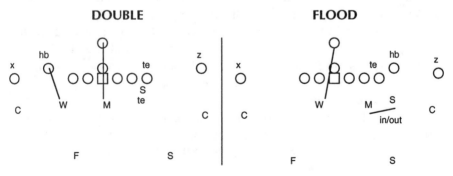

As in cover 2, regardless of the front (**UNDER** is shown above), in cover **2 MAN** the outside linebacker must adjust his position to jam and delay receivers. The diagram on the left above shows **DOUBLE** formation, and **WILL** adjusts to the outside, to carry out the assignment of the defense. The diagram on the right shows **FLOOD** formation, and **SAM** adjusts to carry out the assignment of the defense. **CP:** As the linebacker adjusts, he must keep in mind his responsibility—get depth and maintain vision for the run or pass. Depending on the distance, the MIKE and SAM may want to go man to man rather than in and out on the TE and SB.

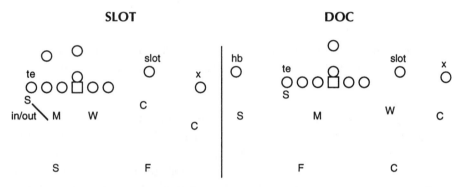

The **TWO-MAN SLOT** adjustments as shown above on the left are the best for both the run and pass. The **DOC** adjustment in the diagram on the right is the same as shown in cover 2, which makes them both look similar.

D. Cover 8 Man

As mentioned in our discussion of 8 ZONE, **COVER 8** can be either a MAN or ZONE call. **COVER 8 is a basic four-deep call.** Cover 8 MAN was one of the basic coverages used when I was with the Baltimore Colts in 1964 (discussed earlier in the section on ZONE coverage).

What you see, or think you see, on a tape or film does not always tell the complete story. This is particularly true in studying coverage, because you do not have the opportunity to see the coverage versus all pattern combinations. This is true in cover 8, because there are certain drops by SAM, MIKE, WILL, and the STRONG SAFETY that would resemble a ZONE drop, depending on the action of the offensive player. It is extremely important to keep this point in mind when studying a coverage.

Each team needs to understand and properly execute both ZONE and MAN principles. They can be taught and used successfully in all defensive packages.

UNDER 8

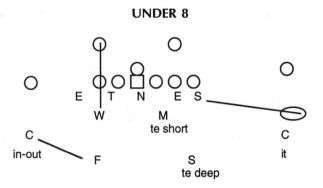

- **Position: SAM.**
- **Alignment: Backer support**—outside shoulder of TE. If TE is flexed, drop off the line of scrimmage at a depth to see both the TE and offensive tackle and the backfield triangle.
- **Key:** TE, strong back, "Z."
- **Assignment: On pass**—begin drop to **short outside zone** ("oh"), see #3, cover **medium and wide** flare man to man. N/T—continue drop to outside zone. SEE QB, react to BALL. **CP:** If TE is on diagonal, cover from depth. Short side of field jam #2, then sloop. (Sloop is a term used to explain the action of the linebacker as he works to the outside area.)
- **Slot:** WILL assignments, #4 man to man.

- **Position: MIKE.**
- **Alignment:** By front called (UNDER, EVEN, 30).
- **Key:** Strong back, TE, backfield triangle.
- **Assignment: On pass, #3 inside**—man to man on close or delay. **#3 outside**—SEE #2, cover #2 on shallow inside route (Rex/Lex). **#3 blocks**—SEE #3 and #2, drop to short inside zone strongside, #3 delay man to man. **Frank action**—drop to short inside zone weakside. SEE both #3 and #4, react to inside route (circle/delay) man to man. **2 short and 2 deep**—weakside on frank action with WILL. (MIKE and WILL are the two short defenders. The WEAK CORNER and WEAK SAFETY are the two deep defenders.)
- **Slot:** Pass responsibility is the same.

- **Position: WILL.**
- **Alignment:** By front called (UNDER, EVEN, 30).
- **Key: Backer support** is normal, with "X" in normal wide position. Corner support versus NEAR or TE.

- **Assignment: On pass, #4 out**—jam #4 and cover man to man (inside-out position). **#4 blocks**—backpedal, locate #5 for curl or other inside route. **Frank action**—jam #4 and drop back and outside. See both #3 and # 4, react to outside route (fan, arrow) man to man. **2 short and 2 deep**—weakside on frank action with MIKE.
- **Slot:** SAM assignments, begin drop to outside zone ("oh"), see #3, cover medium and wide flare man to man. N/T—continue drop to outside zone. SEE QB, react to BALL.

- **Position: STRONG CORNER.**
- **Alignment:** Head-on "Z," five to seven yards deep. **CP:** Alignment will vary by position of "Z."
- **Key:** Backer support—"Z," TE, SB to QB.
- **Assignment: On pass**—inside technique on **#1 man to man**.
- **Slot:** STRONG SAFETY assignments, slot man to man deep.

- **Position: STRONG SAFETY.**
- **Alignment:** Take a position a shade outside the TE, five to seven yards deep. TE flex, a shade inside.
- **Key:** Backer support—TE, SB, "Z," SEE QB and backfield action.
- **Assignment: On pass**—**#2 man to man on medium and deep routes**. **#2 on diagonal route outside** (D)—drop at angle to outside, work through #1 for diagonal take-off (DTO). **Frank action**—move to inside position on #2, be alert for "pop" pass.
- **Slot:** WEAK CORNER assignments, in/out deep with WEAK SAFETY on #4 and #5.

- **Position: WEAK SAFETY.**
- **Alignment:** Take a position by field position. Favor the formation and wide side. Ten yards deep.
- **Key:** SEE backfield triangle and "X."
- **Assignment: On pass, #4 blocks**—drop straight back, then to middle. SEE QB and #5 on inside route. N/T—play the ball. **#4 out**—in and out deep on #5 and #4 with WEAK CORNER. **Frank action**—2 short and 2 deep with W/C.
- **Slot:** Pass responsibility is the same.

- **Position: WEAK CORNER.**
- **Alignment:** Head-on "X," five to seven yards deep.
- **Key:** Backer support, SEE "X" and WB to QB.

- **Assignment: On pass**—outside technique on **#5 man to man. #4 out and #5 on inside route**— trail and check #4 on deep route outside (arrow take-off (ATO). Stay deep, in and out with WS. **Frank action**—2 short and 2 deep with WS.
- **Slot**: STRONG CORNER assignments, inside technique, #1 man to man.

Adjustment Calls

PINCH: A term used to double the TE by MIKE and the STRONG SAFETY.
- **Assignment: SAM**—#3 man to man. **Frank action**—stay man to man on #3. **MIKE**—#2 man to man on inside routes. **#2 releases outside**— drop to middle of field and SEE inside routes of #3 and #1. **Frank action**—#2 man to man on inside routes. **STRONG SAFETY**—#2 man to man outside on medium and deep routes. **#2 diagonal**—work at an angle outside for diagonal take-off (DTO). **#2 releases inside**— trail, help MIKE deep, SEE #2 and #3. **STRONG CORNER**—#1 man to man. Move to bump position. **WEAK CORNER and WEAK SAFETY**—may play regular **EIGHT** or use **VISE** technique on #5 by game plan.

SLIP: A term used to guarantee "oh" cut responsibility for **SAM**.
- **Assignment: MIKE** will **slip the #2** on inside and medium routes and cover the #3 man to man on all routes. **STRONG SAFETY**—#2 man to man an all releases. **#2 diagonal**—cover like regular cover 8 man.

The following adjustment calls are **weakside calls** only:

OZZ: A term to use a **double-zone technique** weakside for **WILL, WEAK CORNER**, and **WEAK SAFETY**.
- **Assignment: Strongside** the **strong corner, strong safety, SAM**, and **MIKE** will continue to play COVER 8 MAN as defined. **CP: On frank action**, MIKE will play a double-zone technique.

JET: A term to use a **double–single technique** weakside for **WILL, WEAK CORNER**, and **WEAK SAFETY**.
- **Assignment: Weakside** the WEAK CORNER is man to man on #5. WILL is man to man on #4, and the WEAK SAFETY is deep help for the WC and WILL. **Strongside** the **strong corner, strong safety, SAM**, and **MIKE** will continue to play COVER 8 MAN as defined. **CP: On frank action**, MIKE will cover the second back weakside. May play in/out with WILL by call before snap if formation alerts you to the possibility.

Front Notes

Because of SAM's assignment, he must be in a backer support position on the line of scrimmage. There is no other alignment that will allow him to reach his responsibility. Even in this position he sometimes is late getting to the "oh" as defined. In **30**, you can mix and match the designated blitzer to fit the need versus the offensive protection. OVER can never be used because of the position of SAM. To repeat, SAM must be on the line of scrimmage in a backer support position.

Adjustment Notes

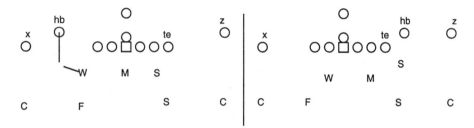

The diagram above shows **COVER 8 MAN** versus **DOUBLE**. Pass responsibilities require that **WILL** and **SAM** cheat their positions. **WILL** has the back, man to man, with help deep. **SAM** must work to the outside "oh," unless a **HOLD** call is made. The **HOLD** call gives **SAM** the **TE** man to man. (This also allows SAM to maintain his position behind the line.) The diagram on the right above shows **COVER 8 MAN** versus **FLOOD**. This is a good mixture. **CP:** On the strongside, by plan, it must be decided how to play the TE and the strong back. Is it an outside release or an inside release? If by alignment the back is outside, which is SAM's man? The MIKE will help the SS on shallow inside routes by the TE. If it is decided that it is an inside release, the MIKE will play the inside receiver man to man, SAM will drop to the outside "oh" zone, and the SS will cover the back man to man. The coverage definition calls for the first identification. However, the type of receiver is always of importance and cannot be overlooked.

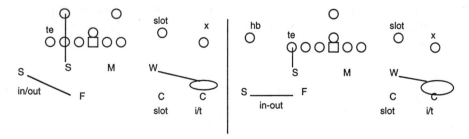

The diagram on the left above shows the adjustments for **slot**. The front begins as **UNDER**, but the formation forces **SAM** and **WILL** to adjust. **WILL**, the strongside linebacker, takes the SAM assignments, and **SAM**, the weakside linebacker, takes the WILL assignments. The same is true for the secondary. The diagram on the right shows the **DOC** formation for **COVER 8 MAN**.

E. Cover 9

COVER 9 is a man coverage. Like SEVEN, NINE is a double-digit call that goes with **EIGHT MAN**. Like TWO, EIGHT can be used as an individual call or can be paired with **NINE**, to be used versus the **SLOT** formation.

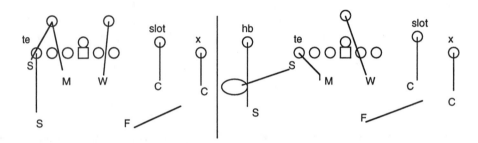

The diagram on the left above shows the alignment and basic assignment for **COVER 9** versus the **SLOT** formation. The diagram on the right shows **COVER 9** versus the **DOC** formation. Because of the offensive personnel, the game plan may say return to **EIGHT MAN** versus **regular**. Flexibility is important and must always be considered in the game plan. **Cover 9**, when paired with cover 8, offers this flexibility.

- **Position: SAM.**
- **Alignment:** A shade outside the shoulder of tight end. If TE is flexed, drop off the line of scrimmage at a depth to see both the TE and offensive tackle and the backfield triangle.
- **Key:** Tight end, running lane, backfield triangle.
- **Assignment: On pass**—begin drop to **short outside zone** ("oh"), see #4, cover **medium and wide** flare man to man. N/T—**continue drop to outside zone**. SEE QB, react to BALL. **CP:** Short side of field jam #5, then sloop. **CP:** TE on diagonal, cover from depth.

- **Position: MIKE.**
- **Alignment:** By front called (UNDER, EVEN, 30).
- **Key:** Weak back, TE, backfield triangle.

- **Assignment: On pass, #4 inside**—man to man on close or delay. **#4 outside**—SEE #5, cover #5 on shallow inside route (Rex/Lex). **#4 blocks**—SEE #4 and #5, drop to short inside zone strongside, #4 delay man to man.

- **Position: WILL.**
- **Alignment:** By front called (UNDER, EVEN, 30).
- **Key: Safety or corner support by plan.**
- **Assignment: On pass, #3 out**—jam #3 and cover man to man (inside-out position). **#3 blocks**—see back, backpedal to hook area. **Frank action**—work weakside, get depth, look for inside breaking receivers.

- **Position: STRONG CORNER.**
- **Alignment:** By call ("KICK") inside technique on #1.
- **Key: #1.**
- **Assignment:** #1, man to man.

- **Position: SLOT CORNER.**
- **Alignment:** By call ("KICK") inside technique on #2.
- **Key: #2.**
- **Assignment:** #2, man to man.

- **Position: STRONG SAFETY.**
- **Alignment:** Head-on to outside of tight end.
- **Key: Backer support, tight end, running lane, backfield triangle.**
- **Assignment:** Tight end man to man, do not charge diagonal. CP: Tight end blocks, HOLD, SEE the action. You have help short outside by SAM and inside by MIKE.

- **Position: WEAK SAFETY.**
- **Alignment:** Over the offensive tackle to the strongside.
- **Key: QB, slot, and X."**
- **Assignment:** By call—"KICK" technique, work to the deep outside, TWO-MAN technique, half of field strongside.

Adjustment Calls Used Strongside on Cover 9

KICK: The standard call for **NINE** versus **SLOT**. Both the **STRONG CORNER** and the **SLOT CORNER** move to an inside technique (TWO-MAN technique). The **WEAK SAFETY** is over the top.

PINCH: Call that doubles the **slot** between the **SLOT CORNER** and the **WEAK SAFETY**. The **STRONG CORNER** has the "**X**" man to man, with an inside technique.

CLAMP: Call that doubles the **WEAK BACK**, between the **WILL** and the **SLOT CORNER**. The **WEAK SAFETY** has the **slot** man to man.

FIST: Call that doubles the "**X**," between the **STRONG CORNER** and the **WEAK SAFETY**. The **SLOT CORNER** has the **slot** man to man.

Cover 9 is a good call to go with cover 8 man as a mixture. Cover 8 man is good as a single call, but the ability to use cover 9 gives the flexibility necessary to properly defense offensive personnel. Also, it should be noted that cover 9 has been used successfully versus regular formations. Cover 9 can still be used versus regular formations with the calls that are described above; however, I suggest its use only versus **SLOT**. The decision is up to the staff, based on what is needed to fill the defensive package. Time, experience, and the need are all factors that must be considered in making the decision. Whatever decision is made, however, you must **make sure** that you can **properly teach** and **practice the technique** to be successful. If this means only two or three coverages, then so be it, but do them well. If you can teach and absorb more, so much the better.

F. 31

31 Zee

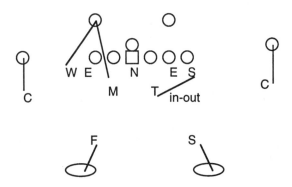

- **Position:** SAM.
- **Alignment:** Take a position head-on the TE.
- **Key:** Corner or safety by game plan, TE, and SB.
- **Assignment: On pass, strong back present**—in/out on #2 and #3 with TED. **#2 outside releases**—cover man to man. **#2 and #3 both outside release**—hold off #2, SEE #3, cover #2 man to man. **#2 inside releases and #3 outside**—cover #3 man to man. **#2 inside releases and #3 blocks**—JAM #2, SEE #3, HOLD for draw, screen and checkdown. **#2**

and #3 both release inside—cover #2 man to man. **No strong back present**—lock TE, cover man to man.

- **Slot:** Pass responsibility is the same, in/out on #4 and #5 with TED. **CP:** Stay with TWO-MAN concept by game plan.

- **Position: TED.**
- **Alignment:** 31 front alignment.
- **Key:** SB and TE.
- **Assignment: On pass, strong back present**—in/out on #2 and #3 with SAM. **#2 outside releases and #3 blocks**—HOLD for draw, screen, checkdown. **#2 and #3 both outside release**—cover #3 man to man. **#2 inside releases and #3 outside**—cover #2 man to man. **#2 inside releases and #3 blocks**—cover #2 man to man. **#2 and #3 both release inside**—cover SB man to man. **No strong back present**—cover #3 man to man.
- **Slot:** Pass responsibility is the same, in/out with SAM on #4 and #5. **CP:** Stay with two-man concept by game plan.

- **Position: MIKE.**
- **Alignment:** 31 front alignment.
- **Assignment: Pinch** (a term used with 31 ZEE to double #4 by MIKE and WILL). **MIKE**—in/out with WILL on #4. **#4 blocks**—HOLD for draw, screen, checkdown. **#4 releases outside** (wide)—work outside to curl, SEE #4 and #5. **#4 releases close**—cover man to man. **Frank action**—stay in/out with WILL on #4. **Counteraction**—cover first back weakside with WILL.
- **Slot:** Pass responsibility is the same, in/out with WILL on #3. **CP:** Stay with TWO-MAN concept by game plan.

- **Position: WILL.**
- **Alignment:** Crackback, giant. **CP:** Vary but stay close to line of scrimmage.
- **Assignment: Pinch** (a term used with 31 ZEE to double #4 by WILL and MIKE). **WILL**—in/out with MIKE on #4. **#4 blocks or releases close**—work outside to curl, SEE #4 and #5. **#4 releases outside** (wide)—cover man to man. **Frank action**—stay in/out with MIKE on #4. **Counteraction**—cover first back weakside with WILL.
- **Slot:** Pass responsibility is the same, in/out with MIKE on #3. **CP:** Stay with TWO-MAN concept by game plan.

- **Position: STRONG CORNER.**
- **Alignment: Take a position head-on "Z,"** no more than five yards deep. You **must be within the five-yard area** to JAM and **reroute** the receiver. This is very important in **COVER 2 MAN** technique as used in **ZEE.**

- **Key: Corner support**—"Z," TE, SB, SEE QB and ball. **CP**: Support will be by game plan (corner or safety).
- **Assignment: On pass**—before snap, move to an inside (kick) technique. **HOLD, jam and FORCE** #1 outside, take away the inside route, **cover #1 man to man. CP**: Be aware of your alignment and the line of scrimmage.
- **Slot**: #2 man to man, inside technique. **CP**: Stay with TWO-MAN concept by game plan.

- **Position: STRONG SAFETY.**
- **Alignment**: Take a position a shade outside the TE, at least seven yards deep. Your distance may vary depending on the split of "Z."
- **Key**: Corner support—"Z," TE, SB, QB, and ball. **CP**: Support will be by game plan (corner or safety).
- **Assignment: On pass**—**deep half of field strongside**. Gain depth to three yards inside the numbers. Read receivers on your side, SEE BALL. Play deep to short, react to ball.
- **Slot**: Pass responsibility, deep half of zone strongside.

- **Position: WEAK SAFETY.**
- **Alignment**: Take a position ten yards deep on the weakside offensive tackle. The offensive formation may alter your alignment and depth.
- **Key**: Corner support—"X," WB, QB, and ball. **CP**: Support will be by game plan (corner or safety).
- **Assignment: On pass**—**deep half of field weakside**. Gain depth to three yards inside the numbers. Read receivers on your side, SEE BALL. Play deep to short, react to ball.
- **Slot**: Pass responsibility is the same, deep half of zone weakside.

- **Position: WEAK CORNER.**
- **Alignment: Take a position head-on "X,"** no more than five yards deep. You **must be within the five-yard area** to JAM and **reroute** the receiver. This is very important in **COVER 2 MAN** technique as used in **ZEE**.
- **Key: Corner support**—"X," WB, SEE QB and ball. **CP**: Support will be by game plan (corner or safety).
- **Assignment: On pass**—before snap, move to an inside (KICK) technique. **HOLD, jam and FORCE** #5 outside, take away the inside route, **cover #5 man to man. CP**: Be aware of your alignment and the line of scrimmage.
- **Slot**: Pass responsibility is the same, #1 man to man, inside technique.

TWO-MAN calls may be used on **31 ZEE. KICK** as described is regular. **VISE** may be called as a variation on #1 or #5. VISE is an in-and-out technique on the receiver, involving the S/CORNER and S/SAFETY or the F/SAFETY and W/CORNER.

As noted in the **SLOT** assignments, we stay with the **TWO-MAN** principle. CORNERS will cover the two wide receivers, and the linebackers will cover the TIGHT END and the two BACKS. By game plan, this is possible **as long as the TE remains in a normal alignment**. If the TE flexes or a back moves outside away from the **slot**, the coverage must **make a decision by the game plan**.

- **Option 1**: Stay with assignment as described above. SAM covers the flexed TE or the back that moves outside away from the **slot**.
- **Option 2**: Rotate the secondary to the flexed TE or the back that moves outside away from the **slot**. **SS covers the TE or the back that moves outside. WS rotates with SC and they divide the deep half zone of the field. WC and SAM cover #1 and #2 man to man.** The decision is a personnel matchup, whichever you prefer. There are other options to check (change) the coverage.

31 Cover 1

Although we have run out of "Z" words, **31 COVER 1** needs to be a part of the coverage package.

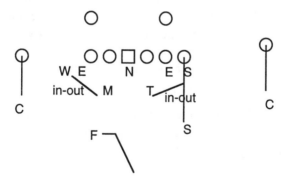

- **Position**: SAM.
- **Alignment: Backer support—outside shoulder of TE.** If TE is flexed, drop off the line of scrimmage at a depth to see both the TE and offensive tackle and the backfield triangle.

- **Key**: TE, running lane, and backfield triangle.
- **Assignment: On pass—in/out on #3 with TED. #3 blocks or closes circle**—work out to slot area. SEE #3 and #1. **#3 releases wide**—cover man to man. **Frank action**—drop with depth to inside, look for inside breaking receivers. **CP: Counteraction,** in/out on first back with MIKE.
- **Slot**: Pass responsibility is the same, in/out #4.

- **Position: TED.**
- **Alignment**: 31 front alignment. Position may vary because of formation and coverage responsibility.
- **Key**: Strong back with SAM and backfield triangle.
- **Assignment: On pass—in/out on #3 with SAM. #3 blocks**—HOLD for draw, screen, checkdown. **#3 releases close inside**—cover man to man. **#3 releases outside**—destroy #2 on inside route and work through #2 to slot area (SEE all receivers). **Frank action**—destroy route, look for gimmick (wide) route of #3.
- **Slot**: Pass responsibility is the same, in/out #4.

- **Position: MIKE.**
- **Alignment**: 31 front alignment. Position may vary because of formation and coverage responsibility.
- **Key**: Weak back with WILL and backfield triangle.
- **Assignment: On pass—in/out on #4 with WILL. #4 blocks**—HOLD for draw, screen, checkdown. **#4 releases close inside**—cover man to man. **#4 releases outside**—drop with **depth. SEE #4 and #5** and **work to slot area (SEE all receivers). Frank action**—in/out on #4 with WILL. **Counteraction**—in/out with WILL on first back weak.
- **Slot**: Pass responsibility is the same, in/out #3.

- **Position: WILL.**
- **Alignment**: 31 front alignment. Position may vary because of formation and coverage responsibility. Crackback position is better for assignment.
- **Key: Backer support** is normal, with "X" in normal split position. Weak back.
- **Assignment: On pass—in/out on #4 with MIKE. #4 blocks or releases close inside**—drop with depth, SEE #5 and #4, and work to slot (SEE all receivers). **#4 releases outside**—cover #4 man to man. **Frank action**—in/out on #4 with WILL. **Counteraction**—in/out with WILL on first back weak.
- **Slot**: Pass responsibility is the same, in/out #3.

- **Position:** STRONG CORNER.
- **Alignment:** Take a position **head-on "Z,"** five to seven yards deep.
- **Key:** Backer support, "Z," and QB. **CP:** Alignment will vary by position of "Z."
- **Assignment: On pass—outside technique, man to man on #1.** You have help in the deep middle.
- **Slot:** #2 man to man.

- **Position:** STRONG SAFETY.
- **Alignment:** Take a position **one yard outside of** TE, five to seven yards deep.
- **Key:** Backer support—TE and backfield triangle.
- **Assignment: On pass—cover #2 man to man,** outside technique.
- **Slot:** Pass responsibility is the same.

- **Position:** WEAK SAFETY.
- **Alignment: Head-on the weakside tackle,** ten yards deep. **CP:** Alignment may vary by formation and field position.
- **Key:** SEE QB and ball.
- **Assignment: On pass—**the **deep middle,** you are **FREE,** play from deep to short. Be in position to make a play on the deep pass, you are the center fielder.
- **Slot:** Pass responsibility is the same.

- **Position:** WEAK CORNER.
- **Alignment:** Take a position **head-on to "X,"** five to seven yards deep.
- **Key:** Backer support, "X," and QB. **CP:** Alignment will vary by position of "X."
- **Assignment: On pass—outside technique,** man to man on #5. You have help in the deep middle.
- **Slot:** Pass responsibility is the same, #1 man to man.

31 Zero

31 ZERO is not needed because of the "PINCH" technique on #3 and #4.

31 Ace

31 ACE is a combination coverage, with five underneath man to man and three-deep zone coverage. It is a good change-up to take away the short patterns with zone coverage deep.

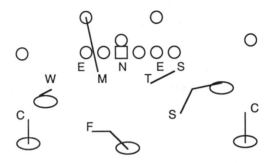

- **Position**: SAM.
- **Alignment**: Take a position head-on the TE.
- **Key**: Safety support, TE, and SB.
- **Assignment**: **On pass, strong back present**—in/out on #2 and #3 with TED. **#2 outside releases**—cover man to man. **#2 and #3 both outside release**—hold off #2, SEE #3, cover #2 man to man. **#2 inside releases and #3 outside**—cover #3 man to man. **#2 inside releases and #3 blocks**—JAM #2, SEE #3, HOLD for draw, screen, checkdown. **#2 and #3 both release inside**—cover #2 man to man. **No strong back present**—lock TE, cover man to man.
- **Slot**: Pass responsibility is the same, #4 and #5 in/out.

- **Position**: TED.
- **Alignment**: 31 front alignment.
- **Key**: SB and TE.
- **Assignment**: **On pass, strong back present**—in/out on #2 and #3 with SAM. **#2 outside releases and #3 blocks**—HOLD for draw, screen, checkdown. **#2 and #3 both outside release**—cover #3 man to man. **#2 inside releases and #3 outside**—cover #2 man to man. **#2 inside releases and #3 blocks**—cover #2 man to man. **#2 and #3 both release inside**—cover SB man to man. **No strong back present**—cover #3 man to man.
- **Slot**: Pass responsibility is the same, #4 and #5 in/out.

- **Position**: MIKE.
- **Alignment**: 31 front alignment.
- **Key**: Guard and backfield triangle.
- **Assignment**: **On pass**—**#4 man to man. #4 blocks**—clamp for draw, screen. **Frank action**—stay man to man. CP: May go in/out with TED.
- **Slot**: Pass responsibility is the same, #3 man to man.

- **Position: WILL.**
- **Alignment:** 31 front—vary alignment, "I," or out position by formation and down and distance.
- **Key: Backer support**—backfield triangle, "X."
- **Assignment: On pass**—**same as ZEKE, short outside zone on weakside**, except with **#5 inside** cover #5 man to man to middle of field. **CP:** Divide the field with the STRONG SAFETY.
- **Slot:** #2 man to man, #2 on diagonal, get depth, locate #1 on inside route.

- **Position: STRONG CORNER.**
- **Alignment: Outside technique** on "Z," five to seven yards deep.
- **Key: Safety support,** "Z," TE, SB. SEE QB to ball.
- **Assignment: On pass**—**deep outside zone on strongside.** You have inside help shallow and deep on strongside. Play outside routes of #1, #2, and #3 man to man. React and play through receiver from outside-in on inside routes of #1, #2, and #3.
- **Slot:** STRONG SAFETY assignments, short outside slot on strongside. SEE #1 and #2, both inside, cover outside of #1 and #2 to middle of field.

- **Position: STRONG SAFETY.**
- **Alignment: A shade outside of TE,** five to seven yards deep.
- **Key: Safety support**—TE, SB, "Z" to QB and ball.
- **Assignment: On pass**—**same as 3 SKY, short outside slot on strongside**, except with **#1 inside** cover #1 man to man to middle of field. **CP:** Divide the field with WILL.
- **Slot:** WEAK CORNER assignments, deep outside zone on weakside.

- **Position: WEAK SAFETY.**
- **Alignment:** Take a position **ten yards deep on the weakside offensive tackle.** The offensive formation may alter your alignment and depth.
- **Key: Backfield triangle,** QB and BALL.
- **Assignment: On pass**—**deep middle zone.** SEE QB and all receivers, play from deep to short. Take **deep inside route of #1, #2, and #3** strongside or **deep inside route of #5 and #4** weakside.
- **Slot:** Pass responsibility is the same.

- **Position: WEAK CORNER.**
- **Alignment: Outside technique** on "X," five to seven yards deep.
- **Key: Backer support**—"X," WB. SEE QB to ball.
- **Assignment: On pass**—**deep outside zone on weakside.** You have inside help shallow and deep on weakside. Play outside routes of #5 and #4

man to man. React and play through receiver from outside-in on inside routes of #5 and # 4.

- **Slot:** STRONG CORNER assignments, deep outside zone on strongside.

DEFENSIVE BACK FUNDAMENTALS: MAN-TO-MAN AND ZONE TECHNIQUE

This section is written as if addressing the defense directly. As a defensive back, you must understand that our philosophy in terms of coverage is to use a mixture of coverages with disguise alignments to make the quarterback hesitate. Our goal is to use both **ZONE** and **MAN-TO-MAN** coverage. To do this, you must have a complete understanding of your responsibility. By studying and working hard, you can improve and become the best.

As a member of the secondary, you are an intricate part of the total success of the defense. Together with the linebackers, you have a run responsibility and a pass responsibility. Coordination between the two groups is necessary to develop a successful pattern. The secondary is the last line of defense to prevent the long run and the long pass. Both can be controlled by proper alignment, proper technique, good tackling, and just plain desire. Failure in execution can mean that the opponent scores a touchdown.

Studying and working to improve are vital to you as an individual player and to the overall success of the team.

1. Know your assignment and the assignment of your teammate, and how the two fit together in the coverage pattern.
2. Know the check-off, and relay the check-off both visually and verbally.
3. Disguise is an important part or our success within the coverage.
   a. Have proper pre-snap movement.
   b. Know when to and when not to disguise.
4. Work on your technique daily, and improve to become the best. Proper technique will enable you to play smart and help you in all situations.
5. Nothing takes the place of studying and knowing your opponent. It is important that you study the outstanding players at your position.

A. Stance

1. Shoulders parallel to the line of scrimmage.
2. Outside foot forward.
3. Weight on forward foot.

4. Hips dropped and knees bent.
5. Arms hanging loosely in front.
6. Alert and ready to react. (**Man to man**—eyes focused on the receiver on a spot between the numbers and the waist. **Zone**—have vision, SEE the receiver, pick up the QB.)

B. Alignment

1. Five to seven yards deep.
2. Your inside foot on the receiver's outside foot.

Your alignment will vary based on the location of the receiver, your assignment within the defense, and the game plan.

The following drills will help you improve your coverage technique, position on the receiver, and backpedal. Equally important, they will help give you the confidence that you have the ability to cover. We begin close and gradually increase the distance. Our goals are to develop confidence and improve technique.

MAN-TO-MAN PASS COVERAGE: TECHNIQUES AND DRILLS

A. Two-Yard Buddy Drill

- **Purpose**: To emphasize the necessity of an alert, balanced stance; to eliminate the drop step and perfect the start.
- **Method**:
  1. **Receiver**: Take a two-point stance and, on your own time, sprint as hard as you can for seven yards.
  2. **Defender**: Take a comfortable stance two yards from the offensive man, outside foot up, inside foot back, hips dropped, head up, arms flexed, alert, and ready to move. Eliminate a false step on the movement of the offensive man. Our goal in this drill is to keep the offensive man from getting even for at least five yards.

B. Five-Yard Buddy Drill

- **Purpose**: To develop the ability to backpedal and establish the ability of the defender to backpedal throughout the "move area."

- **Method**
  1. **Receiver**: Take a two-point stance and sprint as hard as you can until you get even with the defender, but no longer than 20 yards.
  2. **Defender**: Take a comfortable stance, five yards off and slightly outside of the receiver. Begin your backpedal on movement by the receiver and continue until he gets even with you. Proper development of the backpedal technique will keep the receiver from getting even for at least 20 yards (this may be adjusted to 15 yards depending on a player's skill).

A note on the drill: The receiver coach may want to use the receivers in this drill. However, in a teaching situation, I like to keep only the defensive backs in the drill. As the backs improve, the receivers can be added from a competitive standpoint.

As players improve in the buddy drill, various routes are added. Emphasis remains on proper position on the receiver and maintaining the proper technique. If a player is having a problem, I sometimes take him aside and walk through the drill with him until he fully understands. Maintaining position and route recognition are the keys to good coverage. The only way to improve is through study, practice, and hard work.

C. Position Maintenance Drill

- **Purpose**: This drill, at half- to three-fourths speed, is designed to groove a defender's position-maintaining ability.
- **Method**:
  1. **Receiver**: At half speed, run a varying route upfield in a subtle attempt to gain a head-up position on the defender.
  2. **Defender**:
     a. Backpedal and maintain your original lateral position, which may be either inside or outside.
     b. Next, backpedal and adjust your original position to gain and maintain the opposite of your original alignment (e.g., out to in or in to out). **CP**: Stress peripheral vision and focus on the receiver, but see as much as possible.

D. Route Progression Drill

- **Purpose**: This drill is designed to develop route recognition and proper cutoff path to the reception area.

■ **Method**

1. **Receiver:** This drill starts at three-fourths speed and increases to a full-speed drill as proficiency is developed. The receiver will run a progression of routes determined by the position of the defender:

INSIDE 　　　　　　　　　　**OUTSIDE**

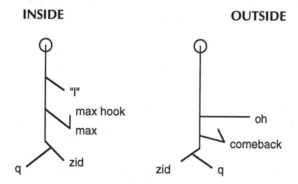

Run these routes in progression, until an awareness of proper cutoff path is developed. Then mix the routes up.

2. **Defender**

a. **Inside technique:** Take a position **five yards** deep on the receiver's **inside shoulder.** Have your **outside foot up** and inside foot back to give you an easy inside opening. As the receiver comes off the line, **backpedal and maintain position** on the receiver, as well as your inside attitude. **Avoid being turned** to the outside. Keep your body attitude so as to be able to **see the quarterback and the receiver.** Know where the receiver is going to catch the ball (reception area or **RA**). For example, if the RA is on the "I," sprint in a straight line parallel to the line of scrimmage and beat the receiver to the RA. **Become the receiver.** Never allow the offensive man to move out of your peripheral vision.

As you sprint to the RA, if the **receiver changes his course** (e.g., "I" to "I" take-off), you must take the **easiest and most direct path** to the new RA. Again, attempt to cut off and control the offensive man. Normally, **take-offs are run from short or shortened medium routes** and are easily sensed if you have good peripheral vision. The max, max hook, post, and Z in deep are played like the "I." Remember not to be turned to the outside when you have an **inside position** and the receiver comes off the line at an angle. **Never lose your inside attitude.** Turn and go only when you have an idea of where the RA is.

Off the post, or Z in deep move, will come the Q or corner route. This route is played like the take-off. It means that you have started your sprint to the Z in deep RA when the Q shows you must redirect your sprint to the Q RA. Take the easiest and most direct route possible. This may mean turning your back on the quarterback. Again, sprint to cut off and control the offensive man.

The **comeback off of the take-off** is a matter of not losing the receiver from your vision and reaction. This is a time-consuming pattern which gives the defender time to react.

The short **crossing pattern** is played like any other inside route. Remember that the **RA is on the other side of the field**. Do not trail the receiver as he maneuvers around the linebackers. Take a straight-line path to the RA. Cut off the receiver.

In summary, **inside technique** means that you are responsible primarily for the inside and deep routes of receivers, with reaction to the short and medium outside routes.

b. **Outside technique**: Take a position five to eight yards deep on the receiver's outside shoulder. See through the receiver to the quarterback. You have primarily responsible for outside to deep. Follow the receiver on short and medium inside routes. Your route progression is (1) "oh," (2) Z in deep, (3) corner, (4) "oh" take-off, (5) comeback.

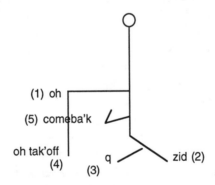

Your objective is the same as for the inside technique:
1. Maintain proper technique on the receiver.
2. Recognize the route and know the RA.
3. Cut off and control the receiver on routes of primary responsibility; intercept or break up the pattern.
4. Intercept.
5. React to routes of secondary responsibility.

The same teaching technique that we used with the inside technique can be used to teach the outside technique. In the outside technique, the defender is basically in an off alignment, with vision in an outside alignment. However, position on the receiver, maintaining position, and route recognition involve the same techniques. In defenses that require an outside technique, the defender will have help in the deep middle or shallow middle.

E. Bump and Run Technique

- **Purpose**: This is a tight coverage used in the field or at the goal line to take away quick passing and to give the defender a change-up in technique.
- **Method**: Take an inside tight position on the receiver (generally the **inside shoulder** of the receiver and **one yard deep**). Face the receiver, and concentrate on him alone. **Always check to make sure that you are not offside.** Disguise your position; move up late. Likewise, when you are off, show "bump" and move back to regular. However, when disguising, **do not be caught moving forward at the snap.** Whatever your final alignment, you must be **set and ready to play on the snap.**
  1. **Receiver releasing inside**: Shuffle your feet to maintain position. Force the receiver outside. If possible, deliver a hand shiver up and under the receiver in a rising manner as quickly as possible. Do not roll your hips with the jam. Flatten the receiver inside. Focus your eyes on the wide receiver's inside number. Keep your shoulders parallel to the line of scrimmage.
  2. **Receiver releasing outside**: Do not attack. See him commit to a direction and take a cutoff path. Rules permitting, **jam** to knock him off stride. Use your inside hand primarily on the jam. If you overcommit to the jam on an outside release, you let the wide receiver upfield and you are beat. Work to get in front of anything inside of the deep route. Stay inside on outside routes.
  3. At the **goal line**, make it difficult for the receiver to get into the end zone. Delay him as much as possible. Don't give him free access. As he crosses the goal line, **move to a position between the receiver** and the **passer**. Intercept or get the knockdown—**WIN!**
- **HOLD**, be patient, and make the receiver commit. (You should be almost flat-footed. The idea is to stay between the wide receiver and the goal line when you are out in the field.)

OUTSIDE RELEASE

lead, cross over,
then contact

INSIDE RELEASE

open, cross over,
and contact

FAKE OUT, COME IN

lead, open to inside
crossover, then contact
and get in front of the
receiver, never trail

DRIVE INSIDE

contact, recover and
open, cross over, and
bump again

■ Study your opponent. (Most wide receivers will fake a jab step inside when going outside. Expect this and do not react to the first move.)

INDIVIDUAL PASS DEFENSE TECHNIQUE

A. Set Position

1. **Feet**: Staggered or parallel, looking in at the quarterback.
2. **Body and arms**: Drop hips, weight on forward foot, arms bent at the elbows. Be alert and relaxed. Do not put hands on hips or knees.

B. Alignment

Basic alignment depends on the defense called, the formation, position on the field, the tendency of the offense, and the game plan.

1. **Strong safety**: Five to seven yards deep. Alignment depends on defense called.
2. **Weak safety**: Ten yards deep, favoring the wide side of the field.
3. **Corners**: Five to seven yards deep. Inside or outside technique, depending on the defense called.
   a. Bump and run: One yard deep, inside shoulder of the receiver.

4. **Strong safety and weak safety**: Alignment will be by the defense called.
5. **Linebackers**: Alignment will be by the defense called.

C. Move to Your Point

This is the spot to which a defender moves while diagnosing the offensive play.

1. **Set point**: Hold your position until you are sure of the play.
2. **Lateral point**: A shuffling action parallel to the line of scrimmage. Slide; do not cross your feet.
3. **Vertical point**: A controlled backpedal action away from the line of scrimmage as the play is diagnosed.

D. When Moving to the Point

Do not move too soon. When the receiver moves laterally, move when the receiver is even with you. Keep position on the receiver. Move downfield when the receiver is even with the linebacker (three to five yards away).

E. While Moving to the Point

Diagnose the play. Is it run or pass?

1. **Focus on eligible receivers**. SEE your key. **KNOW** if your key blocks or releases. Do not guess!
2. **See action of ineligible players** (guards/tackles). If the play is diagnosed as a pass, get into position to cover your receiver and play the ball (man coverage). If zone, get to your area and be ready to react to the ball.
   a. Use proper keys:
      - Corners: Z, TE, SB, X, WB
      - Strong safety: TE, SB
      - Weak safety: X, WB

   If the play is diagnosed as a pass in man coverage, get into position to cover your receiver and play the ball. If the coverage is zone, get to your area and be ready to react to the ball.

F. Position on Receiver

1. **Position varies with technique**: outside, inside, and bump and run.
   a. Inside: A shade inside the receiver, five to seven yards deep

    b. Outside: A shade outside the receiver, five to seven yards deep.

    c. Bump and run: Inside shoulder and one yard off the receiver.

    d. Vertical position: Not closer than three yards or farther off than five yards.

    e. Alignment: By technique.

2. **When free**:

    a. Deep backs **TALK!** Play quarterback's eyes. Break on the ball.

3. **Footwork for position**: Move in a manner so as to always be under control.

    a. First movement is a controlled backpedal. Don't turn your hips. Make the receiver commit before you start to run with him.

    b. When forced to run before the receiver commits, run under control. Use a combination run and slide. Face the same direction as long as possible. Make the receiver "show" before you commit yourself.

    c. After the receiver has committed, play technique. Know the route progression. Beat the receiver to the reception area.

    d. When the receiver changes direction, bring yourself under control and maintain technique.

G. Go for the Ball

1. Look at the passer and the ball. Concentrate and focus on the passer and see the receivers with your peripheral vision. Maintain technique on your receiver.

2. When the ball is thrown, break to the reception area. Learn to judge where you can meet the ball at its highest point. Get to the interception spot as quickly as possible and play the ball at its highest point.

3. **Go for the ball with both hands**:

    a. Fight for the ball. When it's in the air, it's ours!

    b. Look the ball into your hands (pop the head down).

    c. Play through the receiver as he catches the ball on short passes. Strip the ball (under and up).

    d. **Cradle technique**: Play through the receiver the same as making a "face in the numbers" tackle. Drive the **lead** or **cradle arm** around the receiver's waist. The other arm is the **slap** or **knockdown arm**. If the receiver catches the ball, you have him "cradled" to make the tackle and strip. All defenders must perfect this technique. **CP:** If you use the lead arm as the slap or knockdown arm, the receiver will slide off and you will miss the tackle, resulting in a longer gain or even a touchdown. As an example, if you are approaching the receiver from the right, the left arm is the **lead** or **cradle** arm and the right arm is the **trail** or **slap** arm.

4. **On a high pass, play up and over the receiver.** Never go around a receiver. Play through him.
5. Knock the ball out of the receiver's hands if it is a catch.
6. When the ball is thrown, converge on the receiver. **RUN TO THE BALL!**
   a. **Intercept or tackle!**

H. Points to Stress in Coverage

1. Set yourself and keep low. Maintain your backpedal as long as possible.
2. Maintain proper technique on your receiver.
3. Know the route progression. Beat the receiver to the reception area.
4. **INTERCEPT.**
5. Communicate.
6. Deep backs play the PASS first.
7. Linebackers play the RUN first and the pass second.

HOLD AND JAM TECHNIQUE

This technique is used in **ZONE** coverages where it is imperative that we **funnel** the receiver to the inside or **force** the receiver to the outside.

- **Purpose:** To delay and reroute the receiver and prevent him from getting downfield free.
- **Method:** Disguise alignment.
  1. **Funnel technique:** Five yards deep and a shade outside of the receiver.
     a. **HOLD:** Feet squared away, facing the receiver, hips low, body under control. Be ready to move laterally as the receiver approaches you. Hold an outside position on the shoulder of the receiver.
     b. **JAM:** See the numbers. Jam the receiver, funneling him to the inside. Be patient, be under control, and SEE your target. Do not lunge at the receiver; make him commit.
     c. **AFTER JAM:** Move to your responsibility, reading on the move. **If there is a back out,** be alert to react when the **ball is thrown.** **If there is no back out,** continue to get depth, as you drop to your responsibility. Be alert for the screen.

    d. **BALL is thrown**: React immediately. A split-second delay can be the difference between no gain and a big gain.

2. **Force technique**: The same technique as described above will be used to force the receiver outside. Again, it is imperative to **HOLD**, **JAM**, MOVE, and READ as you take your responsibility.

The success of **ZONE** coverage depends largely on the awareness and reaction of the linebackers and the secondary defenders using the **FUNNEL** or **FORCE** technique. For this type of coverage to be successful, the receiver must be rerouted and delayed and the timing of the route destroyed. This will cause the quarterback to look elsewhere to throw. Making the quarterback hesitate gives the line an additional step and the opportunity to SACK or HURRY the throw. This is another example of the defensive team working together and depending on each other for total success.

- **Progression of technique: funnel or force**
  1. HOLD.
  2. JAM.
  3. MOVE and READ as you go.
  4. Back out—be alert to react up when the ball is thrown.
  5. No back out—continue to deepen in area and be alert for screen.
  6. BALL in the AIR—react immediately.

TRAIL TECHNIQUE

This is a TWO-MAN, VISE call, and 8 JET technique. The technique is used in MAN coverage to give tight coverage on receivers by the linebackers and secondary.

- **Purpose**: A tight inside technique. Man coverage technique to mix with the zone coverage funnel technique described above.
- **Method**: From a basic alignment, move to an inside technique, no deeper than five yards, on or before the snap. Disguise; do not show too soon. Practice will enable you to (1) move to an inside technique before the snap or (2) move to an inside technique on the snap.
  1. **Trail technique**: Take a position with your **inside foot up** and an inside position on the receiver. **Be patient** with your inside foot. Do not move it until the receiver is forced to your outside. JAM the receiver; hold inside position. See him, concentrate on him, wall him

off, clamp from inside, and TRAIL the receiver on his inside hip. Turn with the receiver, and focus on the near hip. Parallel his moves. Track him constantly until you hear the "BALL" call or "feel" the ball is near. Study the receiver's hands and eyes; they will tell you if he is the intended receiver. Be prepared to explode through the ball and the receiver. **Strip** and **tackle**. If the ball is not thrown to your receiver and there is no "RUN" call, locate and REACT to the BALL.

- **Progression of technique**:
  1. MOVE to inside technique.
  2. HOLD—be patient.
  3. JAM—force the receiver outside and use the trail technique.

COMMUNICATION

Communicate before and during the play.

- Before the snap:
  1. Identify the formation and the tendency.
  2. Identify the personnel and the tendency.
- During the play:
  1. Corners—talk the route of the wide receiver.
     a. "IN" when he goes in.
     b. "OUT" when he goes out.
     c. "CHINA" on the hitch by the "X" and the corner route by the "slot."
  2. Safeties—when playing cover 2, talk the route of #2 and #4.
     a. "DRAG" on short crossing route.
     b. "IN" on deep in.
     c. "OUT" on deep out.
  3. All secondary players:
     a. "PASS" when the play is diagnosed as a pass.
     b. "BOOT" on the naked or bootleg pass.
     c. "BALL" when the ball is thrown.
     d. "BALL, BALL, BALL" when the ball is about to be caught.

The words used above are examples of calls that the coach would like to stress as important to the secondary. Obviously, it is important for the coach to use the same terminology that the team uses. There is no need to create new terminology unless absolutely necessary.

BLITZ COVERAGE

A. Cover 4

Following our discussion of ZONE and MAN coverage, in this section we discuss basic BLITZ coverage. There are two basic blitz coverages: four and five. **Cover 4** is the term that describes the STRONG CORNER, STRONG SAFETY, WEAK SAFETY, and WEAK CORNER covering #1, #2, #4, and #5. The SAM or strongside linebacker has #3.

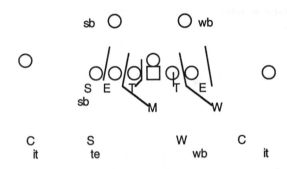

Deuce Coverage (Two- or Three-Man Weakside Blitz Coverage)

- **Position: SAM.**
- **Alignment: Head-on the TE.** Alignment may vary by support call, safety or backer.
- **Key**: Safety support, TE, backfield triangle.
- **Assignment: On pass—#3 man to man, inside technique. Flow**—second back (trio coverage). **#3 blocks to you**—engage. **#3 blocks or releases away**— come under your DE—FREE BLITZ.

- **Position: MIKE and WILL.**
- **Alignment: By alignment called** (UNDER, EVEN, OVER, 30).
- **Key**: Snap of the ball and the gap called.
- **Assignment: On pass**—move on the snap, penetrate the pocket, rush the passer. If you are the outside rusher, contain the passer.

- **Position: STRONG CORNER.**
- **Alignment**: Take a position **five to seven yards** deep, **inside technique on "Z."**

- **Key:** Support by call, **safety** or **backer.** "Z" to QB and ball.
- **Assignment: On pass—#1 man to man,** inside technique, NO INSIDE POST HELP!
- **Slot: #2 man to man,** inside technique, NO INSIDE POST HELP!

- **Position: STRONG SAFETY.**
- **Alignment:** Take a position **five to seven yards** deep, **inside technique on TE.**
- **Key:** Support by call, **safety** or **backer.** TE to QB and ball.
- **Assignment: On pass—#2 man to man,** inside technique, NO INSIDE POST HELP!
- **Slot:** Coordinate with the WEAK SAFETY, DEUCE or TRIO coverage.

- **Position: WEAK SAFETY.**
- **Alignment:** Take a position **five to seven yards** deep, **inside technique on WB.**
- **Key:** Support by call, **backer** or weak safety. WB to QB and ball.
- **Assignment: Deuce call. On pass—#4 man to man,** inside technique, NO INSIDE POST HELP!
- **Slot:** Coordinate with the STRONG SAFETY, DEUCE or TRIO coverage.

- **Position: WEAK CORNER.**
- **Alignment:** Take a position **five to seven yards** deep, **inside technique on "X."**
- **Key:** Support by call, backer or weak safety. "X" to QB and ball.
- **Assignment: On pass—#5 man to man,** inside technique, NO INSIDE POST HELP!
- **Slot: #1 man to man,** inside technique, NO INSIDE POST HELP!

Front Notes

If **30** is the front call, SAM has coverage, and TED, MIKE, and WILL have blitz assignments. The secondary will have the same assignments as described.

Adjustment Notes

COVER 4 calls for the four secondary players to have coverage and the strongside linebacker. The outside blitzer on the weakside or strongside will have a second back coverage. The blitz from **COVER 4** can be picked up offensively, but it creates one-on-one blocks and forces a back to block. It is a good blitz to use in run/pass situations. In pass-only situations, the called blitz will normally involve more people to beat the protection.

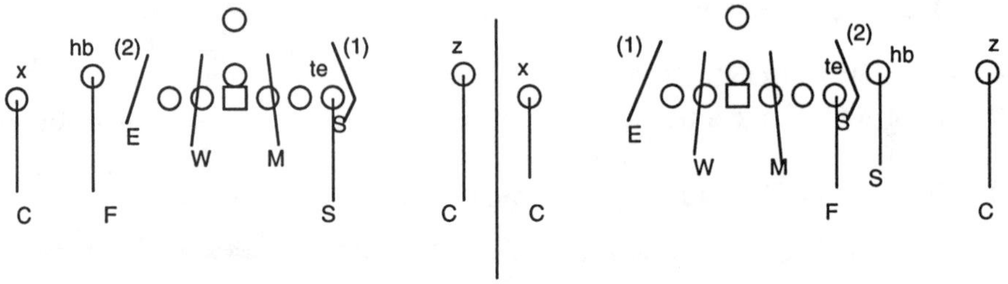

The diagram on the left above shows **COVER 4** versus **DOUBLE**. The two **CORNERS** have coverage on "X" and "Z." The **WEAK SAFETY** has coverage on the HB, and the **STRONG SAFETY** has coverage on the TE. **SAM** has coverage on the first back strong, and the **DE** on the weakside has the remaining back. Versus **FLOOD** (diagram on the right above) or any strong formation, the coverage is **FIVE**. The two safeties move to the strongside and have coverage on the HB and TE (man to man or in/out, depending on the distance). **SAM** has the second back, and the **DE** weakside has the first back. In both diagrams, **MIKE** and **WILL** are free blitzers.

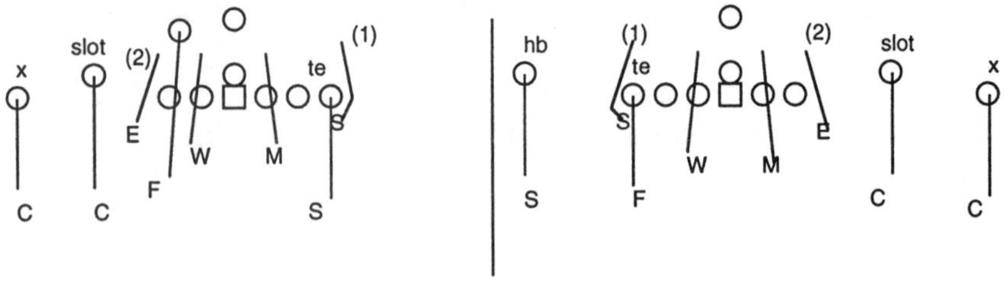

The diagram on the left above shows **FIVE** coverage on the strongside formation. The **DE** has the second back, and the **SAM** has the first back weakside. The diagram on the right above shows **FOUR** coverage versus the **DOC** formation. The **SAM** has the first back, and the **DE** has the remaining back to his side. Again, the **MIKE** and **WILL** are free blitzers. **CP:** SAM and the DE need to communicate with the two safeties to coordinate their coverage. Basically, if the coverage is to you, SAM or the DE has second back coverage. If the coverage is away from you, you have first back coverage.

B. Cover 5

Trio Coverage (Two- or Three-Man Strongside Blitz Coverage)

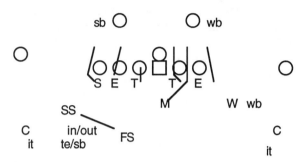

TRIO means the STRONG SAFETY and WEAK SAFETY are in/out on #2 and #3 strongside. SAM is the free blitzer. WILL has coverage on the WB.

- **Position: SAM.**
- **Alignment: Head-on the TE.** Alignment may change by blitz call.
- **Key:** TE and snap of the ball.
- **Assignment: On pass**—move on the snap, penetrate the C gap, rush the passer, break the pocket. If you are the outside rusher, contain the passer.

- **Position: MIKE.**
- **Alignment: By alignment called.**
- **Key:** Snap of the ball and the gap called.
- **Assignment: On pass**—move on the snap, penetrate the pocket, rush the passer. If you are the outside rusher, contain the passer.

- **Position: WILL.**
- **Alignment: By defense called.**
- **Key:** Running lane, backfield triangle (weak back, #4).
- **Assignment: On pass—#4 man to man**, inside technique.

- **Position: STRONG CORNER.**
- **Alignment:** Take a position **five to seven yards** deep, **inside technique on "Z."**
- **Key:** Support by call, **safety** or **backer.** "Z" to QB and ball.
- **Assignment: On pass—#1 man to man**, inside technique, NO INSIDE POST HELP!
- **Slot: #2 man to man**, inside technique, NO INSIDE POST HELP!

- **Position:** STRONG SAFETY.
- **Alignment:** Take a position a shade outside the TE, five yards deep.
- **Key:** Safety support, TE, backfield triangle.
- **Assignment: On pass—in/out on #2 and #3 with WEAK SAFETY** (trio coverage). **Outside release of #2 or #3**—man to man on outside receiver, inside technique. **Both #2 and #3 outside**—outside receiver, man to man. **#2 releases and #3 blocks or releases away**—rush passer, contain FREE BLITZ. **CP:** If #3 blocks to you, engage.
- **Slot:** Coordinate with WEAK SAFETY, DEUCE or TRIO coverage.

- **Position:** WEAK SAFETY.
- **Alignment:** Take a position seven yards deep, head-up to inside the TE.
- **Key:** Safety support, TE.
- **Assignment: On pass—in/out on #3 and #2 with STRONG SAFETY** (trio coverage). **Outside release of #2 or #3**—man to man on inside receiver, inside technique. **Both #2 and #3 outside**—inside receiver man to man. **#2 releases and #3 blocks or releases away**—#2 man to man, inside technique.
- **Slot:** Coordinate with STRONG SAFETY, DEUCE or TRIO coverage.

- **Position:** WEAK CORNER.
- **Alignment:** Take a position five to seven yards deep, inside technique on "X."
- **Key: Backer support,** "X" to QB and ball.
- **Assignment:** On pass—**#5 man to man,** inside technique, NO INSIDE POST HELP!
- **Slot: #1 man to man,** inside technique, NO INSIDE POST HELP!

Adjustment Notes

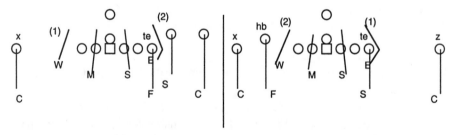

The diagram on the left above shows **FIVE** coverage. Both safeties move to the strongside versus **FLOOD.** The **DE** has the second back, and **WILL** has the first back weakside. **MIKE** and **SAM** are free blitzers. The diagram on the right shows a **DEUCE CALL** on the strong blitz versus **DOUBLE**. The **DE** has the first back, and **WILL** has the second back weakside.

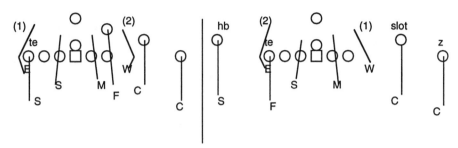

The diagram on the left above shows **COVER 5** versus the strong formation. **WILL** has the second back, and the **DE** has the first back. The diagram on the right shows a **DEUCE CALL** on the blitz versus **DOC** formation. The **DE** has the second back and **WILL** has the first back.

In Chapter 4, we will look at specific blitzes and the coverage required. There are basically two types of blitzes: (1) run/pass and (2) pass only. The **run/pass** blitz is used in basic run/pass situations (first down, second and short to medium). **Pass only** is used in second and long or third and long situations.

4

BLITZ (UNDER/OVER/30) AND BLITZ COVERAGE

Blitzes are organized into what are referred to as **run/pass** blitz and **pass-only** blitz. These terms mean exactly what they say. The **run/pass** blitz is a first- or second-down type of blitz that is designed to be called in situations when a run or pass is expected. The **pass-only** blitz is a third-down type of blitz that is called in situations when a pass is expected.

The difference between the two is based on a philosophy of defense. The **run/pass** blitz gives good run support outside, and the inside gaps are accounted for by the line and linebackers. This type of blitz usually brings one or two defenders, based on the formation. The coverage is blitz coverage that is called **deuce** and **trio**. This was discussed in Chapter 3 on coverage and will be defined in greater detail in this chapter. This blitz usually brings six rushers and covers with five. The offense should have the pickup for the **run/pass** blitz, but one-on-one situations are created and the defense must win one on one.

The **pass-only** blitz gives up a little outside run support and attempts to bring a defender from the secondary to give the offense a pickup problem. This type of blitz will bring more than six and cover with the number remaining. What I will refer to as a "KEY" blitz will be used. This means that the defender will "KEY" the offensive blocker, usually a back. If he blocks, the defender will blitz and engage the blocker. If he releases, the defender will cover. In this type of blitz, the defense is trying to get a defender "free" on the quarterback.

With the liberal substitution rule and changing of personnel on every down, it now boils down to a matchup in personnel. Simply put, if two backs and a TE (two TEs and one back) are in the game (run personnel), it's time to call the **run/pass** blitz. If pass personnel are in the game (three or four wide receivers), the **pass-only** blitz is the best call versus the offense. The blitz is a great call if it works, but if it is picked up, and the quarterback has time, the secondary coverage must be at its best. The secondary is one on one, with no help. The help comes from sending more defenders than the offense can block or from the rusher who wins one on one to force a quick throw or quarterback sack.

The rush is a very significant factor in all pass defense situations. Pressure on the passer is important, and the rush must be properly coordinated. We will begin with a study of the blitz from the UNDER and OVER fronts and then move to the 30 front. Before leaving this chapter we will also discuss the blitz with substituted personnel and the now popular ZONE blitz that we hear so much about today.

FIVE-MAN BLITZ

A. Under Cinko

The first blitz that we will discuss is a basic blitz from the **UNDER** front. It is called **CINKO**, and it is a five-man blitz, by formation. I first became

UNDER CINKO (five-man blitz, by formation)

aware of this possibility when I was with the San Diego Chargers. Dale Lindsey, our linebacker coach, had success with this blitz. It fit our philosophy of sending five people, plus it involved our two best blitzers. We added it to our package, and it proved very successful and useful to us in our scheme. The huddle call tells us that we will blitz a LB in addition to the four linemen. The blitzer is determined by the offensive formation.

- **Position**: SAM.
- **Alignment**: Same as UNDER front.
- **Key**: Backer support, tight end, running lane, backfield triangle.
- **Assignment**: Backer support. **By formation**—blitz D GAP on **strong, split, and I**. **On pass**—rush passer, contain. **Weak and one back**—cover (TE) #2.

- **Position**: MIKE.
- **Alignment**: Same as UNDER front.
- **Key**: Same as UNDER front.
- **Assignment**: B GAP, first back your side.

- **Position**: WILL.
- **Alignment**: Same as UNDER front.
- **Key**: Same as UNDER front.
- **Assignment**: By formation. **Strong, split, and I**—cover first back your side. **Weak and one back**—blitz through weakside A or B GAP by call. **On pass**—rush passer, break pocket. **CP**: On A-gap call, expect the center to turn on you. WIN one on one.

- **Position**: S/END.
- **Alignment**: Same as UNDER front.
- **Key**: Same as UNDER front.
- **Assignment**: Same as UNDER front.

- **Position**: NOSE TACKLE.
- **Alignment**: Same as UNDER front.
- **Key**: Same as UNDER front.
- **Assignment**: Strongside A GAP. **On pass** —rush passer, break pocket.

- **Position**: W/TACKLE.
- **Alignment**: Same as UNDER front.
- **Key**: Same as UNDER front.

- **Assignment**: Weakside B or A GAP by call. **On pass**—rush passer, break pocket. **CP**: On all weak and one-back formations make sure you charge wider and take offensive guard with you. WILL drives through the A GAP.

- **Position**: W/END.
- **Alignment**: Same as UNDER front.
- **Key**: Same as UNDER front.
- **Assignment**: C GAP. **On pass**—rush passer, contain.

- **Position**: S/CORNER.
- **Alignment**: Head on "Z."
- **Key**: Safety support, "Z."
- **Assignment**: Backer support. **On pass**—outside technique #1 man to man. Inside help in middle of field.

- **Position**: S/SAFETY.
- **Alignment**: By call, backer or safety support.
- **Key**: Tight end, running lane, backfield triangle.
- **Assignment**: Backer support. By formation, two backs and one back—same as 10 coverage.

- **Position**: W/SAFETY.
- **Alignment**: Same as 10 coverage.
- **Key**: Same as 10 coverage.
- **Assignment**: Same as 10 coverage.

- **Position**: W/CORNER.
- **Alignment**: Head on "X."
- **Key**: Backer support, "X."
- **Assignment**: Backer support. **On pass**—outside technique #5 man to man. Inside help in middle of field.

Other Calls for Sam and Will on Cinko

SAM will blitz on SPLIT, STRONG, and "I" formation. WILL blitzes on WEAK and all one-back sets (double, flood, doc, and tiger).

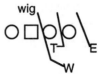

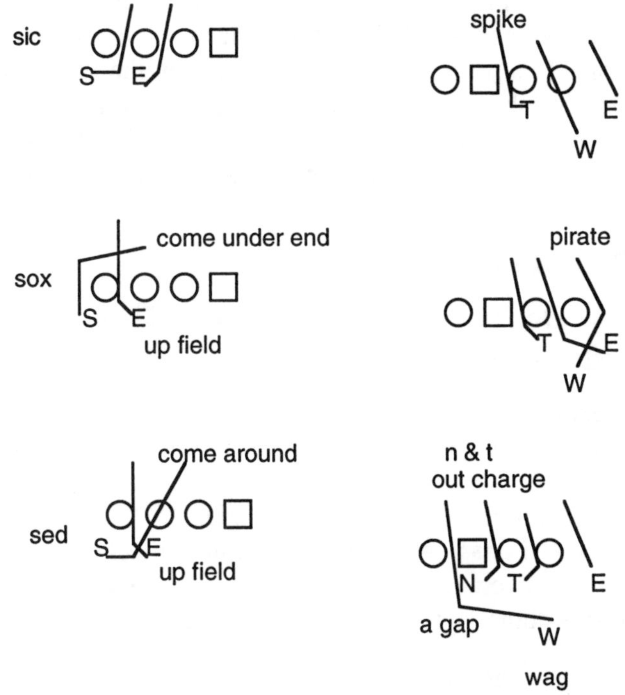

sic

spike

come under end

sox

up field

pirate

come around

sed

up field

n & t
out charge

a gap

wag

All calls will be set by the game plan and may vary by formation and down and distance.

B. Under Sod

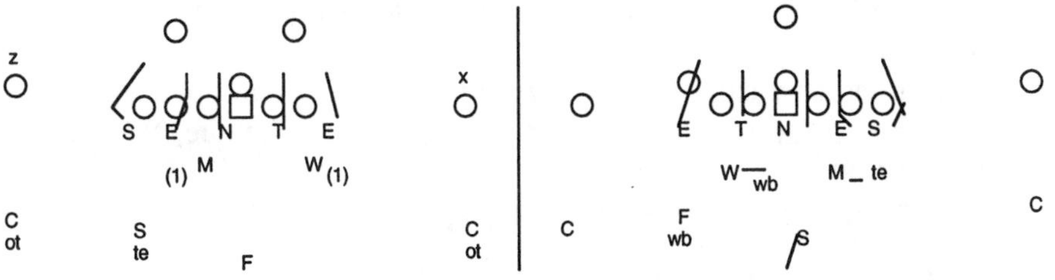

UNDER SOD is good on all formations. The diagram on the left above shows the coverage on all two-back formations. MIKE and WILL have coverage on the first back. The corners have an outside technique, man to man on "Z" and "X." The S/S has the TE man to man, and the W/S is free in the middle of the field. The other change that I want to call to your attention is the charge of the S/S end. The charge is what is referred to as a "tuff" charge and is automatic on UNDER SOD.

The diagram on the right above shows the coverage adjustment for DOUBLE, a weakside one-back formation. The two safeties spin on all one-back formations. In a weakside one-back formation, the W/S will adjust. In a strongside one-back formation (FLOOD), the S/S will adjust.

The lineman (S/S END, NOSE, W/S TACKLE, and W/S END) may use their ME, "U," TOM, and TOMY rush games as called for in the game plan.

SIX-MAN BLITZ

A. Cover 4 (Deuce Coverage—Two- or Three-Man Weakside Blitz Coverage)

- **Position:** SAM.
- **Alignment: Head-on** TE—alignment may vary by support call, safety, or backer.
- **Key:** Safety support—TE, backfield triangle.
- **Assignment: On pass—#3 man to man**, inside technique. **Flow**—second back (trio coverage). **#3 blocks to you**—engage. **#3 blocks or releases away**—come under your DE; FREE BLITZ.

- **Position:** MIKE and WILL.
- **Alignment: By alignment called** (UNDER, EVEN, OVER, and 30).
- **Key:** Snap of the ball and the gap called.
- **Assignment: On pass**—move on the snap, penetrate the pocket, rush passer. If you are the outside rusher—contain the passer.

- **Position:** STRONG CORNER.
- **Alignment:** Take a position **five to seven yards** deep, **inside technique on "Z."**
- **Key:** Support by call—**safety** or **backer.** "Z" to QB and ball.
- **Assignment: On pass—#1 man to man**, inside technique, NO INSIDE POST HELP!
- **Slot: #2 man to man**, inside technique, NO INSIDE POST HELP!

- **Position:** STRONG SAFETY.
- **Alignment:** Take a position **five to seven yards** deep, **inside technique on TE.**
- **Key:** Support by call—**safety** or **backer.** TE to QB and ball.
- **Assignment: On pass—#2 man to man**, inside technique, NO INSIDE POST HELP! **FLOW**—in and out on #2 and #3 with W/SAFETY (TRIO coverage).
- **Slot:** Coordinate with the WEAK SAFETY, DEUCE or TRIO coverage.

- **Position**: WEAK SAFETY.
- **Alignment**: Take a position **five to seven yards** deep, **inside technique on WB.**
- **Key**: Support by call—**backer** or **weak safety**. WB to QB and ball.
- **Assignment: Deuce call. On pass—#4 man to man**, inside technique, NO INSIDE POST HELP! FLOW—in and out on #2 and #3 with S/SAFETY (TRIO coverage).
- **Slot**: Coordinate with the STRONG SAFETY, DEUCE or TRIO coverage.

- **Position**: WEAK CORNER.
- **Alignment**: Take a position **five to seven yards** deep, **inside technique on "X."**
- **Key**: Support by call—**backer** or **weak safety**. "X" to QB and ball.
- **Assignment: On pass—#5 man to man**, inside technique, NO INSIDE POST HELP!
- **Slot: #1 man to man**, inside technique, NO INSIDE POST HELP!

Front Notes

If 30 is the front call, SAM has coverage, and TED, MIKE, and WILL have blitz assignments. The secondary will have the same assignments as described.

Adjustment Notes

COVER 4 calls for the four secondary players to have coverage and the strongside linebacker. The outside blitzer, on the weakside or strongside, will have a second back coverage. The blitz from **COVER 4** can be picked up offensively, but it creates one-on-one blocks and forces a back to block. It is a good blitz to use in run/pass situations. In pass-only situations, the called blitz will normally involve more people to beat the protection.

The diagram above shows **COVER 4** versus **DOUBLE**. The two **CORNERS** have coverage on "X" and "Z". The **WEAK SAFETY** has coverage on the HB, and the **STRONG SAFETY** has coverage on the TE. **SAM** has coverage on the first back strong, and the **DE** on the weakside has the remaining back. Versus **FLOOD** or any strong formation, the coverage is **FIVE**. The two safeties move to the strongside and have coverage on the HB and TE (man to man or in/out, depending on the distance). **SAM** has the second back, and the **DE** weakside has the first back. In both diagrams, **MIKE** and **WILL** are free blitzers.

SLOT   DOC

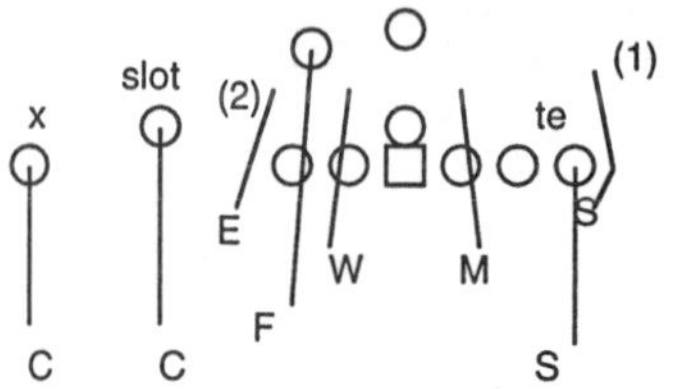

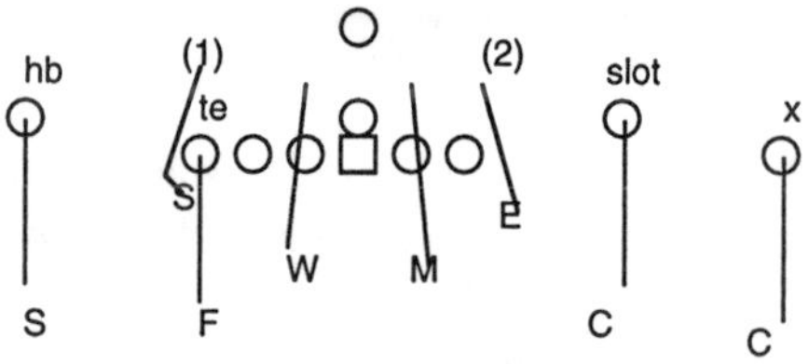

The diagram on the left above shows **FIVE** coverage on the strongside formation. The **DE** has the second back, and the **SAM** has the first back weakside. The diagram on the right shows **FOUR** coverage versus **DOC** formation. The SAM has the first back, and the **DE** has the remaining back to his side. Again, the **MIKE** and **WILL** are free blitzers. **CP:** SAM and the DE always need to communicate with the two safeties to coordinate their coverage. Basically, if the coverage is to you, SAM or the DE has second back coverage. If the coverage is away from you, you have first back coverage.

B. Cover 5 (Trio Coverage—Two- or Three-Man Strongside Blitz Coverage)

- **Position: SAM.**
- **Alignment: Head-on TE.** Alignment may change by blitz call.
- **Key:** TE and snap of the ball.
- **Assignment: On pass**—move on the snap, penetrate the D, C, or B gap by call, rush passer, break pocket. If you are the outside rusher—contain the passer.

- **Position: MIKE.**
- **Alignment: By alignment called.**

- **Key**: Snap of the ball and the gap called.
- **Assignment: On pass**—move on the snap, penetrate the pocket, rush passer. If you are the outside rusher—contain the passer.

- **Position**: WILL.
- **Alignment: By defense called.**
- **Key**: Running lane, backfield triangle (weak back, #4).
- **Assignment: On pass—#4 man to man**, inside technique.

- **Position**: STRONG CORNER.
- **Alignment**: Take a position **five to seven yards** deep, **inside technique on "Z."**
- **Key**: Support by call; **safety** or **backer**. "Z" to QB and ball.
- **Assignment: On pass—#1 man to man**, inside technique, NO INSIDE POST HELP!
- **Slot: #2 man to man**, inside technique, NO INSIDE POST HELP!

- **Position**: STRONG SAFETY.
- **Alignment**: Take a position a shade outside the TE, five yards deep.
- **Key**: Safety support, TE, backfield triangle.
- **Assignment: On pass—in and out on #2 and #3 with WEAK SAFETY** (trio coverage). **Outside release of #2 or #3**—man to man on outside receiver, inside technique. **Both #2 and #3 outside**—outside receiver, man to man. **#2 releases, #3 blocks or releases away**—rush passer, contain FREE BLITZ. **CP: #3 blocks to you**—engage.
- **Slot**: Coordinate with WEAK SAFETY, DEUCE or TRIO coverage.

- **Position**: WEAK SAFETY.
- **Alignment**: Take a position seven yards deep, head-up to inside the TE.
- **Key**: Safety support, TE.
- **Assignment: On pass—in and out on #3 and #2 with STRONG SAFETY** (trio coverage). **Outside release of #2 or #3**—man to man on inside receiver, inside technique. **Both #2 and #3 outside**—inside receiver man to man. **#2 releases, #3 blocks or releases away**—#2 man to man, inside technique.
- **Slot**: Coordinate with STRONG SAFETY, DEUCE or TRIO coverage.

- **Position**: WEAK CORNER.
- **Alignment**: Take a position five to seven yards deep, inside technique on "X."

- **Key: Backer support, "X" to QB and ball.**
- **Assignment: On pass—#5 man to man,** inside technique. NO INSIDE POST HELP!
- **Slot: #1 man to man,** inside technique. NO INSIDE POST HELP!

Adjustment Notes

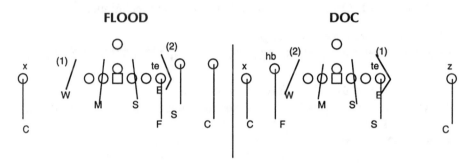

FIVE coverage is shown above. In the drawing on the left, both safeties move to the strongside versus **FLOOD**. The **DE** has the second back, and **WILL** has the first back weakside. **MIKE** and **SAM** are free blitzers. The diagram on the right shows the strong blitz versus **DOUBLE** (deuce coverage). The **DE** has the first back, and **WILL** has the second back weakside.

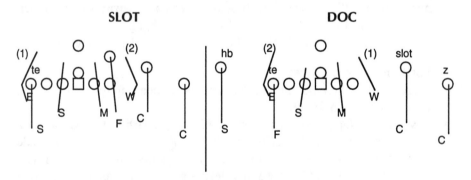

The diagram on the left above shows **COVER 5** versus the strong formation. **WILL** has the second back, and the **DE** has the first back. The diagram on the right shows the blitz versus **DOC** formation (deuce coverage). The **DE** has the second back, and **WILL** has the first back.

C. Under SWILL Blitz (Sam and Will)

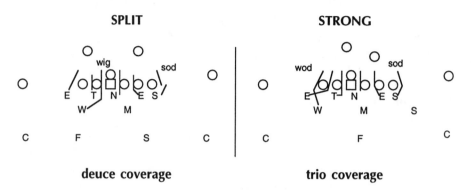

SPLIT   STRONG

deuce coverage   trio coverage

- **Position: S/END.**
- **Alignment:** Same as UNDER front.
- **Key:** Offensive tackle.
- **Assignment:** On the snap of the ball, take a "tuff" charge through the inside shoulder of the offensive tackle. B-gap responsibility. **On pass**—rush passer, break pocket.

- **Position: NOSE TACKLE.**
- **Alignment:** Same as UNDER front.
- **Key:** Center and strongside offensive guard.
- **Assignment:** Penetrate strongside A gap into running lane. **On pass**—rush passer, break pocket.

- **Position: W/TACKLE.**
- **Alignment:** Same as UNDER front.
- **Key:** Offensive guard.
- **Assignment:** By call—**WIG** = penetrate weakside B gap. **On pass**—rush passer, break pocket. **CP:** WOD is drawn in the diagram above on the right.

- **Position: W/END.**
- **Alignment:** Same as UNDER front.
- **Key:** Offensive tackle, running lane, and backfield triangle.
- **Assignment:** By call—**WIG** = weakside C gap. **On pass**—rush passer, contain. WOD = weakside B gap.

- **Position**: SAM.
- **Alignment**: **Backer support**—head-on to outside the tight end.
- **Key**: **Backer support**—SOD key, running lane, and backfield triangle.
- **Assignment**: **Backer support. On pass**—rush passer, contain. CP: You have reverse and bootleg responsibility.

- **Position**: MIKE.
- **Alignment**: Same as UNDER front.
- **Key**: SEE through the offensive line to the backfield triangle.
- **Assignment**: Back and ball keys and responsibility. A, B, C, and D gap in progression. **On pass**—by formation. **Split, weak, and I**—DEUCE coverage, man to man on strong back. **Strong**—weak back, man to man. CP: On **flow** strongside—play the run and cover the second back.

- **Position**: WILL.
- **Alignment**: Same as UNDER front.
- **Key**: By call. WIG—weakside A gap. WOD—weakside C gap.
- **Assignment**: By call—WIG or WOD. **CP**: On WOD, you have contain.

- **Position**: STRONG CORNER.
- **Alignment**: Inside technique on #1.
- **Key**: Backer support. SEE "Z."
- **Assignment**: Backer support. **On pass—by formation (weak, split, I, and strong)**, #1 man to man.
- **Slot**: #1 man to man.

- **Position**: STRONG SAFETY.
- **Alignment**: Head-on the tight end.
- **Key**: Backer support—tight end and backfield triangle.
- **Assignment**: Backer support. **On pass—by formation** (DEUCE coverage). **Split, weak, and I**—tight end man to man. **Strong** (TRIO coverage)—in and out on strong back and tight end with WEAK SAFETY. **CP**: On **FLOW**—in and out on #2 and #3 with W/SAFETY.
- **Slot**: You have W/CORNER assignments.

- **Position**: WEAK SAFETY.
- **Alignment**: **By formation. Weak**—be in a position to support weakside. **Split and I**—be in position to go strongside on FLOW. **Strong**—TRIO alignment.
- **Key**: W/S support with "X" wide. Corner support versus near ("X" is tight or second TE). **By formation** (DEUCE coverage). **Weak**—SEE weak back and near end. **Split and I**—SEE backfield triangle, on FLOW see

tight end and SB in progression. **Strong** (TRIO coverage)—SEE the backfield triangle.

■ **Assignment**: Backer support. **On pass—by formation. Weak, split, and I** (DEUCE COVERAGE)—in and out with WEAK CORNER on weak back and near end. **Strong** (TRIO coverage)—in and out with STRONG SAFETY on first receiver inside of TE, SB. **FLOW**—in and out on #2 and #3 with S/SAFETY.

■ **Slot**: Assignment is the same.

■ **Position**: WEAK CORNER.

■ **Alignment**: **By formation**. W/S support when "**X**" **is wide**—shade inside #5. Corner support **versus near** ("X" is tight or second TE)—shade outside near.

■ **Key**: **By formation**. W/S support when "**X**" **is wide**—SEE "X." Corner support **versus near end**.

■ **Assignment**: W/S support or corner support. **On pass—by formation.** "**X**" **is wide**—man to man. **Versus near (weak, I, and split)**—in and out with W/S on near and weak back. **Strong**—near man to man. On **FLOW**—near man to man.

■ **Slot**: #2 man to man.

In both **deuce** and **trio** coverage, there is no HELP deep. Each secondary defender must take an inside technique and, by game plan design, play a **tight bump technique** or play **back-off** at a depth of about five yards. Whatever the alignment, there are certain offensive alerts of which the secondary defender must be aware.

If the alignment is a **tight bump technique**, the defender must prevent the inside release. By doing this, the primary offensive alert is the "**fade**" (a quick "take-off" deep). If the alignment is **back-off**, the defender must be alert for the **quick inside** ("i" cut) route. A good inside technique is important, but an accurate pass on time is difficult to defend. In many cases, all the defender can do is make the tackle and strip the ball.

THREE-MAN-LINE BLITZ

A. 55 Combo Blitz

The **55 COMBO BLITZ** is a basic 30 BLITZ. With SAM and WILL committed, TED and MIKE have coverage. The secondary uses ONE coverage technique and assignments. The weak safety is free to help in the middle of the field.

SPLIT

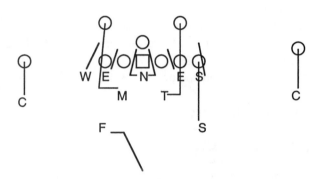

- **Position**: SAM.
- **Alignment**: Backer or safety by call.
- **Key**: Tight end, running lane, and backfield triangle.
- **Assignment**: SOD is regular (SED and INDIAN are other possible calls).

- **Position**: TED
- **Alignment**: Same as 30 front.
- **Key**: Guard and backfield triangle.
- **Assignment**: Back and ball key and responsibilities. **On pass**—first back your side, man to man on all two-back formations. **One back**—coordinate with MIKE on #3 and #4.

- **Position**: MIKE.
- **Alignment**: Same as 30 front.
- **Key**: Guard and backfield triangle.
- **Assignment**: Back and ball key and responsibilities. **On pass**—first back your side, man to man on all two-back formations. **One back**—coordinate with TED on #3 and #4.

- **Position**: WILL.
- **Alignment**: Backer support, on the line of scrimmage.
- **Key**: Offensive tackle, running lane, and backfield triangle.
- **Assignment**: WOD is regular. (STR and WES are other possible calls.)

- **Position**: S/END.
- **Alignment**: Same as 30 front.
- **Key**: Tackle.
- **Assignment**: Two gap. **On pass**—SOD, use inside move and break pocket. (SED and INDIAN are other possible calls.)

- **Position:** NOSE TACKLE.
- **Alignment:** Same as 30 front.
- **Key:** Center and both guards.
- **Assignment:** Two gap. **On pass**—take either gap and break pocket.

- **Position:** W/END.
- **Alignment:** Same as 30 front.
- **Key:** Tackle.
- **Assignment:** Two gap. **On pass**—WOD, use inside move and break pocket. (WES and STR are other possible calls.)

- **Position:** S/CORNER.
- **Alignment:** Head-on "Z."
- **Key:** Safety support, "Z."
- **Assignment:** Safety support. **On pass**—#1 man to man.

- **Position:** S/SAFETY.
- **Alignment:** By call, safety or backer support.
- **Key:** Tight end, running lane, and backfield triangle.
- **Assignment: Safety support. On pass**—#2 man to man.

- **Position:** W/SAFETY.
- **Alignment:** Initial position by plan, move to middle of field, ten yards deep.
- **Key:** QB and backfield triangle.
- **Assignment:** Safety support. **On pass**—deep middle, play from deep to short. You are the center fielder.

- **Position:** W/CORNER.
- **Alignment:** Head-on X."
- **Key:** Backer support, X."
- **Assignment:** Backer support. **On pass**—#5 man to man.

55 Combo Calls Strongside

SED is a change in assignment between SAM and S/END. SAM comes inside the END through the B GAP and breaks the pocket. S/END steps outside and drives upfield to contain. Safety support.

   INDIAN is a change in assignment for both SAM and S/END. SAM drives inside through the C GAP and contains the QB. Safety support. S/END drives through the B GAP and breaks the pocket.

Weakside Calls

WES is a change in assignment between WILL and W/END. WILL comes inside the END through the B GAP and breaks the pocket. W/END steps outside and drives upfield to contain.

STR (straight) is a change in assignment with WILL and W/END. WILL on the line of scrimmage drives through the butt of the offensive tackle to ensure the B GAP and breaks the pocket. W/END steps around WILL and drives upfield to contain. **CP:** WES is probably better in a pass situation. STR is good versus the pass or run.

B. 54 Combo Blitz

This is the same coverage as 55 for the secondary. MIKE and TED are the designated blitzers, and SAM and WILL have coverage. The 54 is a better pass-only blitz because SAM and WILL must vary their alignment versus various formations to carry out their coverage responsibility. The 55 is a good call versus the run or pass.

The normal blitz calls for 54 are TIC and MIC. However, it has been my experience that this does not present the offense with a pickup problem. A stunt pattern that has been most effective for me in this case is **DOUBLE TAC away from the TE. DOUBLE MOE** is **toward the TE.** Other combinations may be used with TED and MIKE.

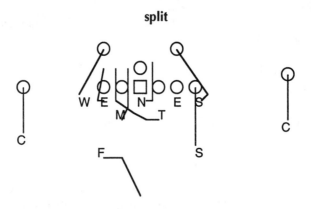

Double Tac (Away from the TE)

- **Position:** SAM.
- **Alignment:** By support pattern (backer, safety). Formation and coverage responsibility for SAM will determine support call.

- **Key**: TE, running lane, and backfield triangle.
- **Assignment**: Support pattern. **On pass**—first back your side man to man on all two-back formations. **One back**—coordinate with WILL on #3 and #4.

- **Position**: TED.
- **Alignment**: Same as 30 front.
- **Key**: Guard and backfield triangle.
- **Assignment**: By blitz call. **On pass**—**double TAC**, move to position behind NOSE and drive around MIKE through B GAP, break pocket.

- **Position**: MIKE.
- **Alignment**: Same as 30 front.
- **Key**: Guard and backfield triangle.
- **Assignment**: By blitz called. **On pass**—**double TAC**, drive through weakside A GAP, penetrate, break pocket. **CP: Double MOE** may be called. Both TED and MIKE will work together on strongside. TED will penetrate strongside A GAP, and MIKE will drive around TED through B GAP.

- **Position**: WILL.
- **Alignment**: By support pattern (backer).
- **Key**: Running lane and backfield triangle.
- **Assignment**: Support pattern. **On pass**—first back your side man to man on all two-back formations. **One back**—coordinate with SAM on #3 and #4.

- **Position**: S/END.
- **Alignment**: Same as 30 front.
- **Key**: Tackle.
- **Assignment**: Two gap. **On pass**—rush passer, contain.

- **Position**: NOSE TACKLE.
- **Alignment**: Same as 30 front.
- **Key**: Center and both guards.
- **Assignment**: Two gap. **On pass**—take gap away from call and break pocket. **Double TAC** take strongside A GAP. **CP:** Double MOE take weakside A GAP.

- **Position**: W/END.
- **Alignment**: Same as 30 front.
- **Key**: Tackle.
- **Assignment**: Two gap. **On pass**—rush passer, contain.

- **Position**: S/CORNER.
- **Alignment**: Head on "Z."
- **Key**: By support call (backer, safety), "Z."
- **Assignment**: Support pattern. **On pass**—#1 man to man.

- **Position**: S/SAFETY.
- **Alignment**: By call, safety or backer support.
- **Key**: Tight end, running lane, backfield triangle.
- **Assignment**: Support pattern. **On pass**—#2 man to man.

- **Position**: W/SAFETY.
- **Alignment**: Initial position by plan, move to middle of field, ten yards deep.
- **Key**: QB and backfield triangle.
- **Assignment**: By support pattern. **On pass**—deep middle, play from deep to short. You are the center fielder.

- **Position**: W/CORNER.
- **Alignment**: Backer support, head-on "X."
- **Key**: By support call (backer, safety), "X."
- **Assignment**: Backer support. **On pass**—#5 man to man.

C. 97 Trio Blitz

This is a blitz by SAM and TED strongside. Again, the combinations are the stunt patterns which create a problem for the offensive pickup. The one shown, INDIAN TOE, has proven to be effective.

SPLIT

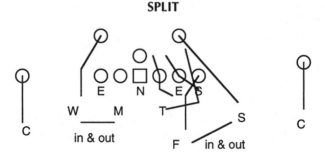

- **Position**: SAM.
- **Alignment**: Head-on the TE.
- **Key**: Tight end, C GAP, running lane.
- **Assignment**: Drive through butt of offensive tackle, penetrate C GAP. **On pass**—continue inside, break pocket.

- **Position**: TED.
- **Alignment**: Same as 30 front.
- **Key**: C GAP, offensive tackle, tight end, running lane.
- **Assignment**: Move to the outside, drive around SAM and upfield, D GAP. **On pass**—rush passer, contain.

- **Position**: MIKE.
- **Alignment**: Same as 30 front.
- **Key**: Guard and backfield triangle.
- **Assignment**: Back and ball key and responsibility. **On pass**—in and out with WILL on #4 on all two-back formations. **One back**—deuce coverage, coordinate with WILL on #3. **CP**: MIKE man to man on #3, WILL drop for depth, SEE receivers by plan. TRIO coverage, in and out on #4.

- **Position**: WILL.
- **Alignment**: Giant or crackback, vary position by plan.
- **Key**: Backer support, offensive tackle, running lane, backfield triangle.
- **Assignment**: Backer support. **On pass**—in and out with MIKE on #4 on all two-back formations. **One back**—deuce coverage, coordinate with MIKE on #3. **CP**: MIKE man to man on #3, WILL drop for depth, SEE receivers by plan. TRIO coverage, in and out on #4.

- **Position**: S/END.
- **Alignment**: Same as 30 front.
- **Key**: Tackle and B GAP.
- **Assignment**: Drive through butt of offensive guard, penetrate B GAP. **On pass**—continue inside, break pocket.

- **Position**: NOSE TACKLE.
- **Alignment**: Same as 30 front.
- **Key**: Center and both guards.
- **Assignment**: Two gap. **On pass**—take gap away from call and break pocket.

- **Position**: W/END.
- **Alignment**: Same as 30 front.
- **Key**: Tackle
- **Assignment**: Two gap. **On pass**—rush passer, contain.

- **Position**: S/CORNER.
- **Alignment**: Head-on "Z," five yards deep, move to inside technique (trio coverage).
- **Key**: By support call (backer, safety), "Z."
- **Assignment**: Support pattern. **On pass**—#1 man to man, inside technique.

- **Position**: S/SAFETY.
- **Alignment**: By call, safety or backer support.
- **Key**: Tight end, running lane, backfield triangle.
- **Assignment**: Support pattern. **On pass**—trio coverage, in and out with W/SAFETY on #2 and #3 on all two-back formations. **One back**—coordinate with W/SAFETY by formation, Deuce coverage on #2 and #4. **CP**: Trio coverage, in and out on #2 and #3.

- **Position**: W/SAFETY.
- **Alignment**: Initial position by pian. Trio coverage—move to strongside in position to cover in and out with S/SAFETY. Deuce coverage—move to weakside in position to cover #4.
- **Key**: QB and backfield triangle.
- **Assignment**: By support pattern. **On pass**—trio coverage, in and out with S/SAFETY on #2 and #3 on all two-back formations. **One back**—coordinate with S/SAFETY. Deuce coverage on #2 and #4. **CP**: Trio coverage, in and out on #2 and #3.

- **Position**: W/CORNER.
- **Alignment**: Head-on "X." Move to inside technique (trio coverage).
- **Key**: Backer support, "X."
- **Assignment**: Backer support. **On pass**—#5 man to man, inside technique.

D. 86 Deuce Blitz

This is a blitz by MIKE and WILL weakside. Again, the combinations are the stunt patterns which create a problem for the offensive pickup. The one shown, **MIC-END WOD**, has proven to be be effective.

SPLIT

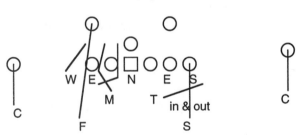

- **Position**: SAM.
- **Alignment**: Backer support.
- **Key**: Tight end, running lane, and backfield triangle.

- **Assignment**: Support pattern. **On pass**—in and out with TED on #3 on all two-back formations. **One back**—trio coverage, coordinate with TED on #4. **CP**: TED man to man on #4, SAM drop for depth, SEE receivers by plan. Deuce coverage, in and out on #3.

- **Position**: TED.
- **Alignment**: Same as 30 front.
- **Key**: Guard and backfield triangle.
- **Assignment**: Back and ball key and responsibility. **On pass**—in and out with SAM on #3 on all two-back formations. **One back**—trio coverage, coordinate with SAM on #4. **CP**: TED man to man on #4, SAM drop for depth, SEE receivers by plan. Deuce coverage, in and out on #3.

- **Position**: MIKE.
- **Alignment**: Same as 30 front.
- **Key**: Guard and backfield triangle.
- **Assignment**: Move to LOS, SEE ball, on snap penetrate weakside B GAP. **On pass**—rush passer, break pocket.

- **Position**: WILL.
- **Alignment**: Crackback, giant, vary alignment by plan.
- **Key**: Backer support, offensive tackle, running lane, and backfield triangle.
- **Assignment**: Move to the LOS, SEE the ball. **On pass**—rush passer, contain.

- **Position**: S/END.
- **Alignment**: Same as 30 front.
- **Key**: Offensive tackle.
- **Assignment**: Two gap. **On pass**—rush passer, contain.

- **Position**: NOSE TACKLE.
- **Alignment**: Same as 30 front.
- **Key**: Center and strongside A gap.
- **Assignment**: Two gap. Take gap away from call. **On pass**—rush passer, break pocket.

- **Position**: W/END.
- **Alignment**: Same as 30 front.
- **Key**: Offensive tackle and by call. MIC-END, weakside A GAP.
- **Assignment**: SEE ball, on snap, two-gap charge, step around MIKE and penetrate A GAP. **On pass**—rush passer, break pocket.

- **Position**: S/CORNER.
- **Alignment**: Head-on "Z," five yards deep, move to inside technique (deuce coverage).
- **Key**: By support call (backer, safety), "Z."
- **Assignment**: Support pattern. **On pass**—#1 man to man, inside technique.

- **Position**: S/SAFETY.
- **Alignment**: By call, backer or safety support.
- **Key**: Tight end, running lane, backfield triangle.
- **Assignment**: Support pattern. **On pass**—deuce coverage on #2 on all two-back formations. **One back**—coordinate by formation with W/SAFETY, deuce coverage on #2 and #4. **CP**: Trio coverage, in and out on #2 and #3.

- **Position**: W/SAFETY.
- **Alignment**: Initial position by plan. Deuce coverage—move to weakside in position to cover #4. Trio coverage—move to strongside in position to cover in and out with S/SAFETY on #2 and #3.
- **Key**: QB and backfield triangle.
- **Assignment**: By support pattern. **On pass**—deuce coverage, cover #4 on all two-back formations. **One back**—coordinate by formation with S/SAFETY, deuce coverage on #2 and #4. **CP**: Trio coverage, in and out on #2 and #3 with S/S.

- **Position**: W/CORNER.
- **Alignment**: Head-on "X," five yards deep, move to inside technique (deuce coverage).
- **Key**: By support call (backer, safety), "X."
- **Assignment**: Support pattern. **On pass**—#5 man to man, inside technique.

E. 57 S/Safety Trio Blitz

As the term indicates, we try to keep it simple and use the terms we learned in the beginning (#5 = blitz, #7 = TED, and the S/SAFETY addition calls for S/SAFETY and TED to blitz). SAM has coverage, and the STRONG SAFETY becomes the designated blitzer with TED. This blitz ties in with the backer support position for the S/SAFETY. He can move up and back from this position to disguise when called to blitz.

SPLIT

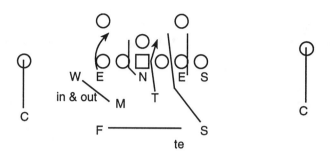

- **Position:** SAM.
- **Alignment:** Same as 30 front.
- **Key:** Tight end and near back.
- **Assignment:** Backer support pattern. **On pass**—#3 man to man on all two-back formations. **One back**—change to 57 combo.

- **Position:** TED.
- **Alignment:** Same as 30 front.
- **Key:** Strongside A GAP, guard and center.
- **Assignment:** Move to head-on guard, SEE the ball, on snap penetrate the A GAP. **On pass**—rush passer, break pocket.

- **Position:** MIKE.
- **Alignment:** Same as 30 front.
- **Key:** Guard and backfield triangle.
- **Assignment:** Back and ball key and responsibility. **On pass**—in and out with WILL on #4 on all two-back formations. **One back**—change to 57 combo.

- **Position:** WILL.
- **Alignment:** Giant or crackback, vary position by plan.
- **Key:** Backer support, offensive tackle, running lane, backfield triangle.
- **Assignment:** Backer support. **On pass**—in and out with MIKE on #4 on all two-back formations. **One back**—change to 57 combo.

- **Position:** S/END.
- **Alignment:** Same as 30 front, except align more head-up to outside.
- **Key:** Tackle.
- **Assignment:** C GAP. **On pass**—rush passer, contain.

- **Position:** NOSE TACKLE.
- **Alignment:** Same as 30 front.
- **Key:** Center and weakside A GAP.
- **Assignment:** Weakside A gap. **On pass**—penetrate A gap, rush passer, break pocket.

- **Position:** W/END.
- **Alignment:** Same as 30 front.
- **Key:** Tackle.
- **Assignment:** Two gap. **On pass**—rush passer, contain.

- **Position:** S/CORNER.
- **Alignment:** Head-on "Z."
- **Key:** Backer support, "Z."
- **Assignment:** Backer support. **On pass**—move to inside technique, #1 man to man.

- **Position:** S/SAFETY.
- **Alignment:** Head-on the tight end, five to seven yards deep.
- **Key:** Tight end, strongside B GAP.
- **Assignment:** Time your movement, SEE the ball, drive through B GAP. **On pass**—penetrate, rush passer, break pocket. **One back**—change to 57 combo.

- **Position:** W/SAFETY.
- **Alignment:** Initial position by plan, move to strongside in position to cover tight end man to man.
- **Key:** Tight end, QB, and backfield triangle.
- **Assignment:** Backer support. **On pass**—TRIO coverage, #2 man to man on all two-back formations. **One back**—change to 57 combo.

- **Position:** W/CORNER.
- **Alignment:** Head-on "X."
- **Key:** Backer support, "X."
- **Assignment:** Backer support. **On pass**—move to inside technique, #5 man to man.

F. 59 S/Safety Trio Blitz

This is basically the same as 57 S/SAFETY, except it involves SAM and the S/SAFETY. TED has coverage, and SAM and the S/SAFETY are the designated blitzers. The blitz with the strong safety outside ties in extremely well with safety support. Here, the S/SAFETY may move up and back to disguise his alignment when he is called to blitz. The alignment problem exists with the W/SAFETY assignment. He must be in position to cover the TE on the snap.

SPLIT

- ■ **Position**: SAM.
- ■ **Alignment**: Same as 30 front.
- ■ **Key**: Tight end and C GAP.
- ■ **Assignment**: Safety support pattern, drive through C gap off the butt of the offensive tackle. **On pass**—penetrate, break pocket. **One back**—change to 59 combo.

- ■ **Position**: TED.
- ■ **Alignment**: Same as 30 front.
- ■ **Key**: Guard and backfield triangle.
- ■ **Assignment**: Back and ball key and responsibility. **On pass**—#3 man to man on all two-back formations. **One back**—change to 59 combo.

- ■ **Position**: MIKE.
- ■ **Alignment**: Same as 30 front.
- ■ **Key**: Guard and backfield triangle.
- ■ **Assignment**: Back and ball key and responsibility. **On pass**—in and out with WILL on #4 on all two-back formations. **One back**—change to 59 combo.

- ■ **Position**: WILL.
- ■ **Alignment**: Giant or crackback, vary position by plan.
- ■ **Key**: Backer support, offensive tackle, running lane, backfield triangle.
- ■ **Assignment**: Backer support. **On pass**—in and out with MIKE on #4 on all two-back formations. **One back**—change to 59 combo.

- ■ **Position**: S/END.
- ■ **Alignment**: Same as 30 front.
- ■ **Key**: Tackle and B GAP.

- **Assignment**: Drive through B GAP off the butt of the offensive tackle. **On pass**—penetrate, break pocket.

- **Position**: NOSE TACKLE.
- **Alignment**: Same as 30 front.
- **Key**: Center and weakside A GAP.
- **Assignment**: Weakside A gap. **On pass**—penetrate A gap, rush passer, break pocket.

- **Position**: W/END.
- **Alignment**: Same as 30 front.
- **Key**: Tackle.
- **Assignment**: Two gap. **On pass**—rush passer, contain.

- **Position**: S/CORNER.
- **Alignment**: Head-on "Z."
- **Key**: Backer support, "Z."
- **Assignment**: Backer support. **On pass**—move to inside technique, #1 man to man.

- **Position**: S/SAFETY.
- **Alignment**: Head-on the tight end, five to seven yards deep.
- **Key**: Tight end, strongside D GAP, running lane.
- **Assignment**: Time your movement, SEE the ball, drive through D GAP. **On pass**—rush passer, contain. **One back**—change to 59 combo.

- **Position**: W/SAFETY.
- **Alignment**: Initial position by plan, move to strongside in position to cover tight end man to man.
- **Key**: Tight end, QB, and backfield triangle.
- **Assignment**: Safety support. **On pass**—TRIO coverage, #2 man to man on all two-back formations. **One back**—change to 59 combo.

- **Position**: W/CORNER.
- **Alignment**: Head-on "X."
- **Key**: Backer support, "X."
- **Assignment**: Backer support. **On pass**—move to inside technique #5 man to man.

The two blitzes just described are only good versus a two-back offense. This is basically true on any blitz that involves the S/SAFETY or W/SAFETY. To be fundamentally sound, **57 S/SAFETY** blitz would revert to **57 combo** blitz and **59 S/SAFETY** blitz would revert to **59 combo** blitz. Both of these were discussed earlier.

57 S/SAFETY blitz adjustment versus the one-back formation reverts to **57 combo.**

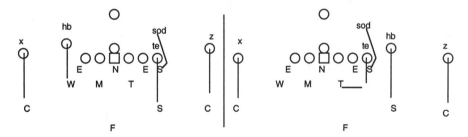

The drawing on the left above shows **57 combo** versus the double formation. On the right is **57 combo** versus the flood formation. Both the **TIC/NOSE** game and the **TIC/END** game are shown. Either game is better than the TIC game.

In the drawing on the left, SAM and MIKE will have the remaining back to the side he blocks or releases. When the back goes away, the free linebacker will get depth in the middle of the field and look for shallow crossing patterns. In the drawing on the right, MIKE and WILL coordinate their coverage on the back in the same manner. SAM has the TE.

59 S/SAFETY blitz adjustment versus the one-back formation reverts to **59 combo.**

The drawing on the left above shows **59 combo** versus the double formation. On the right is **59 combo** versus the flood formation. The SOD game is the best game in all situations. Other possibilities may be used to fit the personnel, but I favor the **SOD** game.

In the drawing on the left, TED and MIKE will have the remaining back to the side he blocks or releases. When the back goes away, the free linebacker will get depth in the middle of the field and look for shallow crossing patterns. In the drawing on the right, MIKE and WILL coordinate their coverage on the back in the same manner. TED has the TE.

I do not like to change a blitz because of the formation, but there are many formation problems when you use a safety blitz versus regular personnel . Because of this, I have found that when a change is necessary, it is best to keep the change as simple as possible. The changes I have used are shown in the above examples.

Any of the calls we have discussed and the stunts may be called from either the four-man or three-man front. I have tried to provide a mixture of both. It is important to realize that the two fronts and their stunts are interchangeable. OVER and 30 with SAM committed (39) are the same fronts. Also, UNDER and 30 with WILL committed (38) are the same fronts. Let's review the similarity in the two 30 and 40 concepts.

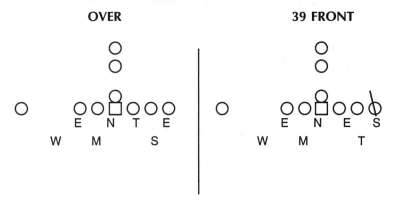

OVER is on the left. **39** is on the right with the SAM committed. The RE is aligned on the offensive guard in the same manner as the OVER TACKLE on the left. The MIKE is aligned away from the TE, and TED is on the side of the TE.

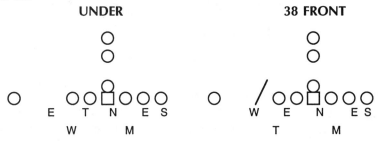

UNDER is on the left. **38** is on the right with the WILL committed. The LE is aligned on the offensive guard in the same manner as the UNDER TACKLE on the left. Also, TED and MIKE have been reversed on the right. This is not necessary, but TED is usually a better cover LB than MIKE. MIKE may take alignment away from the TE if the staff is pleased with his coverage ability.

HALFTIME

Media Relations

Midway through my career, I ran across the *Pocket Guide to Media Success*. Looking back, I wish it had been my good fortune to have found this information during my school years, while attending a clinic, or even while in a media conference. It would have been nice to have had it early in my career. As coaches, we have to deal with the media, in some cases daily. We need to keep certain things in mind as we meet. The media have a responsibility to report the news. The coach has a responsibility to the team, to each individual, and to the school or organization he represents to do all he can to ensure that the news is reported accurately. The pocket guide has proved valuable to me. Looking it over before a meeting helps me tremendously. I share it with you as a reminder to help you to become better prepared as you meet your obligation in conference with the media.

*Pocket Guide to Media Success**

Be Yourself
Don't stiffen up. Relax and share your enjoyment in the sport. Be human.

20 Second Rule
Make your point in 20 seconds or less. Elaborate if there is time, interest or need.

---

* Copyright 1991 Sports Media Challenge, 2700 Coltsgate Road, Suite 203, Charlotte, NC 28211. Reproduced with permission.

Be Precise
Avoid generalities. Use specific examples that clarify and make people care about your view.

Don't Be Baited
Remain calm at all costs.

Don't Use Jargon
Use words that the general public can understand. It builds audiences and fans in the stands.

Don't Forget: You're Always On
If you can see a microphone, camera or reporter's notebook, assume your words and actions are being recorded.

What It Takes to Be No. 1— You've Got to Pay the Price

by Vince Lombardi

Winning is not a sometime thing; it's an all-the-time thing. You don't win once in a while, you don't do things right once in a while, you do them right all the time. Winning is a habit. Unfortunately, so is losing.

There is no room for second place. There is only one place in my game and that is first place. I have finished second twice in my time at Green Bay and I don't ever want to finish second again. There is a second place bowl game, but it is a game for losers played by losers. It is and always has been an American zeal to be first in anything we do and to win and to win and to win.

Every time a football player goes out to ply his trade he's got to play from the ground up—from the soles of his feet right up to his head. Every inch of him has to play. Some guys play with their heads. That's O.K. You've got to be smart to be No. 1 in any business. But more important, you've got to play with your heart—with every fiber of your body. If you're lucky enough to find a guy with a lot of head and a lot of heart, he's never going to come off the field second.

Running a football team is no different from running any other kind of organization—an army, a political party, a business. The principles are the same. The object is to win—to beat the other guy. Maybe that sounds hard or cruel. I don't think it is.

It's a reality of life that men are competitive and the most competitive games draw the most competitive men. That's why they're there—to compete. They know the rules and the objectives when they get in the game. The objective is to win—fairly, squarely, decently, by the rules—but to win.

And in truth, I've never known a man worth his salt who in the long run, deep down in his heart, didn't appreciate the grind, the discipline. There is something in good men that really yearns for, needs, discipline and the harsh reality of head-to-head combat.

I don't say these things because I believe in the "brute" nature of man or that men must be brutalized to be combative. I believe in God, and I believe in human decency. But I firmly believe that any man's finest hour—his greatest fulfillment to all he holds dear—is that moment when he has worked his heart out in a good cause and lies exhausted on the field of battle—victorious.

5

SHORT YARDAGE
AND GOAL LINE

Short yardage and goal line situations are similar to coverage, fronts, and blitzes in a sense. In order to be competitive and to be successful, you need a good mixture available in the defensive package. This does not mean that you use the entire package each week. However, it does mean, for example, that you have the capability of presenting both the even and odd look in both short yardage situations and at the goal line.

This can be accomplished either by using your best first and ten package or by providing a separate package. The separate package can include a little from both; select the best from first and ten, and add the more aggressive short yardage and goal line fronts. There comes a time in every game, and during every season, when you must stop the opponent to win. Both the coaches and the defense must be prepared to make the correct decision.

The correct decision not only means making the proper call, but also means executing the details of the call in the exact manner necessary to be successful. Both require study, preparation, and practice in order to carry out the assignment effectively. This chapter presents a separate package for short yardage and goal line defenses that have proved effective for me over a period of years. I would in no way try to include all of them in the defensive package for a given game or season. Those that best fit the personality of the coach and the team are the ones to consider as the basic package.

FRONTS AND COVERAGE

A. 40 Pinch

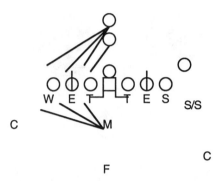

The above diagram shows **COVER 3, S/SAFETY SUPPORT** strongside and **CORNER SUPPORT** weakside. **CP:** By call, with the near back present weakside, the support would be backer.

- **Position: S/S END.**
- **Alignment:** Head-on the strongside offensive tackle.
- **Key:** Offensive tackle.
- **Assignment: Short yardage technique**—on the snap of the ball, charge through the offensive tackle into running lane. **On pass**—rush passer, contain the QB. **CP:** On OVER or UNDER call, if front is to you, your alignment and assignment will be slightly wider through the outside leg of the offensive tackle.

- **Position: S/S TACKLE.**
- **Alignment:** Head-on the strongside offensive guard.
- **Key:** Offensive guard and center.
- **Assignment: Short yardage technique**—on the snap of the ball, charge through the near shoulder of the center. Seal the strongside A gap. **On pass**—rush passer, break the pocket. **CP:** Be alert for the "slip block" (the center reaching to the side of the play to block you and the guard tries to release to your outside for the linebacker), penetrate.

- **Position: W/S TACKLE.**
- **Alignment:** Head-on the weakside offensive guard.
- **Key:** Offensive guard and center.
- **Assignment: Short yardage technique**—on the snap of the ball, charge through the near shoulder of the center. Seal the weakside A gap. **On pass**—rush passer, break the pocket. **CP:** Be alert for the "slip block" (see above for description), penetrate.

- **Position**: W/S END.
- **Alignment**: Head-on the weakside offensive tackle.
- **Key**: Offensive tackle.
- **Assignment**: **Short yardage technique**—on the snap of the ball, charge through the offensive tackle into running lane. **On pass**—rush passer, contain the QB. **CP**: On OVER or UNDER call, if front is to you, your alignment and assignment will be slightly wider through the outside leg of the offensive tackle.

- **Position**: SAM.
- **Alignment**: By support pattern (backer, safety, corner).
- **Key**: Tight end and support pattern.
- **Assignment**: Follow support pattern. **CP**: Your DE has a two-gap assignment, and you have reverse and bootleg responsibility.

- **Position**: MIKE.
- **Alignment**: Head-on the center.
- **Key**: See through the center to the backfield triangle.
- **Assignment**: Back and ball key and responsibility. B, C, and D gap in progression. **CP**: Move tackle to OVER or UNDER front by formation, backfield alignment, and game plan. A, B, C, and D gap in progression.

- **Position**: WILL.
- **Alignment**: By support pattern (backer, safety, corner).
- **Key**: Near end and support pattern.
- **Assignment**: Follow support pattern. **CP**: Your DE has a two-gap assignment, and you have reverse and bootleg responsibility.

B. 40 Over

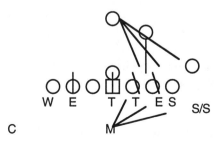

The above diagram shows OVER front, **COVER 3, S/SAFETY SUPPORT** strongside and **CORNER SUPPORT** weakside. **CP:** By call, with the near back present weakside, the support would be backer.

- **Position: S/S END.**
- **Alignment:** Head-on to outside of the strongside offensive tackle.
- **Key:** Offensive tackle and tight end.
- **Assignment: Short yardage technique**—on the snap of the ball, charge through the outside leg of the offensive tackle into running lane. **On pass**—rush passer, contain the QB.

- **Position: S/S TACKLE.**
- **Alignment:** Head-on to outside shoulder of the strongside offensive guard.
- **Key:** Offensive guard and tackle.
- **Assignment: Short yardage technique**—on the snap of the ball, charge through the outside leg of the offensive guard into the running land. **On pass**—rush passer, break the pocket.

- **Position: NOSE TACKLE.**
- **Alignment:** Head-on the center.
- **Key:** Center and both A gaps.
- **Assignment: Short yardage technique**—on the snap of the ball, charge through the center into the running lane. **On pass**—rush passer through the weakside A gap, break pocket.

- **Position: W/S END.**
- **Alignment:** Head-on the weakside offensive tackle.
- **Key:** Offensive tackle.
- **Assignment: Short yardage technique**—on the snap of the ball, charge through the offensive tackle into running lane. **On pass**—rush passer, contain the QB.

- **Position: SAM.**
- **Alignment:** By support pattern (backer, safety, corner).
- **Key:** Tight end and support pattern.
- **Assignment:** Follow support pattern.

- **Position: MIKE.**
- **Alignment: Strong formation**—head-on the center. **Weak formation**—head-on the weakside offensive guard.
- **Key:** See through the center or guard to the backfield triangle.

- **Assignment**: Back and ball key and responsibility. **Strongside formation**—A, B, C, and D gap in progression. **Weakside formation**—A, B, C, and D gap in progression.

- **Position**: **WILL**.
- **Alignment**: By support pattern (backer, safety, corner).
- **Key**: Near end and support pattern.
- **Assignment**: Follow support pattern. **CP**: Your DE has a two-gap assignment, and you have reverse and bootleg responsibility.

C. 40 Under

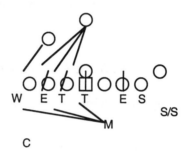

The diagram above shows UNDER front, **COVER 3, S/SAFETY SUPPORT** strongside and **BACKER SUPPORT** weakside. **CP**: By call, with NO near back present weakside, the support would be corner.

- **Position**: **W/S END**.
- **Alignment**: **Head-on to outside shoulder** of the weakside offensive tackle.
- **Key**: Offensive tackle.
- **Assignment**: **Short yardage technique**—on the snap of the ball, charge through the offensive tackle into running lane. **On pass**—rush passer, contain the QB.

- **Position**: **W/S TACKLE**.
- **Alignment**: **Head-on to outside shoulder** of the weakside offensive guard.
- **Key**: Offensive guard and tackle.
- **Assignment**: **Short yardage technique**—on the snap of the ball, charge through the outside leg of the offensive guard into running lane. **On pass**—rush passer, break the pocket.

- **Position: NOSE TACKLE.**
- **Alignment:** Head-on the center.
- **Key:** Center and both A gaps.
- **Assignment: Short yardage technique**—on the snap of the ball, charge through the center into running lane. **On pass**—rush passer through the weakside A gap, break pocket.

- **Position: S/S END.**
- **Alignment: Head-on** the strongside offensive tackle.
- **Key:** Offensive tackle.
- **Assignment: Short yardage technique**—on the snap of the ball, charge through the offensive tackle into running lane. **On pass**—rush passer, contain the QB.

- **Position: SAM.**
- **Alignment:** By support pattern (backer, safety, corner).
- **Key:** Tight end and support pattern.
- **Assignment:** Follow support pattern.

- **Position: MIKE.**
- **Alignment: All formations**—**head-on** the strongside offensive guard.
- **Key:** See through the guard to the backfield triangle.
- **Assignment:** Back and ball key and responsibility. **All formations**—A, B, C, and D gap in progression.

- **Position: WILL.**
- **Alignment:** By support pattern (backer, safety, corner).
- **Key:** Near end and support pattern.
- **Assignment:** Follow support pattern. Alignment and assignment by support pattern.

D. 40 Out

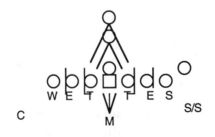

The diagram above shows **COVER 3, S/SAFETY SUPPORT** strongside and **CORNER SUPPORT** weakside. **CP**: By call, with the near back present weakside, the support would be backer.

- **Position**: **S/S END**.
- **Alignment**: Head-on the strongside offensive tackle.
- **Key**: Offensive tackle.
- **Assignment**: **Short yardage technique**—on the snap of the ball, charge through the outside leg of the offensive tackle into running lane. **On pass**—rush passer, contain the QB.

- **Position**: **S/S TACKLE**.
- **Alignment**: Head-on the strongside offensive guard.
- **Key**: Offensive guard.
- **Assignment**: **Short yardage technique**—on the snap of the ball, charge through the outside shoulder of the offensive guard. **On pass**—rush passer, break the pocket.

- **Position**: **W/S TACKLE**.
- **Alignment**: Head-on the weakside offensive guard.
- **Key**: Offensive guard.
- **Assignment**: **Short yardage technique**—on the snap of the ball, charge through the outside leg of the offensive guard. **On pass**—rush passer, break the pocket.

- **Position**: **W/S END**.
- **Alignment**: Head-on the weakside offensive tackle.
- **Key**: Offensive tackle.
- **Assignment**: **Short yardage technique**—on the snap of the ball, charge through the outside leg of the offensive tackle into running lane. **On pass**—rush passer, contain the QB.

- **Position**: **SAM**.
- **Alignment**: By support pattern (backer, safety, corner).
- **Key**: Tight end and support pattern.
- **Assignment**: Follow support pattern.

- **Position**: **MIKE**.
- **Alignment**: Head-on the center.
- **Key**: See through the center to the backfield triangle.
- **Assignment**: Back and ball key and responsibility. Both A gaps. N/T (no one there)—B, C, and D gap in progression.

- **Position**: WILL.
- **Alignment**: By support pattern (backer, safety, corner).
- **Key**: Near end and support pattern.
- **Assignment**: Follow support pattern.

E. 42 Rob/Lee

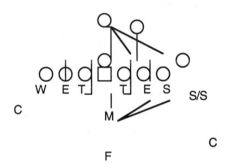

The above diagram is **ROB**, tackle's movement to the **RIGHT**. Coverage is **COVER 3, SAFETY SUPPORT** to the strongside and **CORNER SUPPORT** on the weakside. The ROB or LEE call is usually made first to the offset back, second to the strongside (side of two receivers) versus "I" formation, and third away from the premier running back versus "SPLIT" formation. A fourth consideration would be to handle a special alignment by game plan. The material in this section describes ROB. The LEE call to the strongside would be the same. LEE called to the weakside would be the reverse.

- **Position**: S/S END.
- **Alignment**: Head-on the strongside offensive tackle.
- **Key**: Offensive tackle and tight end.
- **Assignment**: **Short yardage technique**—on the snap of the ball, charge through the outside leg of the offensive tackle into running lane. **On pass**—rush passer, contain the QB.

- **Position**: S/S TACKLE.
- **Alignment**: Head-on the strongside offensive guard.
- **Key**: Offensive guard and tackle to the side of the call.
- **Assignment**: **Short yardage technique**—on the snap of the ball, charge through the outside leg of the offensive guard. **On pass**—rush passer, break the pocket.

- **Position:** W/S TACKLE.
- **Alignment:** Head-on the weakside offensive guard.
- **Key:** Offensive guard and center.
- **Assignment: Short yardage technique**—on the snap of the ball, charge through the near shoulder of the center. **On pass**—rush passer, break the pocket.

- **Position:** W/S END.
- **Alignment:** Head-on the weakside offensive tackle.
- **Key:** Offensive tackle.
- **Assignment: Short yardage technique**—on the snap of the ball, charge through the offensive tackle into running lane. **On pass**—rush passer, contain the QB.

- **Position:** SAM.
- **Alignment:** By support pattern (backer, safety, corner).
- **Key:** Tight end and support pattern.
- **Assignment:** Follow support pattern.

- **Position:** MIKE.
- **Alignment:** Head-on the center.
- **Key:** See through the center to the backfield triangle.
- **Assignment:** Back and ball key and responsibility. **Strongside** A, B, C, and D gap in progression. **Weakside** B, C, and D gap in progression.

- **Position:** WILL.
- **Alignment:** By support pattern (backer, safety, corner).
- **Key:** Near end and support pattern.
- **Assignment:** Follow support pattern. **CP:** Your DE has a two-gap assignment, and you have reverse and bootleg responsibility.

F. 60 Goal Line Blitz

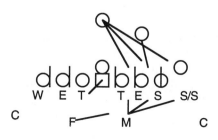

- **Position**: S/S END.
- **Alignment**: Head-up to inside shoulder of the offensive tackle.
- **Key**: Offensive tackle.
- **Assignment**: On snap of the ball, drive through the inside leg of the offensive tackle. Penetrate into the running lane. **On pass**—rush passer, break the pocket.

- **Position**: S/S TACKLE.
- **Alignment**: Head-up to inside shoulder of the offensive guard.
- **Key**: Offensive guard.
- **Assignment**: On snap of the ball, drive through the inside leg of the offensive guard. Penetrate into the running lane. Seal the middle (A GAP). **On pass**—rush passer, break the pocket.

- **Position**: W/S TACKLE.
- **Alignment**: Head-up to inside shoulder of the offensive guard.
- **Key**: Offensive guard.
- **Assignment**: By formation and call by MIKE. On snap of the ball, drive through the near shoulder of the center. Seal the middle (A gap). **On pass**—rush passer, break the pocket.

- **Position**: W/S END.
- **Alignment**: Head-up to inside shoulder of the offensive tackle.
- **Key**: Offensive tackle.
- **Assignment**: On snap of the ball, drive through the inside leg of the offensive tackle. Penetrate into the running lane. **On pass**—rush passer, break the pocket.

- **Position**: SAM.
- **Alignment**: Head-on the tight end.
- **Key**: On snap of the ball, drive through the tight end into running lane.
- **Assignment**: You are FREE, stay square, do not angle. **On pass**—rush passer, contain. **CP**: You have reverse and bootleg responsibility.

- **Position**: MIKE.
- **Alignment**: By formation and pass responsibility.
- **Key**: SEE through the offensive line to the backfield triangle.
- **Assignment**: Back and ball keys and responsibility. A, B, C, and D gap in progression. **On pass**—by formation. **Split and strong**—in and out with S/S on strong back and TE. **Weak and I**—strong back man to man. **Frank**—second back weakside. **CP**: If "Z" is close, in-and-out coverage

is with the S/C, because the S/S has the first receive across his face to the outside. **In the field**, it is best to take the strong back man to man rather than play in/out with the S/S. **CP**: On **FLOW** strongside—play the run and cover the second back.

- **Position: WILL.**
- **Alignment:** Head-up to inside shoulder of the near end.
- **Key:** On snap of ball, drive through the inside shoulder of the near end.
- **Assignment:** You are FREE, stay square, do not angle. **On pass**—rush passer, contain. **CP**: You have reverse and bootleg responsibility.

- **Position: STRONG CORNER.**
- **Alignment: By formation. "Z" is wide**—shade inside "Z," bump and run position. **"Z" is close**—safety support, position is deeper and a shade outside "Z."
- **Key:** Safety support. If **"Z" is wide**, SEE "Z." If **"Z" is close**, SEE "Z," TE, and backfield triangle.
- **Assignment:** Safety support. **On pass**—**by formation (weak, split, I, and strong). "Z" is wide**—"Z" man to man. **"Z" is close**—in and out with MIKE on "Z" and TE. **CP**: On **FLOW**, if "Z" is close, in and out with WEAK SAFETY, because the S/S has the first receive across his face to the outside.

- **Position: STRONG SAFETY.**
- **Alignment:** A shade outside of the tight end.
- **Key: Safety support**, strong back, tight end.
- **Assignment:** Safety support. **On pass**—by formation (DEUCE coverage). **Weak and I**—tight end man to man. **Split**—in and out on strong back and tight end with MIKE. **Strong** (TRIO coverage, MIKE and W/S change alignments)—in and out on strong back and tight end with WEAK SAFETY. **CP**: On **FLOW**, split, I, and strong—first receiver **to cross your face** outside. **CP: Frank action**—TE man to man.

- **Position: WEAK SAFETY.**
- **Alignment: By formation. Weak**—be in a position to support weakside. **Split and I**—be in position to go strongside on FLOW. **Strong**—TRIO alignment.
- **Key:** W/S support if "X" is wide. Corner support versus near. **By formation: Weak**—SEE weak back and near end. **Split and I**—SEE the backfield triangle, on FLOW see tight end and "Z" in progression. **Strong**—SEE the backfield triangle, on FLOW see tight end and "Z" in progression.

- **Assignment: On pass**—by formation. **Weak, split, and I**—in and out with WEAK CORNER on weak back and near end. **Strong** (TRIO coverage, MIKE and W/S change alignment)—in and out with STRONG SAFETY on first receiver inside of TE, SB. **CP:** On **FLOW**, if "Z" is close, in and out with STRONG CORNER.

- **Position: WEAK CORNER.**
- **Alignment: By formation**—W/S support. **"X" is wide**—a shade inside "X," bump and run position. Corner support **versus near**—a shade outside near.
- **Key: By formation.** W/S support if **"X" is wide**—SEE "X." Corner support **versus near end.**
- **Assignment:** W/S support or corner support. **On pass**—by formation. **"X" is wide**—man to man. **Versus near (weak, I, split)**—in and out with W/S on near and weak back. **Strong**—near man to man. On **FLOW**—near man to man.

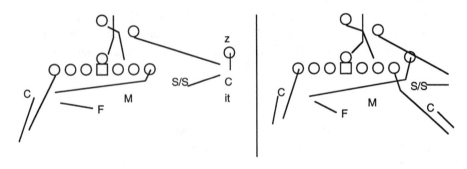

The two diagrams above show **FLOW** (both backs to the strongside) and the coverage pickups versus two formations. The diagram on the left is a STRONG formation with the "Z" in a normal alignment. S/C = the "Z" man to man. The S/S and F/S are in and out on the TE and SB. The **MIKE** plays the run and picks up the second back man to man. The **W/C** is man to man on the near end. **CP:** It is not necessary on a STRONG formation for the MIKE and W/SAFETY to change alignment. The **F/S can remain in the middle** of the formation and still be effective (in and out) with the S/SAFETY or S/CORNER. This leaves the MIKE in a better position to play the run. This is a staff decision based on the tendencies of the offense.

The diagram on the right is a STRONG formation with the "Z" in a close position. The S/C and F/S are in and out on the "Z" and TE. The S/S picks up the SB (first receiver outside). The **MIKE** plays the run and picks up the second back man to man. The **W/C** is man to man on the near end.

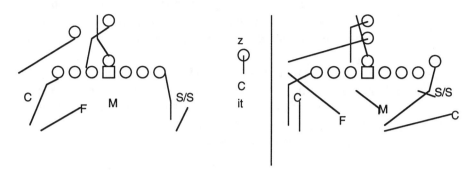

The two diagrams above show FRANK action (both backs weakside). The diagram on the left is a WEAK formation. The W/C and F/S are in and out on the near and weak back. The S/S has the tight end man to man. The S/C has the "Z" man to man. MIKE plays the run and picks up the second back man to man.

The diagram on the right is an "I" formation. The W/C is man to man on the near end. The F/S is man to man on the first back weak. The S/C has the close "Z," and the S/S has the TE man to man. MIKE plays the run and picks up the second back man to man.

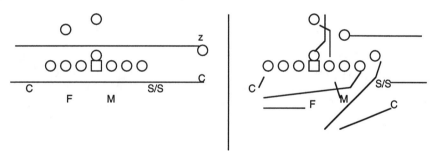

The two diagrams above show movement. The diagram on the left is ZOOM. The S/C goes across with the "Z." The W/C now has the S/S assignments. F/S and MIKE may stay in place or change alignments. Normally, it is better for them to change, because their assignments remain the same. The S/S now has the near end.

The diagram on the right is movement **to FLOOD**. The S/S picks up the SB. The F/S and the S/C are in and out on the TE and Z." MIKE plays the run and takes the second back man to man. The W/C has the near end man to man.

These additional diagrams are provided to help you to better understand the pickups on FLOW and the responsibilities on movement. I have found that the first day back after a game is a good time to review goal line and short yardage formations and backfield actions. There are many offensive possibilities in this area and situation. The defensive coordinator needs to spend as much time as possible on the proper alignment and adjustment to movement. It is something that can be walked through. Learning and reviewing the assignment is a mental drill. The first day back after a game is a good time to review; then pick out one more period during the week to recheck any problems that the next opponent may present. Proper execution in this area and in this situation will result in a win.

The next area we will discuss is the possibilities that exist with the **three-man-line** concept in short yardage and at the goal line. Basically, it begins with SAM and WILL committed, playing MAN or ZONE coverage. The same can also be accomplished with DEUCE coverage.

One advantage of the **three-man line** is that you always have two linebackers behind the line, with the additional possibility of the strong or weak safeties in close proximity. This is not an answer in itself, but it is an opportunity that must be studied within the total package.

G. 55 Cover 2

- ■ **Position**: S/S END.
- ■ **Alignment**: Head-on the offensive tackle.
- ■ **Key**: Offensive tackle.
- ■ **Assignment**: On the snap, drive through the offensive tackle into running lane. **On pass**—rush the passer, break the pocket.

- ■ **Position**: NOSE TACKLE.
- ■ **Alignment**: Head-on the center.
- ■ **Key**: Offensive center.
- ■ **Assignment**: On the snap, drive through the center into running lane. **On**

pass—rush the passer, break the pocket. **CP:** Take either gap, and stay in your lane.

- **Position:** W/S END.
- **Alignment:** Head-on the offensive tackle.
- **Key:** Offensive tackle.
- **Assignment:** On the snap, drive through the offensive tackle into running lane. **On pass**—rush the passer, break the pocket.

- **Position:** SAM.
- **Alignment:** Head-up on the tight end.
- **Key:** Tight end.
- **Assignment:** On the snap, drive through the tight end into running lane. **On pass**—rush the passer, contain. **CP:** Make the tight end release to the outside.

- **Position:** TED.
- **Alignment:** Two yards deep (off the feet of the lineman). Head-on to outside of the offensive guard.
- **Key:** SEE through the offensive guard to the backfield triangle.
- **Assignment:** Back and ball keys and responsibilities. **On pass**—by formation and backfield action. Short inside zone on the strongside.

- **Position:** MIKE.
- **Alignment:** Two yards deep (off the feet of the lineman). Head-on to outside of the offensive guard.
- **Key:** SEE through the offensive guard to the backfield triangle.
- **Assignment:** Back and ball keys and responsibilities. **On pass**—by formation and backfield action. Short inside zone on the weakside.

- **Position:** WILL.
- **Alignment:** Head-up on the near end.
- **Key:** Near end.
- **Assignment:** On the snap, drive through the near end into running lane. **On pass**—rush the passer, contain. **CP:** Make the near end release to the outside.

The **secondary** has the same responsibilities as discussed in Chapter 3 on coverage for **COVER 2**. **CP:** For better run support, refer to the diagram on the right above. The S/S and the S/C have exchanged alignment and assignment.

55 COVER 2 is a good change-up in the field in **short yardage** situations or at the goal line in the **five-yard-line area**.

H. 55 Deuce

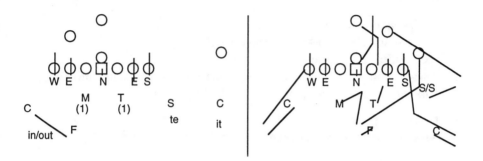

The **55 DEUCE** call, like 55 cover 2, is good as a mixture in any situation. 55 deuce gives a little tighter coverage and is probably thought of more in short yardage or at the goal line.

The diagram on the left above shows the assignments for the back-up pass. MIKE and TED have the two backs man to man. The W/C and the F/S are in and out on the near and weak backs. The S/S has the TE man to man, and the S/C has the "Z" man to man. The diagram on the right above shows TRIO coverage on the STRONG formation. **CP**: With the extra linebacker, MIKE can play the run and then help in the middle of the field for crossing receivers. TED will play the run and take the second back.

- **Position**: S/S END.
- **Alignment**: Head-on the offensive tackle.
- **Key**: Offensive tackle.
- **Assignment**: On the snap, drive through the offensive tackle into running lane. **On pass**—rush the passer, break the pocket.

- **Position**: NOSE TACKLE.
- **Alignment**: Head-on the center.
- **Key**: Offensive center.
- **Assignment**: On the snap, drive through the center into running lane. **On pass**—rush the passer, break the pocket. **CP**: Take either gap, stay in your lane.

- **Position**: W/S END.
- **Alignment**: Head-on the offensive tackle.
- **Key**: Offensive tackle.
- **Assignment**: On the snap, drive through the offensive tackle into running lane. **On pass**—rush the passer, break the pocket.

- **Position:** SAM.
- **Alignment:** Head-up on the tight end.
- **Key:** Tight end.
- **Assignment:** On the snap, drive through the tight end into running lane. **On pass**—rush the passer, contain. **CP:** Make the tight end release to the outside.

- **Position:** TED.
- **Alignment:** Two yards deep (off the feet of the lineman). Head-on to outside of the offensive guard.
- **Key:** SEE through the offensive guard to the backfield triangle.
- **Assignment:** Back and ball keys and responsibilities. **On pass**—SB man to man. On **FLOW**, play the run and cover the second back. **CP:** On flow, you are backed up by **MIKE**, be aggressive.

- **Position:** MIKE.
- **Alignment:** Two yards deep (off the feet of the lineman). Head-on to outside of the offensive guard.
- **Key:** SEE through the offensive guard to the backfield triangle.
- **Assignment:** Back and ball keys and responsibilities. **On pass**—WB man to man. On **FLOW**, play the run. N/T—drop to the middle. **CP:** Be alert for crossing routes.

- **Position:** WILL.
- **Alignment:** Head-up on the near end.
- **Key:** Near end.
- **Assignment:** On the snap, drive through the near end into running lane. **On pass**—rush the passer, contain. **CP:** Make the near end release to the outside.

- **Position:** STRONG CORNER.
- **Alignment: By formation. "Z" is wide**—a shade inside "Z," bump and run position. **"Z" is close**—safety support, position is deeper and a shade outside "Z."
- **Key:** Safety support. If **"Z" is wide**—SEE "Z." If **"Z" is close**—SEE "Z," TE, and backfield triangle.
- **Assignment:** Safety support. **On pass—by formation (weak, split, I, and strong). "Z" is wide**—"Z" man to man. **"Z" is close**—"Z" man to man. **CP:** On **FLOW**, if **"Z" is close**, in and out with WEAK SAFETY.

- **Position:** STRONG SAFETY.
- **Alignment:** A shade outside of the tight end.

- **Key: Safety support,** strong back, tight end.
- **Assignment:** Safety support. **On pass—by formation** (DEUCE coverage). **Weak and I**—tight end man to man. **Split**—in and out on strong back and tight end with MIKE. **Strong** (TRIO coverage)—in and out on strong back and tight end with WEAK SAFETY. **CP:** On **FLOW,** split, I, and strong—first receiver outside. Weak—TE man to man.

- **Position:** WEAK SAFETY.
- **Alignment: By formation. Weak**—be in a position to support weakside. **Split and I**—be in position to go strongside on FLOW. **Strong**—TRIO alignment.
- **Key:** W/S support if "X" is wide. Corner support versus near. **By formation: Weak**—SEE weak back and near end. **Split and I**—SEE the backfield triangle, on FLOW see tight end and "Z" in progression. **Strong**—SEE the backfield triangle, on FLOW see tight end and "Z" in progression.
- **Assignment: On pass—by formation. Weak, split, and I**—in and out with WEAK CORNER on weak back and near end. **Strong** (TRIO coverage)—in and out with STRONG SAFETY on first receiver inside of TE, SB. **CP:** On **FLOW,** if "Z" is close, in and out with STRONG CORNER.

- **Position:** WEAK CORNER.
- **Alignment: By formation.** W/S support, **"X" is wide**—a shade inside "X," bump and run position. Corner support, **versus near**—a shade outside near.
- **Key: By formation.** W/S support, **"X" is wide**—SEE "X." Corner support **versus near end.**
- **Assignment:** W/S support or corner support. **On pass—by formation. "X" is wide**— man to man. **Versus near, weak, I, and split**—in and out with W/S on near and weak back. **Strong**—near man to man. **On FLOW**—near man to man.

Deuce (Trio) Coverage versus Back-Up Pass: Secondary Alignment versus Wide "Z"

To further clarify the assignments, let's take a look at the next two diagrams. The diagram on the left below is the **back-up pass** showing **DEUCE** coverage versus **SPLIT** formation. If it were a **WEAK** formation, **MIKE** would have the **strong back** man to man and the **STRONG SAFETY** would have the **TE** man to man. The **I formation** can be played with either DEUCE or TRIO coverage.

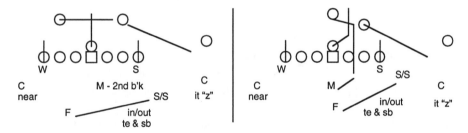

The diagram on the right above shows **TRIO** coverage versus a **STRONG** formation. Here, the F/S is moved strongside to be in and out with the S/S on the **TE** and **strong back**. MIKE is moved weakside and has the **weak back** man to man. The **WEAK CORNER** has **near** man to man. In both diagrams, the **STRONG CORNER** has the "Z" man to man with an inside technique.

The diagrams below show **DEUCE (TRIO) COVERAGE versus flow pass**. The drawing on the left shows the movement on deuce versus the backfield action. The diagram on the right shows TRIO alignment versus the STRONG formation.

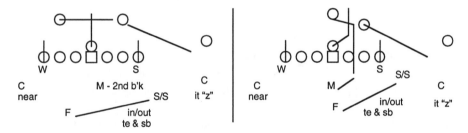

These two diagrams show **FLOW**. On the left is FLOW from **SPLIT** formation. On the right is FLOW from **STRONG** formation. In both cases, the F/S and S/S are in and out on the **TE** and **SB**, and **MIKE** has the second back. The **WEAK CORNER** has the **near** and the **STRONG CORNER** has "Z" man to man.

Deuce (Trio) Coverage: Secondary Alignment versus Close "Z" Formation

The next two diagrams show **SPLIT** and **STRONG** formations versus a **close** "Z." Assignments remain the same for all. The **STRONG CORNER** has the "Z." The diagram on the left below is **DEUCE** coverage, and **TRIO** is shown on the right.

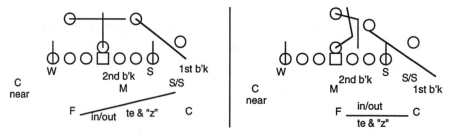

The two diagrams below show **FLOW** with **"Z" in close**. Now the **S/S** has the **first back** (first receiver shallow outside), and the **F/S** and the **CORNER** are in and out on the **TE** and **"Z."** **MIKE** continues to play the **run first**; then he takes the **second back**. The **WEAK CORNER** has the **near**.

These diagrams are provided to enable you to better understand **DEUCE** and **TRIO** coverage. The drawings, plus work on the field, will help the player to execute properly in critical short yardage and goal line situations.

Before leaving this area, let's discuss two more points. First, **55 DEUCE** is played the same way, except you have **one extra linebacker**. Because of this, the extra linebacker may be used in several ways. He can be **free**, and help in the middle, as suggested in the diagram on page 252, or on run action strongside, the TED, as an example, can **run through**, forcing the QB, and the second linebacker (MIKE) may take the coverage.

The second point is that the **"I" formation** can be played as either a **WEAK** or **STRONG** formation. This usually depends on what the opponent does out of the "I." Most of the time, it is a STRONG running and passing formation, but this may differ from team to team. "I" should remain flexible and be adjusted from game to game.

I. 64 Goal Line Blitz

This is an inside call, where the two tackles take the A GAPS. The F/S and MIKE blitz in the B GAPS. On an outside call, the two tackles take the B GAPS, and the F/S and MIKE blitz in the A GAPS.

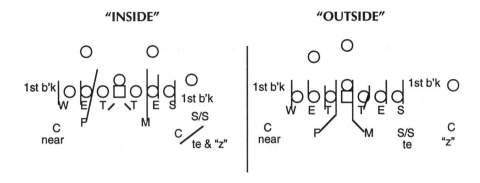

- **Position**: S/S END.
- **Alignment**: Head-on the offensive tackle.
- **Key**: Offensive tackle, C gap.
- **Assignment**: On the snap of the ball, drive for inside leg of tight end. Drive upfield, penetrate. **On pass**—rush passer; if back releases on your side, contain the QB. **CP**: If second back releases to your side, cover man to man.

- **Position**: S/S TACKLE.
- **Alignment**: Head-on the offensive guard.
- **Key**: Offensive guard, A gap.
- **Assignment**: Seal the inside A gaps with the W/S tackle (you have the QB sneak). **On pass**—rush passer, break pocket. **CP**: On **"outside call,"** drive through inside leg of offensive tackle.

- **Position**: W/S TACKLE.
- **Alignment**: Head-on the offensive guard.
- **Key**: Offensive guard, A gap.
- **Assignment**: Seal the inside A gaps with the S/S tackle (you have the QB sneak). **On pass**—rush passer, break pocket. **CP**: On **"outside call,"** drive through inside leg of offensive tackle.

- **Position**: W/S END.
- **Alignment**: Head-on the offensive tackle.
- **Key**: Offensive tackle, C gap.
- **Assignment**: On the snap of the ball, drive for inside leg of near end. Drive upfield, penetrate. **On pass**—rush passer; if back releases on your side, contain the QB. **CP**: If second back releases to your side, cover man to man.

- **Position**: SAM.
- **Alignment**: Move late to backer support position.
- **Key**: Backer support.
- **Assignment**: Backer support. **On pass**—first back to your side man to man.

- **Position**: MIKE.
- **Alignment**: By formation (SPLIT, WEAK, "I," STRONG).
- **Key**: B-gap strongside.
- **Assignment**: Drive through B gap and locate ball. **On pass**—rush passer, break pocket. **CP**: On **"outside call,"** drive through A gap.

- **Position**: WILL.
- **Alignment**: Move late to backer support position.
- **Key**: Backer support.
- **Assignment**: Backer support. **On pass**—first back to your side man to man.

- **Position**: STRONG CORNER.
- **Alignment**: Bump and run position, a shade inside of "Z."
- **Key**: SEE "Z."
- **Assignment**: Backer support. **On pass**—"Z" man to man. **CP**: If "Z" and TE are close, call in/out with STRONG SAFETY.

- **Position**: S/SAFETY.
- **Alignment**: Move late to backer support position.
- **Key**: Tight end and backfield triangle.
- **Assignment**: Backer support. **On pass**—tight end man to man. **CP**: If "Z" and TE are close, call in/out with STRONG CORNER.

- **Position**: WEAK SAFETY.
- **Alignment**: Show DEUCE or TRIO coverage, alignment by formation.
- **Key**: B-gap weakside.
- **Assignment**: Drive through B gap and locate ball. **On pass**—rush passer, break pocket. **CP**: On **"outside call,"** drive through A gap.

- **Position**: WEAK CORNER.
- **Alignment**: Move late to backer support position.
- **Key**: Near end and backfield triangle.
- **Assignment**: Backer support. **On pass**—near end man to man.

J. 70 Goal Line Blitz

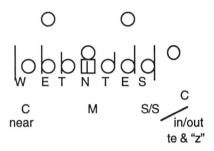

70 is a **substituted defense**. An extra lineman is substituted for a defensive back. Depending on the offensive personnel, a **CORNER** would usually come out and the **WEAK SAFETY** will play the position on the **near end**.

- **Position**: S/S END.
- **Alignment**: Head-on to outside of the offensive tackle.
- **Key**: Offensive tackle.
- **Assignment**: On the snap of the ball, drive through the inside leg of the tight end. Drive upfield, penetrate. **On pass**—rush passer; if back releases on your side, contain the QB.

- **Position**: S/S TACKLE.
- **Alignment**: Head-on to outside of the offensive guard.
- **Key**: Offensive guard.
- **Assignment**: On snap of the ball, drive through the inside leg of the offensive tackle. **On pass**—drive upfield, break the pocket.

- **Position**: NOSE TACKLE.
- **Alignment**: Head-on the center.
- **Key**: Offensive center.
- **Assignment**: On snap of the ball, drive through the center, penetrate the running lane. **On pass**—drive upfield, break pocket.

- **Position**: W/S TACKLE.
- **Alignment**: Head-on to outside of the offensive guard.
- **Key**: Offensive guard.
- **Assignment**: On snap of the ball, drive through the inside leg of the offensive tackle. **On pass**—drive upfield, break the pocket.

- **Position:** W/S END.
- **Alignment:** Head-on to outside of the offensive tackle.
- **Key:** Offensive tackle.
- **Assignment:** On snap of the ball, drive through the inside leg of the tight end. Drive upfield, penetrate. **On pass**—rush passer; if back releases on your side, contain the QB.

- **Position:** SAM.
- **Alignment:** Move late to backer support position.
- **Key:** Backer support.
- **Assignment:** Backer support. **On pass**—first back to your side man to man.

- **Position:** MIKE.
- **Alignment:** Stack behind NOSE.
- **Key:** SEE through interior offensive line into backfield triangle.
- **Assignment:** Back and ball keys; A, B, C, and D gap in progression. **On pass**—second back strongside or weakside.

- **Position:** WILL.
- **Alignment:** Move late to backer support position.
- **Key:** Backer support.
- **Assignment:** Backer support. **On pass**—first back to your side.

- **Position:** STRONG CORNER.
- **Alignment:** Bump and run position, a shade inside of "Z."
- **Key:** SEE "Z."
- **Assignment:** Backer support. **On pass**— "Z" man to man. **CP:** If "Z" and TE are close, call in/out with STRONG SAFETY.

- **Position:** S/S SAFETY.
- **Alignment:** Move late to backer support position (head-on the tight end).
- **Key:** Tight end and backfield triangle.
- **Assignment:** Backer support. **On pass**—tight end man to man. **CP:** If "Z" and TE are close, call in/out with STRONG CORNER.

- **Position:** WEAK CORNER.
- **Alignment:** Move late to backer support position (head-on the near end).
- **Key:** Near end and backfield triangle.
- **Assignment:** Backer support. **On pass**—near end man to man.

This is a good defensive package for short yardage and the goal line. **60, 64,** and **70** are best from the **five yard line in**; however, in a "must" situation,

60 is useable in the field. However, in the field, **MIKE** should take the SB man to man and the S/S should take the TE man to man (no in/out). **70** may also be used in the field in critical situations.

The key is preparation and practice. There are many offensive formations available in this situation. Defensively, you must be capable of matching personnel and executing properly. It is a time to **set the tempo** for the game and the season.

K. Cover 2 Snug

Before leaving the chapter on goal line defense and coverage, it is important to discuss the mix of blitz, man, and zone coverage. To be successful, all three variations of coverage must be available in the package. Zone coverage is very important in this area because, realistically, it is the key breaker. Blitz and man coverages are similar in many respects. Both have the same strengths and weaknesses.

The zone mixture that I like best is double zone or cover 2. Cover 2 has the pre-snap look of both man and blitz, which is very important in this area. Even after the snap, depending on the pattern, the look is similar to man coverage. There are several differences that should be noted for cover 2 in this area of the field. To differentiate cover 2 in this area and cover 2 in the field, cover 2 in the goal line area is called **2 SNUG**. It is cover 2, but the techniques vary because of the area on the field and the distance that must be covered.

- **Position**: SAM.
- **Alignment**: Head-on the TE.
- **Key**: TE, backfield triangle, corner support.
- **Assignment**: **Strongside slot area**—SEE release of #2. Drop one yard in front of goal line. **#2 inside or lateral outside**—jam, destroy release. Basic 2 coverage reads—no deeper than one yard from goal line. Cover man to man all receivers in your area. **#2 vertical outside**—jam, zone strongside slot area. Do not chase vertical routes. SEE QB, be alert for #1 on shallow inside route or crossing routes by weakside receivers. **CP**: Cover crossing routes to boundary. **#2 vertical and #3 wide or to flat**—man to man on #3. **FRANK or FLOW**—basic cover 2 reads.
- **Slot**: WILL assignments.

- **Position**: MIKE.
- **Alignment**: By front called.
- **Key**: Center, guard, and backfield triangle.

- **Assignment: Strongside hook area**—key #3 release. Drop one yard in front of goal line. **#3 inside release**—jam, destroy all routes by #3 man to man in your area. **#2 vertical and #3 wide or to flat**—alert SAM, work to slot area. **CP:** Be alert for delay or crossing routes from the weakside.
- **Slot:** Same assignment.

- **Position: WILL.**
- **Alignment:** By front called.
- **Key:** Offensive tackle, backfield triangle, corner support.
- **Assignment: Weakside slot area**—key release of #4. Drop one yard in front of goal line. **#4 inside–lateral outside**—jam, destroy release. Basic two coverage reads. No deeper than one yard from goal line. Cover man to man all receivers in your area. **#4 vertical outside**—jam #4, zone weakside slot area. SEE QB, be alert for #5 on shallow inside route or crossing routes by strongside receivers. **CP:** Cover crossing routes to boundary. **FRANK or FLOW**—basic cover 2 reads.
- **Slot:** Move out to SLOT, SAM assignments.

- **Position: STRONG CORNER.**
- **Alignment:** Outside technique on "Z," five yards deep. **CP:** Depth may vary by field position.
- **Key:** Corner support, "Z," "Y," SB to ball.
- **Assignment: Short outside zone on strongside.** Outside funnel technique, five yards deep. Drop one yard from goal line, unless man to man versus vertical. Key release of #2. **#2 inside–outside release**—basic two coverage technique. Jam #1. **#2 outside vertical**—man to man #1 or out routes. **CP:** Cover shallow route inside route of "Z" to the numbers.

- **Position: STRONG SAFETY.**
- **Alignment:** A shade outside of "Y," five to seven yards deep. **CP:** Depth will vary by field position.
- **Key:** Corner support, "Z", "Y," SB to QB.
- **Assignment: Deep half of field strongside.** Drop one yard from goal line unless man to man versus vertical. Key release of #2. **#2 inside–outside release**—basic two coverage technique. **#2 outside vertical**—man to man on route. Maintain outside technique.

- **Position: WEAK SAFETY.**
- **Alignment:** Five to seven yards deep. **CP:** Depth will vary by field position.
- **Key:** Corner support, "X," WB to QB.

- **Assignment: Deep half of field weakside.** Drop one yard from goal line, unless man to man versus vertical. Key release of #4. **#4 inside–outside release**—basic two coverage technique. **#4 outside vertical**—man to man on route. Maintain outside technique.

- **Position: WEAK CORNER.**
- **Alignment:** Outside technique on "X," five yards deep. **CP:** Depth may vary by field position.
- **Key:** Corner support, "X," WB to ball.
- **Assignment: Short outside zone on weakside.** Outside funnel technique, five yards deep. Drop one yard from goal line, unless man to man versus vertical. Key release of #4. **#4 inside–outside release**—basic two coverage technique. Jam #5. **#4 outside vertical**—man to man #5 vertical or out routes. **CP:** Cover shallow inside route of "X" to the numbers.

With **2 SNUG** as part of the goal line coverage package, you will have the mixture of coverage that is important for success. 2 SNUG may actually become the number one choice at the goal line, which actually makes the mixture of man and blitz more reliable. I have emphasized a mixture of coverage in every area, but there is no area more important than at the goal line. Stop the **SCORE**, change the tempo, and gain the momentum for a victory.

6

SUBSTITUTED PASS COVERAGE

Other than the rule changes to restrict the defense, nothing during my coaching career has changed the game more than offensive substitutions by situations. Many teams go immediately to situational substitutions on any down. Primarily, it indicates to the defense an intention to throw the ball. However, a running threat remains a possibility by down and distance. The defensive signal caller must be aware not only of the down and distance but, equally important, the offensive personnel in the game. As a note to the signal caller, I always needed help from the coach in the coach's box or a coach on the sideline with the substitution and the personnel involved. My concentration was on the call and my vision was focused on the signal caller on the field. In San Diego, one of the best at this was John Hinek, director of college scouting. He usually saw it first and was accurate. He has since been promoted to business manager. Somebody else must have recognized his talent and ability.

PERSONNEL NUMBERING

45	Four linemen, two linebackers, five defensive backs
46	Four linemen, one linebacker, six defensive backs
47	Four linemen, seven defensive backs

35	Three linemen, three linebackers, five defensive backs
36	Three linemen, two linebackers, six defensive backs
37	Three linemen, one linebacker, seven defensive backs

KINGS formation: Three wide receivers, one TE, and one back. Is the back a pass threat, a run threat, or both? (This is important if the opponent is using different personnel.)

QUEENS formation: Three wide receivers and two backs. This presents a different problem to the defense. This is equally as strong passing, but probably somewhat more of a run threat.

JACKS formation: Four wide receivers and one back.

SPREAD (no backs): From all the above, movement may occur by the back, which creates another look for the defense.

When I was in San Diego, we played a team that had an outstanding TE. He had wide receiver catching ability but below average blocking ability. He usually played every down; however, in one game in particular, he was moved in and out of the lineup. We were alert to this possibility and adjusted with a run defense when he was out of the game and a pass defense when he was in the game.

I recall a similar situation in another game, where the TE was aligned normal or flexed. We had noticed this in our game study and prepared to meet the challenge. We did so by making a double call. On **TE tight**, we played a run-type defense. On **TE wide**, we played a pass-type defense. Sometimes this was with **regular** personnel (two wide receivers, one TE, and two backs), and other times it was with **KINGS** personnel (three wide receivers, one TE, and one back). The TE's position was our key, the double call was effective, and we were successful in gaining the edge to win.

PASS COVERAGE

A. Cover 1 Robber

Cover 1 rules are played as we learned in regular coverage. In regular coverage, MIKE sometimes has the ROBBER assignment. In cover 1 substituted, the safeties show a two-deep look, and then one of the safeties becomes the robber.

KINGS

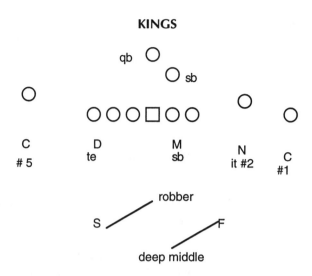

- **Position: WILL/DIME.**
- **Alignment:** Head-on to outside the TE. By support call.
- **Key:** TE.
- **Assignment:** #4 man to man. **CP:** Expect deep middle help by safety. Do not expect help from the robber.

- **Position: MIKE.**
- **Alignment:** Head-on to outside of the SB.
- **Key:** SB.
- **Assignment:** #3 man to man, outside technique.

- **Position: NICKEL.**
- **Alignment:** Inside technique on #2.
- **Key:** #2.
- **Assignment:** #2 man to man. **CP:** Expect no help from robber on shallow inside route.

- **Position: STRONG CORNER.**
- **Alignment:** Bump and run.
- **Key:** #1.
- **Assignment:** #1 man to man. **CP:** Expect deep help from safety. If robber takes your man on inside route, replace the robber and look for inside routes.

- **Position: STRONG SAFETY.**
- **Alignment:** Show cover 2 alignment.

- **Key**: QB and ball, #1 and #2 strongside, #5 weakside.
- **Assignment**: Robber—cover middle area ten yards deep for crossing receivers. Work outside-in. Read QB and react to ball. **CP**: Know yardage needed for first down.

- **Position: WEAK/SAFETY.**
- **Alignment**: Show cover 2 alignment.
- **Key**: QB and ball.
- **Assignment**: Deep middle of field, favor the formation. Read QB and react to ball.

- **Position: WEAK CORNER.**
- **Alignment**: #5 bump and run.
- **Key**: #5.
- **Assignment**: #5 man to man. **CP**: Expect deep help from safety. If robber takes your man on inside route, replace the robber and look for inside routes.

B. Cover 2—Five Short, Two-Deep Zone

For cover 2 to be effective, it is important for all receivers to be jammed and rerouted. The outside receivers must be funneled inside. The inside receivers must be jammed and forced outside. Reroute and delay them from entering the deep middle of the field. If played properly, cover 2, along with a mixture of TWO MAN, will create problems for the offense. To be successful, you must make the QB hesitate.

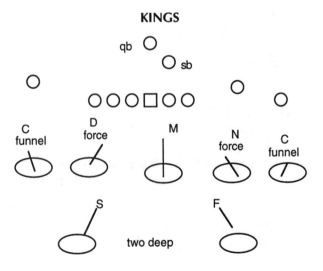

KINGS

- **Position:** DIME.
- **Alignment:** Off the line of scrimmage and inside the TE. SEE TE and backfield triangle. If TE flexes, drop off line of scrimmage and inside.
- **Key:** Corner support—TE.
- **Assignment:** Jam and force the TE outside. Short inside zone on weakside. SEE #4 and #5—drop straight back. SEE the pattern as you drop, get depth. Locate #5 and #2 and 3 on crossing pattern. Frank action—HOLD, destroy pattern, be ready to attack gimmick.

- **Position:** MIKE.
- **Alignment:** Space alignment with DIME. Favor side of one back.
- **Key:** #2 and #3 as you gain depth in the middle of the field.
- **Assignment:** Zone middle area. Get depth with inside receiver of #2 and #3, square up, and attack ball. SEE QB, play the ball. Frank action—favor weakside, SEE receivers. Get depth, square up, attack ball.

- **Position:** NICKEL.
- **Alignment:** Head-on to inside of SLOT.
- **Key:** Corner support, #2
- **Assignment:** Force #2 outside, SEE SB as you work to SLOT, gain depth.

- **Position:** STRONG CORNER.
- **Alignment:** Head-on to outside or #1.
- **Key:** Corner support, #1
- **Assignment:** Funnel #1 inside, gain depth in short outside zone. Take away the "oh" and fade. SEE #3 and #2. N/T—cushion with depth, square away, react to ball.

- **Position:** STRONG SAFETY.
- **Alignment:** 10 to 12 yards deep, approx. 2 yards inside numbers.
- **Key:** Corner support, #4 to #5, QB and ball.
- **Assignment:** Deep half of field.

- **Position:** WEAK/SAFETY.
- **Alignment:** 10 to 12 yards deep, approx. 2 yards inside numbers.
- **Key:** Corner support, #2 to #1, QB and ball.
- **Assignment:** Deep half of field.

- **Position:** WEAK CORNER.
- **Alignment:** Head-on to outside or #1.
- **Key:** Corner support, #1

- **Assignment**: Funnel #1 inside, gain depth in short outside zone. Take away the "oh" and fade. SEE #3 and #2. N/T—cushion with depth, square away, react to ball.

C. Cover 2 Man—Man Under (Trail Technique), Two Deep

It is very important to mix TWO MAN with cover 2. TWO MAN is an aggressive MAN coverage. Cover 2 MAN challenges the receivers, and defensively we must develop this concept. We must force the offense to beat TWO MAN.

As in regular cover 2, the support call may be either safety or corner by the game plan. Here again, the best pass defense is safety support. That allows the corner to focus on his assignment first. As stated earlier, the safety may be a fraction late in support. However, it is my belief that in this situation we call the best pass coverage.

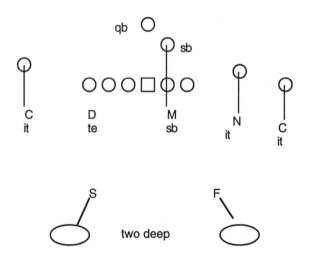

- **Position**: DIME.
- **Alignment**: Off the line of scrimmage and inside the TE. SEE TE and backfield triangle.
- **Key**: Support by game plan—safety or corner. SEE #4.
- **Assignment**: #4 man to man.

- **Position**: MIKE.
- **Alignment**: Space alignment with DIME. Favor side of one back.
- **Key**: #3 and backfield triangle.
- **Assignment**: #3 man to man.

- **Position**: NICKEL.
- **Alignment**: Inside technique on #2.
- **Key**: Support by game plan—safety or corner. SEE #2.
- **Assignment**: #2 man to man.

- **Position**: STRONG CORNER.
- **Alignment**: Inside technique on #1.
- **Key**: Support by game plan—safety or corner. SEE #1.
- **Assignment**: #1 man to man.

- **Position**: STRONG SAFETY.
- **Alignment**: 10 to 12 yards deep, approx. 2 yards inside numbers.
- **Key**: Safety support, #4 to #5, QB and ball.
- **Assignment**: Deep half of field.

- **Position**: WEAK/SAFETY.
- **Alignment**: 10 to 12 yards deep, approx. 2 yards inside numbers.
- **Key**: Safety support, #2 to #1, QB and ball.
- **Assignment**: Deep half of field.

- **Position**: WEAK CORNER.
- **Alignment**: Inside technique on #5.
- **Key**: Support by game plan—safety or corner. SEE #5.
- **Assignment**: #5 man to man.

Adjustments Used with Two Man

KICK, as described, is regular. The **strongside calls** are as follows. "**VISE**" may be called as a variation on #1 or #5. It is an in-and-out technique on the receiver, involving the CORNER and SAFETY. "VISE" should be played with corner support. "**CLAMP**" is an in-and-out call on #2 between the NICKEL and SAFETY. "CLAMP" would change the support call to NICKEL (backer) support.

The **weakside call,** "**VISE**," is between the CORNER and SAFETY.

D. Cover 6 Sky

KINGS formation

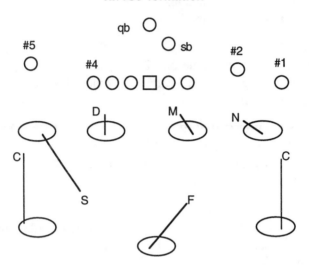

- **Position**: **DIME**.
- **Alignment**: Off the line of scrimmage and inside the TE. SEE TE and backfield triangle.
- **Key**: Weak safety support, SEE #4 and #5.
- **Assignment**: Short inside zone on weakside.

- **Position**: **NICKEL**.
- **Alignment**: Off the line of scrimmage and slightly inside the SLOT receiver. Be at a depth to SEE the SLOT and the backfield triangle.
- **Key**: Backer support (NICKEL), SEE the SLOT and the backfield triangle.
- **Assignment**: Short outside zone on the strongside.

- **Position**: **STRONG CORNER**.
- **Alignment**: A shade outside of #1, five to seven yards deep.
- **Key**: Backer support, SEE #1 and 2.
- **Assignment**: Deep outside zone on strongside.

- **Position**: **STRONG SAFETY**.
- **Alignment**: Show two-deep alignment weakside.
- **Key**: Weak safety support (STRONG SAFETY).
- **Assignment**: Short outside zone on weakside.

- **Position**: **WEAK CORNER**.
- **Alignment**: A shade outside of #5, five to seven yards deep.

- **Key**: Backer support, SEE #4 and 5.
- **Assignment**: Deep outside zone on strongside.

E. Cover 8 Zone

This is a special ZONE concept with three short and four deep.

KINGS

- **Position**: DIME.
- **Alignment**: Off the line and slightly inside the TE.
- **Key**: Backer support, SEE #4 and backfield triangle.
- **Assignment**: Short inside zone. **#4 is vertical**—work through #4 to #5. **#4 is short**—cover man to man from depth of about ten yards or depth by down and distance.

- **Position**: MIKE.
- **Alignment**: Space alignment with DIME. Favor side of one back.
- **Key**: SEE #3 and backfield triangle.
- **Assignment**: Short inside zone. **#3 vertical**—drop him to S/S, look for inside routes of #1 and #2. **#3 short**—cover man to man. **#2 and #3 outside**—cover #3 man to man.

- **Position**: NICKEL.
- **Alignment**: Shade inside of SLOT, five to seven yards deep. Have enough depth to see SLOT and backfield triangle.
- **Key**: Backer support, SEE QB, SLOT, and backfield triangle.
- **Assignment**: Get depth. **#2 is vertical**—look up #1. **#2 is short**—cover man to man from depth.

- **Position**: STRONG CORNER.
- **Alignment**: Head-on #1, five to seven yards deep.
- **Key**: Backer support (NICKEL)—#1 and #2.
- **Assignment**: Deep quarter of outside zone on strongside.

- **Position**: STRONG SAFETY.
- **Alignment**: Take a position by field position, ten yards deep.
- **Key**: Backer support—SEE #4 and #5, QB, and backfield triangle.
- **Assignment**: Deep quarter of inside zone on weakside. SEE all weakside receivers, #4, and #5.

- **Position**: WEAK SAFETY.
- **Alignment**: Take a position by field position, favor the formation, ten yards deep.
- **Key**: SEE #1, #2, QB, and backfield triangle.
- **Assignment**: Deep quarter of inside zone on strongside. SEE all strongside receivers, #2, and #1.

- **Position**: WEAK CORNER.
- **Alignment**: Head-on #5, five to seven yards deep.
- **Key**: Backer support, SEE #5 and #4.
- **Assignment**: Deep quarter of outside zone on weakside. SEE #4, #5, and cover the widest and deepest from outside-in.

F. Anchor Zone

This is a three-deep, four-underneath zone, always keeping two linebackers behind the line. MIKE and DIME will be the hook defenders.

KINGS

- **Position:** DIME.
- **Alignment:** Weakside offensive B gap and backfield triangle.
- **Key:** Strong safety support—SEE backfield triangle and QB.
- **Assignment:** Short inside zone on weakside.

- **Position:** MIKE.
- **Alignment:** Strongside offensive B gap and backfield triangle.
- **Key:** SEE backfield triangle and QB.
- **Assignment:** Short inside zone on strongside.

- **Position:** NICKEL.
- **Alignment:** Off the line of scrimmage and slightly inside the SLOT receiver. Be at a depth to SEE the SLOT and the backfield triangle.
- **Key:** Backer support (NICKEL), SEE the SLOT and the backfield triangle.
- **Assignment:** Short outside zone on strongside.

- **Position:** STRONG CORNER.
- **Alignment:** A shade outside of #1, five to seven yards deep.
- **Key:** Backer support, SEE #1 and 2.
- **Assignment:** Deep outside zone on strongside.

- **Position:** STRONG SAFETY.
- **Alignment:** Show two-deep alignment weakside.
- **Key:** Weak safety support (STRONG SAFETY).
- **Assignment:** Short outside zone on weakside.

- **Position:** WEAK CORNER.
- **Alignment:** A shade outside of #5, five to seven yards deep.
- **Key:** Backer support, SEE #4 and 5.
- **Assignment:** Deep outside zone on weakside.

Notice that the STRONG SAFETY and WEAK SAFETY have been interchanged in alignment and assignment. In substituted defenses, I normally like to keep the STRONG SAFETY on the side of the TE for better run support. This allows the WEAK SAFETY to use his ability in pass coverage. The same is true with the DIME position. The DIME should be the best defensive back with a linebacker mentality and defensive back pass coverage skills. The MIKE should be your best linebacker for both the run and the pass.

When I was with the San Diego Chargers, we never wanted to take Junior Seau off the field. He was an excellent linebacker versus the run. Plus he had the quickness and strength to cover the best back coming out of the backfield. He and our strong safety coordinated the calls and made sure we were aligned properly.

ANCHOR ZONE is a zone defense that keeps two linebackers behind the line for good run defense, and **ONE KEY** is a man coverage that keeps two linebackers behind the line. This gives you both zone and man coverage, which allows two linebackers to remain behind the line. This, along with the other coverages, provides an excellent substituted package.

G. One Key

KINGS

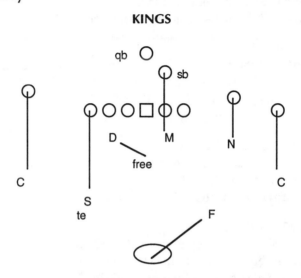

This is a ONE-COVERAGE assignment defense. The free linebacker becomes the ROBBER (DIME, as indicated above). If the remaining back is in the middle, MIKE or DIME will key and cover the back as he releases to the side of their alignment. The STRONG SAFETY has the TE. The WEAK SAFETY is free in the deep middle.

"BUNCH" ADJUSTMENTS IN MAN-TO-MAN COVERAGE

Our first call is **stay with your man** (see next page). When using this, be sure to align on separate levels so that the defender can run through and not be picked.

The next option is **"lock banjo"** (see next page). We will **"lock"** the receiver on the line of scrimmage and **"banjo"** the first inside and the first outside.

If four defenders are involved, we can use the zone call **"OZ"** (see next page). This is a good call with **two short** and **two deep**. MIKE and NICKEL have the first in and the first out. The WEAK SAFETY and the CORNER have the second in or the second out.

STAY WITH YOUR MAN

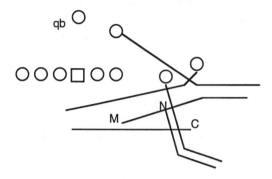

"LOCK BANJO"
Lock the receiver on the line of scrimmage, banjo the first in and first out

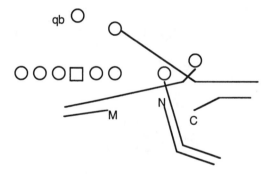

"OZ"
M = first in, N = first out, F = second in, C = second out

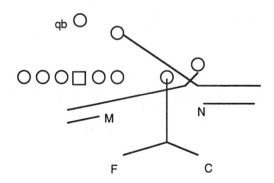

There are many possible "BUNCH" pickup combinations. However, it has been my experience that if you try to use many more than the three that I have discussed here, then problems develop. First of all, practice time is a factor. Next, it is difficult to learn and perfect more than two or three. Again, keep it simple, and learn and know the assignment. The better a player knows the assignment, the better he will execute it. Like anything else, if you prove you can handle the "BUNCH" patterns, the offense will look for another plan of attack.

SUBSTITUTED BLITZ DEFENSE

45, 46, 47, 35, 35, and **37** personnel calls are used as defined in substituted coverages. **NICKEL** is the fifth back, **DIME** is the sixth back, and **QUARTER** is the seventh back.

The blitzes from this personnel are what was referred to earlier as a PASS-ONLY BLITZ.

A. 45 Dog—Cover 1

In **46**, **DIME** would replace **WILL**. In **47**, the **DB** would replace **MIKE**.

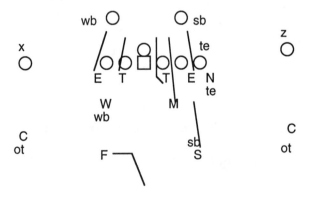

MIKE is designated dogger

The called dogger is NICKEL, MIKE, WILL, or STRONG SAFETY. The term applies to the STRONG SAFETY or WEAK SAFETY by plan. **Cover 1** is the coverage. The **STRONG SAFETY** (WEAK SAFETY) takes the called dogger's man. The WEAK SAFETY is FREE. Both CORNERS are man to man on "X" and "Z" with an outside technique with help in the DEEP MIDDLE. The line will use their RUSH GAMES. In the diagram above, the **MIKE** and **RT** may exchange gaps by call.

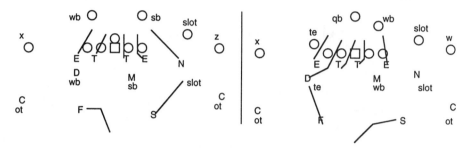

QUEENS formation is shown in the diagram on the left above. The NICKEL is the called dogger. The STRONG SAFETY covers the SLOT. The DIME and the MIKE have the two backs.

KINGS formation is shown in the diagram on the right above. The DIME is the called dogger. The WEAK SAFETY has the TE, and the NICKEL has the SLOT. The line will use their RUSH GAMES. The diagram shows the OVER front. The line is moved away from MIKE and to the DIME to protect the DIME versus the run. **CP**: The STRONG SAFETY by plan may take the TE, and the WEAK SAFETY would be assigned the deep middle.

B. Double Dog—Cover 1

QUEENS formation is shown in the diagram on the left above. In **DOUBLE DOG** strongside, MIKE is the declared dogger (**bear call**), and NICKEL keys the SB. If the SB blocks MIKE, the NICKEL becomes the FREE dogger. If the SB releases, the NICKEL covers the SB. If the SB releases weakside, the DE has the second back weak.

KINGS formation is shown in the diagram on the right above. In **DOUBLE DOG** weakside, the WEAK SAFETY is the declared dogger (**bull call**), and the DIME keys the TE. If the TE blocks the W/S, the DIME becomes the FREE dogger. In this diagram, there is no second back strongside. If there were, the DE would have the assignment.

C. Backer Dog Opposite—Cover 1

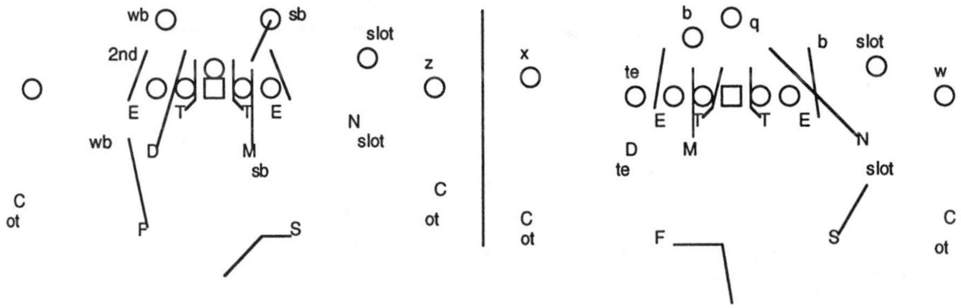

QUEENS formation is shown in the diagram on the left above. In BACKER DOG OPPOSITE, MIKE (the declared rusher right [**bear call**]) reads the SB as he rushes. If the SB blocks MIKE, he engages. If the SB releases to the side of MIKE, he covers. If the SB releases away, MIKE is the free rusher. The **BACKER OPPOSITE** is **DIME** (first cover man opposite MIKE is the free dogger). If the SB releases to the side away from MIKE, the DE has second back coverage or the remaining back to his side. The WEAK SAFETY by assignment and alignment takes the first receiver opposite MIKE.

KINGS formation is shown in the diagram on the right above. In BACKER DOG OPPOSITE, MIKE (the declared rusher left [**bull call**]) reads the remaining back as he rushes. If the back blocks MIKE, he engages. If the back releases to the side of MIKE, he covers. If the back releases away, MIKE is the free rusher. The **BACKER OPPOSITE** is **NICKEL** (first cover man opposite MIKE is the free dogger). If the remaining back releases away from MIKE, the DE has the second back or remaining back coverage.

D. 45 Inside Blitz

Able is the A gap, and Baker is the B gap. (In **46**, DIME would replace WILL. In **47**, the DB would replace MIKE.)

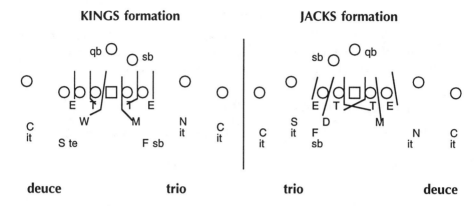

The diagram on the left above is INSIDE BLITZ (Able). The diagram on the right is the Baker with the tackles in a "TOM" or "TOMY" game. The coverage is DEUCE on the side of two receivers and TRIO on the side of three receivers.

E. 45 Double Key Blitz

In **46**, DIME would replace WILL. In **47**, the DB would replace MIKE.

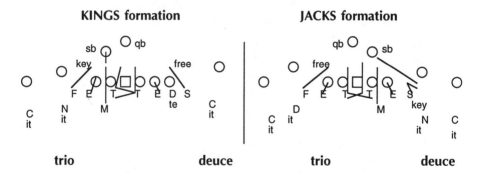

The diagram on the left above is DOUBLE KEY, which means that the two safeties on the end of the line key the back to their side. If he blocks (MIKE), the safety on that side is FREE. If he releases, the safety will cover. The blitz coverage is TRIO or DEUCE coverage. The two tackles use a "TOM" or "TOMY" game to ensure the middle versus the quick trap. Any movement to the right or left by the strong back is covered by the safety to the side of the movement.

I have found the DOUBLE KEY BLITZ to be very effective, due not only to the blitz but also to the "check-off" possibility. In other words, if the QB checks, the defense will check to a regular coverage. There are several possibilities, and we will take a look at the different checks.

F. 45 Double Key—Omaha Blue

OMAHA denotes the blitz is checked. BLUE denotes the coverage (cover 3).

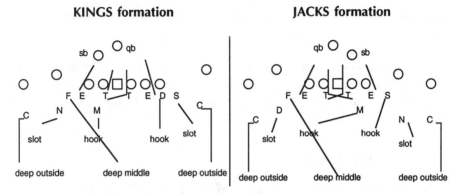

Like everything else, I try to keep the assignments as simple as possible. The CORNERS take the **deep outside** on their side. The WEAK SAFETY always takes the **deep middle**. The second defender in takes the slot on that side. The third defender (not counting the WEAK SAFETY) takes the hook area. The OMAHA call is a definite part of the DOUBLE KEY package. A decision is made weekly on the coverage to be used. BLUE (cover #3) is shown above.

G. 46 Double Key—Omaha Two Man (Vise)

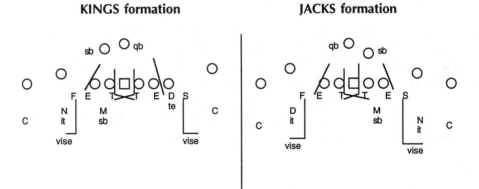

The left and right is the OMAHA call with TWO MAN VISE coverage. The two safeties will get depth and will be the inside defender on the VISE call. The CORNERS remain on the outside defender. The DIME and NICKEL have the TE and SLOT man to man with an inside technique, and MIKE has the strong back. With the decision to use TWO MAN in the OMAHA call, the decision may also be made to change the VISE to the best receiver or the favorite receiver on the offensive check-off. Using **COVER 3** or **TWO MAN** as the check-off coverage puts additional pressure on the offense as they prepare a check-off play. Originally, only cover 3 was used in the OMAHA package, but experience showed that a variation was needed. TWO MAN VISE was the change-up that was needed to maintain the defensive advantage.

ZONE BLITZ

The next part of the PASS-ONLY BLITZ package is the very popular **ZONE BLITZ** package. This package was made popular recently by the Pittsburgh Steelers and other clubs. As I mentioned earlier, we stumbled on the concept when I was with the Miami Dolphins. Kim Bokamper was an outside line-backer, and we moved him to defensive end to strengthen our pass rush. While at end, we would call coverage to him, drop him to the hook area, and blitz the two linebackers on his side. It was successful in two regards—from a rush standpoint and Kim was successful in knocking down passes by his drop and path. Developed by Dick LeBeau, defensive coordinator for the Cincinnati Bengals, and others, the concept now is more refined, and it creates quick outside pressure on the QB.

A. Nickel Zone Blitz

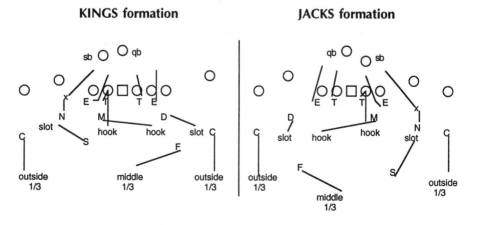

NICKEL ZONE BLITZ is a four-man rush, four-short, and three-deep ZONE coverage. The NICKEL must communicate his alignment (roger on the right or lucky on the left) to the front and linebackers. The NICKEL takes his alignment, and the three-deep coverage is locked. The end on the side of the blitz uses a RAM charge into the B gap. The tackle on the side of the blitz engages the offensive guard and drops to the HOOK on his side. MIKE has the HOOK assignment away from the drop tackle. The DIME and the S/S have SLOT assignments. The CORNERS and the W/S are the three-deep defenders.

Next is the **DIME ZONE BLITZ**. It is the same as NICKEL, except DIME is the designated blitzer. The same rules that apply to NICKEL now apply for DIME. DIME makes the roger or lucky call, and the coverage is locked. The end on the side of the call is in a RAM charge into the B gap. The tackle on the call side is the engage and hook tackle. MIKE has the HOOK assignment away from the call or drop tackle. The NICKEL and the safety to the side of the call have the SLOT assignment. The CORNERS and the safety away from the call are the three-deep defenders.

B. 45 Dime Zone Blitz

KINGS formation   **JACKS formation**

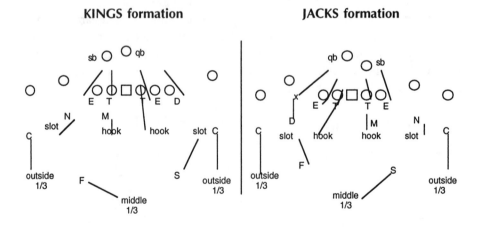

C. Double Sting Cover 2

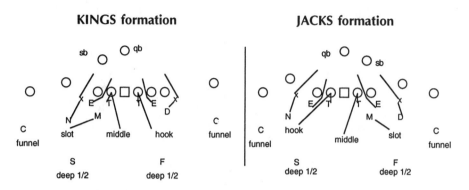

DOUBLE STING cover 2 is a ZONE BLITZ with cover 2. Both NICKEL and DIME are the designated blitzers. It is a four-man rush with five underneath and two deep. The NICKEL and DIME take their normal alignment. Both ends take a RAM charge into the B GAP to their side. MIKE takes his regular alignment (on the remaining back) and makes a call (right or left) to give direction to the tackles (right = the tackles come out to the right). (Example: See the diagram on the left above.) Both CORNERS funnel the receiver inside. The S/SAFETY and W/SAFETY have regular cover 2 assignments. The coverage is locked on any movement by the receiver to the other side. Stay cover 2, CORNERS stay on their side. The hook and slot defenders must adjust depending on the final formation.

The above ZONE BLITZES are basic. There are other combinations, and as the package is developed, adjustments will be made to take advantage of the personnel on defense. The ZONE BLITZ can best be developed and carried out through the three-man-line concept. This is true because there are more linebackers and more combinations are possible. In addition, there are fewer linemen dropping in the three-man concept. An example of the three-man-line concept is shown next.

D. 30 Double Sting Cover 2

KINGS formation

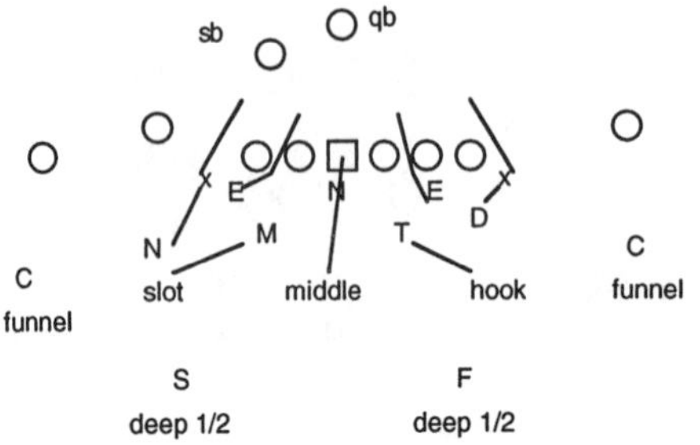

JACKS formation

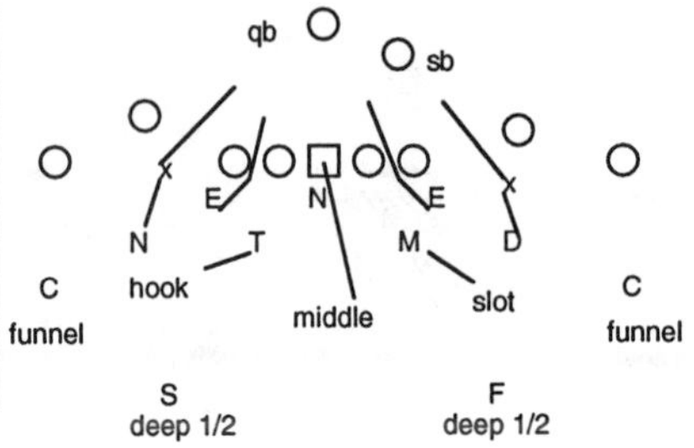

The diagram above is one example of the three-man-line **ZONE BLITZ** concept with **cover 2**. There are many combinations from the three-man line because of the number of linebackers.

E. 30 Dime Zone Blitz Cover 3 and 30 Nickel Zone Blitz Cover 3

30 DIME ZONE BLITZ cover 3

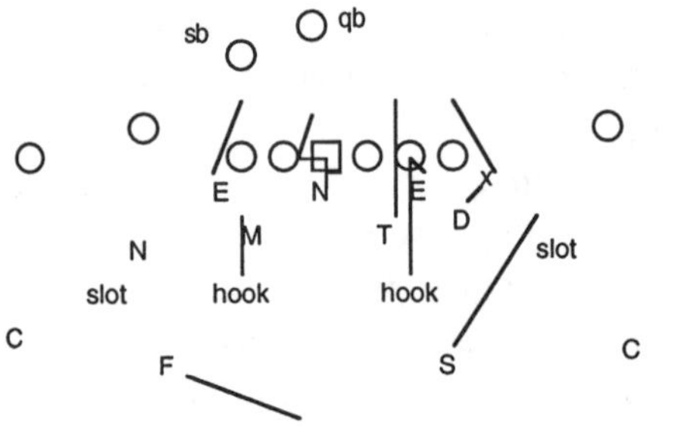

30 NICKEL ZONE BLITZ cover 3

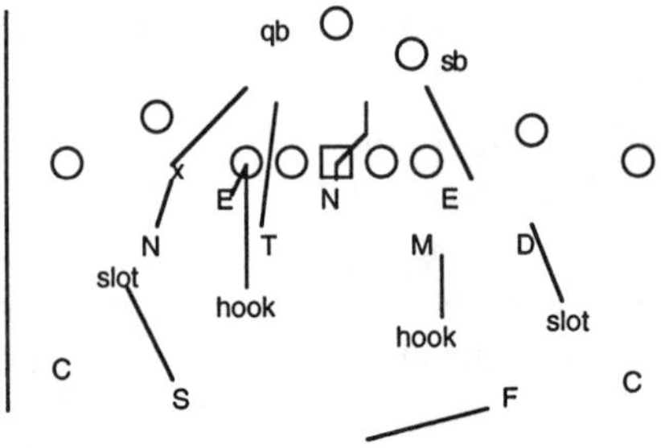

The diagram on the left above is **DIME ZONE BLITZ** cover 3. TED and the DIME are the designated blitzers. The safety to the call has the slot. The end on the side of the call engages the tackle and drops to the hook. MIKE has the hook away from the call. The NICKEL has the slot away from the call.

The diagram on the right above is the **NICKEL ZONE BLITZ** cover 3. TED and the NICKEL are the designated blitzers. The safety to the call has the slot. The end on the side of the call engages the tackle and drops to the hook. MIKE has the hook away from the call. The DIME has the slot away from the call.

These examples should give you an idea of the combinations that are available. The ZONE BLITZ with either **cover 3** or **cover 2** has proved to be very effective. Each team will probably continue to run its own version which best fits its personnel. It is an opportunity for the defense to gain an advantage, and it enables the defense to pressure the quarterback without using BLITZ coverage.

Both the PASS ONLY and ZONE BLITZ are basic ideas and have been used successfully. The main idea in the blitz in general is to take advantage of the protection and to create one-on-one pickups. In setting up the game plan, it is very important to study the opponent's protection and use the type of blitz or stunt that takes advantage of the offensive blocking pattern. What has been presented here is basic and can be easily adjusted to provide the best stunt within the blitz call. Like every detail that we have discussed, the blitz package must be practiced and must fit a team's personnel.

7

SPECIAL SITUATIONS

The topics in this chapter are important to the success of the defensive package. In many ways, they can be considered the "little things" that help a team reach its goals. Often they are the difference between winning and losing. They are a part of preparation, and they must be reviewed weekly, practiced, and included as part of the game plan.

TWO MINUTES TO GO

An important part of every ball game is the **last two minutes** in either half. Many a game is won here. It is imperative for the team to know the rules in the two-minute phase. When is time out—when the clock starts, with the snap, or with the referee's whistle? Time-outs must be saved for the two-minute period. Note that the official rules for college or high school football may differ from those discussed in this section.

A. Clock Starts with the Snap of the Ball

1. Change of possession
2. Expiration of time-out
3. Incomplete pass
4. Penalty (if team committing the infraction has time-outs remaining)
5. Play out of bounds

6. Signal for start of two-minute period
7. Due to crowd noise

B. Clock Starts with the Referee's Whistle

1. Time-outs taken in excess of three
2. Measurement for first down unless clock is otherwise stopped
3. Undue pileup and delay unpiling
4. Removal of injured player (if no time-out is available, ten seconds is run off the clock)

The team that can handle itself through this period without confusion and frustration will be the champion. The offense is trying to conserve as much time as they possibly can by going out of bounds to stop the clock. They also conserve time by calling one or more plays in the huddle and hurrying back to the line of scrimmage to put the ball in play. Play begins as the referee whistles the ball in play.

C. General Rules and Guides

1. Keep the ball carrier or receiver in bounds.
2. **Stall**—especially the lineman. Lay on the pile. Be slow to get up. However, be onside when the referee whistles the ball in play. Be alert for the down **marker** as you move back to the line of scrimmage.
3. Watch the ball—move with the ball. **An offside penalty stops the clock.**
4. If we are ahead by two touchdowns or more, we will be in a prevent type of defense. It is mandatory that we:
   a. **JAM** and reroute receivers. Line up correctly and play the proper technique.
   b. **Destroy the pattern**, causing the QB to hesitate.
   c. **LBers and DBs**—all defenders must have good depth in alignment. Good vision—react to the ball.
   d. **Linemen**—use your games. Never be blocked one on one.
5. Play through the receiver—under and up. **Knock the ball loose.**
6. **Know the situation—down and distance, position on the field**—and always know the **exact time remaining.**
7. We will use regular personnel or substituted personnel (NICKEL, DIME, or QUARTER). **Know our plan** when you begin the series. Be alert for the change in personnel.
   a. Best front (pass rush).

b. Best coverages (we will mix).

c. Best pass-only blitz, if needed. Be prepared to STAY or CHECK-IT.

D. The Offensive Strategy

1. The offensive **strategy changes as field position** and **time remaining change**. If the opponent has the **full two minutes**, they will use a combination of zone passes, draws, and screens. They will be trying to **move the ball conservatively** and take advantage of our coverage and pass rush. The defense has to be especially alert. Emphasis should be on **converging on the ball carrier**, keeping the ball carrier in bounds, and **making good tackles**. We do not want to gamble in this situation. **Force** the offense to go the long way and make a **mistake**.

2. If the offense has only **one minute or less** remaining with **50 or more** yards to go, their strategy changes. They will **work to the sidelines**, using patterns where the receiver has a chance to get out of bounds. This is where we must have a good bracket on the receiver and keep him in bounds. Turn the ball carrier inside, and keep the clock running.

3. **In desperation**, the offense will send all receivers deep and throw into the end zone. They try to create a **jump-ball** situation—a catch or a batted ball for a touchdown or at least an interference penalty. Our jumpers must be prepared to cover the receiver and **intercept** or **knock the ball down (NO TIP)**. Play the ball—the back defender and the front defender look for the batted ball.

4. To win, we must JAM all receivers and we must have depth. The deep backs must **never** allow anyone to get behind them. Keep everything in front. **Proper alignment** and **proper coverage technique** are very important. Know down and distance and time remaining.

5. A defensive **penalty stops the clock** and **awards yardage** to the offense. Play smart. We do not want to encourage the opponent with a careless penalty.

6. **Defensive signal caller** on the field—call time-out only when instructed to do so by the head coach.

E. The Defensive Strategy When Behind

1. We must **get the ball**. Cause a fumble or three and out to force a punt.

2. Every down is like **short yardage**.

3. **Aggressive fronts**—first man make the tackle, second and third under and up. Strip—force the minus play.

4. Our best **run support and coverage**. Usually the opponent will use two or three TEs.
5. **Run/pass blitzes**.

F. The Two-Minute Plan

Are we in regular personnel or substituted? In normal situations, it is best to begin this period with substituted personnel. Whatever the situation, players must be alert on the sideline to make the change quickly. Near the end of the half or game, players must be alert for **LAST PLAY CALL** (approximately ten seconds remaining) and wide bunch formation.

If there is no **LAST PLAY CALL**, players will play the defense called. If there is a LAST PLAY CALL but no wide bunch formation, then we will play the defense called. We will only play LAST PLAY CALL versus a wide bunch formation in anticipation of the "Hail Mary" pass play.

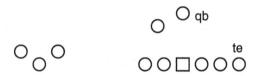

Wide bunch formation but NO LAST PLAY CALL: Play the defense called. The TE may be normal or flexed.

LAST PLAY CALL: Play 30 with a FOUR-DEEP alignment or 46 with a FOUR-DEEP alignment.

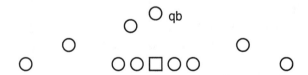

LAST PLAY CALL but **NO wide bunch alignment**: Play the defense called.

The purpose of the **LAST PLAY CALL** versus the wide bunch formation is to place our team in the best position possible versus the "Hail Mary" pass. On any other play, react to the ball and receiver or the ball carrier. Make the tackle.

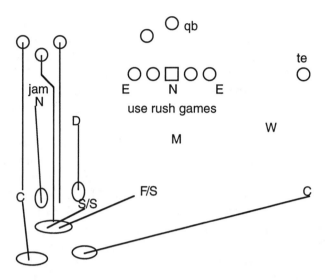

The **NICKEL** must **JAM** the lead receiver. The **WILL** must align normal or gain width and depth on "flex" by the TE. **MIKE** has good depth in the middle. The line as noted must use their rush games. Our **JUMPERS** are the S/S and F/S (the most athletic players we have available, which includes the players on offense). When the ball is thrown, both CORNERS must run to the ball. The CORNER to the side of the throw positions himself behind the ball. The CORNER away positions himself to the side. Both look for the TIP. The **DIME** and **NICKEL** run with the receivers and look for the forward TIP.

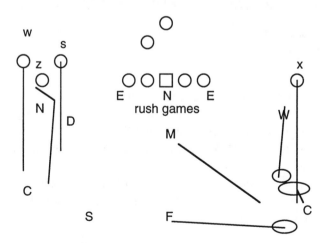

The diagram above shows how to play the ball when it is thrown to the one receiver side. **WILL** tries to reroute the receiver and runs deep to look for the TIP in front. The **CORNER** is the **JUMPER**. The **F/S** looks for the TIP behind the JUMPER and protects the goal line. MIKE and the other deep defenders will run to the ball when it is thrown. The **F/S** must have enough depth (at or near the goal line) and must be in position to react to the side to which the ball is thrown.

As you select personnel for the LAST PLAY CALL, make sure that your best JUMPERS are jumping for the ball. Then assign the other responsibilities: Who looks for the TIP in front? Who looks for the TIP behind? Ideally, to the side of the BUNCH, you need two JUMPERS, two in front looking for the tip, and two behind looking for the tip. To the side of the one receiver, you need one jumper, one in front for the tip, and one behind for the tip. After the personnel are assigned, proper execution is the key. That can only be established through practice.

Like every other phase of the defensive package, these situations must be reviewed and practiced weekly. The two-minute period must be practiced as a game situation at least twice each week. In the time remaining, the score, including down and distance, must be a part of every play. This is true for the offense as well as the defense and has been true for every team with which I have been affiliated. I might add that the two-minute practice has always been one of the most competitive practices of the entire week.

DEFENSE VERSUS GROUP FORMATIONS

A group formation is any wide formation that includes interior linemen. Use the following to defend when a **GROUP** shows:

1. Automatic 3 CLOUD or 3 SKY coverage to the side of the group.
2. Automatic slide to the side of the group.
3. CORNER/SAFETY support to the side of the group.
4. SAM/DE have cut-back responsibility.
5. DE (four-man) or SAM/WILL (three-man) lines up on the inside of the group.
6. Remaining linemen at the ball will adjust to a three-man-line alignment.
7. DT (four-man) or DE (three-man) adjusts to the group, if the formation is three or less.

By following these basic principles, a team will always be prepared to defense an unusual formation. Several examples of alignment versus various group formations are shown in the following diagrams.

FOUR-MAN-LINE ADJUSTMENTS

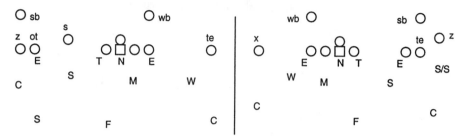

THREE-MAN-LINE ADJUSTMENTS

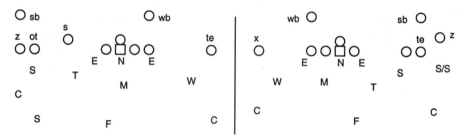

A team must always be aware of the possibility of a **GROUP** formation. It should always be included in the game plan and reviewed weekly. One surprise GROUP formation a week in the defensive team period should be sufficient. If the opponent has shown a tendency toward GROUP formation, then more time needs to be spent in review.

UNBALANCED LINE ADJUSTMENTS

As we review special situations and formations, there is one other area that needs to be covered by the staff for the defensive package: the **UNBAL-ANCED LINE**. This shows up every now and then (maybe more in college) when a pro offensive coordinator tries to surprise the defense with an unbalanced line. To be prepared, and to decide how to play versus this formation, it should be a part of the game plan.

The simplest way is to line up on the ball. We do that defensively all the time, and to do that versus the UNBALANCED LINE makes sense. However, if the opponent has shown the unbalanced line in earlier games, which may mean that it is a part of their offense, you may want to align **on the ball** and **align on the man**. This has always been my policy. After all, if the offense is not sure, they may be reluctant to show the alignment.

A mixture is valuable in many ways, and this is another example of why a mixture of fronts, coverages, and blitzes is important.

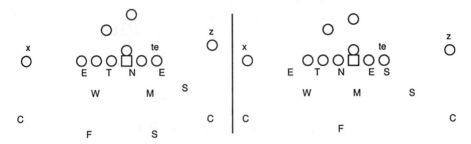

The diagram on the left above shows the **UNDER** front aligned on the **BALL**. When the **FRONT** is aligned on the **BALL**, the coverage should be a weakside coverage. This combination keeps the defense balanced and fits perfectly versus the offensive formation. The example shows **UNDER 8** or **2**. The diagram on the right shows the **UNDER** front aligned on the **MAN**. When the **FRONT** is aligned on the **MAN**, the coverage should be a strongside coverage. The example shows **UNDER 3 SKY**.

The diagram on the left above shows the **OVER** front aligned on the **BALL**. When the **FRONT** is aligned on the **BALL**, the coverage should be a weakside coverage. This combination keeps the defense balanced and fits perfectly versus the offensive formation. The example shows **UNDER 8** or **2**. The diagram on the right shows the **OVER** front aligned on the **MAN**. When the **FRONT** is aligned on the **MAN**, the coverage should be a strongside coverage. The example shows **UNDER 3 SKY**.

With the two plans discussed, the defense will be well prepared to handle the **UNBALANCED LINE** when surprised or when the offense uses it as a part of their offensive plan. I would like to leave one more tip with you before moving on: The **BLITZ**, for simplicity, should be aligned on the **BALL**. This keeps the **blitz paths** the same and simple for the defensive personnel. It also allows for the proper use of DEUCE or TRIO coverage based on the offensive formation.

8

DISCIPLINE, MOTIVATION, AND STEP-BY-STEP TEACHING

DISCIPLINE

A. What It Means and How to Achieve Success

There are many different ways to address discipline and motivation. In fact, there are probably as many different ways as there are coaches. In the final analysis, it is up to the individual in charge: What he believes. What he expects. How he communicates. What he will tolerate. And what is beyond compromise.

Rules vary from team to team. We had rules when I was in high school, in college, in the Marine Corps, an assistant and head coach in college, an assistant and head coach in professional football, and a director of athletics at a major university. But regardless of the situation and the rules, we still had our problems, as most teams do.

Quite simply, discipline means doing things right and having the self-control to follow through. In all group situations, there are rules, regulations, and policies which are designed to ensure success. It is expected that they will be fair and will be followed. While some may not agree with them, each individual is expected to establish the habits necessary for success.

297

Part of discipline is a positive attitude, to establish a "can do" frame of mind as opposed to a "can't do" approach. Yes, there will be problems, but we can control the approach we take to find the solutions.

The distractions that interfere with performance need to be eliminated. When I was in high school, two distractions were cigarettes and occasionally alcohol. During those years, I never recall hearing about drugs. Today, tobacco and alcohol are prevalent among high school and college students, as are drugs in some instances. The same is true in professional athletics. Although there has been a steady decline in smoking by the athlete in recent years, the "chew" or "dip" has become popular. Although the professional athlete is older, the problems are the same or worse. In college, missing classes is the symptom of a problem. In professional football, the symptoms are being late for meetings, failure to meet weigh-in assignments, and missing curfew during training camp or the night before a game.

In high school and college, the penalty for breaking a rule is physical—up early (5 or 6 A.M.), extra running, running the stadium steps, or more one on one. In professional football, the penalty is financial. All fines are approved by the Players Association before the season starts, with final approval from the NFL office. As director of athletics, I met with the college coaches and encouraged them to be fair, be specific, and emphasize scholarship. We had a drug council, made up of faculty, the team doctor, administrators, and students. The drug prevention program was confidential and centered around random drug testing. Cases were discussed, but names were withheld from the student members.

The NFL has had its own testing program for several years. One test is administered to everyone (coaches, players, and staff) before the start of the season. From then on, testing is random based on a certain percentage of team members. Abusers are tested more often, and I believe that, for the most part, the program is effective.

There definitely is a need for rules in football. Ideally, the staff, administration, and players should be part of the discussion on rules, so that they have an opportunity to offer input. That is very important. Including all parties concerned in the decision-making process helps to make the entire program more realistic and acceptable.

One topic that needs to be included in the discussion of rules is revoking the privilege to participate. It is my firm conviction that sometimes the only penalty that gets a player's attention is to say, "You can't play." In the final analysis, "you can't play" gets the attention of the player when all else fails. That holds true for the high school, college, and professional athlete. Coaches and administrators finally seem to be waking up to this type of reprimand.

There is no doubt in my mind that the "can't play" penalty will get the athlete's attention. Together with counseling, it is a step toward solving the problem and returning the individual to active participation as a player and a good citizen.

People of good character are needed by all successful organizations, teams, and programs. Everything you do is a reflection on you, your family, the team, and the entire organization. Character includes the moral strength and dependability to overcome adversity and win. How one performs as an individual is reflective of one's character.

B. Rule Violations and Fines

The following list represents standard rule infractions. I have intentionally not indicated the amounts of the fines.

1. **Overweight** (failure to meet reporting or weekly weight)—fine is per pound per day
2. **Unexcused absence** from mandatory off-season meeting
3. **Unexcused absence** from a scheduled meeting (team, position, practice, training room, doctor, transportation)
4. **Late for any scheduled meeting**
5. **Unexcused absence from curfew**
6. **Late for curfew,** up to 30 minutes after scheduled time (more than 30 minutes late is defined as an absence)
7. **Unexcused absence for scheduled promotional activity** (public relations office)
8. **Late for a scheduled promotional activity**
9. **Failure to report an injury** to the trainer or team doctor (an injury must be reported no later than the next day following a game or practice)
10. **Loss of all or part of the playbook**
11. **Leaving the bench area to enter a fight on the field**
12. **Conduct detrimental**—repeated violations as defined by the head coach will result in escalation of the fine (Conduct detrimental is any type of behavior detrimental to the team and the organization and may result in a **fine and suspension** for a period of time to be defined.)

The only legitimate excuse for a missed appointment is personal or immediate family illness or problems. The player should notify the coach as soon as possible (the coach should provide each player with his office and home phone numbers).

Fine money can be donated to charity. The captains should meet with the squad and then recommend charities to the head coach.

C. Team Rules

1. It is each player's responsibility to **be on time** for all scheduled activities.
2. **Curfew** is 11:00 P.M. during training camp, on road trips, and at home. Lights are to be out by 11:15 P.M. A player is late for curfew if he is not in his room or has a guest in his room after 11:00 P.M.
3. **Women** are not permitted in a player's room (at training camp or the hotel) at any time.
4. Unauthorized use of **drugs** is prohibited.
5. Players are not permitted to associate with **gamblers** or frequent places where gambling occurs.
6. At no time will a player be allowed to have in his possession at training camp or in the locker room **firearms** or other deadly **weapons**.
7. **Radios, stereos, and televisions** should be played at a low sound level. Players should be considerate of their neighbors and will be informed if the sound is too loud, If the volume is not turned down, the player or players will be fined. (This problem has been alleviated somewhat with the use of earphones.)
8. **Transportation** will leave on time—**the coach's time**. There will be no head count or unnecessary waiting. Allow plenty of time for unexpected delays. A player who misses transportation must supply his own, via the fastest available means. Players are responsible for being on time to all meetings and practices. We will always travel as a team.
9. Players are responsible for all **personal expenses** incurred on road trips. These expenses must be paid upon leaving the hotel.
10. Official **weigh-in** will be on Thursday of each week. If a player is over his assigned weight, he will be fined and reweighed each successive day until he reaches his assigned weight. Be on time for weigh-ins.
11. Following a **road game**, all players must return home with the team, unless excused by the head coach.
12. No **alcohol** is allowed in the dormitories and never in excess in public. No hard liquor is allowed at any time.

The above team rules are provided as an example to help you to better understand the problems encountered and how the professional team attempts to handle discipline. As a college coach, I had a similar group of rules. The main difference was the punishment, which was physical instead of monetary. For example, if a player was overweight, I would read his name and the amount he was over. The squad made it so tough on the player that he was embarrassed, and the problem was usually corrected as a result of the squad's attitude toward the individual.

People want and expect discipline. They want and expect it from their parents, from their schools, from their jobs, and from their coaches. In many instances, they also want and expect discipline from their peers.

The above examples of discipline for the professional athlete are only a sample of the areas that are usually a part of the player's responsibility. I reemphasize the "can't play" suspension as the only form of discipline that gets the repeated violator's attention. I am glad to see this type of penalty being used more and more. Coaches, administrators, and governing bodies have finally come to realize that it may be necessary to suspend a player.

TEACHING: A PART OF MOTIVATION

The ideas expressed in this section have proven successful for me over the years. If I were to accept another coaching position, I would put these ideas into action again.

First and foremost, find out as much as is humanly possible about your assistant coaches and players. Get to know them and their families. Learn their likes and dislikes. Ask their opinions, and listen to their thoughts concerning a decision. All good relationships have both a professional and a social aspect. If one aspect is injured, the other will hold the relationship together.

It is definitely easier to develop and maintain a relationship with the staff than with the players, especially the social aspect. But you do have help in developing your relationship with the players. Each assistant is responsible for his group. By working with the assistants and discussing each player, the coach and the assistant will develop a working philosophy for each individual. The phrase "everybody on the same page" is important to the relationship and everything we do. Establish trust. Treat each team member fairly. Maintain an open-door policy. Involve people in making decisions. Compliment success, and redirect performance that needs to be improved.

Think back to when you were a player or an assistant. What did you expect? How important was it to you to be aware of what was going on? Did you like to be involved? The answers to those questions will help you address the issues being discussed here.

A. Preparation Is Basic to Performance

To have a good practice, both the players and coaches must be prepared. In many cases, there is a lack of preparation by the players and at times on the part of the coaches. This often carries over into lack of preparation for a game. Preparation is the work one does in getting ready for practice. It is work done off the field, at home, or in meetings prior to practice. It is accomplished with the aid of a coach or alone as an individual. To have a good practice, time must be spent in preparation. This is true for the teacher/coach as well as the student/player. Thought, study, and visualization are all part of the preparation process. Practice without proper preparation is like playing a game without practice. Sometimes when we see a game film, we wonder how much practice was involved.

In many cases, the student/player, or even the teacher/coach, must be taught how to prepare. The technique is foreign to many young players and coaches. This is particularly true of visualization. What does the word mean? How do you do it? Why is it important? It took me several years to fully understand the "what," "how," and "why" of visualization. It has been shown that the mind does not know the difference between visualizing and actually doing a technique or assignment. When I realized the importance of this point, I immediately began to visualize as part of my preparation. I continue to use the technique to this day, and nothing has helped me as much in my preparation. Visualization has been an important part of preparing this book. Visualizing what I wanted it to be and how I wanted to present the material was helpful to me. Simply put, visualization is forming a mental image or picture in your mind of what you want to accomplish. A player can visualize the proper technique used in making a tackle, just as a student can visualize the proper technique in presenting a speech to a class. Both are preparation in getting ready for the actual activity, and both are necessary for success. If you aren't already using visualization, begin to visualize today as part of your preparation.

B. Ability to Read

Another factor that has a bearing on preparation is the reading ability of the student/player. As the teacher/coach, the question you must ask yourself is, "Can the student/player read and understand the playbook well enough to study it?" This was always one of my main concerns with incoming rookies. I strongly believed that it was important for me to understand the reading and comprehension level of the rookie. At our first meeting, we would open the playbook and take turns reading aloud. I would begin and then call on both veterans and rookies. It may have been a way to keep their attention on the material being covered, but, more importantly, it gave me some indication of the reading level of the new players. In other words, I needed to find out if I could be reasonably sure that every player would be able to comprehend the assigned reading material. Most could, but every year or two one of our more promising rookies had difficulty. This was good information to have, because if those recruits were going to help us, we had to find another way to teach them. We could not rely on an assignment to read the playbook as a method to teach the individual.

The walk-through became a popular substitute to help solve this problem, and it also immediately became part of the step-by-step approach to learning. The walk-through has been an integral teaching aid on every team with which I have been involved. It was a review that reinforced the veteran, and it proved to be an extremely important teaching aid to the new player. As coaches, we are always looking for ways to move our team ahead, to gain the edge, and to be totally prepared. On the teams I coached, the walk-through, meetings, and individual preparation all became a part of our total package prior to practice.

C. The Three P's

Each person must make a commitment to accept individual responsibility to do everything possible to **prepare**, **practice**, and **play** in the best possible manner. The first "P" is **preparation**—off the field, reviewing the scouting report, studying the tapes of the opponent, and each individual studying the player he will be opposite. Next is coming to **practice** prepared to review the things the coaching staff will present to help the player improve. As the player improves, he is also preparing himself to **play** the game. By reviewing different situations, the player becomes more aware of what he needs to know to be successful. A player who has properly **prepared** and **practiced** efficiently has an opportunity to **play** effectively and contribute to a win. Many players must learn how to do these things, in which case patience on the part of the staff is very important.

D. Step-by-Step Teaching

To be a good teacher or coach, first you must have **knowledge** of the subject matter, and then you must be able to **demonstrate that knowledge**. This is best accomplished by breaking down the assignment or technique being taught using a step-by-step approach. For example, there are several individual steps in catching a ball: (1) **look the ball into your hands**; (2) **catch the ball in your hands**; (3) **put it away** (pop your head down), **hand over the point**; and (4) **use a cross-body action** as you run to protect the ball from being knocked loose. By breaking the assignment or technique down into small parts, players have a better opportunity to learn the total picture.

The same is true of alignment, stance, the defensive charge, tackling, or any technique that you want to teach. A great example defensively is what is referred to as the defensive progression. The **defensive progression** must be executed in order. It begins with **alignment**, then **stance, movement on the ball** (the charge), **control the blocker, locate the ball** (shed the blocker), **pursue**, and **tackle**. If, for example, a player attempts to locate the ball before he controls the blocker, he will more than likely be blocked. The offensive player will have an opportunity to put his head by the defensive player's shoulder.

E. Practice Is the Proving Ground

The assignment or technique that has been taught must be practiced. The final part of the teaching process is **evaluation**. Compliment a player or student who has achieved and been successful. Make him aware that he has done what you wanted. If a player fails to achieve, then a correction must be made and the player redirected. In either case, it is important to compliment or redirect as quickly as possible. Do it now, not tonight, tomorrow, or after the game—but **now**, as soon as possible.

Sometime during the teaching period, a fundamental principle of learning takes place: Kilpatrick's theory of learning. Kilpatrick said, "You never learn anything until you accept it to act upon" (in other words, until you accept it to actually do). The actual "doing" may occur today, tomorrow, next week, next month, or never. We have all known "head-nodders." Those are players who nod their heads and agree with everything being said. However, when it is time to apply the assignment or technique in a game situation, they fail to accomplish the task. They were seemingly in agreement, but they had failed to learn. They did not "accept it to act upon."

F. Don't Guess

One way to be effective in jumping a player ahead is to play a game with him. The name of the game is DON'T GUESS. I explain to the player what I mean, and I explain to the player what I expect. The rules are simple. If I ask the player a question and he does not know the answer, he is to say, "I don't know." It doesn't take very many "I don't knows" for the player to quickly learn that he needs to prepare better, which in a way is Kilpatrick's theory of learning—"accepting it to act upon" or accepting it to do. The question usually revolves around the use of the **eyes**. If the player has a definite person to see in the offensive formation, the question might be: "What did the TE do?" "What did the 'Z' do?" "What did the offensive guard or tackle in front of you do?" You get the point. Be definite, and ask definite questions—questions that you have stressed as the coach.

Next, place the player in a controlled practice situation and show him the formation or play that you want him to see and react to properly. Why a controlled situation? There is only one reason: as the coach, you want the player to experience success, to gain confidence, and to get the "feel" of proper execution. Step-by-step teaching and visualization are important to learning and successful execution.

Step-by-step teaching has proven successful in every area of learning. For example, the San Diego Police Department uses the step-by-step approach to teach rookies. Many of the procedures involve the safety of the individual and are therefore a "must" in the field. The same importance is placed on the assignment and techniques that are taught in defensive or offensive football.

PRACTICE

What is practice? Practice is time on the field that normally is divided into several parts. Those parts are warm-up, individual, group, and team. The warm-up and team periods are generally scheduled. Depending on the day and the objective, the individual and group periods may or may not be a part of a practice. In some cases, one position may be involved in an individual period and other positions may be involved in a group period.

The **warm-up** is just what the word implies. It can consist of formal calisthenics, stretching, and some form of jogging or running. I like the squad to be together during this period, but it is often divided by individual positions. In either case, the assistants need to be involved by walking around and encouraging individuals in their group to follow the leader. This is the reason why I like to have the squad together, because this is the first opportunity to develop a **team concept**, where each individual accepts responsibility for carrying out his assignment. Indeed, the assignment could be an exercise, stretching, or some other warm-up activity. The important thing is that the initial emphasis is on **listening**, following a command, and **working together** to a successful completion. It is teamwork, it is discipline, and there is nothing more pleasing to observe than a group working together in unison to accomplish an objective.

In the **individual period**, each assistant has his position and works on the little things necessary for the player to achieve the ultimate goal. We hear a lot about goals. We all have them—but we seldom hear about the "little things" that can help us accomplish our goals. The individual period is a teaching period, a technique period. Defensively, the line may be working on movement on the ball, the linebackers may be working on controlling the blocker, and the defensive backs may be working on their footwork and how to change direction. Pick out one, two, or at the most three techniques to work on during this period. Keep the period moving quickly, but always compliment performance or redirect if necessary. As the warm-up period was the beginning of the team concept, the individual period is the beginning of the step-by-step teaching approach. Successful performance is complimented, and performance that needs improvement is redirected. It is important to establish **now** that each attempt is an opportunity to **win** and to be successful. Equally important is immediately establishing the desire to be the best and to do it right the first time. Perfect practice is the byword.

Group work is the next part of practice. Pass offense versus pass defense is practice that involves the passing game. Seven on seven (the offensive line and backs versus the defensive line and linebackers) develops the running game and run defense. Half-line passing emphasizes the right side of the formation throwing against the left side of the secondary or the right side of the formation running plays versus the left side of the defensive line and linebackers. All have merit and are necessary to improve. It is a full-speed learning period with no tackling. The offense and the defense work together to carry out their assignments.

A. Work Against Each Other

Contrary to what some may believe, the best defensive period for me has been versus the number one offense. It may even be defined as an offensive period. It is good for the defense because the offense is working to time up the pass or the run. We are playing our defense and, if necessary, giving the offense the variation they need to see. This is better for the defense than working against an offense using cards to describe the action. When using cards, the offensive coaches are using their backups and sometimes even borrowing defensive players or kickers to fill in. The timing is off, the picture is poor, and the work is an assignment review—but very little else. In Miami, Wednesday was offensive day, and it was our best defensive day.

Even if we had to change parts of our coverage or play a different front, it remained our best defensive day. As coaches, we convinced our players of the importance of seeing plays run correctly at the proper tempo. The next day, Thursday, was defensive day. By the time we got to the team period, the backups, extra defensive players, and kickers were usually all involved, giving us a picture of the opponent's anticipated play. We worked against each other again on Friday. We usually worked in shorts, but our red zone period was one of the best. Defensively, we were working against the best. At times, we needed to make a coverage adjustment to give the offense an accurate picture of the opponent. Whatever the case, it remained a great defensive period. The sessions on Wednesday and Friday helped us to improve. As long as we didn't lose ground on Thursday, we were okay.

This method and theory of work may be difficult to visualize, especially in college. At the college level, with increased numbers and the presence of scout teams, it is probably necessary to work off of cards to ensure the play or defense is run properly. The same may even be true in high school. The problem is that the offense uses makeup personnel versus the defense, and the defense uses makeup personnel versus the offense. What develops is a half learning situation. As defensive coaches, we try hard to develop a learning attitude even though we are giving the offense a picture of the opponent's defense. This is very difficult when using makeup personnel and cards to show the charges and assignments. It may be difficult to imagine, but a Wednesday offensive day practice in Miami was an excellent period for the defense. Another example was our two-minute practice. We always worked against each other using our own offense and defense. There was never a more competitive period, and it was very profitable for both sides.

All coaches are faced with a limited amount of teaching time. Working against each other gives a team more time to improve and be the best. The San Diego Chargers proved it in the AFC championship game against the Pittsburgh Steelers to win the right to play in Super Bowl XXIX. The game came down to the two-minute period. The Steelers moved the ball, but the Chargers were perfect on fourth down inside the ten. Dennis Gibson, our middle linebacker, got the knockdown and we advanced. We had practiced the situation many times versus our number one offense and were prepared when the situation developed in the game.

Being successful in working against each other in a learning situation, with a learning attitude, requires a staff that believes in the system. "How to" must also be taught. Very few players, regardless of who they are or where they have been, have participated in this type of practice. It is not difficult; for example, if it is an offensive period, the defense will align and take the proper charge. There is solid initial contact, but the offense is allowed to run the play. There is no tackling. Emphasis must be placed on staying on your feet. With the reduction in college scholarships, more and more college programs will begin to use the pro method of practice, especially in the spring. Hopefully, the spring experience will carry over to the fall. The same is true of the high school program that is limited in numbers. All I can say is try it—it will help you to improve and be the best.

The final practice period is **team work**. The procedure has already been discussed and the pros and cons justifiably considered. No tackling is involved, and every action is as near full speed as possible, with limited contact. Both the offense and defense can benefit. As I mentioned, this method was our best defensive day in Miami. True, both the defense and the offense will need to add the plays or alignments necessary to give special attention to the respective unit, but this can easily be accomplished within the framework of the practice. The benefit to the unit is establishing the full-speed tempo needed to prepare for game-like situations. Also, this type of team practice requires the coaches to make short and to the point comments in complimenting or redirecting. This in itself is important, because in many ways it involves the procedure necessary on game day.

B. Game Day/Game Plan

It is game day. We have prepared, we have practiced, and now it is time to "add the emotion" necessary to perform and to measure our performance in competition. Each week we see games played where there is a lack of emotion. As coaches, we must strive to teach the importance of emotion and help the players reach the desired level that is needed to perform successfully. "Adding emotion" must be taught in practice, just like any other technique. Every drill requires a certain amount of emotion, and you can stand back and quickly observe the player who possesses or the player who lacks true emotion. There are varying degrees of emotion. Some have the necessary "added emotion," and others need to be redirected. You cannot wait until game day and suddenly turn the emotion on by flipping a switch. Many of the great players whom I have observed exhibit a practice tempo similar to that on game day. Two who come to mind immediately are Jerry Rice and Junior Seau. Both as nearly as possible simulate game day actions as they practice.

The SARA principle is a problem-solving technique used by the San Diego Police Department, among other organizations. The acronym SARA represents a four-step process: **scanning**, **analysis**, **response**, and **assessment**. Game day is the response. Response is the result of scanning (gathering information on the opponent) and analysis (examination of the information). Assessment occurs after the game.

The game plan is a composite of the fronts, coverages, and blitzes that will be used by down and distance and position on the field. The score and the time remaining are always factors but seldom create a problem that has not been addressed in the plan. Special situations are also covered in the game plan—two minutes before the half and at the end of the game, unusual formations, unbalanced line, and group formations. Other reminders may also be listed for the signal caller's convenience.

You never know when a play will win a game. Therefore, each play must be approached as if it were the most important. Success on a play brings celebration, but you must quickly put the celebration behind you and get ready for the next snap. Poor performance on a play brings disappointment, and you must just as quickly put the disappointment behind you and get ready for the next snap. This philosophy is the key to success. Get ready to play each down, and be the best that you can be. At least half of the problems that develop during a game are the result of poor focus or poor attention to detail. Success demands 110% focus and effort on each play. Even partially thinking about what happened on the play before, whether successful or unsuccessful, hurts your opportunity to win.

C. Three Out of Five Is a Must

Take advantage of each opportunity. You cannot let an opportunity slip out of your grasp. That only encourages the opponent. How does a player take advantage of an opportunity? He takes advantage of an opportunity by learning his assignment and successfully carry it out at least three times out of five opportunities. Why do I base success on five opportunities? The answer is that the number five is a meaningful number to discuss with the individual and is easy to remember. If every member of the unit dedicates himself to this one principle, then the defense will have the proper pattern. Five for five would be a superb performance, and four out of five is certainly a winner, but three out of five still gives you a chance to win. Players can think in terms of five opportunities and strive for success.

D. Football Is a Physical and a Mental Game

At times, a player may lose a physical battle because his opponent is stronger or quicker. The purpose of off-season and in-season work is to develop the physical capability to enable players to win their share of the physical battles.

But they must also **win the mental battle**. An individual or a unit that misses an assignment has lost the mental battle. When a player loses the mental battle, he does not have the opportunity to win the physical battle. He hits the wrong man or the wrong gap. He covers the wrong man or runs the wrong route. No one will judge him on how well he performed physically if he misses his assignment and loses the mental battle. Players and coaches work hard to **eliminate the missed assignment**. This philosophy begins in the first meeting as a defense and continues throughout preparation, practice, and play. It is the trademark of a winning team.

In discussing the mental phase, I try to accomplish several things. The first is how we teach to help us accomplish our objective. The second is to emphasize and reemphasize the mental approach to the game. This begins in the team meetings, is extended to the warm-up, and continues throughout the entire practice. I stress daily the important of lining up properly. Without proper alignment, an assignment is missed before the ball is snapped. In other words, the player has no opportunity to carry out his assignment. It is a mental error, with no opportunity to win the physical battle. This type of error negates all the effort and emotion that the player has exerted. Perfect practice develops perfect play.

There are many more **mental errors** than physical errors in a game. In my opinion, there is no excuse for the mental error. "Nothing but air" causes a player to make a mental error. What is a mental error? A mental error is lining up on the wrong man, lining up in the wrong gap, hitting the wrong man, running the wrong path, taking the wrong drop, or covering the wrong man. There is no physical action involved in a mental error, but the numbers are significant. If you keep the total number of missed assignments in the range of five to eight per game, you have an opportunity to contribute to the win defensively. If the numbers reach double digits, you have to be fortunate to have an opportunity to contribute to a win. In most cases, the offense cannot score enough points to overcome the mental lapse of the defense.

Football is a **team** game. No individual player on either side of the ball can be totally responsible for the success of the unit. The **team concept** must be taught; it is not inherited or passed on by osmosis. Each player must first of all believe in himself. Next, he must believe in the person playing in front of him, beside him, and behind him. And the people in those positions must believe in him. What do I mean by "believe"? Each player must believe that he will successfully carry out his assignment and that the other players will successfully carry out their assignments. By working together, a proper defensive pattern will develop on every play, and the result will be a physical battle.

On the **first series,** the first question that needs to be asked is: "Is it like we planned?" If it is, the game plan is working. If offensive changes were made, the next question is: "Do we need to adjust?" If the answer is yet, what changes need to be made? Those are decisions that must be made during the first series and each series thereafter. Then, when the defense comes off the field, the coaches get the defense together and make the adjustment. I never like to make a major adjustment with the defense on the field. I do not like to be surprised, and I most certainly do not want to surprise the defense. In fact, I am reluctant to make a major decision (one that we have not anticipated or practiced) even on the sideline. I usually wait until the half for that type of change, when I have the opportunity to talk to the team, discuss the change, and answer questions. By making the change in the locker room, I can more easily make sure that "everybody is on the same page." If a change is needed, make it immediately, and remember to compliment good performance and correct or redirect poor performance.

Making a change or adjusting quickly is one reason why I like a **complete game plan.** By that I mean a game plan that covers all situations and has the flexibility of options. At times, the assistant coaches would tell me that we were putting too much into our plan. And we probably were. However, I never liked to remove the basic fronts, coverages, or blitzes from our plan. I always liked to have our basic plan available every week. From week to week, we might add a front adjustment, a coverage adjustment, and a blitz adjustment, but we never eliminated what I considered to be our basic package. Some of the assistants with whom I worked probably never understood what I meant by "our basic package." Their thinking was that we were giving the players too much. I tried to reduce the material, but I must admit that I sometimes felt we were too limited. I always felt good when we had anticipated properly, were prepared, and had practiced the assignment. I mention this because I think it is a very real situation. By recognizing it early, the staff has time to make the best decision possible. There comes a time in every game when you need flexibility, and options give you the flexibility to make a change and redirect.

Halftime during the season and the play-offs is about 12 minutes and close to 30 minutes or more during the Super Bowl (because of the halftime show). Twelve minutes is long enough and close to 30 minutes is much too long. Now that I have retired, I enjoy listening to the commentators talk about what is happening and what needs to be accomplished at halftime. Most of the time, their suggestions were probably handled between series on the sideline. Let's review the procedure I followed at halftime.

First, the **coach in the coach's box** draws on the board any problems that developed in the first half. These are usually on the board when the team arrives from the field, and it is usually the material that I and the other staff members asked to be placed on the board. After looking at the problem(s) and making any necessary comments, I then turn to the other coaches and ask if they have anything to add. After their comments regarding their positions, I take a minute or two to summarize and briefly explain what we must accomplish in the second half. If we must "shut 'em out" in the second half to win, every member of the defense must know it. Everyone must be aware of the facts, whatever they may be. Then it is usually time for the head coach to say "all up" and to summarize for the entire team. During the summary, an official comes in and says, "It's time to go." The equipment man opens the door, and off we go for the second half.

The procedure for the **second half** is similar to the first. Both the offense and the defense make adjustments, and after everyone settles down, it becomes a matter of who does the best job in physically and mentally carrying out their assignment in a game situation. After all, it is only a game, and the team that carries out its assignment the best is usually in position to win.

The reporters and television analysts don't understand this. They are in the dressing room after the game asking what the secret was. If they can find none, then it is their job to create one for the 11:00 broadcast and the next morning's headline. And then what do we do as coaches? We can't wait to see the tape—to see what really happened to our well-devised and well-thought-out game plan. This is our period of assessment.

PRACTICE SCHEDULE

There are many different approaches to the practice schedule. To keep things simple, I have assigned each day a number, working through the week to game day.

A. Day #1

- View game tape before practice and meet in groups by position.
- **Equipment**: Helmet, shorts, and jersey. Tape before each practice.
- **Loosen by position or as a team**: I like to loosen as a team rather than by position. Loosening as a team is another opportunity to do things together. The players can still be in their groups, with the assistant coach circulating through the group and encouraging the players to follow the leader.

- **Break into groups by position**: Review the game tape for mistakes and any new learning that will be added for the next opponent.
- **Team period (defense)**: Approximately ten plays to review mistakes and new material versus offensive formations and favorite plays.
- **Team period (offense)**: Same period as defined above. Approximately ten plays.
- **Team together**: Two-minute review (depending on the number of plays, one group or two groups). Approximately 15 to 20 minutes.
- **Break into groups by position**: Run gassers three times (over and back equals one) on the watch. **Receivers and defensive backs**, 30 to 35 seconds; **running backs, quarterbacks, and linebackers**, 35 to 40 seconds; and **linemen**, 40 to 45 seconds. Sixty seconds rest between each gasser. Meet with coach after running.

B. Day #2

- **Meet before practice by group** (offense/defense) and take on game plan. After the game plan, meet by position to review opponent's tape and tape of yesterday's practice.
- **Equipment**: Full pads.
- **Loosen**: After loosening, finish with team starts (defense and offense).
- **Break into groups by position**: Individual work by position (include tackling).
- **Combination period (defense)**: Line and linebackers versus offensive line and backs (seven on seven) drill. Eight plays—opponent's favorite inside runs. Defensive backs—safeties with line and linebackers. Corners with coach or with receivers in one-on-one drills. Quarterback and receivers—time up individual routes.
- **Combination period (offense)**: Same as defined above. Approximately eight plays. Eight plays versus defensive line and linebackers. Eight plays—inside runs and off-tackle.
- **Pass offense and defense**: Emphasis on offense—12 plays. Emphasis on defense—12 plays. As much as is practical, use team terminology and numbering.
- **Offense and defensive lines**: Pass protection and pass rush.
- **Team period (defense)**: Twelve plays, run/pass blitz and pass-only blitz.
- **Team period (offense)**: Fifteen plays, off-tackle, sweeps, play pass, screens, and draws.
- **Break into groups by position**: Run gassers three times. Meet with coach after running.

C. Day #3

- Meet before practice by position, review opponent's tape and tape of yesterday's practice.
- **Equipment**: Full pads.
- **Loosen**: After loosening, finish with team starts (defense and offense).
- **Break into groups by position**: Individual work by position (include tackling).
- **Combination period (defense)**: Line and linebackers versus offensive line and backs (seven on seven) drill. Eight plays—opponent's favorite inside runs. Defensive backs—safeties with line and linebackers. Corners with coach or with receivers in one-on-one drills. Quarterback and receivers—time up individual routes.
- **Combination period (offense)**: Same as defined above. Approximately eight plays. Eight plays versus defensive line and linebackers.
- **Pass offense and defense**: Emphasis on offense—12 plays. Emphasis on defense—12 plays. As much as is practical, use team terminology and numbering.
- **Offense and defensive lines**: Pass protection and pass rush.
- **Team period (defense)**: Fifteen plays, opponent's offense, run and play pass.
- **Team period (offense)**: Eight to ten plays versus run/pass blitz and pass-only blitz; 12 plays—sweeps, play pass, screens, and draws.
- **Break into groups by position**: Run gassers three times. Meet with coach after running.

D. Day #4

- Meet before practice by position, review opponent's tape and tape of yesterday's practice.
- **Equipment**: Shorts and shoulder pads with helmet.
- **Loosen**: Finish with team starts (defense and offense).
- **Break into groups by position**: Individual work by position. Linemen—movement on the ball. Linebackers—pass drops. Defensive backs with receivers and quarterbacks.
- **Combination period**: Red zone passing.
- **Pass offense and defense**: Emphasis on offense—12 plays. Emphasis on defense—12 plays. As much as is practical, use team terminology and numbering.
- **Offense and defensive lines**: Pass protection and pass rush. Offensive and defensive line review.

- **Team period (defense)**: Fifteen plays, opponent's offense, run and drop-back pass.
- **Team period (offense)**: Fifteen plays, best run plays plus screens and draws.
- **Two-minute review**: At least one time for the #1 offense versus the #1 defense.
- **Break into groups by position**: Defensive line and offensive line meet with coaches. Quarterbacks and receivers throw individual patterns versus the defensive backs at the goal line. Remaining quarterbacks, all running backs, and tight ends throw individual patterns in the field versus the linebackers. **CP**: The tight ends may be divided between the receivers at the goal line and the running backs.

E. Day #5

- Meet before practice by position, review tape of yesterday's practice.
- **Equipment**: Shorts and helmet. Watch special team tape as a team.
- **Loosen**: On own, review offense/defense plus kicking game review.
- **Team period**: Eight plays—opponent's offense versus defense. Eight plays—offense versus opponent's defense.
- **Kicking review**: Punt and punt return, kickoff and kickoff return, field goal and field goal rush, extra point and extra point rush.
- **Meet together**: Coach announcements plus game comments.
- **Night meeting**: Meeting for an hour is a great time to tie up the loose ends. It is another opportunity to review a partial game tape of something that needs to be stressed (may use parts of several games). Finish the time with a review of the game plan, including substitution alerts.
- **Snack (buffet style)**: Immediately after the meeting.

F. Game Day

The pre-game meal (buffet style) is usually four hours before game time. Thirty minutes before the meal is a good time for chapel services and mass. The only meetings are individual meetings by the coaches or group meetings by the offense or defense. The special teams met yesterday, so there should be no need to meet again as a group, although players can meet individually with coaches if necessary. Any meetings should be immediately after the pre-game meal and should last no longer than 30 minutes. The shorter the better, and then only to make final comments valuable to the entire group. A coach may want to meet with certain individuals immediately afterward, and this should be encouraged if necessary. This is also a good time to remind the players what time the bus leaves for the stadium and give them any other necessary information.

The above practice plan can, of course, be adjusted from time to time. However, practice days #2 and #3 should remain full pad days. You need to maintain the contact edge, and that can easily be done by wearing full pads on those days. If you need to lighten up the schedule, do that on day #1 and possibly go without shoulder pads on day #4.

Time is a factor for many programs at the college and high school level. The practice program can be adjusted to fit the time schedule. By all means, make sure that you cover the most important areas on the field, even if it is only a walk-through.

VIDEO EVALUATION: A USEFUL TEACHING AID

Coaching is one profession where you can pull out a videotape, turn it on, begin looking at it, and soon see something you did not notice in an earlier viewing. Why would you notice something new? For one thing, it probably was not on your mind to look for the technique, fundamental, or whatever you noticed for the first time in the previous viewing. By viewing a tape, you can find something new and different that you did not see before. This has happened to me and to all coaches, if they are honest about it.

Before studying a tape, know **what you want to look for** as you view it. Make a list of the things you want to see. Run a play back and forth until you find each item on your list. Then go to the next play and follow the same procedure. It may take more time than you are accustomed to spending, but it will be time well spent. When you have completed the project, you will have a record, and you will not need to look at that tape again for the same material. This is similar to the procedure followed in grading the offense, defense, or special teams. Specific items listed on a form are graded and the information is recorded.

For example, when grading a defensive lineman, the following items need to be studied and evaluated on every play: the **stance** (proper alignment as defined by the defense), the **charge** (did the player move on the ball), **control the blocker** (did the player stay square and keep the blocker's head from going past his shoulder), **locate the ball** (shed the block), **pursue** (did the player take the proper angle to the ball), and **tackle**. In grading, each defensive player is evaluated on the techniques required in his position. If, for example, a player lined up on the guard and should have been on the center, that would have resulted in a missed assignment. On a missed assignment, a player has no opportunity to show what he is capable of achieving. His work on that particular play versus the offense is over.

The videotape is the best tool a coach has to determine that a technique taught in practice is being used in the game. Is the player stepping with the proper foot? Is he aligned at the proper depth? Is he taking an inside technique or an outside technique as required by the defensive call? Is he reacting properly to the back and ball keys? These are all important items that need to be continually reviewed in the tape to make sure that the player is using them in a game situation.

What I am suggesting may be a new concept to some, perhaps not in grading a play, but it is certainly a new idea to use the same procedure every time you watch a tape. First define what it is you want to see. What is the purpose? There are many answers. Coaches use tapes in grading, in scouting an opponent, in scouting a player, and in gaining additional information. It is this last phase that haunts many of us, and we spend endless hours searching tapes for answers. Planning ahead and making a list before turning on the tape will prove profitable.

Viewing videotapes is important in the coaching profession. It helps us to evaluate ourselves and it helps us learn. For example, if we are teaching a technique in practice, we expect the technique to be used in the game. If it is, the tape will show that. If it is not, then we need to find out why not. Is it our teaching method? Is it the player? Is the material we are teaching too difficult to be carried out in an actual game situation? Does it just sound good in a meeting or a speech in a clinic? Whatever the purpose, viewing the tape is the assessment part of the SARA technique. Were we successful and did we accomplish the objective?

Let's revisit the SARA technique. **Scanning** is viewing the videotape in an objective manner to answer the questions on your list. **Analysis** is studying the material you gathered from scanning and deciding what it means. If a piece of information is missing, you must return to scanning. This may mean returning to the videotape to find the missing piece, or it may be something that you failed to list or overlooked. **Response** is developing the game plan to be used in the game. **Assessment** is examining the final result.

Studying videotape also helps coaches study and learn about the opponent. Videotape has virtually eliminated scouting the opponent. Now there is only one reason to scout an opponent—to find out about an injured player. How serious does the injury look? Was the injured player treated on the bench? Was he taken to the dressing room? You can see if he returned to the game. If he didn't, what happened to him? Did he leave the dressing room on crutches? Was he walking with a slight limp? Will he play next week? A tape cannot answer the last question, but it can answer everything else about the game.

In making a list, you are organizing your thoughts in terms of what information you want to collect from the tape. You are not wasting time; you are being objective in your search. And most of all, you are answering the questions that you deem important to preparation of the individual, the group, the team, and the game plan.

It is no secret that to be successful, you need a plan—a plan for scanning, a plan for analysis, and a plan for response. Success in these areas will provide the opportunity for success on game day. The next time you look at a videotape, make a list of what you want to see and the information you need, turn on the tape, and go to work. As you view the videotape, record the information. When you finish, you will feel a greater sense of satisfaction. You will have achieved the objective. You will have the information available to find the answer. You will be prepared.

You will also be better prepared and rested for practice, because you have the answers you need. You won't have to stay up all night looking at a tape over and over. You can look at it one time, review your list, record the information, and find the answer. At one time or another, we have all thought, "There must be a better way!" What I am suggesting is a better way to study and evaluate a videotape.

THE EYES LEAD THE BODY

In this chapter, we have discussed discipline, motivation, preparation, practice, evaluation of videotapes, and step-by-step teaching, all of which all important teaching aids for success and winning. Before closing, I would not do the topic justice if I did not spend some time talking about the **EYES**. To be perfectly honest, this discussion of the eyes may be much more important than any other topic I have discussed. In fact, it is so important that this section probably should have appeared first. We have discussed all facets of football—basic information, the signal caller, terminology, fronts, coverage, and the techniques involved in playing and coaching. I have used the word "**SEE**" many, many times. Often it appeared in uppercase letters, because it is the **key** to everything we do every day. The EYES are important—how we use them, what we see, what it means to us, what they help us to accomplish, and even what problems they keep us from experiencing. All of the above contribute to the proper use of the EYES. All sports depend on muscular movement. It is the EYES that lead and control the body and its muscular movement. In general terms, the EYES are probably the best teaching aid available to coaches.

My first conscious thought about the EYES centered around my parents and Dr. Stern, their eye doctor, when I was eight or nine years old. One of my parents was farsighted and one was nearsighted. Dr. Stern's comment to my parents was, "I can't wait to see how Bill's eyes turn out." He never lived to find out, and in my mid-thirties I began to need glasses to read and to see the film clearly in my work.

A. A Teaching Aid to Qualify as an Expert

My next recollection concerning the EYES was when I was in high school, playing football and later basketball. Blanton Collier, my coach, often talked about the EYES in describing the techniques of playing the game. I was an offensive guard and tackle, and I remember in pulling to lead the play I was taught to first locate the defender and to follow the defender up to the point of contact. In making contact, he taught the use of the EYES in hitting the spot—the belt buckle at the bend of the body (under the shoulders and above the waist). By picking out the defender and focusing on a part of him, my target was a specific spot. Success was improved by following the instruction of Coach Collier, and failure to properly use the EYES often resulted in a missed block. I was lucky that there was no film or tape to record my "got man" or "missed man" for the archives.

While in Marine Corps boot camp, the EYES again became a factor in my success as my training advanced to the rifle range. I was trained to fire the M-1, and after training I had to qualify. One of the keys to success was not only your firing position, but picking out a spot within the bull's-eye, which, if done properly, narrowed your margin of error and made you more accurate. The EYES, and what you were looking at, were the key to qualifying and success. This concept was not entirely new to me, and I found it interesting that many of the coaching points that I had learned from Coach Collier were similar to what my drill instructor and range coach were telling me. There is no doubt in my mind that the early application of and appreciation of the use of the EYES that I learned at Paris High was helpful to me on the rifle range at Parris Island, South Carolina.

Qualifying was exciting. From various distances, you were asked to fire at the target. I was doing well, and the final attempt was at 500 yards. I checked my sling, and I checked my elbow. At that distance, everything had to be perfect and in alignment. Next, you had to sight properly, pick out a spot inside the bull's-eye, and squeeze the trigger. I was perfect and qualified as an expert. I know Dr. Stern and Coach Collier would have been proud. I used my EYES, and my EYES helped me to achieve success.

B. Use the Eyes to Gain the Edge

Later, while attending Miami University in Ohio, I had the opportunity, while on vacation, to watch Coach Collier, then an assistant coach with the Cleveland Browns, grade films of the Browns' games. He used a hand-cranked viewer to study the action of each player, gave the player a grade on each technique, and recorded the breakdown. In each case, the EYES were an important part of the grade. What did the player see? What should he have seen? Did he react appropriately? It was obvious that many errors were the result of not picking out a spot to hit. Observing the grading technique reemphasized to me the use of the EYES and their importance in football and all activities. For example, if you are walking down the street and an obstruction is in your path, you make an adjustment. You walk around it or over it, but you don't fall over the obstruction. And you do all of this without a thought; it is second nature for you to adjust. You see the problem and make the adjustment. The same mechanism that allows us to adjust in everyday life also helps us to adjust in football or any sport. In tennis, you are supposed to bend your knees when hitting a low ball. This may be true, but if the EYES are watching the ball meet the racquet, the body will automatically adjust in order to hit the ball properly. The EYES lead and control the body and its muscular movement. You automatically sense the problem and adjust. As I learned in every endeavor, picking out a specific spot on the target helps to narrow the margin of error. In the final analysis, picking out a spot gives you a greater opportunity to be successful. It gives you the edge needed to win.

Upon my release from the service in 1947, I returned to the University of Kentucky to continue my education and play football. I soon found out that I was undersized as a lineman and not fast enough to succeed as a back or receiver. Veterans were returning almost daily for tryouts, hoping for a scholarship. Recognizing my situation, and with Coach Collier's guidance, I received an offer from Miami University in Oxford, Ohio. My early training, along with the Miami experience, prepared me for a life in coaching that I wanted and was fortunate enough to attain.

Coaching first at Miami and then at Ohio State with Woody Hayes in 1951 jump-started my career. In 1954, I had the opportunity to join Cleveland Browns assistant Blanton Collier at the University of Kentucky for eight years. It was here that proper use of the EYES really became alive in my coaching career. In coaching the offensive line, and later the defensive line, the EYES became a teaching aide in every technique we taught. Blanton Collier was first of all a teacher, and his application of the technique was learned through frame-by-frame study of films as an assistant with the Browns. He graded every position, and in doing so, the proper use of the EYES became more and more evident as a key to success in every technique. Both this and Kilpatrick's theory of learning were indeed important factors. Kilpatrick said, "You never learn anything until you accept it to act upon." You can nod your head and agree with everything that is said, but you never learn an assignment or a technique until you make yourself carry it out in a game situation.

C. The Eyes and the Receiver

For the next two years, I had the opportunity to join Coach Tommy O'Boyle at Tulane University. My initial assignment in 1962 was to coach the "lonesome end." It was a new experience. I could use the ball, but the thing that interested me more was the opportunity to include the EYES in my coaching. The EYES were a large part of my emphasis in coaching the offensive and defensive line. Now, it would be possible to use the EYES to a greater degree.

To work with the receivers was an opportunity to use everything that I had learned about the EYES. Knowledge of how the EYES lead and control the muscular movement of the body was very helpful to me. We worked daily on catching the ball in the hands and "popping the head down" to ensure that the players kept their EYES on the ball until after they made a catch. We also stressed placing the hand over the point of the ball and putting the ball away in a cross-body action. "Popping the head down" is the key to catching, and it ensures that the player keeps his EYES on the ball during the catch.

D. The Eyes and Defense

In 1963, John Rauch, our offensive coordinator at Tulane, became the head coach at Oakland. Our offense changed, and my assignment changed to defensive coordinator. The assignment also included coaching the linebackers. Here again, the EYES were just as important in defensive football as they had been with the offensive linemen and receivers. As a defensive player, and especially as a linebacker, it is important to pick out a spot to hit and to use peripheral vision in carrying out the assignment. The good athletes probably do a lot of things naturally, but using the EYES properly will make them more effective.

It was from this initial experience, plus others with the Miami Dolphins and Don Shula and later with Bobby Ross and the San Diego Chargers, that I maintain that the defensive coordinator should coach the linebackers. That statement will no doubt raise many eyebrows, because most coordinators are "walk-around" coaches with no specific position. In the last few years, we have even seen more coordinators in the coach's box. This may be fine for offensive coordinators, but the defensive leader needs to be on the sideline, close to the action, so he can feel the tempo of the game. Locating the ball is very important in defensive play, and to be the best, a player must use his EYES effectively.

Coaching the linebackers is an ideal assignment for the defensive coordinator. Why? The answer is simple when you take the time to think about the assignment of both the linebackers and the defense. The linebackers are involved with both the running game and the passing game. They must fit perfectly in both situations. Being the coordinator places you in close contact with the players, and the techniques, and the strategy involved with their responsibilities. I cannot leave this area without mentioning one other point. The place for the defensive line coach and linebacker coach to stand while working with their positions in practice is in front of the players. This means standing behind the offense, listening to the play called, and watching the reaction of the defensive players as the play is run. Again the EYES play a part. From in front, the coach can **see** the EYES of the player and make sure that he is seeing his key and looking at the blocking pattern properly. Looking in the right direction and seeing the right things is at least half the battle defensively. Adding the physical and emotional aspects will give the player the edge needed to win.

The bottom line is that throughout my career, I have come to recognize the importance of the use of the EYES. The experiences and opportunities highlighted here were valuable to me in learning and developing a philosophy of coaching and teaching that has survived over a period of time—four decades to be exact. If you find only one or two things I have presented helpful, I will consider my efforts a success.

9

DEVELOPING A
GAME PLAN:
THE KEY TO SUCCESS

Like everything else in football, there is more than one way to develop a game plan. Experience has taught me that, above everything else, a coach needs to have the best information possible to prevent an obvious error. How do you do that? Let's revisit SARA, a technique that was discussed earlier, which I learned in working with the San Diego Police Department.

The principles in SARA provide a method to obtain the information necessary to develop a game plan. The "S" is for **scanning**. What does scanning mean? It means watching tapes of the opponent and recording the information you find. It means recording what the opponent likes by **down and distance**. For example, suppose you are looking at first down. Does the opponent run? If so, do they run inside or outside? Do they pass? If so, do they use play action or drop back? Do they use draws and throw screen passes? The same information is gathered on second and third down. Those downs can also be broken down by down and distance. In other words, what does the opponent like on second and long, second and short, third and long, third and medium, third and short, and fourth down?

Next is **field position**. What does the opponent like when backed up inside their own 20 yard line? What do they like between the 20 and mid-field to the 50? What do they like from mid-field to the 20? What do they like from the ten in to score? Does the score make a difference in their play selection? For example, do they run more if they are ahead? Do they pass more if they are behind? When do they like the gimmick play—on first, second, or third down? Where on the field do they like the gimmick play?

This last area may not be important at all levels of competition, but it is extremely important at the professional level. When does the opponent substitute and on what down? What type of substitutions do they make—three wide receivers and a tight end, four wide receivers, or two tight ends and two wide receivers? Do they stay with regular personnel on third down? Is the quarterback under the center or in the shotgun alignment?

For many years, I always reviewed the **hash marks** to see if the opponent had a tendency to run to the wide side or into the sideline. Even after the hash marks were moved in and aligned with the goalposts, some teams had a hash mark tendency. With the hash marks as they are in college and high school, most teams have a hash mark tendency. It is helpful to know this in preparing the game plan.

Another observation that is useful is the **pattern of the offensive coordinator's call**. Some have no pattern, almost like they are pulling a call out of a hat. Others have a definite pattern to their calls. They may run 70% or more on first down, or they may pass 70% on second and long, with an occasional draw for balance. For example, I found that one team in particular had a pattern that gave the offensive team balance, but it also revealed an identifiable pattern. The caller did the following: If there was a run on first down and second down was seven or more, they would pass. If there was an incomplete pass on first down, the second and ten call would be a run. Normally, when the game was even, the caller alternated his calls on first down: run–pass–run–pass or pass–run–pass–run. Second and short was a run call an extremely high percentage of the time, unless it was second and six. On second and six, an occasional pass would show up. Third and long was a high percentage pass down, with an occasional draw or screen. Third and short was a run, with a play action pass at times on third and two. The pattern that was most useful to me was the one on first and second down. It was so strong that I based every first -and second-down call on the run/pass tendency. This example illustrates the importance of scanning and the proper use of analysis in developing the game plan.

Returning to SARA, after scanning comes "A," for **analysis**. Analysis means studying the information you have recorded and coming to a conclusion as to what it means. You may see a trend immediately, or you may not see a trend. Both are meaningful and helpful in your game preparation and practice. Analysis is gaining a true understanding of what the opponent is thinking and trying to accomplish. It thoroughly describes the intent of the opponent. The opponent may have been successful in one game and may have had difficulty in another. Analysis will let you concentrate on the situations where the opponent was successful. Proper analysis will show you the true picture, and you will be prepared to develop the game plan.

After scanning and analysis comes "R," for **response**. The response is the game plan, which includes preparing the plan, practicing the plan, and executing the plan during the game. In my opinion, you begin with your basic package. You study each area—the fronts, the coverages, and the blitzes—to see how each fits versus the information you have available. You may decide to use more over and fewer under fronts or more under and fewer over fronts. The same is true as you look at coverage. Cover 2 looks good, and you must decide what type of mixture is best. Maybe you need to consider cover 8 and cover 10 more. As you look at your blitz package, the main concern is finding something that will take advantage of the opponent's pass protection in a pass situation or help you stop the run in a run situation.

Is **something new** needed? Oftentimes, the answer is no. All that is needed is to call a certain line stunt more versus formation A, but not versus formation B. All of the coverages may be good, but cover 2 and cover 8 may need to be stressed more, with a mixture of cover 10 in run situations. The run/pass blitz package may be good, but it may be necessary to study what is best versus the opponent's substituted personnel in pass-only situations. The zone blitz package may be good, but what else, if anything, is needed? As a philosophy, I would rather have a little too much during the week and not use it on game day than not have enough. It is also a good idea to have a little something new each week. A new wrinkle helps to get the players' attention and it definitely requires added concentration. Both are important during preparation and practice during the week.

It is also important to **anticipate the unusual**. The unbalanced line, group formations, and the no-huddle offense are all part of the defensive package, and each must be reviewed during the week to ensure proper preparation. Each week, the team must have good work in two-minute situations, and the LAST PLAY call and alignment must be reviewed.

Last, but by no means least, is the **substitution plan**. Each player must be aware of the situation and a possible substitution and must listen intently for the call— jumbo, nickel, dime, or regular. I have always stressed that if you are involved in any substitution situation, you must be with the signal caller at all times. Along this same line, each player must be aware of who he backs up in case of injury. If #1 is not able to enter the game, #2 must be up and ready.

The last letter in SARA, "A," is for **assessment**. Assessment is the final result. Was the defense successful? What needs to be adjusted? All four pieces—scanning, analysis, response, and assessment—are part of preparing the game plan. Adjustments must be made immediately. Discuss a problem between series or at halftime. And remember to compliment and encourage if performance is good and to correct and redirect if performance is poor. **Do it now**, not after the game.

THE SIGNAL CALLER

The more I thought about coaching and the problems encountered, the more I came to the conclusion that a section of this book should be devoted to the signal caller. It may be as important as any other topic that I have discussed. I hesitate to say more important because, to me, the players are the key to everything we accomplish. I have learned through experience that there are times when a better call could have been made, but because of the players' belief in the call, as well as their emotion and execution, the call was successful. With a sense of humility, I do believe that the signal caller is important to the ultimate success of the defensive team. With this thought foremost in my mind, it is appropriate that I give the subject the attention and respect it deserves.

Success as a unit depends on each individual and how well he masters his assignment. As a player masters his individual assignment, he must strive to learn how to fit into the overall defensive call. It is only when he attains this knowledge and ability that the team can begin to reach the level of production necessary to win.

The defensive team must **stop the score**, whether a touchdown or a field goal. Statistics are used in many ways. Oftentimes, they can be rationalized to fit the desired result. In the final analysis, defensive success will be measured by the points scored. Weekly results should be posted, and how the defense ranks in all areas needs to be discussed. The team must strive to be the best. If the defense needs a shutout to win, then the team must be capable of producing a shutout. This is the attitude that must be developed and believed.

A. Down and Distance

Football at every level is a game of down and distance. Throughout each game, the defense will be confronted with first and ten more than any other situation. A win on first down will force the offense to "play your game." The signal caller and the entire defense must know the down and distance and what is required to win. **Three plays and out** is the objective. The defense, as a group, must understand what is required to play each down and distance category. The key to defensive success is **get the ball and come off the field**.

First and ten. The defense must force the opponent into second and long. To do this, the opponent must be held to three yards or less. While each game will depend on the strategy of the opponent, the majority of teams will attempt to establish the running game along with play action passes. By mixing fronts and primary run support, and by moving lineman through the use of charges, the defense can be effective in winning the first and ten battle. First and ten is a run and play pass down. Coverages and blitzes will be mixed, with emphasis on those that give the defense good run support and protection against the play action pass. Many times, a defense wins by knocking the ball carrier back and not letting him fall forward. The hitting and attack style of defense must be a part of every play.

Second and long (seven or more). The defense has more flexibility in this situation. The offense is more limited and must catch up. Most teams will use the pass with an occasional draw, screen, or gimmick type of play to gain the advantage. With this tendency, the defense needs to continue to mix fronts and provide a balanced rush. Line stunts (games) must have good contain, plus be good versus draws or gimmick traps. The linebackers and secondary defenders must work hard to force the pass to be caught in front of them and make the tackle. This also is a good down to mix tight man coverage. This type of coverage will be good versus the backs, and it will provide a good mix on the wide receivers. A win makes it third and long.

At times, offensive teams will strive for a mixture by throwing on first down. If the pass is incomplete, they will run on second and long. In my opinion, they use this philosophy to gain balance in their offensive calls. Whatever the reason, it points out the need to study and analyze the offense. The defensive signal caller needs as much information as possible to adequately prepare. He must anticipate what the offense will do. Knowledge of the offensive thinking is of the utmost importance in making the call.

Third and long (five or more). With a good call, and proper execution, the defense comes off the field. Most teams will rely on their passing game. They may change personnel to take full advantage of the opportunity. The defense must play this situation as a pass-only down and react to anything else that develops. First and foremost, the defense must make certain that the matchup in personnel is correct. The entire defense must know the distance needed for a first down. The linebackers and secondary in particular must be conscious of the yardage needed. The front must exert maximum pressure on the passer to get the sack or force a hurried throw. Coverage and blitz will be mixed, but the signal caller must keep in mind the offensive tendency and game situation. This is a pass-only down. Who does the opponent like? What type of route do they use? The pass defenders must strive to get the interception or the knockdown. If there is a completion, it must be limited to an area where the defenders can attack, make the tackle, and strip the ball. The defense must get the ball and come off the field. Penalties, missed tackles, and missed assignments prevent the defense from being successful.

Second and short (five or less). If the offense makes five to nine yards on first down, they have the advantage, and it is second and short. This down and distance is a lot like first down, except that some teams will go for the touchdown on a play action pass. Mix the fronts, and use the charges that will force a loss or create a big play. The coverages will be similar to those used on first down. It is important to have good quick run support, but the deep secondary must keep in mind the play action "bomb." This is a situation that the defense must work hard to avoid. If second and short is continually coming up, it is usually a sign that the defense is not controlling the line of scrimmage. The offense is winning, knocking the defensive line off the ball, and creating running lanes. Whatever the reason, the defense must know what and why and make the correction immediately.

I realize that I have not mentioned **second and medium**. The reason is that I honestly do not know what the term means, so I eliminated the phrase from my thinking. However, in reviewing the offensive calls, if I saw that the offense made a clear distinction, then I would make note of the call. In most cases, the calls on second and six or second and five fall into either a second and long category or a second and short category. This has been my thinking throughout the years. Realistically, we are only talking about one or two yards at the most. In some games, second and six will not even come up.

Third and short (two or less). Know the offensive personnel in the game. Are they regular or substituted? The defensive calls are limited. A mix is still good, but the signal caller must keep in mind what is best. The defensive line, and linebackers if committed to the run, must have the type of charge required to play the defense called (regular or under and up). The secondary must SEE and focus directly on their run/pass key. If their key blocks, they must first react to play the run. If a pass develops, they must react to play the pass. If their key releases, they must first react to play the pass. If a run develops, they must react to play the run. The defensive players must have great mental discipline in this situation. Make the offense earn the yardage—no cheap gains. We have all experienced an offside penalty, because of a hard cadence or a missed tackle in this situation. Either one allows the offense to maintain possession and continue the drive. Depending on the game situation, there may be a time when it is best to play the pass first or give the first down running, regroup, and start over. Know the plan, anticipate, be correct, and come off the field.

Third and medium (five, four, or three). The tendency of the offense is very important on this down and distance. This is generally a pass down, with the type of route that will ensure the first down (individual route or bunch type). If the offense decides not to pass, then the run is usually a gimmick-type run (trap) that takes advantage of the front. Through the years, there have been teams that have extended medium to third and two. So again, the offensive breakdown is important to the signal caller. Knowing what to expect is necessary to defensive success. Anticipate, be prepared to play, rush, and cover. And be alert for the gimmick.

Fourth and long (two or more). We cannot leave down and distance without discussing this situation. It is the last play, the desperation play—an offensive must and a defensive must. It is either a gimmick formation or a regular formation. The entire defense must know the distance required to maintain possession or to score a touchdown. The front has to provide containment and maximum pressure on the passer. Their assignment is to get the sack or to hurry the throw. The coverage must get the interception or cause the knockdown. If there is a completion, the pass defenders must be in a position to attack, tackle, and strip the ball. Tipped balls can be dangerous. The defense must work to prevent the tip, outjump the opponent, and knock the ball down. Depending on the time remaining and the situation, the defense must be prepared to adjust the secondary alignment to protect the goal line. In this alignment, the underneath coverage will align deeper, for better vision and to be a factor on balls thrown into the end zone. Expect the deep throw, the hook lateral, or other plays designed to keep the ball alive.

Fourth and short (one). Similar to fourth and long, this is another opportunity to win and come off the field. **Time** remaining, the **score**, and **position on the field** are all important. If it is a must-win situation, the best call is easy. Use the best you have available. What worked earlier in the game?

What was a problem earlier? All of these factors must be considered. Again, this is an opportunity to make the play that wins the game.

I vividly remember a call I made on fourth and short versus the Washington Redskins in Super Bowl XVII. It is one of those calls that I would like to reach out and grab back. We called time-out to discuss the situation. It was getting late (10:01 remaining), at about the Redskin 43 yard line. After discussing the situation, it was my decision to play the best short yardage defense, stop 'em, and come off the field. The result was that John Riggins ran off the Dolphins' left tackle for a touchdown. I can still see him running. True, we missed a tackle, but I should never have put our defensive back in that situation. I never like to second guess, but I wish I would have had sense enough to give our players a better opportunity to be successful. Looking back, with ten minutes remaining, we gambled with our call to stop the Redskins and get the ball for our offense. If we had been successful, it could have been a call that helped win the game. We were not successful, and the play sealed the victory for Washington.

B. Field Position

Field position, along with down and distance, is another factor that must be considered in making the defensive call. Every team will have a philosophy that is evident in the various playing areas. These tendencies will vary with the game situation, but the signal caller and team must be aware of the offensive thinking. Football is a game of field position. The team that can gain and maintain field position has the advantage. It is the responsibility of the defense to win the battle. The job of the defense is to gain field position for the offense by forcing a punt or by taking the ball away.

Inside the 20.   When the defense has the opponent backed up, the objective is to keep them in this area. Force the error. Create confusion. Force the punt. Gain field position for the offense. Some teams will try to "grind it out," while others will attempt the play action pass and throw the "bomb" in this area. The signal caller and defensive team must know the tendency of the opponent. Aggressive fronts with a variation of charges will help stop the run. Sound aggressive coverages will help the defense to be successful and force the punt. A turnover in this area will usually result in the opportunity for a defensive score or points for the offense.

Twenty to mid-field (change-up area).   The offense will utilize their basic plan and will show the tendency to run, pass, or both, depending on their philosophy. The objective of the defense is to stop the offense from crossing mid-field. Force them to turn the ball over, either by making an error or by punting. For the defense, this is the "change-up area." The defense must continue to vary the fronts and use their best charges. Strong emphasis needs to be placed on concealing the coverage and breaking any tendencies the defensive team may have established. (Example: This is a good blitz or fake blitz area.)

Mid-field to the ten.   This is the offensive scoring zone, the green zone, or any other term used to describe the area more definitely. The defense refers to this area as the **red zone**, which means that the defense must stop the drive, force the loss, or drive the offense out of scoring range. Aggressive play and aggressive calls are important. Use the calls that the defense executes best. In this area, the defense does not want to fool the offense; they want to beat the offense physically. Once the offense is inside the 30 yard line, the defense must "make things happen." Use the front, charge, coverage, and blitz calls that will force a loss or a turnover. This is no time to experiment. **Use the best calls** and take advantage of the defensive personnel. The signal caller and the team must be aware of the opponent's favorite run and favorite receiver. This also may be a gimmick area for some teams. It is important that the defense keep its poise and play the defense as defined.

Ten to the goal line.   In this area, the defense is in a position to stop the score and win the game. Refusing to be scored on will set the tempo for the game and often for the season. Tendencies are important. How does the opponent get into the end zone? Do they punch it in, or do they try for a quick score? Who do they rely on as a ball carrier or a receiver? Do they change personnel? This is a physical battle, and the defense must **be the best**. The signal caller should place the defense in the best position to win and not concern himself with tendencies.

When I think about that last sentence, my thoughts go immediately to the San Diego Chargers' goal line stand versus the Pittsburgh Steelers in the 1994 AFC championship game. The defense had played well throughout the game, and our offense finally tied the game and then put us in front 17–13 in the fourth quarter. Now it was time for the defense to take charge and seal the victory. Pittsburgh received the kickoff and began their drive. They made a first down by inches several times and were moving the ball down the field. They needed a touchdown to win, so we continued to make our best calls to force them to make an error. Finally, it was fourth and three, with less than a minute remaining, on the Pittsburgh nine yard line. What should we do? We had established tendencies; we liked to play a zone. What call should we make? Should we call a blitz, man coverage, or go with our best? I made the call—we would repeat our zone call. A thousand "what ifs" ran through my mind. The ball was snapped, and Neil O'Donnell dropped back and threw quickly to the right for the back running a close circle. Dennis Gibson, our middle linebacker, played it perfectly. He got the knockdown, and the San Diego Chargers were on their way to Super Bowl XXIX in Miami. Previous to the call, I had thought about considering the possibilities. But I knew in my heart what we had practiced and perfected since the beginning of training camp, so my decision was easy—it was based on what we knew and had practiced and played in that situation many times during the year. Afterward, in talking about the call with the players, they said they had actually expected the zone call. Why? Because they had confidence in their assignments and their ability to make the play. I did not surprise them and try to outguess the opponent or pull something out of a hat. I relied on what we knew and what we had practiced and played through the year. We made the play and won the game—the biggest game to date in the history of the San Diego Chargers.

C. Game Situations

The **score** of the game, the **time** remaining, and who has the **momentum** all must be considered in making the defensive call.

You are ahead.   The opponent is "playing your game." Continue with your plan, mix fronts, mix coverages, prevent the cheap score, and give the opponent every opportunity to make an error.

Tied or one touchdown behind.   It is essential to maintain poise and be totally aware of the situation. Be more selective and more aggressive and gain the momentum. Select defenses (fronts, coverages, blitzes) that will prevent the offense from controlling the ball. Win on first down. Get the ball and come off the field.

Behind by two touchdowns or more.   It's time to regroup. Recognize the situation and what must be accomplished to regain the momentum. Try to understand what has happened to put your team in this situation, and figure out what you must accomplish to win. Choose the fronts, coverages, and blitzes that, when properly executed, can result in quick turnovers or scores for the defense. You are in trouble—it's time to gamble. To win, the defense must allow no more points and must get the ball for the offense. The defense must make things happen, force errors, and change the tempo. Often in this situation, all that is needed is added emotion. Football is an emotional game, and emotion can make things happen. More emotion will help the defense execute better and play more physically. Individually, each player has to **want** to win more than the opponent. That's emotion, and it is exactly what is needed to be successful. Nothing takes the place of carrying out the assignment with emotion.

Two minutes in the half or the game

* **You are ahead**: Maintain your poise and play sound, normal defense. Force the offense to go the "long way"—no cheap gains. The defense must play maximum rush and pressure the quarterback. Get the sack or hurry. All coverages must force all passes, if completed, to be caught in an area where the defenders can attack the receiver, tackle, and strip the ball. It is very important to keep the clock running (keep the ball carrier or receiver in bounds). Stay alert for the no-huddle offense. All players must be alert to communicate with the bench for the defensive call. And everyone must **know the plan**.
* **You are behind**: The defense needs to get the ball. Prevent the first down or cause a fumble. Select the fronts, coverages, and blitz that will make things happen. In most cases, the defense will go to a short yardage or goal line type of blitz alignment. The opponent will generally try to maintain possession with basic runs. Know the rules that affect the clock in the two-minute period. What stops the clock? What starts the clock?

D. General Thoughts and Suggestions

1. **Study the tendencies** that have been established by the opponent. What are they trying to accomplish? The coach must be knowledgeable about the opponent and be able to teach that information to the defensive unit. The players must learn about their opponent.
2. Know the **strength** and **weakness** of the defensive unit.
3. If there is a problem, what is the reason? Is it an **assignment breakdown** or a **physical breakdown**? Make the defensive team aware of a problem as soon as possible.
4. Recognize a problem and **make the correction**. Make an adjustment that will enable the defense to be effective.
5. **NEVER** wait to make a correction. Make it **now**. Make the change that will win a championship.

The general philosophy presented here has proven useful to me in college and professional football. It is my belief that the philosophy is applicable at all levels. Down and distance, field position, and game situations are the same at all levels. It is the individual philosophy of the teams that varies. One team will throw more on first down or run more on third and long. Another team will do the opposite. These differences are normal. Remember that a team's tendencies may change when the team is ahead or behind. The signal caller must recognize the situation that created the change in tendency.

I have enjoyed my role as the signal caller. Some of my calls were successful, and there are a few I would like to have back. Some were changed when the defensive caller on the field recognized something that I didn't anticipate or see. I always gave the field defensive caller (a linebacker or safety if the change involved coverage) the freedom to make a change. When the defense is properly prepared, the leader on the field is qualified to make a change. The only thing I ever asked was that he have **a reason** for making a change.

It is imperative that the defensive coordinator (signal caller) be present on the sideline, where he is in a position to "feel the tempo" of the game. Also, he is in a better position to make a correction or quick decision to substitute. I am beginning to see too many coordinators in the coach's booth. They have good height and can see, but the action is different in the coach's box than it is on the field. The coach needs to be on the sideline if for no other reason than to make the quick call or change that is often necessary. I am comfortable with a coach in the coach's booth alerting me to something that he has observed. Usually, it is something that happened on the other side of the field. Between series, I discuss with each coach his thoughts concerning the next series. It is important to involve everyone. During halftime, I ask each coach to give a quick summary of his position to the squad. Then, I take that information, add my thoughts, and review what we must accomplish in the second half.

Being the signal caller was exciting and is a part of the game that I truly miss. In retirement, I have been involved with the San Diego Police Department in training Field Training Officers. Members of this elite group of officers are assigned to work with rookies coming out of the police academy. My assignment was to talk with the officers about coaching and teaching techniques. In the beginning, I wondered, "Why me?" But I soon realized that regardless of the profession, we all have similar problems as we work with people. Being involved with the police department has introduced me to their problem-solving technique, which was developed by Herman Goldstein in his book *Improving Policing: A Problem-Oriented Approach*. This technique was of particular interest to me because it is similar to the information the signal caller must find, study, and use effectively. Goldstein named this problem-solving technique SARA. The term is used continually in police work today. It is not just jargon. It is meaningful and very useful in the concept of "problem-oriented policing," which means solving the problem that is creating a disturbance.

SARA is the same technique that is used by the signal caller in studying the opponent. The caller gathers information (**scanning**); studies the information, determines what it means, and recognizes a pattern (**analysis**); makes a defensive call (**response**); and examines the result (**assessment**). Was the call successful? If a piece of information is missing, then the signal caller must return to scanning and analysis.

To make the proper response or the proper call, the scanning and analysis by both the policeman and the signal caller must be free of error. Both the policeman and the signal caller must have the best information available. I share this information with you because, as coaches, we go through the same basic procedure. However, the term SARA has made the process more meaningful to me. It is a step-by-step procedure to find the right answer.

Take pleasure in being the signal caller. There is no other assignment in the game that will bring you as much satisfaction. One last reminder: call the defenses that you know and have practiced. Be prepared for each situation. Approach each play as if it were the most important play in the game. Each call must reflect this attitude.

STEALING SIGNALS: BE ALERT AND BE AWARE—IT DOES HAPPEN

Because of several experiences that came to my attention during my career, there is no doubt in my mind that defensive signals, which obviously are useful to the offense, can be stolen. The larger problem may be in getting the information into the game. However, this too is possible with proper coordination.

When I was with the Baltimore Colts, I was working in the coach's box with the late Don MeCafferty. Don was the offensive coordinator for the Colts, and I was the defensive line coach. Don was connected to John Sandusky on the sideline, and I was connected to Charley Winner and later to Chuck Noll. Don helped me when we were on defense, and I helped Don when we had the ball. One of the ways that I helped Don was by watching the defensive signal caller and trying to pick up the defensive call. If there was only one signal caller, it was relatively easy, but the one problem that surfaced immediately was that at times I could not tell exactly when the field signal caller was looking. To solve the problem, I enlisted the help of an additional member or our organization. As I watched the coach on the sideline, my partner would watch the field signal caller and continue to repeat, "He is looking, he is looking, he is looking. STOP." "STOP" meant that the field signal caller had stopped looking. Therefore, every action previous to the STOP command was a part of the signal from the coach to the field signal caller.

At that time, our offensive coaches were only interested in the blitz signal. When I learned the blitz signal, I alerted Don. He in turn alerted John Sandusky, who in turn alerted the offensive tackle who was in the huddle to his side. The tackle then alerted the quarterback. If everything worked to perfection, the best pass would be called with the best protection. If the information arrived late, it still might be valuable to the quarterback. He might, under various circumstances, change the play at the line or throw quickly to the receiver who was reading his blitz key. Most of the time, this system was very effective. At times, it would be difficult to get the blitz signal if one team did not use the blitz as much as others. However, once you learned the signal, it was merely a matter of transferring the information to the huddle.

I remember one game where I went an entire half without getting the signal. What made it even worse was that the team was blitzing more than usual. I had the front signal and the coverage signal, but I had missed the blitz signal. As we started the second half, I immediately recognized the front signal as I saw the coach cross his feet. I knew what I had missed.

Another coach smoked a lot on the sideline. His blitz signal was striking a match and lighting his cigarette. I think he had an idea we were getting some information, and he was trying to conceal the blitz signal.

The key was to have someone watch the field signal caller and repeat, "He is looking, he is looking. STOP." That kept it simple. It was specific, and the call was definite. There was no guesswork. The information still had to be given to the quarterback in the huddle, and John and his offensive tackles developed a system that was effective.

With that experience, I went to Miami and immediately used another player to work with me in signaling the field signal caller. That worked well, but then I stumbled on the fact that one opponent was taking pictures of our signals. The scout would sit across the field from us and take pictures. He had a great file. I never knew how he got the information to the huddle, but when playing his team I would intentionally wait until the quarterback put his head down in the huddle before I made a call. We played the team twice a year, and I suddenly realized that the quarterback was looking at me as I was looking at him. When our eyes met, it brought a smile from both of us.

This experience taught me that the second caller should be moved to another area on the sideline. I tried this several times but never felt comfortable with the procedure. I never liked to give the signal too early, so I just added a third caller. Each caller would signal, and the live caller could be changed by series, by quarter, or however we chose.

Upon arriving back on the sideline with the San Diego Chargers, I continued to use the same method, but again I learned that a scout for another division team was filming my signals. This never really concerned me because there was no way to know who the live caller was. The assistant coach was the offensive line coach as well as the signal stealer. He left the team after a year and joined another division team. Knowing this, I was particularly careful and always used three callers in games against him. During one game, I noticed a new face in the chain gang. He was staying particularly close to the three of us to learn who the live caller was. I kidded my coaching friend about his assignment, and after he sent an accomplice to spy on us, I really gave him a hard time. His team beat us once, but not because of stealing a signal.

If you are calling signals alone, then wait as long as possible before you signal. However, although the technique I used in Baltimore was effective, the best method to prevent signals from being stolen is to use two callers in different locations on the sideline but still in line with the field caller's vision. Regardless of the method used, be aware of the possibility that the opponent may have the defensive call.

OVERTIME

MY COACHING CAREER

My family encouraged me to recap my career in coaching and athletics administration. I have tried to share with you why and how I made coaching my profession, people who had an impact on my career, and highlights of a career in professional and college athletics that spanned 45 years.

The Formative Years

I have been very fortunate to be able to do the things I wanted to do at the time I wanted to do them. This was true from the very beginning and throughout my career until I retired from the San Diego Chargers in February 1995. First of all, I was fortunate to grow up in Paris, Kentucky. My parents were always very supportive and basically let me make the decisions I wanted to make. They guided and directed me in a manner that made it seem like I made every decision on my own. However, I am certain that if they thought I had made a poor decision, they would have stepped in to point me in a better direction. My second bit of good fortune was to have Blanton Collier and his assistant, Dick Butler, as my high school coaches. With Coach Collier leading the way, I was exposed to the best athletic background any young man could want. At that time, he was better known as a basketball coach. Although basketball is and always will be "king" in Kentucky, those of us in the football program knew better and realized we were being coached by the best.

All of this became more meaningful during my senior year in high school. Our schedule was cut short in 1944 because of World War II. We traveled by car (families saved their gas ration cards for road trips) and by train and completed our season undefeated with a squad of about 15 players—no two platoon, no defense and offense, just one team with a substitute for every two or three positions. Our record was 4–0. We were a proud group.

Thoughts of a college education were very much in my mind. I considered at various times pharmacy and law and along the way thought I might like to coach, but I didn't know if I would ever have the opportunity.

After football season came basketball, and I was busy getting ready. During this time, the University of Kentucky showed some interest in me, as did Auburn University. One of the Auburn assistant coaches was from Georgetown, Kentucky, a neighboring city to Paris, and I am sure that was why Auburn was interested. I was invited to visit, but it was just too far and I did not make the trip. My Uncle Lucian, a Centre College graduate, was an influence during this time. Bo McMillan, a former Centre great, was coaching at Indiana and arranged for me to visit. My Dad and I made the trip to Bloomington on a snowy winter weekend, saw a basketball game, and toured the campus. On the way home, we stopped by the Athletic Club in Indianapolis to talk with Coach McMillan. We had a good visit and returned to Paris.

During basketball season, Coach Collier was called into the service and entered the Navy. No one thought he would have to go because he was married and had three daughters, but knowing him, he wanted to be a part of the effort for our country. Coach Butler had already joined up, and we had a new coach, Eddie Reynolds. Eddie, Blanton, and Dick had all been good friends. Eddie had coached at Bourbon County High School (Paris is the county seat of Bourbon County), but the team was disbanded for the duration of the war.

We were lucky in Paris to have enough players to support the football and basketball programs. Like other high schools, we had lost players to the service, but there were still enough to play a schedule. Unfortunately, our basketball team didn't enjoy the same success as our football team, but we appreciated the efforts of Coach Reynolds. We fought through the district, advanced to the regional tournament, and lost to the eventual state champion. I fouled out about midway through the second half. Basketball was over, and it was time to get ready for college football.

The University of Kentucky continued to show interest in me, and I decided to accept a scholarship offer: tuition, room, board, books, and $15.00

a month for laundry. That was the standard athletic scholarship at the time in the Southeastern Conference.

Attending the University of Kentucky

I entered the University of Kentucky in the summer of 1944, in time for football practice. I had unsuccessfully tried to talk my parents into giving me permission to volunteer for military service, as many of my friends had. No way did I want to be drafted. The Marine Corps was my choice, but all the talking in the world and all the arguments I could think of would not sway my parents. They were determined that I finish high school and begin college. Finally, as a compromise, they consented to give their permission sometime in December, before my eighteenth birthday.

Most of the players entering Kentucky were freshman, with a few transfers from schools that had disbanded their sports programs because of the war. There were also several players who had been rejected for military service because of physical problems. However, the problems were not severe enough to prevent them from participating in football.

With the summer about over and the fall approaching, the season was about to begin. We had three coaches. A.D. Kirwan was the head coach and had been for several years. His two assistants were Athletic Director Bernie Shively, a former All-American Guard at Illinois, and Rome Rankin, the former head coach at Eastern Kentucky. Eastern was one of the schools that had disbanded its program, and Rome came to Kentucky and brought several players with him.

We played a reduced schedule, two games against Tennessee and one game against each of the other teams in the conference. It was an educational experience, both academically and athletically, but I always had that date in December in the back of my mind. I was sworn in on December 13, 1944 in Cincinnati, but I was not called up immediately. In March 1945, I received my orders to report to Parris Island, South Carolina, for boot camp. My dream was finally coming true.

United States Marine Corps

Boot camp at Parris Island, and the Marine Corps in general, was a great experience. Looking back, I think everyone should have the experience. Teamwork was one point that was continually emphasized. It had been stressed to me in high school, but that was nothing compared to the way it was stressed in boot camp. Teamwork, dependence on each other, following orders, and learning how to take care of yourself were part of the everyday routine. How to take care of your rifle, how to shoot properly, and following orders were a must. There was much to learn, but teamwork and dependence on each other were key factors in earning the "anchor & globe" (the Marine Corps Insignia). When boot camp was finally over, it was time for advanced training.

Advanced training meant Camp Lejeune, North Carolina, and Heavy Weapons School. In simple terms, that meant machine guns, Browning automatic rifles, and mortars. For a kid from a small Kentucky town, things were getting serious.

When training was over, I awaited my orders. They soon arrived, and I boarded a train with the rest of the troops for San Diego and Camp Pendleton. We headed west from North Carolina, through Atlanta and then New Orleans. I firmly believe that we went through every small town in Texas. Someplace in Arizona or New Mexico, our leaders decided we needed some physical activity. The train stopped in the middle of nothing but sand, cactus, and sagebrush, and we exercised and ran. Our leaders were pleased to see that no one had forgotten how.

The trip took about four or five days, and the Forty-Niners during the gold rush couldn't have been any happier than we were to arrive in California. Camp Pendleton was our new home, but not for long. It seemed like no one knew what to do with us, and we knew what that meant—run, run, run. Luckily, our final orders arrived in a few days, and we officially became known as the 79th Replacement Draft. We went by truck to the port of San Diego, boarded a ship, and were on our way.

Our first stop was Hawaii, where we learned about President Truman's decision to drop the atomic bomb on two Japanese cities. The war in Europe had ended while we were in training at Camp Lejeune and was about to end in the Pacific. We stayed at a Marine camp outside of Honolulu and waited. We spent our time on work details and playing cards, in particular hearts.

A veteran of previous trips to the Pacific bunked in our tent, and we soon learned that he wanted to take all the hearts, including the queen, every game. This may have been my first exposure to real defense—give up a little but STOP THE SCORE. The Marine Corps finally decided what to do with us, and it was off to Guam.

Aboard ship, it was eat, sleep, and play more hearts. The weather was a little rough on the trip, and I had a new experience—seasickness. They say you are supposed to continue to eat, but how I'll never know. Nevertheless, we all survived and arrived in Guam, where again our time was spent on work details and playing hearts. We looked forward to our new orders, and soon it was time to move on. Back aboard ship, we passed Saipan and Tinnan. The scuttlebutt was that we were headed for China.

China it was. We anchored off Taku and went ashore for further assignment. I was assigned to "C" Company, First Engineer Battalion, attached to the Seventh Regiment, First Marine Division. The division had just returned from Okinawa, and we were their first replacements. They were happy to see us, because it meant that some would be heading home. Headquarters for the Seventh Regiment, along with "C" Company of the First Engineers, was in Pei-tai-ho Beach.

Pei-tai-ho Beach was a two-day train ride from Tientsin, with an all-night stop in Tang-shan. We shared a car with several well-to-do Chinese, but the rest of the train was crowded with peasants who slept in the baggage racks between cars and relieved themselves out the car doors or out the windows. This was our introduction to China, but we were glad to be there and looked forward to our new assignment.

Pei-tai-ho was a railroad stop, not far from Shan-hai-kuan, where the Great Wall meets the sea. We were stationed in a large former hospital complex about halfway between the railroad and Pei-tai-ho Beach proper. Pei-tai-ho Beach was a resort, so we were told, and many foreign countries had their summer embassies in the area. It must have been a summer resort, because no ambassador would want to be caught there in the winter. It was December 1945, on the bay of Po Hai, which is the northern section of the Yellow Sea. The sea was frozen as far out as you could see, and the cold winds from Manchuria were blowing. Nevertheless, those of us who were members of the 79th Replacement Draft were glad to arrive at our new home.

Our division's assignment, as we saw it, was twofold: first, to repatriate the Japanese and, second, our presence in North China was to prevent the Chinese Communists from moving south from Manchuria. The first was probably the official reason, but we thought the second was our main objective. As an Engineer Battalion, it was our responsibility to keep the rail line open and to keep the cinder-graded airport landing strip open and operating, along with any normal road maintenance jobs. From time to time, someone (supposedly the Communists) would destroy a railroad bridge, and it was our job to repair the bridge and keep the track open.

Gradually, things began to settle into a daily routine. The Japanese were returned to their homes, and our maintenance duty came in spurts. Some weeks we were busy, and other times our only job was to polish the equipment. Our company was a close-knit group. One day, when our group was repairing a bridge, we met a Chinese boy of eight or nine. He returned to the compound and stayed with us. I have often wondered where he is and what he is doing today.

Sometime in early 1946, I was promoted to sergeant, to fill a vacancy created by veterans returning home. My spec number matched the need, and our officers believed in filling the needs of our company as required in the table of organization. My promotion brought about a transfer, and I was reunited with several members of the disbanded 79th Replacement Draft.

Return Home and Return to School

In the fall of 1946, it was my turn to return to the States. Before leaving China, I was offered a promotion to staff sergeant if I would sign over. I appreciated the show of confidence in me, but I was too intent on returning home and resuming my education. I shall always be thankful for my tour of duty in the Marine Corps. It was my good fortune to have had outstanding training, as well as some great experiences. I believe the training and active duty as a Marine helped me more than anything else to mature. Most of all, it made me understand and realize the importance of working together to accomplish a goal. As a Marine, there is a great degree of dependence on each other. The individual has a responsibility to carry out his orders, not only for his own protection and the satisfaction of his superiors, but also for the protection and satisfaction of his platoon, company, battalion, regiment, and division. I had been aware of the word "teamwork" in high school, but I saw the term in action in the Marine Corps. Experiencing the meaning of teamwork firsthand jump-started my coaching career.

I returned to Paris, Kentucky, in November 1946 and to my athletic scholarship at the University of Kentucky in January 1947. It was a busy first few months, with both classes and football, although football was limited to conditioning drills. Many veterans were returning to school, as were players who had been on the team the year before. There were a few familiar faces, but most were strangers, and all of us were battling for recognition.

It soon became evident to me that I was in a "no-win" situation. Players were continually coming and going. A new group would come in each week and join us in the workouts. Some would be asked to stay, and others were sent home. Then a new group would come in the next week. I came to realize that I was just not big enough to be a lineman, and I knew long ago that I did not have the ability to play in the backfield or to be a receiver. Finally, I made a decision. I dropped the workouts, continued in school, and began to look for another school where I might have a better opportunity to play.

Looking for advice, I visited with my former high school coach, Blanton Collier, who was now an assistant coach with Paul Brown and the Cleveland Browns. He knew me and understood my thinking and said he would help me make a decision. He mentioned two colleges that he thought I should consider: Xavier University in Cincinnati and Miami University in Oxford, Ohio. Both were good schools, and both had outstanding football programs and coaches.

With this plan in mind, I continued my education at Kentucky but now had the time to review my situation and make the best decision in terms of my future. I made plans to talk with Coach Ed Kluska, the head coach at Xavier. I was somewhat familiar with Xavier but had several questions concerning my opportunity there. I talked with Coach Kluska a couple of times on the phone, and he expressed an interest in my joining the program. I felt good about the opportunity.

Around mid-March, I had the opportunity to visit Miami University, talk with the coaches, and watch a day of spring practice. Oxford is a small college town about 25 miles northwest of Cincinnati. Miami University had, and still has, a great reputation as an academic institution. In addition, several prominent coaches, including Paul Brown, Weeb Ewbank, and Earl Blaik, among others, called Miami their alma mater. Sid Gillman was the head coach, and George Blackburn was one of the assistants. Both were easy to talk to. I enjoyed watching the practice and could see immediately that the players were enjoying the experience. I stayed with two of the players that evening and talked with them about the school and the football program. The next morning, I met with Coach Blackburn, and he assured me that I would have an opportunity to play. It was a great two days, and it was helpful for me to see the campus, meet the players, and generally experience the atmosphere at the college and Oxford.

Upon returning home, I continued to think about the pluses and minuses. Both colleges had discussed with me the possibility of entering in the summer to practice football and to become acclimated before the fall semester. I finally made a decision. It was Miami University, and I must say that it was one of the best decisions I have ever made. I felt that way in the spring of 1947, and I feel that way today, some 50 years later.

Attending Miami University

Attending Miami University in Oxford, Ohio provided me with an opportunity and background vital to my desire to coach. I had three head coaches in three years: Sid Gillman, George Blackburn, and Woody Hayes. I know of no one who has had better teachers and coaches to direct them in learning and understanding football. This was true not only from a technical standpoint, but the three also provided an outstanding background in how to motivate and how to do the "little things" necessary to be successful and to win. Again, the players played a part. I was there with Ara Parseghian, Carmen Cozza, Bo Schembechler, John Pont, and many, many others, all with the desire to learn the fundamentals and to coach. This role was nothing new for Miami University. Paul Brown, Earl Blaik, Weeb Ewbank, and many others preceded us and helped establish a tradition that continues today.

Miami University remains an academic leader in teacher education and is rated among the "best buys" among the nation's public universities. The demands placed on me in that the beautiful setting helped to mold my thoughts and directed me toward success as a student–athlete and later as a coach and athletic administrator. I earned my B.S. in education in 1950 and received my M.Ed. in school administration in 1954.

Looking Back, I Was Well Prepared

My preparation was now complete. I often think of the advantages I had over the years. In my early years, my parents encouraged me to be the best and to be self-sufficient, yet guided me with a loving hand. I was also fortunate to be coached in high school by Blanton Collier. It has often been said that Coach Collier was at the head of the class in the technical aspects of football. This was true in both defense and offense, and many of his contributions to the offensive side are still apparent today. He was ably assisted by Dick Butler, who in his own right took a different path with an administrative career in professional baseball. Paris High School was a learning experience under the best tutelage possible, with Dr. Lee Kirkpartrick as superintendent; Dr. F.A. Scott as principal; and Blanton Collier, Dick Butler, and Eddie Reynolds as coaches. The teachers were demanding yet understanding. An aspiring young person could not ask for a better foundation.

Next in my preparation was the United States Marine Corps. I had discipline, but the Corps built on that and made me more aware of my commitment to my teammate, my fellow Marine. I was dependent on him, and he was dependent on me. This is what I have more recently defined as the "**true team concept.**" Coach Collier taught me that "you can accomplish a lot of things if you don't care who gets the credit." The Marine Corps put that statement into practice.

Upon returning to civilian life, I took advantage of the G.I. Bill, completed my education at Miami University, and learned from the best coaches in the game. I also played with some of the best people in any situation. Many were just like me, looking for an opportunity, and they found it on the fields of Miami University.

Coaching at Miami University

After graduating from Miami University in January 1950, I was asked to join Woody Hayes' staff at Miami as offensive line coach. It was a break for me, because many coaches never have that kind of opportunity, especially immediately after graduation. My first year coaching was a success and was unique in many respects. In particular, it placed me in the role of coaching many of the players who had been my teammates the year before.

The staff included John Brickles as backfield coach as well as director of athletics. Bill Hoover was the end coach, Bill Wehr had the guards and linebackers, Woody Wills was the defensive coach, and Ara Parseghian was the freshman coach. We completed the season with a 9–1 record that included a 28–0 shutout of the Cincinnati Bearcats in our final game. The win over Cincinnati was particularly important to all of us because the Bearcats were coached by three of our former coaches—Sid Gillman, George Blackburn, and Joe Madro—and several players were former teammates. Cincinnati had left the Mid-American Conference to play as an independent, and we were the conference champions. Our record was good enough for a bowl bid to the Salad Bowl (now the Fiesta Bowl) in Tempe, Arizona, to play against Arizona State. We prepared well, working hard during Christmas vacation in a heated Quonset hut, to get ready for the Tempe/Phoenix weather. Our preparation paid off with a 34–21 win.

The victory was important for Woody Hayes. He had been head coach at Denison University and had a 14–5 record over a two-year period at Miami. This earned him a place on the list of names being considered for head coach at Ohio State University when Wes Fesler was fired after the loss to Michigan. Speculation centered around Paul Brown, Sid Gillman, Harry Strobel (who had been a member of Fesler's staff), and Woody. The media made the most of the opportunity. As it turned out, Paul Brown dropped out, and Woody picked up support from within and outside the university. After the dust settled, Woody Hayes was selected as the nineteenth football coach at Ohio State University.

Coaching at Ohio State University

I was invited to go to Columbus with Woody as offensive line coach. It was a once-in-a-lifetime opportunity, and I will always be grateful to Woody for asking me to be a part of his staff in 1951. We started immediately to install our version of the split-T offense. The Buckeyes had been a single wing team for many years, and changing over kept us busy. The personnel were up to our expectations, but the first year can best be defined by the phrase "growing pains." Not only did we change to the "T" formation, but Woody's style was distinctly different from Wes Fesler's. The change was difficult for many of the upper classmen, but they worked hard to do what we asked. We finished in fifth place in the Big Ten with a 4–3–2 record.

The next year was better. The players felt more comfortable with the "T," and we were joined by an outstanding freshman class. Our 6–3 record gave us a third place finish in the Big Ten. We beat Michigan for the first time since 1949 (with a 27–7 win) and were on our way. We repeated our 6–3 record in 1953, and that class and the 1952 group proved to be the foundation of the 1954 Rose Bowl team and the beginning of Coach Hayes' success at Ohio State.

Our original staff remained intact. Doyt Perry, a successful and extremely popular high school coach, joined us as backfield coach. Bill Hess, another successful high school coach, joined us as freshman coach. Gene Fekete, Esco Sarkinnen, and Harry Strobel stayed on from the former staff. It was an outstanding group. Also, the renowned Ernie Godfrey stayed on as recruiting coordinator and helped on the field, especially with the place kickers. He had coached at Ohio State since 1929, from the days of Sam Willaman, Francis Schmidt, Paul Brown, Carroll Widdoes, Paul Bixler, and Wesley Fesler, and worked with Woody through 1961. He was truly the "dean" of Ohio State coaches, and we were very fortunate to have him with us. For me, it was an opportunity to learn the art of place kicking, and the useful tips he taught remain with me today.

Coaching at the University of Kentucky

In 1954, I had the opportunity to join Blanton Collier, my former high school coach, at the University of Kentucky. I don't think Woody ever forgave me for leaving, because he had given me a great opportunity initially. But, as has been true throughout my career, I was presented with the specific opportunity I desired at the time. The Lord has surely blessed me and looked after me, and I thank him every night for his guidance and direction and the opportunities that were made available to me. The decision to go to Kentucky was a good one in many ways. As an offensive line coach, I continued to learn, and the experience of working with Coach Collier was a definite advantage.

We had a good group of coaches in the beginning. However, only two of us (Ermal Allen and me) stayed with Coach Collier throughout his eight-year tenure. Dom Fucci, John North, and Ed Rutledge joined our staff in 1956. Sometime in late 1956 or early 1957, I met Betty Jane, my wife to be, and we were married on August 24, 1957. In 1959, Bob Cummings, Norm Deeb, Howard Schnellenberger, J.R. "Abe" Shannon, and Don Shula joined our staff.

That was also the year that I asked to have my coaching assignment changed to the defensive line. A vacancy developed when Matt Lair, who had been with us from the beginning, left to join the Texas A&M staff. I felt that I needed experience on the other side of the ball, but Bob Cummings, formerly of Vanderbilt and Georgia Tech, joined us to coach the defensive line. I had to wait for my chance until Bob left to return to Vanderbilt in 1961. I moved to defense, and Chuck Knox joined our staff to coach the offensive line.

As it turned out, 1961 was my final year at Kentucky. Coach Collier was fired and returned to the Cleveland Browns after posting a respectable 41–36–3 for a .531 average for eight years, including a winning 5–2–1 record and two shutouts (23–0 in 1955 and 20–0 in 1959) against arch-rival Tennessee. Five coaches have succeeded Coach Collier, and none has put together a winning season. Neither the university nor the fans ever fully realized the type of program that Blanton Collier provided because football does not receive the attention that basketball enjoys at the University of Kentucky.

The assistants were also fired, and the staff scattered. Ermal Allen joined the Dallas Cowboys, John North joined LSU, Ed Rutledge returned to high school coaching, Norm Deeb returned to graduate school to earn his doctorate in education, and "Abe" Shannon returned to coaching baseball. Only Chuck Knox was retained on the new staff. The University of Kentucky Football Media Guide continues to list Chuck Knox, John North, Howard Schnellenberger, Don Shula, and me as former assistants who later became head coaches in the National Football League. Leeman Bennett, a former quarterback and graduate assistant on our staff in 1961, also became a head coach in the NFL. All but Chuck were a part of Coach Collier's 1959 staff.

Fired and Unemployed: A Time to Decide!

This period of unemployment gave me the opportunity to evaluate my career. I continually asked myself whether I should continue coaching. I even went so far as to study real estate. My father-in-law, Melvin Carter, was a successful realtor. I got my broker's license and immediately entered a holding pattern.

On a cold winter night in February 1962, the phone rang. It was Coach Tommy O'Boyle from Tulane University in New Orleans. (I had interviewed with him and Athletic Director Horace Renegar at a coaches convention in

Chicago.) He asked me, "What have you done?" I replied, "Nothing. What have you done?" He responded, "Nothing." Then he asked whether I had ever been to New Orleans. I hesitated a moment and said no. He asked me to visit and talk with him. This time there was no hesitation on my part, and arrangements were made for my visit.

It was a great visit and the beginning of a friendship with Tommy and Rosemary O'Boyle that lasts to this day. I had actually met Coach O'Boyle when he was an assistant with the University of Miami in 1959. I was an assistant with Kentucky, and we were playing the Hurricanes in the Orange Bowl. My assignment was a phone in the end zone bleachers, and 30 feet to my right was Coach O'Boyle with the same assignment for Miami.

Tulane University and the Decision to Make Coaching My Career

All of us from the Kentucky staff landed on our feet and probably benefited from the decision to fire us. At the time, we were told not to come around the office, so we met daily at the soda fountain in a local drugstore. We dubbed ourselves the "Untouchables," and for many years we met annually to celebrate our dismissal.

I landed at Tulane University with Coach Tommy O'Boyle's staff. Tommy put together a good group of coaches, including Jim Carmody. Doug Hafner, Jim Royer, John Rauch, Fred Wallner, and Don Watson. At the time, Tulane was struggling in the powerful Southeastern Conference, and Tommy and our staff had the job of restoring respectability. This was an opportunity for me to work with the "lonesome end." Johnny Rauch, of Georgia fame and later head coach of the Oakland Raiders, had been part of the "lonesome end" offense at the U.S. Military Academy. He was now the offensive coordinator at Tulane, and we proceeded to put in the unbalanced line, "lonesome end" offense. Coaching the "lonesome end" was a new experience for me and the first time I had the opportunity to use the ball in my coaching.

In 1963, when Johnny Rauch was selected as head coach of the Oakland Raiders, our offense changed and we had some coaching changes as well. W.D. "Dub" Fesperman, George McKinney, and Johnny Menger joined our staff, and I was named defensive coordinator and linebacker coach. This was my first title and a definite career opportunity. At the time, I didn't realize just how much of an opportunity. The two years that I was with Tommy and his wife, Rosemary, were two of the happiest years in my young coaching career, even though we were 0–10 the first year, which was a new experience for me. Nevertheless, we worked hard and felt we were improving. In 1963, we were 1–8–1, with a victory over South Carolina in Columbia and a tie with Vanderbilt. We reduced our points allowed on defense from a high of 293 in 1962 to 191 points in 1963, a real sign of progress.

The next year began with the increased enthusiasm that comes with an opportunity to improve. John Symank, who had just completed his career as a defensive back with the Green Bay Packers, joined the staff. It was the beginning of a long relationship. Later, John and his wife, Sarah, were with me in New York with the Giants and then at LSU. I do not know a more loyal person than John Symank.

Before spring practice, opportunity came knocking, and I was off to the Baltimore Colts to join Don Shula's staff. Don and I had been on the staff at Kentucky in 1959. He left the next year to join the Detroit Lions and was named head coach of the Baltimore Colts in 1963.

Baltimore Colts

The 1964 Baltimore staff was small in number compared to present-day staffs. There were just two of us on defense. Charley Winner was the secondary coach and coordinated the defense, and my assignment was the defensive line. Charley worked with the linebackers on pass defense, and I worked with them on the running game. Offensively, Don McCaffery was the backfield coach, John Sandusky was the offensive line coach, and Dick Bielski was the receiver coach. We all shared an office on the third floor with Coach Shula. When the offensive coaches looked at a film, Charley and I would study the other team's defense. Likewise, when we looked at a film, the offensive coaches would study the other team's offense. When Don got a phone call, we would evacuate the room and visit with Keith Molesworth and Upton Bell in the personnel office. When Don finished his call, we would return to our desks for further film study or discussion.

There was great togetherness on the staff. We drove to the office together, we worked together, and we drove home together when the day was over. We usually had lunch, plus a game of "liar's poker," at a small restaurant next to our office.

My initial assignment was to review the defensive line keys and rewrite them in our language. This forced me to study the film and catch up on our defense and to study the other defenses in the league to learn where we differed. Our training camp was in Westminster, Maryland, on the campus of Western Maryland College. After training camp, we had to spend several weeks at a private school (McDonogh) until baseball season was over. Then we moved into the visitors' dressing area at Memorial Stadium, which consisted of a locker room, a small training room, and a smaller equipment room. Next to the locker area was the team meeting room, divided by a sliding curtain to separate the offense and defense.

Success came quickly in 1964. We had a veteran team, and Coach Shula provided the leadership. We finished the season with a 12–2 record. The division championship gave us the opportunity to play the Cleveland Browns for the NFL Championship against Coach Collier, for whom both Don and I had worked at Kentucky. Cleveland won the game 27–0, and my first year in professional football was over. We had been successful but were disappointed with outcome of the final game.

The next two years, we were close but a little short. In 1965, we were 10–3–1 and lost in the Western Division play-off to Green Bay 13–10. That gave us a berth in the famous play-off game for losers in Miami, where we beat Dallas 35–3. It was good to finish strong, but the Green Bay loss was a disappointment. We had played well during the year under difficult circumstances due to injuries to quarterback John Unitas and Gary Cuozzo. Tom Matte, a former quarterback at Ohio State, was a running back for us, and he stepped in as our quarterback. His ability, along with the use of a "wrist band" to aid in calling plays, made for an exciting finish. Our defense played well. At the end of the overtime period, the Packers kicked a very suspect field goal that was ruled good. Film of the kick showed that it was off to the left. However, at that time there was only one official aligned under the goalpost crossbar. He signaled good, and the referee behind the kicker confirmed his decision to end the game. Green Bay won 13–10 and continued to the NFL championship game. At the Rules Committee meeting the next spring, the rules were changed so that two officials would be aligned under the goalpost, one on each side in a position to look upward to rule if the ball is in or out. The officials remain in that position today.

My family began to grow in 1965. Son David joined us on August 6, and I immediately began to work on his stance and starts.

After the 1965 season, Charley Winner, who worked with me on defense, was named head coach of the St. Louis Cardinals football team. Chuck Noll, a former guard with the Cleveland Browns and then a defensive coach with the San Diego Chargers, was named as his replacement.

In 1966, we were 9–5 and again earned a berth in the Miami losers' game, where we defeated the Philadelphia Eagles 20–14. We finished the 1967 season with an 11–1–2 record but were short of earning the right to play for "The Ring."

My family grew again in 1968 with the addition of our daughter, Mary Susan, born February 29. It was the beginning of a great year.

We finished the 1968 regular season with a 13–1 record, which put us in the Western Conference championship game against Minnesota. We beat the

Vikings 24–14 and advanced to the NFL championship game in Cleveland. This time it was our turn. We defeated the Browns 34–0 to win the right to advance to **Super Bowl III**. It was a great year and a great opportunity, but a disappointing finish versus the New York Jets. We lost 16–7. It was the first Super Bowl win for the new American Football League and a great win for Coach Weeb Ewbank and the entire Jets team. A day or two before the game, quarterback Joe Namath guaranteed the victory in the media. He predicted the win, and he produced. Another interesting sidelight developed when Bubba Smith, our defensive end, showed up at practice wearing white shoes. In those days, only Joe Namath and a few others wore white shoes. We were concerned because we did not want a distraction that would affect the team's focus. It seems that Bubba had just wanted to express himself. He enjoyed the attention but returned to black shoes for the game. Today, showing up in black shoes would attract the same attention.

The next year brought many changes. The NFL and AFL merged in 1969, and realignment found Baltimore, Cleveland, and Pittsburgh in the new American Football Conference of the NFL. Defensive assistant Chuck Noll was named head coach of the Pittsburgh Steelers. Bob Boyd retired as a player after the 1968 season and was immediately asked to replace Chuck as defensive backfield coach for the Colts. The best we could accomplish in the 1969 season was an 8–5–1 record. In many respects, the season resembled a roller coaster, up one week and down the next. We lost our first two games, won three, lost one, won two, lost one, won two, tied one, lost one, and won the last. It was definitely not a typical year for the Baltimore Colts.

Don's record at Baltimore was 73–26–4 for 1963 to 1969. The record when I was with the Colts and Don was 65–20–4, and we allowed 225 points in 1964, 284 in 1965, 226 in 1966, 198 in 1967, 144 in 1968, and 268 in 1969, our final year at Baltimore.

As various accounts attest, Coach Shula's relationship with owner Carroll Rosenbloom was never the same after the loss to the Jets. Carroll's friends never let him forget the loss, and he in turn never let Don forget it. That no doubt played a part in Don's decision to listen to other offers. He eventually accepted an offer from the Miami Dolphins and was named head coach on February 18, 1970. In April, NFL Commissioner Pete Rozelle awarded Baltimore the Dolphins' first-round draft choice for 1971. The move was complete, and Don announced his staff several days later.

Joining the Miami Dolphins

The Dolphins' staff was a great group. Howard Schnellenberger was the offensive coordinator, Monty Clark was the offensive line coach, and Carl

Taseff was the offensive backfield coach. I was given an opportunity as defensive coordinator. Mike "Mo" Scarry was the defensive line coach, and Tom Keane, a holdover from the former staff, was named defensive backfield coach.

A staff of six is comparatively small by today's numbers. Most staffs today consist of 12 to 15 coaches. The additional slots have opened up more job opportunities for coaches. But I have often wondered, why the increase? First, most teams have added a special teams coach. In Baltimore and Miami, those duties were handled by Coach Shula and the staff, although Don did eventually add a special teams coach in Miami. I fully understand the need. More and more importance has been placed on the special teams, and a special teams coach is necessary in today's game. The other major change was the assignment of the coordinators. Today, they are what I call "walk-around coaches," and I was just that on my return to the sideline with the San Diego Chargers in 1992. As a rule, the coordinator has no position to coach. The advantage is more time to organize and to observe the offensive or defensive positions. But I wonder if that advantage outweighs the responsibility of coaching a position.

By coaching a position, you are actively involved with the other position coaches, and I believe you are in a better position to coordinate the offense or defense. I feel the same way about the coordinator being in the coach's box instead of being on the sideline on game day. Maybe the offensive coordinator needs to be upstairs, but the defensive coordinator needs to be on the sideline. I know from firsthand experience (I was upstairs for my six years at Baltimore) that the action on the field is very different from the action in the coach's box upstairs. Today, it is interesting to see several head coaches take on the game day responsibility of offensive coordinator. Mike Holmgren is doing it at Green Bay, Lindy Infante did the same thing at Indianapolis, and Kevin Gilbride has recently accepted the role with the Chargers. They may have an assistant with the title, and I am sure they receive information from the coach's box (which we all need at times), but it is obvious that they are making the final decision on the play called. In the early years at Miami, Howard Schnellenberger and Coach Shula worked together in a similar manner.

In the beginning at Miami, most of our time was spent deciding how and what we wanted to teach. Many different ideas were presented based on experience with various successful organizations. Howard had been with the Los Angeles Rams, Monty had been a player with the Cleveland Browns, and Carl joined us from the Detroit Lions. Defensively, "Mo" Scarry came from the Washington Redskins, in addition to a long career as a pro player and a college assistant and head coach. Tom was the holdover from the previous staff, and he was very valuable in making us aware of the personnel. Many of our early discussions actually involved the entire staff. That was the way we had worked in Baltimore, and it had been successful. Offensive coaches contributing to the defense and defensive coaches contributing to the offense made for a very tight group. When a final decision was made, it was ours, because we had been involved in making it.

Next came the pre-training camp workouts with the players who were in town. This period helped the coaches and players get acquainted. It enabled the players to learn a little about our plans and what we expected, and it helped the coaches learn more about the players, their abilities, and their willingness to work. As always, some players were consistent in their attendance, and some needed to be encouraged. Each week a new face or two would appear as word got around that we were working out. By the start of training camp, both players and coaches had a good idea of what to expect and were anxious to begin.

Training camp opened on July 12, 1970, and we began by timing everyone in the 40-yard dash and 60-yard shuttle. In between were the bench press, a few deep breaths, and pull-ups. The final exam came in the form of a 12-minute run, to see how much ground each player could cover. It was the answer to conditioning and how much a player had accomplished in the off-season. Some excelled, some were satisfied with a middle-of-the-road pace, and a few lagged behind. The idea was to "keep moving"—words that were heard over and over.

Practice began with players who had failed the 12-minute test. Everybody had to endure the pain. Next came the regularly scheduled morning workout, with emphasis on the running game and the play action pass. After lunch and a rest, the afternoon session consisted mainly of the passing game, plus screens, draws, and special plays. Defensively, practice time and new learning were planned in the same manner, with run defense, middle drill, half-line, and a team period in the morning and pass defense, one on one, seven on seven, and a team period in the afternoon. Both coaches and players looked forward to dinner.

After dinner, it was time for the rookies to perform. At one time or another, each was asked to sing his college song. Some knew the words and could carry a tune, and others ad-libbed the words in a less than melodic voice. There were always a few who didn't know they had a school song, but they weren't off the hook. They had to select a favorite melody, which at times was better than listening to some of the school songs. After some free time, it was time for the regularly scheduled night meeting.

The night meeting alternated between a walk-through on the field and a classroom session. In the classroom, film of the afternoon practice was reviewed. (Film of the morning practice was reviewed in the afternoon meeting before hitting the field for the afternoon practice.) After studying the film, new learning for the next day was reviewed. Each player had his notebook open and followed the instruction. After a short lecture, a diagram or a description was presented on the overhead projector, followed by questions, answers, and further explanation. A short meeting the next morning was used to review the material discussed the previous evening.

To me, the walk-through was the best form of instruction. It was a learning period on the field, where actual situations were reviewed. It might be a situation that had developed in the afternoon or morning practice, or it could be the introduction of material that had been presented in the afternoon and needed to be repeated. As coaches under the direction of Coach Shula, we were striving for discipline and for perfection in learning and execution. Without proper discipline and proper learning, execution suffers.

The Early Years at Miami

We weren't exactly an immediate success. We lost the first game in 1970, won the next four, and lost the next three. After eight games, we were 4–4. I remember sitting in the dressing room at Franklin Field in Philadelphia after our fourth loss. We had played well at times and had the opportunity to win, but we did not take advantage of it on either offense or defense. We had scored 17 points against the Eagles—the most that we had scored on offense—and lost. Defensively, we had allowed 24 points, which was considerably less than we had allowed in our other losses. Don came in, looked around, and said, "We are going to keep working. Now let's get out of here." Nothing more needed to be said. We showered, packed, and boarded the bus.

The next week, we played the Saints and won 21–10. We were now 5–4. Then the Colts visited, and we won 34–17. It was our revenge for a 35–0 loss in Baltimore three weeks earlier. The victory over the Colts started a streak of successive wins over the Falcons, Patriots, Jets, and Bills. We were 10–4 and earned a spot in the play-offs. Our success was short-lived however, as we lost to Oakland 21–14.

Our first year was complete. We had overcome adversity, we were together as a team, and we had improved. We all saw the opportunity that the future presented. With continued hard work and determination, we could "gain the edge" and win.

Each of the next three years presented a challenge. In our opening game in 1971, we tied Denver 10–10. The day before the game, there was so much snow on the field that we could not work out, but game day was beautiful. We won in Buffalo the next week, but returned home and lost to the Jets the following week. Three games into the season, our record was one win, one loss, and one tie. Then we began a streak of eight straight wins, but we stubbed our toe versus the Patriots in New England and the Colts in Baltimore. We ended the season with a 27–6 win over the Packers in the Orange Bowl to finish 10–3–1. It was our second ten-win season, our first AFC East title, and our second play-off opportunity.

The first play-off game was in Kansas City on Christmas Day. We arrived the day before, visited the field, returned to the hotel, and had our usual team meetings and snack. December in Kansas City can mean any type of weather, but we were fortunate. It was cold, but the field was in good shape, considering the possibilities. Kansas City jumped out to an early 10–0 lead in the first quarter, and we tied it up in the second quarter. Both teams scored twice in the third and fourth quarters, which meant "sudden death" overtime. No one scored in the first overtime period, although both teams had opportunities. We missed a field goal, and Nick Buoniconti, our middle linebacker, blocked an attempt by Jan Stenerud. Stenerud had also missed an earlier attempt in regulation time. We continued to play up and down the field. Each team was trying to think of something to do to win the game. Finally, Bob Griese called a counter play for Larry Csonka, who carried for 29 yards to the Chiefs' 36. That put Garo Yepremian in position to win it with a 37-yard field goal. (The goalposts were on the goal line in those days; they were moved to the end line in 1974.) With 7:40 elapsed in the second overtime, Garo kicked the field goal for a 27–24 win. It was the longest game in professional football: 82 minutes and 40 seconds.

The Kansas City win placed the Dolphins in the AFC championship game versus the Colts on January 2, 1972 in the Orange Bowl. We had played Baltimore twice that year. We won the first meeting in Miami 17–14, and Baltimore beat us 14–3 in the second game. We scored in the first quarter to lead 7–0, and it was still 7–0 at halftime. A 62-yard interception return by Dick Anderson in the third quarter made the score 14–0. When the ball was deflected by cornerback Curtis Johnson, Dick picked up his blockers and weaved his way to score behind a wall of six open field blocks. He was quoted as saying, "My eyes were popping as I ran. I have never seen so many people land on their heads." We scored again in the fourth quarter to make the final score 21–0. Interceptions by Dick Anderson, Mike Kolen, and Jake Scott contributed to our win.

Our next stop was New Orleans and **Super Bowl VI** versus the Dallas Cowboys. It was a total disaster. The Cowboys had a good day running the football. Although we held Roger Staubach to 119 yards passing, he continued to scramble and come up with yardage to maintain possession of the football. Double zone coverage would generally make him hesitate, but I sometimes wondered if it was worth it. He was such a good athlete that he could avoid the rush, make the first down, and maintain possession, which is exactly what he did. Another factor, and not an excuse, is that sometimes a team that reaches its goal of getting to the Super Bowl does not play well in the game. That's what happened to the San Diego Chargers in Super Bowl XXIX versus the San Francisco 49ers. Getting to the Super Bowl is quite an accomplishment. The excitement and adulation during the week of the game make it difficult to keep focused, especially in a team's first appearance. Experience makes one realize that getting there is just another step toward the ultimate goal—a world championship. Super Bowl VI was definitely a learning experience for Miami. It made us realize the importance of winning the "big one." The dressing room was quiet after the game. We didn't need anyone to remind us what we needed to accomplish.

The Greatest Season Ever: 17–0

After a good off-season and training camp, we were ready to begin the 1972 season. We had the privilege of opening in brand new Arrowhead Stadium in Kansas City, and it was just as hot on September 17 as it had been cold on Christmas Day in 1971. Luckily, the sun was to our back, and the press box gave us shade on the sideline. Coach Hank Stram and the Chiefs were in the sun, but they probably got more television coverage because they were across from the camera. (The opponent sideline changed sometime later. When I returned to Arrowhead Stadium in 1981 with the Dolphins and later with the Chargers, the sideline opposite the press box was assigned to the opponent. Luckily, those games were in November and December, and the sun felt good on those windy fall days.)

The 20–10 victory at Kansas City was **win #1**. It was a good beginning, and we immediately focused on our next game. We beat the Oilers 34–13 for **win #2**. The third game was versus the Vikings in Bloomington. It was a real struggle, but we pulled it out in the end by a score of 16–14 for **win #3**. Game four versus the Jets in New York ended 27–17 for **win #4**. The Chargers came to town for game five. Bob Griese was injured early in the game, and it didn't look good. Earl Morrall, the veteran who had helped us in Baltimore, entered the game, and we beat the Chargers 24–10 for **win #5**. Tests revealed that Bob had dislocated his right ankle and broken his right leg. Earl was now the man to lead us. Next we played the Bills at home. It was a real shoot-out. Both teams moved the ball up and down the field. First one team scored and then the other. In the end, we prevailed 24–23 for **win #6**. A trip to Baltimore got us a 23–0 shutout for **win #7**.

Looking back, we were happy to be 7–0 midway through the season, but we realized we had much work ahead of us. A return match against the Bills in Buffalo was next. We all remembered the scare at home, but we were prepared and defeated the Bills 30–16 for **win #8**. The next three games were at home in the Orange Bowl. The home crowd cheered us to a 52–0 shutout over the Patriots for **win #9** and **Coach Shula's 100th win**. We beat the Jets 28–24 for **win #10**, and a 31–10 Monday night game versus the Cardinals was **win #11**. Three games to go! The Patriots in New England in December are always a problem, and this game was no exception. We were happy to leave with a 37–21 victory for **win #12**. The next week at Yankee Stadium was a cold, dreary, rainy day. We struggled early but beat the Giants 23–13 for **win #13**.

By now, the media, our fans, and just about everyone was beginning to realize what was at stake. The coaches and players all recognized the situation and knew what we had to do to make it happen—keep our focus, keep preparing as we had been doing weekly, and play our best when the whistle blows. The Colts were our guests, and we had to be ready to play. We were and got **win #14**. The 16–0 shutout on December 16 was a little sweeter for me because it was my birthday.

We quickly put thoughts of an undefeated season out of our minds as we began our preparation for the Cleveland Browns and the AFC play-off game scheduled for December 24 at home. The game would be no different than many of our other games during the year. Teams took pride in getting ready to play the undefeated Dolphins, and the Browns played inspired football.

It was a twist of fate that the coach on the other sideline was Blanton Collier—my high school coach, the coach for whom both Don and I had worked at Kentucky, the best man at my wedding, the coach who had beaten Baltimore in 1964 for the NFL Championship, the coach who led the Browns in 1968 when Baltimore defeated them for the NFL Championship. A lot was on the line.

Despite leading 10–0 at halftime and four interceptions (one by Doug Swift, two by Dick Anderson, and one by Curtis Johnson), the Dolphins trailed 14–13 with 8:11 to play. At that point, Earl Morrall engineered an 80-yard drive with a couple of completions to Paul Warfield, and an 8-yard run on a trap up the middle by Jim Kiick scored the go-ahead touchdown with 4:56 remaining. Dolphins linebacker Doug Swift sealed **win #15** when he intercepted his second pass from Cleveland quarterback Mike Phipps. It was on to the AFC championship game at Three Rivers Stadium on December 31, 1972.

The temperature in Pittsburgh was 63 degrees, unusually warm for that time of year. Both teams were coming off of impressive seasons, and the score was 7–7 at the half. The Dolphins had scored on a daring fourth-down run from punt formation by Larry Seiple. Bob Griese replaced Earl Morrall at quarterback to begin the second half, just 11 weeks after he had broken his leg. Pittsburgh scored first and the Dolphins trailed 10–7. Griese ignited the offense in the third quarter with a 52-yard pass to Paul Warfield and directed 80- and 49-yard drives, with Jim Kiick scoring on rushes of 2 and 3 yards to put the Dolphins ahead 21–10. Terry Bradshaw closed the gap to 21–17 with a 71-yard drive. Our victory was sealed with an interception by Nick Buoniconti at mid-field with 2:30 remaining. (Linebacker Mike Kolen had also intercepted a pass earlier.) We earned **win #16** and a trip to the Los Angeles Coliseum versus George Allen and the Washington Redskins in Super Bowl VII.

Normal procedure was one week of practice at home and one week at the site, and that year was no exception. The Redskins were coming off of a good year, with a solid and productive offense and an excellent defense. This game would be a real challenge. We needed our week of practice at home, even though we had been preparing since September 12. We needed to review our plans for the Redskins, but we also needed to use the time to relax and get healthy. We had no serious injuries in the AFC championship game, but the constant pounding over 16 weeks takes its toll. Also, the time gave Griese an extra week of work. He had played well in the second half of the Pittsburgh game, and we knew another week would have him at the top of his game. Plus, as we learned in Super Bowl III and Super Bowl VI, there are many distractions at the site of the game.

We arrived in Los Angeles and proceeded to our lodging. According to the schedule given to us by the NFL office, we were to use the Rams' training facility. Although it was a good facility with ample fields, locker room, and meeting rooms, a school across the street overlooked the practice area and was of some concern to us in terms of privacy. Picture day was first on the schedule, and when it was over, Don, Howard, and I visited other possible sites to see what other practice areas might be available. Howard had been a member of the Rams' coaching staff with George Allen, and he knew the area. We finally found a great location. The field was below ground level. To ensure privacy, one of our photographers doubled as security by walking the top of the stadium and surveying the area.

Now that we had a new facility, we were ready to begin our preparation. Our schedule was simple. We took the bus from our hotel in Long Beach to the Rams' locker rooms, dressed, and then reboarded the bus and headed to our new practice facility. Our practices went well. There was the usual excitement that accompanies a Super Bowl, but there was also a seriousness of purpose that was good to see. After practice, it was back on the bus, back to the locker room for a refreshing shower, and then a film session to study the Redskins.

In one film session late in the week, we looked at the Redskins' offense versus the Giants. As a staff, we had studied the film earlier and made a note to be sure to show it to the squad. As we always do when we study an opponent, we looked for various ways other teams had adjusted and defended against the Washington offense. Showing both the good plays and the errors that other teams make helps us to emphasize the things we need to accomplish to be successful. Such was the case in the Giants–Redskins film. It vividly showed the play of nose tackle John Mendenhall. He literally refused to be blocked by the Redskins' center and slid along the line of scrimmage making play after play. It was a great example of what the nose tackle could do and needed to do versus the Redskins' offense. They were an outstanding inside running team, and the Giants were successful in shutting them down because of Mendenhall.

As we watched the film with the defense, each coach ("Mo," Tom, and I) sat with his group. I ran the projector and reversed it as a coach or player requested. "Let's see that again" was heard often during the session. That was a good sign and was evidence that no one had "one foot in the parking lot" (a phrase Coach Shula often used to describe a poor practice by a player). Every player was interested in learning more about the Redskins. As we watched the Giants, I took extra time to point out the play of Mendenhall to our nose tackle, Manny Fernandez. I wanted to create in Manny's mind an image of what John had accomplished and how his play was a big factor in the total Giants' defense. We continued watching without saying much. When John made a good play, I would reverse the film and look at the play again. I did not want to overemphasize the play of the nose tackle, but if I could establish an image in Manny's mind, it would build his confidence and competitiveness. I wanted him to say, "I can do it better." At the same time, the other coaches were pointing things out to their players in the same manner.

When the session ended, the players and coaches were free to spend a night with their families and friends. My mother was in town, along with my Uncle Reuben and his daughter, Diane. And of course my wife, Betty Jane, and our two children, David and Mary Susan, were there. We all looked forward to relaxing and enjoying the time together. During the season, there is never enough time to spend with one's family. It is one of the problems of coaching.

Saturday was our final practice. We reviewed the kicking game, plus five or six plays by the offense and defense. After practice, we had more free time, a meeting with the media, some family time, and a final check of the game plan and the defensive calls.

Finally it was Sunday. The day began with chapel service, the pre-game meal, the ride to the Los Angeles Coliseum, going to the locker room, walking the field, and visiting with coaching friends from the other team. Pre-game warm-ups began with kick returners, kicker, punters, receivers, and quarterbacks out. I always go out early with our specialist to watch the other specialists work. In particular, I like to watch the kicker to see the snap and his get-off time, distance, and height. That Sunday was no different except that I noticed that the Redskins' kicker's toe seemed to be more pointed than normal. Rumors had been floating around all year that he tied up his toe, and I thought it looked like a possibility. I said something to the official, who proceeded to have the kicker remove his shoe. My suspicion was wrong. His toe was very heavily taped, but it was not tied up. All was legal (although I like to think that I created some doubt in the kicker's mind that resulted in a missed field goal attempt.) The remaining players came through the tunnel and took there places for the warm-up.

Super Bowl VII was a record crowd of 90,182. The first quarter saw Howard Twilley, an original Dolphin, team up with Bob Griese for a 28-yard touchdown pass. The score was 7–0 at the beginning of the second quarter. In the second quarter, Griese connected with Paul Warfield on a 57-yard bomb for what we thought was our second touchdown, but it was nullified by an offside penalty. A 32-yard interception return by linebacker Nick Buoniconti set up the Dolphins' second score later in the half as Jim Kiick rammed it into the end zone from the one. The halftime score was 14–0 Miami as both teams returned through the tunnel to their respective locker rooms.

The second half began as a battle in the trenches, back and forth, with neither team able to establish a consistent attack. The same type of physical battle continued into the fourth quarter. Each team had its chances, but neither was able to capitalize. Early in the fourth quarter, our offense stalled, and Garo Yepremian was called on to kick a 49-yard field goal. Then something bizarre happened. When his kick was blocked, Garo somehow ended up with the ball and tried to throw a pass—to whom no one will ever know. The anticipated throw was ruled a fumble. Mike Bass recovered for the Redskins and scored. That made it 14–7 with 12 minutes remaining. The game continued in a physical battle until safety Jake Scott intercepted Billy Kilmer's pass in the end zone and returned it 55 yards to seal our victory and **win #17**. We had three interceptions in the game, two by Jake Scott and one by Nick Buoniconti. Scott was voted MVP, and Manny Fernandez led the line assault on the Redskins' running game with 17 tackles and a quarterback sack. Defensive end Bill Stanfill also had a sack.

It was over! We had an undefeated season with a record of 17–0 and had won Super Bowl VII. After 16 straight wins, anything other than 17–0 would have seemed like a failure.

The next year brought a new challenge. We had proved as a team that we belonged with the best. We had to win Super Bowl VII, and we did. Now we had to prove that we could continue our winning streak. Continue we did, with a 21–13 win over the 49ers on a hot and humid day in the Orange Bowl. It was the first time that we had opened the season at home, plus it was a one o'clock kickoff. To the best of my knowledge, every game after that was scheduled for four o'clock until late October or November. The next week we visited Berkeley and lost 12–7 to the Raiders. Our streak had been broken. There was nothing to do but start another.

And that we did, as we put together a streak of ten wins by defeating the Patriots 44–23, Jets 31–3, Browns 17–9, Bills 27–6, Patriots 30–14, Jets 24–14, Colts 44–0, Bills 17–0, Cowboys 14–7, and Steelers 30–26 before losing to the Colts in Baltimore 16–3. We finished the season with a 34–7 win over the Detroit Lions and the AFC East Championship. We were 26–2 over a two-year period, **the best in NFL history**.

The 1973 season brought a special feeling of pride in the defense for the coaches and players. We held our opponents to a record 15 touchdowns, including two consecutive shutouts against Baltimore (our fourth in a row) and Buffalo. We held the Jets and the Colts to three points each. The second time we played the Bills, they scored six points. The Browns scored nine points, and we held Detroit to seven in the final game. In the opener, the 49ers scored 13 points. The second time we met both the Patriots and the Jets and in the game against the Cowboys, we held each team to 14 points. The embarrassing game, although we won, was the 23 points allowed versus the Patriots in the third game of the season. The Oakland game was a physical battle; we only allowed 12 points, but that was too many to help our team win. I have always stressed that if we need a shutout to win, then we must "shut 'em out." The year is a tribute to the players in terms of the way they prepared and the way they played.

We played the Cincinnati Bengals in the play-offs in the Orange Bowl on December 23, 1973. Cincinnati came into the game with an explosive offense, and we knew we had our work cut out for us. We scored first when Bob Griese connected with Paul Warfield for a 13-yard touchdown pass; reliable Garo Yepremian converted, and it was 7–0. The Bengals moved the ball but then stalled, and Horst Muhlmann kicked a 24-yard field goal to make it 7–3. We countered late in the quarter when Larry Csonka scored. Garo converted, and the score was 14–3 at the end of the first quarter.

We knew going into the game that the Bengals had two great receivers in Issac Curtis and Charley Joiner (Joiner later became a receiver coach with the San Diego Chargers). We devised a method to "cut" Curtis at the line of scrimmage. It proved effective early, and we continued to mix the cut technique with the normal jam technique. It is interesting to note that the Rules Committee ruled against the "cut" the following year and made it an illegal maneuver. Bengals Coach Paul Brown was a member of the Rules Committee. We had been a part of a rule change made the following year at least twice now. First, two officials were stationed under the goalpost, one under each upright, and now it was the "no cut" rule. Either we were making progress or the Rules Committee was.

The second quarter opened in much the same manner as the first, with both teams moving the ball. Midway through the second quarter, Mercury Morris scored on a four-yard run, Garo again made good, and the score was 21–3. Things looked good until just before the half, when Griese's pass was intercepted by Bengal safety Neal Craig, who returned the catch for a touchdown. This narrowed our margin to 21–10. A field goal by the Bengals made it 21–13. On the ensuing kickoff, Mercury Morris fumbled and Cincinnati recovered. With only seconds remaining, Muhlmann kicked another field goal, and the half ended with Miami on top 21–16.

We took total control in the second half with a touchdown on a seven-yard pass from Griese to Jim Mandich and field goals in the third and fourth quarters, for a final score of 34–16. Defensively, we kept the Bengals out of the end zone. We held Issac Curtis to one catch for 2 yards, and Joiner had two catches for 33 yards. Our jam and cut technique was successful. Ken Anderson was 14 of 27 for 113 yards. Our Dick Anderson had an interception, and Mercury Morris led the offensive attack with 106 yards in 20 carries.

Next was the AFC championship game versus Oakland in the Orange Bowl on December 30, 1973. Earlier in the season, Oakland had stopped our 18-game winning streak by beating us 12–7 in Berkeley. We realized what was at stake and what it would take to be successful. The first half belonged to us as we led 14–0. In the second half, Oakland battled back and made it 17–10 to start the fourth quarter. In the fourth quarter, Griese directed a 63-yard drive that culminated in a field goal and a 40-yard drive that ended in Csonka's third touchdown. Defensively, safety Dick Anderson forced a fumble by Marv Hubbard at mid-field with six minutes to play. The ten-point fourth quarter made it 27–10. Our reward was a trip to our third consecutive Super Bowl and an opportunity to earn back-to-back Super Bowl victories.

Super Bowl VIII was played in Houston on January 13, 1974. During the off-week, I was contacted by San Diego owner Gene Klein concerning a vacant coaching position. I knew that Mr. Klein was interested because Don had told me earlier that he had asked permission to speak with me. He flew to Miami to meet with me, described the situation in San Diego, and offered me the job. I could not give him a definite answer at the time because the New York Giants had also requested permission to talk with me.

Andy Robustelli was the new general manager of the Giants. We had talked on the phone, and I had asked to meet with Wellington Mara, the owner. When we met a few days later at the Miami Airport Inn, all the things that Andy had said were confirmed by Mr. Mara. Plans were made to get together with Andy in Houston. I had a decision to make. San Diego was interested. I had great respect for Mr. Klein and appreciated his taking the time to fly to Miami to meet me. The Giants were also of interest to me, especially after I had the opportunity to meet with Mr. Mara. The Giants had a great tradition and history in the NFL under the direction of the Mara family. To be honest, the San Diego opportunity was probably a little better financially, but I never believed in basing a decision totally on finances. I felt like I had already made up my mind, but I continued to review the options.

I tried hard during our off-week not to let my discussions interfere with our preparation, and I believe I succeeded. However, as the week progressed, the media got wind of something going on and there were calls regarding what, where, when, etc.

When we arrived in Houston for **Super Bowl VIII**, we were assigned to the Oilers' practice facility. The weather in Houston was unusually brisk, and the facility was not built for cold weather. The week at home had been helpful. Our practices were sharp, and the off-week had been good for our bumps and bruises. As usual, media day was first on the schedule, and I was asked the usual questions concerning our defense. I soon became aware that those questions were only an opening. The main theme centered around my upcoming decision. The media, as usual, seemed to know more about what was going on than I was prepared to discuss. I tried to be as honest and frank as possible, recognizing that reporters have their assignments and are "under the gun" to get the story. That was only the beginning. As the week progressed, I was met before and after practice for updates and the usual round of questions.

Andy Robustelli met with me as planned. I confirmed to him that my meeting in Miami with Mr. Mara was important and that I would join the New York Giants. Earlier I had notified Mr. Klein of my decision, thanked him for his interest, and wished him success in finding a coach. The official announcement would be made sometime after the game, but it probably ranks at the top of the list of all-time worst kept secrets. The media grapevine was accurate, and I was in the position of having to wait until the Giants made an official announcement.

It was game time and we were ready. Our preparation and attention to detail had been good during the off-week, and we had handled the Super Bowl atmosphere in stride. This was our third straight trip, and our demeanor could be described as business-like.

The game at Rice Stadium began in typical Dolphins' style. Our offense took the opening kickoff and put together a 62-yard drive in ten plays, scoring on Larry Csonka's 5-yard smash. Minnesota punted, and the onslaught resumed with a 56-yard, ten-play drive capped by Jim Kiick's 1-yard plunge to make it 17–0. It was midway through the second quarter before the Vikings crossed their 40 yard line. The Minnesota drive stalled at the six when Oscar Reed fumbled and safety Jake Scott recovered. The first half ended, and the teams retired to their respective locker rooms.

The second half began in much the same manner as the first. Good defense and our offense continued to move the ball effectively against the Minnesota defense. A diving catch by Paul Warfield netted 27 yards to set up the third touchdown for Larry Csonka on a 2-yard plunge. That made it 24–0 heading into the fourth quarter. Another Super Bowl shutout was in the making, until Fran Tarkenton scrambled and scored with 1:35 remaining to make the final score 24–7. Csonka was voted MVP, with a Super Bowl record 145 yards in 33 carries. During the three play-off games, our offense rushed for 703 yards and we outscored our opponents 85–33. With the 1973 season over, we had **three consecutive Super Bowls**, with **back-to-back wins in Super Bowl VII and Super Bowl VIII**.

Leaving the field was probably one of my most emotional moments. I knew my time with the Dolphins was over. It had been a great four years. But most of all, I knew that my relationship with Don was going to change. We had worked together since 1964. He had given me the opportunity to coach the defensive line and then to coordinate the defense. I tried to do a good job for him, and I think the record shows that I did. The emotion was more than I could take. As our paths crossed on the way to the locker room, we hugged each other and I cried. I was so appreciative.

The atmosphere in the dressing room was exciting. The players and coaches were a proud group with satisfied smiles as the result of 32 wins in 34 attempts. It was the kind of feeling that goes with a job well done. As a complete surprise to me, I was awarded the game ball by the squad. I had received others in the past, but the game ball from Super Bowl VIII was the best. It was from a great group of guys who totally understood the unselfish attitude and team concept so necessary for success. I keep the ball in the center of other mementos of my career.

The after-game party was equally enjoyable. The Giants had made the announcement. It was official—I was the new head coach for the New York

Giants. There were congratulations and the usual parting words. I spent part of the evening talking with Eugene Davis, our assistant equipment man and general handyman. He had been with us from the beginning and was an extremely loyal individual. He seemed sad that I was leaving, and I explained to him that we would remain friends even though we would be miles apart. He remained with the Dolphins for a number of years, and it was always a pleasure to see him and reminisce.

New York Giants

I returned to Miami with the team, packed a couple of bags, and left in January 1974 for my official introduction in New York as the ninth head coach of the Giants. The program was held at a local restaurant. The media, members of the Giants organization, and other dignitaries were present. However, the one person whose presence totally surprised me was Stanley Barnett, a former Paris, Kentucky, resident who now lived across the river in New Jersey. His support was encouraging and much appreciated. After the program, we walked back to the Giants' office, just so we could talk and enjoy the time together.

Things began to happen almost immediately. The newly formed World Football League began to sign players from NFL teams. Several of our players were involved. It all centered around money and what appeared to be an unusually good opportunity. It was almost like college recruiting all over again. Yankee Stadium was being redesigned, and we would have to play our games in another arena. It was soon determined that Yale Bowl in New Haven, Connecticut, would be our temporary home. The draft was approaching; time with the scouts, studying film, and reports were the order of the day. The organization had decided that we needed a new training and practice facility. After reviewing the previous facility, I was in agreement. It had been an old baseball park and was practically on the Jersey waterfront in the middle of warehouses and other industries. It was depressing just to ride through the area and certainly not a selling point to players being wooed by the World Football League. Andy was scouting new areas, and from time to time I visited sites that he felt were a definite possibility. In between, my time was spent on the phone contacting possible coaches and setting up appointments to interview the previous staff and players who were in the area. It was indeed a time of change. A transition was in order, and I was in the middle of probably one of the most memorable times in the history of the New York Giants.

The Giants were a family-owned team. Ownership had passed from father to oldest son. Upon his death, ownership passed to the next son in the line of succession. The coaching staff appointments had generally followed the same theme. Most had been a part of the family. The Giants were loyal to their people, to their players, and to their coaches. There was no question that I was a departure from that philosophy. I stepped into this position knowingly, but I never fully realized many of the other factors involved.

For example, I never realized until later that a rift was developing between Wellington Mara and his brother's son, Tim Mara. They both owned 50% of the team. Wellington had always been involved in the football operation, but he was supposed to be out of it when Andy Robustelli was hired in 1974. They both had office space in the Giants' downtown office. Wellington seemed to be more involved in the football operation, but I always enjoyed talking with Tim as time permitted. He had an interesting insight into whatever discussion was on the table. I respected both gentlemen and tried to keep them informed about the team and the problems we faced. I appreciated their ideas on possible solutions. I worked directly with Andy, but it was evident from the beginning that Well was active in football decisions and Tim, to my knowledge, was on the sideline.

Our 1974 staff was complete, and we moved to temporary offices in White Plains, New York. Ray Wietecha, offensive line coach, was the holdover. Hunter Enis coordinated the offense, Ted Plumb coached the receivers, Allen Webb (a former Giants player) was our offensive backfield coach, Maxie Baughan coached the linebackers, John Symank coached the defensive backs, Floyd Peters coached the defensive line, Jim Trimble remained as pro personnel director, and Jim Lee Howell and Harry Buffington shared the college personnel scouting along with Rosey Brown, Ken Kavanaugh, and Emlen Tunnell (Emlen died at training camp in 1975). A strange twist developed in the late spring when Maxie Baughan resigned and returned to the Washington Redskins as a player to work with his former coach, George Allen. I always wondered what the true story was surrounding this move. When this happened, Ed Rutledge joined us as linebacker and special teams coach. Our new training facility and coaches' offices were complete at Pace University in Pleasantville, New York, and we were ready for the season. Training camp remained at Fairfield College in Fairfield, Connecticut, for that year, and we had a pre-camp meeting of our draftees at Fordham College.

Like other teams, we lost some players to the World Football League, so many of our rookies had an opportunity to contribute early. This, together with a strike by the Players Association which delayed the veterans from reporting, really gave us a good look at our draftees. We finished the pre-season 2–4, remained healthy, and were ready to start the season.

We opened the 1974 season in Yale Bowl with two tough losses: 13–10 to Washington and 28–20 to New England. The next week we visited Dallas and won 14–6. We felt good about where we were and were looking forward to the next part of our schedule. Then we lost 14–7 to the Falcons at home, lost 35–7 in Philadelphia, lost 24–3 in Washington, and lost 21–7 at home to the Cowboys. After seven games, we were 1–6 and disappointed, because we had not taken full advantage of our opportunities.

The second half of the season began with a 33–27 win in Kansas City. The Jets were next. We had beaten them in the pre-season and were looking forward to the rematch in Yale Bowl. It was a great game, and the score was 20–20 at the end of regulation. Overtime found both teams moving the ball, with quarterback Joe Namath taking a designed bootleg and running it into the end zone for a 26–20 Jets win. In our next five ga.nes, we had some close ones, but close doesn't count. We lost in Detroit 20–19, at home versus St. Louis 23–21, at Chicago 16–13, at home versus Philadelphia 20–7, and lost our final game 26–14 in St. Louis. A season record of 2–12 was not what we had envisioned. There was much work to do to reach the competitive level that was needed.

Looking back, John Hicks (right guard), Tom Mullen (left guard), Clyde Powers (strong safety, who later became director of pro personnel with the Indianapolis Colts), Jim Pietrzak (defensive tackle), Ray Rhodes (wide receiver, who later became head coach of the Philadelphia Eagles), and Steve Crosby (fullback, who later coached in the NFL for many years with Miami, Atlanta, and Cleveland; did college scouting for the Philadelphia Eagles; and presently is the offensive coordinator at Vanderbilt University)—all rookies—played a significant part in the 1974 season. John Mendenhall was an All-Pro selection (he was the nose tackle we had studied in preparation for Super Bowl VII versus the Redskins in 1972). Walker Gillette arrived from the Cardinals to fill a void at wide receiver. Quarterback Craig Morton joined us in a trade with Dallas, but he did not have the supporting cast that was needed. Doug Kotar, a free agent from Kentucky, quickly developed into a dependable running back (he later developed a fatal illness). Dave Jennings, selected off the waiver wire, was the Giants' punter for the next ten years (he is now a sports announcer and last I heard was working with the Jets Football Network). All of these acquisitions helped us, and we felt we were making progress. The future looked bright. We had survived the attack by the World Football League and the strike by the Players Association.

But continued improvement was necessary, and we had to take advantage of all market possibilities. The draft was important, but we had to be aware of upgrading the team through trades and waivers. Our first draft choice went to Dallas in the Craig Morton trade. We traded our third choice to Denver for running back Larry Watkins. We traded our fifth choice to Miami for cornerback Henry Stuckey and traded our sixth choice to Baltimore for starting defensive end Roy Hilton. We strengthened our coaching staff with the addition of Marty Schottenheimer to coach the linebackers and coordinate the defense. Marty had been a player in the NFL and more recently a player–coach with Portland in the World Football League. This addition enabled us to free up Ed Rutledge so he could devote his full attention to special teams.

Training camp was moved to our training and office complex at Pace University, and our home field for the 1975 season was Shea Stadium. Giants Stadium in the Meadowlands complex was under construction, and we were looking forward to our own facility and a permanent home. For 1975, like the previous year, we remained a traveling team.

The early pre-season was a success, with impressive wins over New England (28–14), San Diego (17–7), the Jets (21–20), and Pittsburgh (24–7), but we lost 24–21 to Cleveland in Seattle and 31–13 to Miami. (Due to a Players Association problem, the Miami game was delayed until players from both teams finally met and decided to play.) What a way to get ready for the season. We played like we still had one foot in the locker room. It was not a good tune-up for the regular season.

We opened with a 20–17 win in Philadelphia but lost the next three, 49–13 to Washington, 26–14 to St. Louis, and 13–7 to Dallas. Next was a Monday night game versus Buffalo, which we won 17–14, followed by a 20–13 loss to St. Louis. We beat San Diego 35–24 at home. Then came a series of five straight losses, which put us in a tailspin for a time. We lost 21–13 to Washington, 13–10 to Philadelphia, 40–14 to Green Bay, 14–3 to Dallas, and 21–0 to Baltimore. We regrouped and finished strong with a 28–14 win over New Orleans and a 26–23 win in San Francisco. We finished the season 5–9. There was work to be done. We still needed to upgrade our personnel, but we felt we had improved. We would be moving into Giants Stadium sometime during 1976, and we wanted to be worthy of the complex.

In hindsight, we did not make good use of the draft, as we had the year before. The only player that surfaced and became a starter was defensive end George Martin, an 11th round draft choice from Oregon. Floyd Peters had scouted George in the spring and was convinced that he was a player. Floyd started talking about George early, and we were able to get him in the 11th round. George was a real steal; not only was he a good player, but he was also a great person and had been a member of the 1982 Super Bowl team. The trades gave us strength. Watkins was valuable to us as a running back, Hilton played well as a defensive end, and Henry Stuckey provided depth at defensive back, but they were not the impact players we desperately needed. Other than our trades and 11th round draft choice George Martin, we failed miserably in the draft. This was our lifeline—and we had to make better decisions in the college draft.

Evaluating players is a natural instinct. Some people have it, and others do not. The top evaluators have the instinct. They see something above average or lacking in a top prospect, or they see something that leads them to believe that a lower ranked player can fill a need. One of the best at this is Steve Crosby—the same Steve Crosby who was our 17th round choice with the Giants in the 1974 draft. He helped us pick some solid players with the Dolphins and he helped the Eagles to be more selective.

Defensive line coach Floyd Peters resigned after the 1975 season. Floyd did a good job for us. He had been a former player with the Philadelphia Eagles and an area scout with the Miami Dolphins before joining us in 1974. He was a true professional, and we would miss his contribution to our program. In reviewing possible replacements, John McVay, who had recently joined Andy's staff, recommended Jay Fry. I remembered Jay as a former player and coach at Miami University, and he had been a member of McVay's staff in the World Football League. We talked to Jay, liked his enthusiasm, and asked him to join us as defensive line coach.

When the World Football League folded in the fall of 1975, we began to look at available personnel. Two or our coaches, Jay Fry and Marty Schottenheimer, and John McVay, an assistant with Andy, were former WFL coaches, and we felt we had an edge on knowledge concerning personnel. We brought in a couple of offensive linemen that we thought would help us improve. My only reservation was their lack of size. They had performed well in the WFL, but they definitely lacked the size needed to play in the NFL. Our most important addition was Larry Csonka, former fullback with the Dolphins who had jumped to the WFL for the 1975 season. After the WFL folded, we signed him as a free agent. We felt he had a few good years remaining, and his general presence would definitely be an asset. The 1976 draft was somewhat of an improvement over 1975. Our additions were Troy Archer (who was later killed in an accident), Harry Carson, and Jerry Golsteyn (who injured a knee in the pre-season and never had the opportunity to return to the form he showed prior to the injury). Harry Carson produced immediately and was a part of the Giants' success in the eighties.

The 1976 pre-season was a success. We finished healthy, with a 4–2 record. We lost the first game to New England 13–7 and then put together four wins, including a 16–14 win over the Jets in the last football game played in Yankee Stadium. When the stadium was redesigned, it was no longer practical to use for football. The Jets were coached by Lou Holtz, who had a short career in pro football and returned to college. In four road games, we beat Houston 30–14, Pittsburgh 17–0, Green Bay 20–16, and lost 14–13 to San Diego in our final pre-season game.

When the regular season started, we were still in Shea, but we were optimistic that we would be in Giants Stadium sometime during the year. Our first three games were on the road. We opened at Washington and lost 19–17 in a thriller. Some people point to that game as the one that ruined the season, but I do not believe that theory. Nevertheless, regardless of the reason, we continued our slide. We lost at Philadelphia 20–7 and to the Los Angeles Rams 24–10. The following week, October 10, 1976, was our opening game in Giants Stadium, our new home. Although our stadium was complete, our transition to a competitive football team continued. We lost our debut against the Cowboys 24–14 before a sellout crowd. We returned to the road and lost to Minnesota 24–7. Returning home, we lost to Pittsburgh 27–0, and that was my last game.

After the game, Andy informed me that a decision had been made to go in another direction. It was final on Monday morning, October 25, 1976. I had been hired to resurrect the New York Giants and was disappointed that I had not been given adequate time to do the job. That was my response then and it remains my response today.

In looking back, the Giants needed an immediate fix. They brought in two new faces in 1974, Andy Robustelli as general manager and Bill Arnsparger as head coach. Andy was a Giants' legend from the glory years as well as the owner of a successful travel business. I am certain he felt that he could turn the Giants around. There was a new stadium on the horizon, and management wanted a new team. I think Andy soon realized that changing the direction of a football team that had been sick since the mid-sixties was not an easy task. He tried to help and did what he thought was best. However, many of the same problems remained. With the exception of a few players, the 1974, 1975, and 1976 drafts did not produce the impact player we needed to build a team. We picked good people and they worked hard, but they did not have the ability to play consistently in the NFL. With the exception of George Martin and Harry Carson, the draft never brought us the type of impact player that will play for ten years. Martin and Carson were both in that category, but we needed more. Other than the trade for Morton and Csonka, the others were stopgap players to fill a void. At that time, there were no free agents, just the college draft and trades. Building through the draft takes time and patience. In two years and seven games, the Giants had neither the time nor the patience to give a coach time to build. My replacement was John McVay, who had been hired in early 1976 to work with Andy.

The New York Giants had a new stadium and wanted a new team. When that was not possible, they took the easy route and got a new name to coach the team. Realistically, I accepted the opportunity to coach the Giants, and I take the responsibility for the two years and seven games as coach. I felt that I helped to establish a base, but there was no question that much more work was needed. In those years, the college draft and trades were the keys to rebuilding, and unfortunately both take time.

The Giants' fortunes began to sour in the mid-sixties. The organization did not regain championship status until Bill Parcells took the reins in 1983, after Ray Perkins resigned to go to Alabama. In Parcells' third year, the team was 10–6, followed by 14–2 in 1986 and a first-place finish in the NFC East and a championship in Super Bowl XXI. Recognition for part of this success should go to George Young, who was brought in to replace Andy Robustelli as general manager in 1979. George had a solid background in personnel and football that dated back to his days as a high school coach in Baltimore, a scout, an assistant coach with the Baltimore Colts, and later as director of personnel with the Miami Dolphins. George and Bill Parcells proved to be a perfect fit, and the New York Giants were back as a competitive organization.

Return to the Miami Dolphins

My short vacation allowed me to watch my son's football practice at Bell Middle School in Chappaqua, New York. I had no reason to hide. I was disappointed, but not embarrassed. In the interim, Coach Shula called and asked me to return to the Dolphins. By the Thursday following my release from the Giants, I was at practice with the Miami Dolphins preparing to play the New England Patriots. On October 31, 1976, I was on the sideline calling the defensive signals. We held the Patriots to a field goal and won 10–3.

Six games remained. We beat the Jets 27–7 but then lost three straight, 14–3 to Pittsburgh, 17–16 to Baltimore, and 17–13 to Cleveland. We beat Buffalo 45–27 and lost 29–7 to Minnesota in the season finale. The Dolphins finished 6–8, which was Coach Shula's worst record, and missed the play-offs for the second consecutive year.

We rebounded in 1977. Our 10–4 record gave us a tie for first place in the AFC East, but we lost the tie breaker to the Colts and missed the play-offs.

In 1978, the NFL introduced a new 16-game format. We finished 11–5, tied for the AFC East title, and lost the wild card game to Houston 17–9. We were beginning to improve on defense. We had three shutouts (versus Baltimore, Cincinnati, and Washington) and allowed New England a field goal, Oakland six points, and Baltimore eight points.

We were 10–6 in 1979 and finished in first place in the Eastern Division. We lost the American Conference play-off to Pittsburgh 34–14, and the Steelers went on to win Super Bowl XIV.

An 8–8 season in 1980 brought mixed results. Bob Griese surpassed the 25,000-yard career mark on October 5 versus the Colts, but suffered a sprained right shoulder and was lost for the season. He was replaced by David Woodley, who started the last ten games of the season.

Larry Little and Bob Griese retired in 1981. Coach Shula got career victory 200 versus the Patriots, and the Dolphins were 11–4–1. We won the AFC East, but lost the American Conference play-off game in overtime to the Chargers in a 41–38 thriller.

The strike in 1982 interrupted the season. The season started on September 12, and play stopped on September 21 and did not resume until November 20. We were 7–2. One of the losses was to the Patriots in New England, where work release parolee Mark Henderson cleared a space on the snow-covered field for kicker John Smith's field goal. We defeated the Patriots 28–13 in the playoffs, with four quarterback sacks (one each for Earnie Rhone, Bokamper, Bob Baumhower, and A.J. Duhe) and two interceptions (one each by Don McNeal and Gerald Small). Next we beat San Diego 34–13. We had three sacks, two by Duhe and one by Bokamper. In the AFC championship game, we defeated the Jets 14–0 to win the AFC title. A.J. Duhe intercepted quarterback Richard Todd three times and returned one catch 35 yards for a touchdown. Small and Glenn Blackwood each had one interception, and we had four sacks, two by Bokamper and one each by Bob Brudzinski and Baumhower.

Super Bowl XVII was played in Pasadena, California, at the Rose Bowl on January 30, 1983. It was another match between the Redskins and Dolphins. The game boiled down to one play. After a seesaw start, we went ahead 17–10 in the first half on a 98-yard kickoff return by Fulton Walker— a Super Bowl record. The Redskins kicked a field goal in the third quarter to make it 17–13. On fourth and one on the Washington 43 with 10:01 remaining, John Riggins went outside his own left tackle for a 43-yard touchdown. We missed a tackle on the play, but the player should never have been put in that situation. The final score was 27–17 Washington.

That is the one call in my career that will always haunt me. We took a time-out to discuss the situation. The Redskins were moving the ball, and it was fourth and one at the 43 yard line. Should I call a short yardage defense and stop the Redskins there, or should I call a normal defense and hope that we stop them, but not "sell the farm"? I decided to use a short yardage defense and stop them now, but we failed to stop them, and the result was a score. Riggins had a Csonka-type game against us. He had 166 yards in 38 carries. We had two interceptions versus Joe Theismann, one each by Duhe and Lyle Blackwood, and three sacks, one each by Rhone, Baumhower, and Larry Gordon.

The next year brought change. We drafted Dan Marino, linebacker Larry Gordon died in Phoenix on June 25, and I accepted the head coach position at LSU on December 2, 1983. We were 12–4 and won the AFC East but lost to Seattle in the first round of the play-offs. The season started out like a roller coaster. We won two, lost one, won one, lost two, won four, lost one, and finished with a five-game winning streak to win the AFC East.

Midway through the season, I was contacted by Bob Brodhead, athletics director at LSU, who asked if I would be interested if there were an opening as head coach. I told him that I would be interested if and when the position became open. I put the possibility out of my mind, because it was something I could not control. My responsibility was to prepare our defense to play each week, and I did not want the LSU situation to become a distraction.

The LSU 1983 season ended on November 24 with a victory over Tulane and a 4–7 finish overall and 0–6 in the Southeastern Conference. Soon after, I heard from Bob Brodhead again. He told me that the decision had been made to open up the head coach position. I confirmed my interest and was offered and accepted the job on December 2, 1983. In discussing the situation with Coach Shula, he was very understanding. He permitted me to leave after each of our remaining games to recruit for LSU. That was very important for the LSU football program because of the early signing date. I will forever be grateful to Don for giving me the flexibility. He was confident that I could handle the divided responsibility, and I feel I did so without a problem. For the next three weeks, I would leave after our game, fly to Baton Rouge, and cover an area of the state with Sam Nader (coordinator of LSU recruiting) to visit with prospective student–athletes. I would return to Miami on Tuesday and begin our preparation for the next game. As time allowed, I interviewed prospective coaches in Baton Rouge. Pete Mangurian flew into town one night, and I talked with him about a coaching position at about five in the morning. We had a good meeting, and I was still able to visit an area with Sam and talk to prospects. I was especially proud that the defensive squad reacted positively during this time. They maintained their focus, prepared properly, and played well. It was a definite sign of leadership and maturity within the defensive team and a reflection on coaches "Mo" Scarry and Tom Keane.

After my announcement and discussion with Don, we beat the Oilers 24–17, the Falcons 31–24, and the Jets 34–14 to win the AFC East and a play-off berth versus Seattle. We prepared and were ready to play. But as sometimes happens, a series of events in the game created situations for the offense and defense that were difficult to overcome. The first quarter saw two teams fighting to gain the edge. On our second possession, we started a 12-play, 80-yard drive that ended with a 19-yard touchdown pass from Marino to tight end Dan Johnson, but the extra point was missed. The ensuing kickoff resulted in a 59-yard return that led to a 6-yard scoring pass from Dave Krieg to Cullen Bryant. Seattle kicked the extra point and led 7–6. Our offense immediately retaliated as Marino and Duper hooked up on a 32-yard circus catch for a touchdown. Miami led 13–7 at the half. The second half began the same way as the first. A fumble in Seattle territory early in the third quarter set the Seahawks up for a 50-yard march that featured a 28-yard pass completion and culminated in a 1-yard run by Curt Warner. Seattle regained the lead 14–13.

Early in the fourth quarter, a 27-yard field goal increased Seattle's lead to 17–13. We regained the lead 20–17 following an interception by Gerald Small and an 18-yard return. Woody Bennett scored on a two-yard run with 3:43 remaining. Seattle came right back with a pair of completions from Krieg to Steve Largent for a total of 56 yards, and Warner ran 2 yards for the score. Seattle was back on top 24–20. We fumbled the ensuing kickoff and Seattle recovered, but their offense went nowhere. However, the good field position made a field goal attempt good, and Seattle led 27–20. Another fumble on the next kickoff iced the game and a spot in the play-offs for Seattle for the first time in their eight-year history.

Looking back, when the lead was 20–17 with 3:43 remaining, it was our job on defense to get the ball for our offense and come off the field. We failed and allowed the opponent to score. A defense has to be good enough to do whatever is necessary. It has always been my philosophy that if we need a shutout to win, the defense must play well enough to get the shutout. It was a disappointment. We would not have the opportunity to play for the AFC title and in another Super Bowl. I would be remiss if I did not thank our secretary, Ann Rodriquez, for making sure we had our scouting report and game plan each week. She truly helped us "gain the edge."

LSU Fighting Tigers: Geaux Tigers!

Why was I interested in LSU? The answer is simple. I first became involved with LSU in 1954 when I was an assistant at the University of Kentucky and Paul Dietzel was head coach at LSU (Paul had been a senior at Miami University when I entered in 1947). We had played LSU every year from

1954 to my last year at Kentucky in 1961 and were three out of eight. Our first game was a 7–6 win and our other two wins were both shutouts, 14–0 in 1956 and 3–0 in 1960. I prefer not to mention the other five games. LSU was a good football team in those years. When I left Kentucky after the 1961 season, I went to Tulane, and John North, as assistant at Kentucky, received an offer from LSU. In the early years, the Tulane–LSU rivalry was a good one, but it faded in later years, and now the teams only play each other every other year. I had been impressed with the LSU program under Charley McClendon, and when the opening developed, it was of interest to me.

I had enjoyed college coaching early in my career and thought that LSU and Baton Rouge would be a great place to coach and live. Throughout my career, I made moves in different directions, but they were always moves that I wanted and enjoyed. I looked forward to the coaching opportunity and the excitement at LSU.

When I arrived full-time, my schedule was quite busy. It was important that I continue recruiting, get to know the players, and complete my staff. Those were my priorities. I had a brief meeting with the players after I was announced as head coach. We reviewed our objectives and talked about the importance of doing the "little things" that make big things happen. I was impressed with the players' attitude and looked forward to a more personal get-together.

Recruiting is an ongoing program. I had received a warm welcome in the homes that I had visited and was looking forward to continuing the visits. There is a constant nucleus of outstanding student–athletes in the state of Louisiana, and I wanted them to continue to be the core of our program. The fans there are among the best in college football, and they deserve to cheer for home-grown players. A Saturday night in Tiger Stadium is a spectacular event.

Pete Jenkins, defensive line coach, was the lone holdover from the previous staff. In addition, John Symank, who had been with me at Tulane and the New York Giants, became linebacker coach. Mike Archer, from the University of Miami, became defensive backfield coach. Kurt Schottenheimer, from Tulane University, became linebacker coach. Our defensive staff was complete. Offensively, I had interviewed several coaches while I was in transition. Ed Zaunbrecher, from Wake Forest, became offensive coordinator and quarterback coach (Ed is now the head coach at Northeast Louisiana). Pete Mangurian, from Stanford, was named to coach the center and guards (he later was the offensive line coach with the Denver Broncos, New York Giants, and Atlanta Falcons and is now the head coach at Cornell University), and Jerry Sullivan, from Indiana (but a Miami native), was named receiver coach. Terry Lewis, formerly of the Naval Academy, would coach the tackles. That gave me a good group to help in recruiting, and I took my time before naming the remaining coaches. One reason I did so was because I wanted to review the high school coaches in the state. High school coaches are often overlooked, and I did not want to ignore them. They would be our lifeline, and I wanted them to feel that they were a part of our program.

Recruiting continued to move forward, and we signed 25 outstanding young men to join the program, 19 from Louisiana, 5 from Florida, and 1 from Texas. It was an outstanding class of student–athletes, led by center Nacho Albergamo, guard Eric Andolsek, receiver Wendell Davis, punter and kicker Matt DeFrank, quarterback Mickey Guidry, linebacker Nicky Hazard, kicker Ronnie Lewis, running back Sammy Martin, receiver Mike Mayes, tackle Ralph Norwood, and nose tackle Darrel Phillips.

Jessie Daigle, a former high school coach, joined us as backfield coach, and our staff was complete before spring practice. We completed our football notebook and were ready to begin practice. Spring practice was a success. Our offense, defense, and terminology were in place and we were ready for the fall. The LSU Coaches Clinic held on campus was also successful. The clinic proved to be a great opportunity for all of the staff to get to know the high school coaches. The Louisiana High School Coaches Clinic in Lafayette in July gave us another opportunity to visit with the high school coaches. However, from then until the beginning of fall practice, I wanted to visit as many high schools as possible. In 1984, there were not the stringent rules that are in place now. Today, a new coach has a real problem because of the visiting restrictions concerning recruits and coaches. I have always maintained that a successful veteran coach had a hand in writing the rules.

I had asked the players to prepare physically during the summer. That included a definite reporting weight, distance running for stamina, and starts and sprints for quickness and speed. It was evident on picture day that our squad had worked over the summer, but the next day was the true test. It involved testing each player on his summer work and comparing that with what he had accomplished in the spring. We were a fat team in the spring, and I did not feel that we needed the excess weight in hot and humid Baton Rouge (plus our opening game was a one o'clock start in hot and humid Gainesville, Florida). Size was beginning to creep into college football. We wanted size, but we wanted size that was properly distributed and useful, not a hindrance. I was pleased with our progress and the tests proved the point.

Our first test of the 1984 season was versus the University of Florida in Gainesville. Florida was ranked high (between third and sixth) in the pre-season polls, and we knew we had to be ready. The game proved to be everything we expected and then some. We went ahead 21–14 midway in the fourth quarter, but when we kicked off to the Gators, they showed their superiority. They got the ball on the offensive right hash mark and moved consistently down the field. I can still see it today. We could not stop them, and they scored to tie the game 21–21. We got the ball back with little time remaining, managed to move it to mid-field, and attempted a field goal. It was wide. We had fought a hard battle versus a very good Florida team. A tie is not a win, but I left the Florida game with a good feeling about our team. This was Charley Pell's last game as coach of the Gators. NCAA problems had developed in the off-season, and he was suspended before the next game.

After Florida, we had three non-conference games. We beat Wichita 47–7, Arizona 27–26, and a good Southern California team in Los Angeles 23–3. We worked out Friday afternoon before the game in Los Angeles and had a meeting scheduled for that evening. Some of the players asked to be excused from dinner so they could visit the Hollywood sights and Rodeo Drive. I thought, why not? After all, part of a college education is travel and seeing interesting parts of the country. I did, however, make one point: "Be sure you are on time for our 8 P.M. meeting." At 8 P.M., with every player present, I began our meeting.

A lot of our fans attended the game in Los Angeles. Joe Yates, our public relations director, reminded me to thank them for their support. Our fans were seated in a section on our way to the tunnel, and I did what Joe requested as we passed by. Joe was a real friend and gave me many helpful ideas. Prior to the press conference at which I was announced as head coach, he alerted me to "be sure and say LSU, not Louisiana State University." I came to town saying the full name, and he knew I needed to be redirected. After that, I never hesitated to do what Joe Yates said. He was the best.

Next were five conference games, with Notre Dame in the middle. We beat Vanderbilt 34–27 and Kentucky 36–10 in Lexington. At that point, we were 5–0–1. Notre Dame was next, and they beat us 30–22 in Baton Rouge. Our schedule called for us to finish with four conference games. We were in the SEC race and looked forward to the challenge. We beat Mississippi 32–29 and, as the score indicates, the game was back and forth all night. We beat Alabama in Birmingham 16–14 on a key blocked punt by Michael Brooks. Our last conference game was versus Mississippi State in Starkville. A win meant the SEC championship and a Sugar Bowl bid. We had a good week of practice. We needed it because the Bulldogs were an option team. We needed the work, but what worried me all week was the fact that our picture of the option was not at the same speed that we would see on Saturday. We knew our definition of responsibilities and were as healthy as possible after nine games. Mississippi State had a problem at quarterback and their backup started.

We played well, but not well enough versus a very quick quarterback. We had an opportunity to win but missed a long field goal as the game ended. That gave us an SEC record of 4–1–1. The next week, Auburn lost to Alabama on "Bo" Jackson's wrong-way run, and we were invited to the **Sugar Bowl** versus Nebraska. Our final game of the season was against Tulane in Baton Rouge, and we won 33–15 to complete our season 8–2–1. Nebraska beat us 28–10 in the Sugar Bowl. We had work to do, but our first year was a success.

Our objective the next year was another recruiting class to go with the 1984 group, and all the coaches hit the road. I made a couple of staff adjustments. Kurt left for Notre Dame, and I brought in Mike Nolan to coach the linebackers (the same Mike Nolan who had coordinated the Giants' defense and is now coordinating the defense for the Redskins). With this move, I assigned John Symank to full-time recruiting. He was with us early in the week, left to visit the schools, and met us for the game. We were trying to do everything possible to maintain contact with the high schools in Louisiana and the surrounding area. Mike Archer took on the added responsibility of coordinating the defense, and I brought in Joe Wessel as a graduate assistant to work with our special teams and help Mike with the secondary.

It is very difficult for the secondary coach to coordinate the defense. Foremost, the secondary coach must stand behind the defensive backs and make sure they are in their proper spots. As coordinator, it is best to work in front of the defense. These two areas are in conflict with each other. There is no way a coach can be in two spots at the same time. However, bringing in Joe Wessel enabled us to have the best of both worlds. The move strengthened our recruiting, our special teams, and our defense.

Recruiting was coming along well, and we felt that the class of 1985 would give us two good groups back to back. We signed 26 student–athletes, some of whom could prove valuable to us as freshmen. The group was led by safety Jamie Bice, defensive end Kenny Davidson, defensive tackle Karl Dunbar, linebacker Eric Hill, quarterback Tommy Hodson, safety Greg Jackson, defensive end Clint James, running back Victor Jones, linebacker Oliver Lawrence, running back/wide receiver Tony Moss, and guard Ruffin Rodrigue. Sixteen were from Louisiana, three from Florida, four from Texas, two from Pennsylvania, and one from Alabama.

After spring practice and a successful annual spring clinic, it was time for my trip around the state to visit the high schools. I was looking forward to what we all felt was a good season in the making. The 1985 season began at North Carolina, where we won 23–13. Next was Colorado State, and we won 17–3. Our conference schedule began with the University of Florida coming in, and we lost 20–0. We were completely dominated by the Florida team. They took charge defensively, and we were stymied in every department. It was a wake-up call. We continued our conference play with a 49–7 victory over Vanderbilt; Kentucky fell 10–0, and we beat Mississippi in Jackson 14–0. With two conference games remaining, we were 3–1. Next was Alabama at home, and we tied 14–14. We finished the conference with a 17–15 win over Mississippi State. Our conference record was 4–1–1. We had three non-conference games remaining. We were probably out of the SEC race and the Sugar Bowl, but we felt good about finishing strong and receiving a major bowl bid.

A real test came the following week on a November trip to South Bend. The practice field and the game field were covered with snow, so our Friday practice had to be adjusted. I did not want to go inside, so we took a walk around the stadium and realized that we could practice in the parking lot (we had done that several times in Baltimore when the field was covered and we wanted to work.) The wind was blowing, but the parking lot was only partially covered with snow. There would be no problem with footing. In fact, by the time we were ready to practice, the parking lot was almost clear. We put on soft-soled shoes, sweatpants, sweatshirts, and helmets, and off we went. We worked for about an hour. It was cold and windy, but we survived. We had a good practice, and a feeling of superiority and enjoyment came over the squad.

There was a "smoker" that night for the media, the coaches, friends of LSU who had made the trip, and a select few Notre Dame alumni who had arrived early. During the evening, I was told that Notre Dame had also worked out in the parking lot. I guess they didn't want us to gain the edge.

Conditions the next day were much better. The only snow that remained was around the edge of the field, and the temperature was better—still cold, but better. In our pre-game warm-up, our kicker, Ronnie Lewis, was suffering from the weather. I could tell that he was in no condition to kick. I am glad the situation surfaced during the warm-up, when I had plenty of time to make a decision. I suggested he stay in the locker room, and I told our punter, Matt DeFrank (a Florida native), to get ready. He had kicked in high school and had kicked for us until he became our regular punter. He had great distance as a kicker and was our kickoff specialist. Unfortunately, his field goals weren't always accurate. The game was a typical hard-nosed battle. Both teams moved the ball, but neither could establish any sign of a drive. We were knotted at 7–7. We managed to put a few good plays together and finally got close enough for a field goal attempt. Matt entered the game.

The snap was perfect and he kicked through the ball. It was long enough. It could have been higher, but it cleared the line of scrimmage and crossed over the crossbar. The ball had a slightly different rotation than you normally see, but the kick was good and put LSU ahead 10–7. We continued to play good defense, and we kept Notre Dame from scoring or getting close enough to try a field goal. It was a thrill for us to beat Notre Dame in South Bend. And winning in that weather made the victory even sweeter.

I was in awe of the Notre Dame tradition, especially the locker facilities. The visitors' locker room was what you might imagine, filled with images of Knute Rockne and the other great coaches of years gone by preparing to play the game. Later, when my son David was a graduate assistant there, I had the opportunity to see the Notre Dame locker room. It was slightly more modern, but it still had that feeling of ghosts around every post.

Next was Tulane in New Orleans, and we beat the Green Wave 31–19. We finished the season on December 7 with a 35–15 win over East Carolina for a final record of 9–1–1. The late finish may have been one reason for the snub by the major bowls. The real reason will never be known, but we did receive a bid from the Liberty Bowl to play against Baylor.

Playing in the **Liberty Bowl** in Memphis on December 27 was one of the worst decisions I have ever had a hand in. Memphis was much colder than South Bend. The people of Memphis tried hard to show the players a good time, but the players just didn't want to be there. I didn't help matters when we practiced Christmas morning so we could have the rest of the day off. In hindsight, we should have taken the entire day off. Baylor was happy just to be there and took the day off. You can imagine how we played. I mentioned earlier how at times Coach Shula referred to a poor practice as practicing "with one foot in the parking lot." This game was about as close as I have ever come to playing with "both feet in the parking lot." Baylor won 21–7. We were never in the game. It was definitely not the way I wanted to end the season.

We returned to Baton Rouge more determined. We were totally embarrassed and realized that we had neither prepared nor played up to our ability. We accepted the result and got to work immediately. Recruiting was the number one priority. Texas A&M and Nebraska had suddenly started recruiting in Louisiana. From time to time, Nebraska had been around New Orleans, but this year they seemed to be spreading out across the state. My guess was that their trip to the Sugar Bowl encouraged their participation. Texas A&M hired a former coach or two from Louisiana in an effort to get their foot in the door.

The competition for players became tougher, and we felt that the material in the state was thinner than usual. Our coaches worked hard, but we probably didn't have quite the success that we enjoyed in the first two years. We did, however, sign some impact players that contributed as freshmen and completed successful careers at LSU. The more that I am involved in recruiting and the college draft, the more I come to realize that you never know what a young person will do until you give him an opportunity. Some poor practice players play well in a game, and some good practice players play poorly when the whistle blows. What I look for is the ideal player—one who prepares properly, plays well, and makes an outstanding contribution to his team and school. The term student–athlete is descriptive of this type of player. The young person must first be a good student and then must be a good athlete.

We completed the recruiting process with a good signing class of 23 student–athletes. Ten were from Louisiana, eight from Texas, four from Florida, and one from Alabama. Three players in this class were outstanding: kicker David Browndyke, running back Harvey Williams, and running back Walker "Slip" Watkins. When the final results were in, others had contributed: running back Eddie Fuller, quarterback Sol Graves, tight end Ronnie Haliburton, center Blake Miller, receiver Leon "Tyke" Tolbert, and tight end Willie Williams. Willie later grew into a pro offensive tackle. Tyke was the tight end coach at Northeast Louisiana and recently accepted a position at Auburn University, and Blake Miller is the offensive line coach at Northwestern Louisiana.

Many of the players on the 1986 team had been recruited in 1984. They knew what we expected and were determined to meet the demands. They knew how to prepare, and they had achieved success. A championship was in the back of all of our minds, and we were not going to be denied. Spring practice was good. We gave the young guys a lot of work, which I believed would help us during the year.

As pre-season practice started, the search committee from the University of Florida asked me to interview for the vacant position of director of athletics. I had been contacted by an alumnus in the summer to determine if I would be interested. My response at the time was yes, but I was happy at LSU and wasn't looking to move. I really didn't know what to do. After much thought, I decided to go for the interview. Before making a final decision, I discussed the situation with Chancellor Wharton, Director of Athletics Bob Brodhead, the coaches, and the squad. I explained what had happened and what I wanted to do, with their approval. I received their best wishes and went to Gainesville. The interview was very formal and was handled very well. It was over early enough for me to catch a flight back to Atlanta and then to Baton Rouge and only miss one day of practice. Upon my return, the media met me, and I explained the situation as I knew it. I resumed practice the next day. As far as I was concerned, the subject was behind me and my concentration was on our team and the approaching season. Our practices were good, and my total attention was on the first game and the season.

The season began with a solid 35–17 win over Texas A&M. One of the key plays in the game came in the second quarter when quarterback Mickey Guidry and back Sammy Martin read the blitz for a big gain. From that point on, we were in control. Next was Miami University, my alma mater. I tried all week to get the squad's attention, but failed. Miami has a history of knocking off the favorite once or twice a year. I knew their history because I had been a part of it. I failed to get my message across. By game time, it was raining—a perfect setting for the upset. Three factors were involved: Miami's history, the rain, and the fact that we were coming off of a very emotional win. All contributed to our playing below our capabilities, and we lost 21–12. I had no trouble getting anyone's attention from that point on.

We were 1–1 as we began three straight conference games. We beat Florida 28–17 in Gainesville, Georgia 23–14, and Kentucky 25–16 in Lexington. The team presented my mother, who lived in nearby Paris, Kentucky, with the game ball after the win, and I really appreciated the squad thinking of her in this manner.

We beat North Carolina 30–3 at home. Next came three conference games, beginning with Mississippi. Ole Miss is always a challenge, and this game was no exception. The lead changed several times, and we were in a position to win at the end. We established a good drive, but time was running out. We were in position to kick a field goal that was well within David Browndyke's range, but instead of waiting for fourth down, we lined up on third down on the right hash mark. The snap was good, the hold was good, the kick was up, but it was wide and the game was over. We lost 21–19. It was our first conference loss and our second loss of the season. Our last conference game for the championship was in Jackson versus Mississippi State. Many of the players had been on the team when we lost to the Bulldogs in 1984, and we had no problem getting ready for the rematch. The championship was within reach. We had to beat Mississippi State to win the SEC.

It was one of the best games that the team played in the three years that we were together. We beat the Bulldogs 47–0, and after the win we circled the field to thank our fans. It was a tradition that we had established at Southern California our first year. The fans seemed to like our recognition of their support, and we continued to show it after each victory. On away games, we would go to the section of the stands where our fans were seated and express our appreciation. In Jackson, the entire team joined me to celebrate with the fans.

We won the **SEC championship** but still had two non-conference games remaining and wanted to finish in style. Our objective was to be the best that we could be, and that's how we prepared. The Notre Dame game would be televised, and it was an opportunity to represent our school, our team, and our fans. This was our third game versus Notre Dame and we were 1–1. We beat them 21–19 in a thriller. I helped to make it that way. I was determined to kick to Tim Brown, an excellent receiver and returner. I did, against the wishes of special teams coach Joe Wessel, and it was 0–7 immediately. That was my wake-up call, and we rolled it to him the rest of the night. We contained him as a receiver, but he quickly gained our respect as a returner.

The final game was versus Tulane, and there was no way they were going to embarrass us. We prepared and played well enough to beat them 37–17. After the game, we received a bid from the **Sugar Bowl**. We would play Nebraska again—just lucky I guess. In years past, it was my understanding that the coach helped select the opponent. But times have changed. I guess television ratings and money have more impact.

After the Sugar Bowl announcement, I had an announcement to make myself. I would resign after the Sugar Bowl to join the University of Florida as director of athletics. Chancellor Wharton and Director of Athletics Brodhead had both agreed that it would be best for me to coach through the bowl game. I wanted the announcement to be made immediately after the season because I did not want it to interfere with recruiting. By announcing then, it would be out of the way and we could concentrate on the game and the coaches could begin recruiting. I had also requested that a member of the staff be named head coach, for a smooth transition. We had established a good program and were successful, and there was no need to look elsewhere. This suggestion took a little longer to implement because there are channels to go through. Finally, Mike Archer was selected as my replacement. Mike is now the linebacker coach with the Pittsburgh Steelers.

Our practice began in Baton Rouge, and we went to New Orleans the day after Christmas. Our preparation was intense and we were ready to play the game. We started out well, but Nebraska caught up and never looked back. They beat us 30–15 for the second time in three years in the Sugar Bowl. We finished the season 8–2, with a 5–1 conference record.

Looking back, we had a lot of great student–athletes in our program at LSU. Michael Brooks was named an All-American in 1985 as a junior and was on his way as a senior until a knee injury sidelined him for the season. He was named All-SEC in 1985 by all the news services. Lance Smith was named an All-American in 1984 and All-SEC the same year. Wendell Davis was named All-American in 1986–87 and All-SEC by all the news services in 1987. In addition, he was named a member of the LSU Modern Day Team of the Century. Nacho Albergamo was named All-American in 1987 and All-SEC in 1987 by all the news services. In addition, he was named a member of the LSU Modern Day Team of the Century. Greg Jackson was named All-American in 1988 and All-SEC the same year.

All-SEC first team recognition was awarded to Lance Smith, Dalton Hillard, Roland Barbay, and Norman Jefferson in 1984. In 1985, Dalton Hillard, Michael Brooks, Roland Barbay, and Norman Jefferson were named. And 1986 was a banner year with Wendell Davis, Henry Thomas, Eric Andolsek, Tommy Hodson, Brian Kinchen, Roland Barbay, Toby Caston, and Karl Wilson named.

The student–athletes we recruited continued to receive All-SEC recognition in 1987, 1988, 1989, and 1990. Wendell Davis, Nacho Albergamo, Eric Andolek, Tommy Hodson, Chris Carrier, Darrell Phillips, David Browndyke, and Matt DeFrank were named in 1987. In 1988, it was David Browndyke, Eddie Fuller, Eric Hill, Tommy Hodson, Greg Jackson, Tony Moss, Darrell Phillips, Ralph Norwood, and Ron Sancho. In 1989, it was Tony Moss, Tommy Hodson, and David Browndyke, and in 1990 Blake Miller and Harvey Williams.

GTE Academic All-American honors went to Juan Betanzos in 1984 and to Nacho Albergamo in 1986 and 1987.

LSU Modern Day Team of the Century named Wendell Davis, Eric Martin, Nacho Albergamo, Eric Andolsek, Lance Smith, and David Browndyke to the offense and Henry Thomas, Michael Brooks, and Liffort Hobley to the defense.

A number of Tigers were drafted by the NFL. In 1985, Lance Smith,* Eric Martin,** Jeffrey Dale, Liffort Hobley, and Greg Dubroc were drafted. Dalton Hillard,** Garry James, and Jeff Wickersham made it in 1986. In 1987, Henry Thomas,* Michael Brooks,** Karl Wilson,** Toby Caston (who died during his career), Roland Barbay, and Norman Jefferson were drafted. *Wendell Davis,* Brian Kinchen,* *Eric Andolsek* (who died during his career), *Sammy Martin,** Kevin Guidry, Rogie Magee, and Chris Carrier were picked in 1988. In 1989, *Eric Hill,* Greg Jackson,* Ralph Norwood* (who died during his career), *Mike Mayes, Ron Sancho,* and Rudy Harmon were chosen. *Kenny Davidson,* Karl Dunbar,** Eddie Fuller,** Tommy Hodson,** Ronnie Haliburton, Clint James,* and *Tony Moss* were drafted in 1990. In 1991, *Harvey Williams,* Blake Miller,* and *"Slip" Watkins* were picked.

---

* indicates currently playing, and ** indicates recently retired. Names in italic type are players recruited between 1984 and 1986.

The student–athletes, the university administration, the faculty, the coaches, and the fans are all to be congratulated. Everyone worked together to make LSU an outstanding example of what I call a "true team." My family and I enjoyed our stay at LSU and in Baton Rouge. We had first lived in Louisiana in 1962–63, and when we returned in 1984, we enjoyed every minute. The people of the state wanted the best, and we did our best to give them the best program possible. I am proud of our record: 26 wins, 8 losses, and 2 ties in three years, for a .750 percentage. It is the best record in school history, which dates back to 1909. An **SEC championship** in 1986, **Sugar Bowl** appearances in 1984 and 1986, a **Liberty Bowl** in 1985, and **SEC Coach of the Year** awards in 1984 and 1986 capped off my three years there. I wish Coach DiNardo the best. He and his staff have worked hard to bring the Tigers back. The school and the fans deserve the best.

Director of Athletics at the University of Florida

Several factors played a part in my decision to move to the University of Florida. First, I thought it was a good time for me to get into administration. I had experienced an exciting and successful career on the sideline at both the college and professional level as both an assistant and head coach. Second, administration was of interest to me because I would be working with other coaches and their student–athletes. The problems in intercollegiate athletics seemed to be increasing, and I felt that I could be of help. Third (which probably was actually first), I was tremendously impressed with the University of Florida. There seemed to be a cohesiveness under the direction of President Marshall Criser. Fourth, Gainesville is a college town, with a college atmosphere, and my son was a senior there and my daughter was a freshman.

With these reasons in mind, I joined the University of Florida as director of athletics in January 1987. It was important to me that a premium be placed on academics as well as athletics. I wanted a successful athletic program and equally strong academic excellence among our student–athletes. To help me reach this objective, I asked Larry Fitzmorris, who had been in charge of our academic program at LSU, to join me. When he said yes, I knew I was on the right track. It took time, but between 1989 and 1991 the University of Florida student–athletes earned the most all-academic honors for a three-year period in school history. The academic success did not hurt our athletic success. In each of five years, Florida's combined men's and women's program ranked among the ten most successful in the nation according to *USA Today*.

Next, I wanted to maintain and build the alumni support base that is so important to a successful program. Associate Director Jeremy Foley, Gator Booster Director John James, and his assistant Tom Scott were instrumental in helping me maintain and improve the participation of the private sector. In today's world of intercollegiate athletics, the private sector is the key to a successful program. Gate receipts and student fees alone can no longer be expected to fund the program. With the implementation of Title IX and the additional programs it requires, increased funding is necessary. Add to that continual updating of facilities, and the private sector becomes more and more important in every athletic program. Because of the forward thinking of many former Florida administrators, the university was well ahead of many schools.

Winning always helps, and when an opening developed, it was my job to bring in the best possible coach and staff. If the selection affected the women's program, I spent considerable time with Associate Director Ann Marie (Lawler) Rogers, the women's administrator. Ann Marie, like Jeremy, was very helpful, and I continually relied on both of them, along with Larry Fitzmorris and trainer Chris Patrick. Jon McBride joined us as director of marketing, and Mick Hubert became the new voice of the Gators. These additions, plus holdovers Bill Holloway as ticket director and Norm Carlson and John Humenik in Sports Information, were all key to our successful program.

One of the first additions was "Buddy" Alexander, who joined us as men's golf coach. I had known him when I was at LSU. He was a native Floridian, and I knew he would be a good fit. Beverly Kerney joined us as the women's track coach (she recently left Florida to join the University of Texas), and Mary Wise joined us to coach volleyball. Ann Marie was instrumental in both selections, and both coaches are ranked at the top nationally in their respective sports. Beverly continues to be successful at Texas, and Mary has developed a nationally ranked volleyball program at Florida. My two most important selections were Lon Kruger to lead the basketball program (after taking the team to the final four in 1994, he resigned to accept the head coach position at Illinois) and Steve Spurrier to lead the football program. Steve has built an outstanding program, with a National Championship in 1996, and has signed a new multi-year contract that will take him into the next millennium.

During my five years at the University of Florida, I received tremendous help from the university administration and the athletic association. The University Athletic Association (UAA) is a separate entity and consists of the university president, faculty, and alumni. Gator Boosters, the fund-raising arm of the association, consists of alumni, the athletics director, and other members of the university administration. The UAA and the Gator Boosters work very closely with each other and with the administration. There is a real sense of teamwork among the groups, and it was a real pleasure to be associated with them.

I reported directly to the university president. I knew what he expected and met with him periodically to keep him informed. I do not like to be surprised, and I certainly did not want Mr. Criser to be surprised. After his resignation during my third year, Provost Bob Bryan was appointed interim president. I was happy with his appointment because I had worked closely with him in his position as provost. The line of communication remained basically the same, and I have often said that I could not have worked for two presidents who were more interested and involved than Marshall Criser and Bob Bryan. I knew that the search for the new president would take considerable time, and I felt very comfortable with Dr. Bryan during this interim period.

Dr. John Lombardi was named as the new president. After visiting with him, I knew our relationship would be similar. I appreciated this, because you never know what to expect when someone new comes in. It was especially important to me that I be allowed to attend the deans and administrative directors meeting. Listening to the problems and concerns of the leaders of the university helped me to establish policy for the UAA and continued to strengthen the working relationship among the university, the UAA, and the Gator Boosters. It was a true team concept. This, plus the fan support and the financial support from the private sector, enabled us to give the university, the city of Gainesville, and the state of Florida an outstanding program.

During each of my five years at the University of Florida, the athletic program was ranked in the top ten nationally according to an annual *USA Today* poll. In addition, my tenure saw the completion of the Alfred McKethan Baseball Stadium and the Scott Linder Tennis Stadium, plus a new stadium for track and a 10,000-seat expansion of Ben Hill Griffin Stadium for football. Our student–athletes earned SEC Academic Honor Roll status more times than any conference school had since 1987. Many people were responsible for our success, and I thank them for their part in making it happen.

In early 1992, an opportunity for me to return to the sideline developed. I had enjoyed my work in administration. It was similar to coaching in the way people worked together to accomplish a goal, especially the administrators, the coaches, and the employees with whom I worked on a daily basis. It was great to be around the athletes and their families, but that phase was very similar to what I had always enjoyed. The thing that was different for my wife and me was the number of athletic contests that we were able to attend. We both really enjoyed that part of the job and continue to stay in touch with many of the coaches and athletes. Nothing will ever replace the opportunity to watch the competition at the college level among both the men's and women's programs.

Upon checking into the hotel while attending an NCAA meeting in Anaheim, California, I had a message to call Bobby Ross, the new head coach of the San Diego Chargers. I asked University President Dr. Lombardi and Faculty Representative Nicholas Cassisi for permission to interview. Their replies were positive, and I made plans to meet with Coach Ross a couple of days later in Irvine, California. We had a good meeting, and he asked me to join his staff. I told him that I would like to meet with him again before returning to Gainesville. I updated Dr. Lombardi and Dr. Cassisi and told them that I planned to meet with Bobby again. After the NCAA meetings ended on Friday, we met at the Chargers office. My wife, Betty Jane, was with me, and it was good opportunity for her to meet Bobby and see the facility. After another good meeting with Bobby, my wife and I returned to Gainesville on Saturday. During the trip home and through most of Sunday, I changed my mind a hundred times. I had told Bobby that I would give him an answer on Sunday. Believe me, the time change was very helpful. There is a three-hour difference, and I needed all three hours. We talked as a family. David, our son, was coaching at Alabama A&M, and our daughter, Mary Susan, was home and pushing for a decision. For a young lady who never really cared for football, she was acting like a rabid San Diego Chargers fan. There was no reason to delay. I wanted to return to the sideline, and I had the opportunity to do so with San Diego. I informed Dr. Lombardi, made the call to Bobby, and reported to work in mid-January 1992.

San Diego Chargers: Back to the Sideline

One of the reasons I felt good about returning to the sideline was I knew that I would be working with people whom I knew and respected. Jerry Sullivan, my receiver coach at LSU, was the receiver coach. I knew Carl Mauck, the offensive line coach, from his days as a player in Baltimore. Dale Lindsey, a player at the University of Kentucky when I coached there and later a linebacker with the Browns, would be our linebacker coach. (I tried to hire Dale when I was at LSU, but he wanted to stay in professional football.) I had never worked with Sly Crooms, but I knew him by reputation. John Fox, the secondary coach, had been at Pittsburgh, which gave him an excellent background. I knew Jack Reilly, the quarterback coach, when he was a junior college coach in Southern California. I had interviewed him when I was at LSU, and we had worked out in Jack's facility when we played Southern Cal. The other coaches, George O'Leary, Ralph Friedgen, and Chuck Priefer, had been with Coach Ross at Georgia Tech. It was a good staff, and I thought it would be fun to be a part of the group.

I was right—the next three years were fun. We were 11–5 in 1992 for a first place finish in the AFC West. We beat Kansas City 17–0 in the first round of the play-offs, but lost to Miami 31–0 in the divisional play-off. In 1993, we fell to 8–8 and a fourth place finish in the AFC West. We rebounded in 1994 to finish 11–5 and win the AFC West. We beat Miami 22–21 in the playoff game, which gave us an opportunity to play Pittsburgh for the AFC Championship. We beat Pittsburgh 17–13 and went on to **Super Bowl XXIX** versus the 49ers. We lost to San Francisco 49–26 in what was a poor performance for us in all areas.

Retirement

As a coach, this was my **sixth Super Bowl** appearance over four decades, both NFL records. I gave a lot of thought to my future. Should I try for seven or retire and spend more time with my family and volunteer projects? The more I thought, the more I realized that it was time to retire, and I did so on February 2, 1995. Would I miss it? Yes, especially game day.

In 8 of my 13 years as a defensive coordinator in professional football, our defense was first or second. From 1964 through the 1994, covering 23 years and four decades (with the Colts, Dolphins, and Chargers), our team was ranked first or second in the division 18 times. During this same period, I had the opportunity to participate in 29 play-off games. This included one NFL Championship game (before there was a Super Bowl) and six Super Bowls (at least one in each of four decades—the 1960s, 1970s, 1980s, and 1990s) with three teams—one with Baltimore, four with Miami, and one with San Diego. The Super Bowl appearances were highlighted by the 1972 undefeated 17–0 season and back-to-back wins in Super Bowl VII and Super Bowl VIII.

At the college level, we won one Southeastern Conference championship and made two Sugar Bowl appearances and I received two Coach of the Year awards (1984 and 1986) in three years at LSU. Five years as director of athletics at the University of Florida completes the picture.

However, the many players, coaches, administrators, and owners who were a part of my accomplishments are far more important than the statistics. It is those associations and relationships that will be a part of my memory forever. And nothing will ever replace the memory of the preparation, the practice, and the playing of the game.

I soon realized that there were many opportunities available to me, namely, volunteer work with the San Diego Police Department and with the Stephen

Ministry program of Torrey Pines Christian Church, committee work with the association in the area where I live—and writing this book. All have proven more than enough to keep me busy but allow time for other things I also enjoy. I play tennis at least three times a week. Betty Jane and I have had time to visit our son David, his wife Kim, and their son Stephen in Monroe, Louisiana. In the spring of 1998, David accepted the position as defensive backs coach at Cornell University. Our daughter Mary Susan and her husband Stuart recently moved to Raleigh, North Carolina, where he is the general manager of the Ticketmaster office. Mary Susan is busy decorating.

I have enjoyed sharing my thoughts and experiences with you. I am forever thankful for the many opportunities afforded me and to my many associates who helped make it all possible. In looking back at my career in professional and college athletics, including both the highs and the lows, it was a great ride, with no regrets.

It was such a great ride that I returned to part-time coaching in the spring of 1998 as special teams coach with Cornell University. I could not refuse an opportunity to work with head coach Pete Mangurian (my offensive line coach at LSU) and my son, David. Betty Jane and I are looking forward to the season. She will become a working grandmother, plus we will be closer to Mary Susan and Stuart. Once again, we are fortunate to be a part of the college atmosphere in one of our country's outstanding universities. We are truly blessed.

REFERENCES

- Baltimore Colts Defensive Playbook, 1964–1969
- *Improving Policing: A Problem Oriented Approach,* Herman Goldstein (McGraw-Hill, 1979)
- Indianapolis Colts Media Guide
- Louisiana State University Media Guide
- LSU Football Playbook, 1984–1986
- Miami Dolphins Defensive Playbook, 1970–1973, 1977–1983
- Miami Dolphins Media Guide
- Miami University Media Guide
- New York Football Giants Media Guide
- New York Football Giants Playbook, 1974–1796
- Ohio State University Media Guide
- *Pocket Guide to Media Success,* Sports Media Challenge, Charlotte, North Carolina, 1991
- San Diego Chargers Defensive Playbook, 1992–1994
- San Diego Chargers Media Guide
- Tulane University Media Guide
- University of Kentucky Media Guide
- "What It Takes to Be No. 1," by Vince Lombardi

INDEX